SOCIOTECHNICAL SYSTEMS

SOCIOTECHNICAL SYSTEMS

Factors in Analysis, Design, and Management

Kenyon B. De Greene
Institute of Aerospace Safety and Management
University of Southern California

PRENTICE-HALL, INC.
Englewood Cliffs, New Jersey

Library of Congress Cataloging in Publication Data

DE GREENE, KENYON B
  Sociotechnical systems: factors in analysis, design,
and management.

  Includes bibliographies.
  1. Social policy. 2. Environmental policy.
3. System analysis. I. Title.
HN18.D414   658.4'032   73–3063
ISBN 0–13–821553–7

10 9 8 7 6 5 4 3 2 1

Printed in the United States of America

Prentice-Hall International, Inc. *London*
Prentice-Hall of Australia, Pty. Ltd., *Sydney*
Prentice-Hall of Canada, Ltd., *Toronto*
Prentice-Hall of India Private Limited, *New Delhi*
Prentice-Hall of Japan, Inc., *Tokyo*

To Karola, Brent, Erika, and "Kenerl"—
may we have the wisdom and discipline to ensure their and
the other little folks' "best of times."

It is the best of times, it is the worst of times, it is the age of wisdom, it is the age of foolishness, it is the springtime of hope, it is the winter of despair.

Paraphrased from Charles Dickens

Contents

IV IS ANYBODY LISTENING? THE SUPREME CHALLENGE   345

Preface

The many ailments of all today's societies are symptoms of a common underlying problem—*the failure to comprehend things as a whole. Accordingly, economic, social, personal, and environmental costs are increasingly prohibitive* and program successes increasingly few. There are just not enough resources of any kind to do everything we would like. Today we stand at a fundamental fork in the road and the decisions we make in the following years may well prove irrevocable. If we decide to treat the whole, our varied but apparently isolated and unrelated difficulties should begin to sort themselves out. If instead we decide to continue on our present course, we can expect our programs to have, at best, limited and short-term successes, and, at worst, reinforcing, all-pervasive, and disastrous consequences for all the world and for the future everlasting.

This book, a response to these apparently overwhelming problems, is an introduction to the entire field of sociotechnical systems, and a first book to cover an emerging field definitively. It is interdisciplinary; behavioral science provides an integrating theme. It can also be thought of as a book in "systems science: biological, behavioral, and social" as opposed to "systems science: physical." Both types of books are important to the development of an overall curriculum geared to the problems of today's protean world.

This general purpose book is suggested for a variety of upper division and graduate course adoptions, including management theory, systems management, systems engineering, research and development seminars, public administration, general business management, environmental problems and management, organizational behavior, social dynamics, management policy, and research methodology. It can also be of interest to a wide and varied general market, including the trade market, and hopefully will be of significant educational value for the literate public.

Numerous examples and cases show how managers must face problems, find relationships between technology and people as well as between their organizations and the outside world, and how this information can influence their decisions. The cases for the most part indicate how systems theory and methods, and a bridge between theory and method, can be utilized to ameliorate social, economic, environmental, and political problems engendered by technology. The cases place a considerable emphasis upon contemporary and predicted environmental and social problems, the big issues of the 1970s. It is stressed that a business or organization or political entity cannot be separated from environmental and social effects consequent to its existence. This case-anecdote treatment, as opposed to utilization of *just one* methodology like computer modeling and simulation, is imbedded in summary appraisals and normative discussion.

Throughout the book given areas are reviewed, major points summarized, references provided, and main examples worked through which point out critical features of faulty problem definition, data lack, faulty decision-making, system oversimplification, and use of or lack of systems theories and methods. The many examples collectively represent timeliness, comprehensiveness, uniqueness, and pedagogic value. Chapters 1 through 3 and 8 and 9 emphasize systems and organizational behavior and Chapters 4 through 7 emphasize research and study methodology.

Concern is expressed for the social and political environment in which planning takes place. This includes recognition of the importance of genuine conflicts of interest and the political processes in decision-making. For example, the important tradeoffs between restrictive government control and an organization's freedom to develop, build, or pollute are considered.

The term "sociotechnical system" of course had a very specific meaning as originally defined and used by Emery and Trist of the Tavistock Institute in London. In this book the original concept is greatly extended to include not only intraorganizational and organizational problems, but even more important, large-scale societal problems and political behavior in technological societies. Herein we deal more with high-level management situations than with work situations as was the case of most of the Tavistock writings. Especial emphasis is placed upon the *needs* for *changing* theories, philosophies, concepts, and practices of management. Much attention is thus paid to deficiencies of the "production" and "efficiency ethoses," and the needs to change exploitative, consumption, and commercial behavior.

As a macrosystems effort the success of this book is dependent upon the prior work of hundreds of other authors, much as the success of an Apollo spacecraft is dependent upon the subsystem developments by hundreds of subcontractors and vendors of small components. Whereas the overall framework and integration represented here remain the responsibility of this writer, many of the modules are developments of individual authors. In all cases, attempts have been made to give credit to these input sources. If, because of the sheer mass of material covered, proper credit was omitted, the author submits his humble apologies.

In summary, the major emphases of this book are:

1. A review, comparison, evaluation, and integration of relevant theories, and an advancement of new theoretical concepts.
2. Provision of a behavioral and social "cement" for a wide variety of political, economic, environmental, and technological material.
3. A definition of problems, methods, and data sources and usefulness, and an evaluation of further data needs.
4. An evaluation of technological developments and projections and forecasts thereof, and the impacts of such developments.
5. An interrelating of intra- and extrasystem or organization features associated with people, technology, and environments, whether they be social, physical, or natural ("ecological"). Accordingly, the book is certainly a socio-technical-environmental book, and could be entitled, albeit clumsily, "Sociotechnicoenvironmental Factors in Analysis, Design, and Management."
6. A utilization of complex systems models, including models of society, and determination of at least correlative and at best cause-effect relationships between independent and dependent variables.
7. Determination of principles, particularly predictive principles, for the management of complex organizations, including the management of society.

Finally, although many of the areas considered in this book, for example, ecology and the environment, are currently in the public eye, this book represents a first total *systems* approach to integration and planning. There is today tremendous interest in applying systems techniques to sociotechnical and environmental problems. Nevertheless, many of the standard or established techniques such as operations research, benefit-cost analysis, and Program Planning and Budgeting System (PPBS) may be found wanting and may fall by the wayside. Other techniques must be developed, especially in dealing with "soft," very labile, or extremely complicated and hard-to-define variables. Theory must be advanced, especially in dealing with behavioral and social variables. This then is an essential *raison d'être* of this book: to bring together the fragments and pieces of our problem-solving expertise—up to now physical systems scientists talk the big picture but are not certain how to proceed; behavioral scientists are almost unaware of the challenge; and social scientists lack an understanding of technology.

As such this book can be thought of as a second generation of technology's contributing to the benefit of society. The operations research—management science "effectiveness" and "benefit-cost" approaches can be viewed as a first. Today's job is of course much harder, much more subtle than the promise of the 1960s suggested. Thus, although this is indeed a book on systems science, a book about society and technology and management and government, and a book on conservation, *most of all,* it's a book about you and me, where we are today, and where we're going tomorrow.

It is hoped this book will help you develop, enlarge, or confirm (even in the negative sense) your own sociotechnical philosophy. Are you a doomsday advocate (e.g., there will be widespread death from famine and pollution by the mid-1970s), a pessimist (problems of the utmost severity confront our world and we have limited time, doubting that our capability, given even the best efforts, can solve these problems within our present sociocultural contexts), an optimist (serious but not unsurmountable problems exist, but dedication and application of our expertise will solve major problems within a few decades to a century), or one of those cheerful persons who maintains things have always been about the same throughout mankind's existence—a "Hatlo's History" philosophy—and man has always solved his problems and will continue to do so *as problems arise?* One of the things which certainly must concern each of us is the question to which extent things actually *are* different today. There may be some tough customers to convince.

ACKNOWLEDGMENTS

The author would like to thank four men who helped a great deal in preparation of this book. Their kind help in reviewing both the proposed outline and the full manuscript was invaluable. They are Professor David Lee Bradford, Stanford University; Professor Warren B. Brown, University of Oregon; Dr. Harold H. Frank, University of Pennsylvania; and Professor Herbert A. Simon, Carnegie-Mellon University. I would also like to acknowledge the kind help of Sheryl Fullerton, without whose help this book in its final form would not be possible.

KENYON BRENTON DE GREENE
Woodland Hills, California
March, 1973

I

SYSTEMS, THEORIES, CONCEPTS, DYNAMICS, AND PROBLEMS

Part I begins with an overview of the structure and function of complex systems in general, and of the problems associated with the study of such systems. This is followed by an overview of general systems and related theories, and specific sociotechnical theories. Deficiencies in theory in describing the properties and predicting the behavior of complex systems are interpreted. The main dynamics of socio-technical-environmental interaction are then discussed. A behavioral connective tissue or integration is stressed. This part concludes with a consideration of the implications for systems management of essentially exponential technological and social change, and impact by and on the social and natural environments.

1

The Systems Framework:
An Overview

INTRODUCTION AND DEFINITIONS

This book is about systems science. It deals with systems—or the need for systems—at the "complex" level of hierarchy. These systems are composed of multifarious elements or constituents: people, vehicles, computers, power plants, buildings, roads, and so forth organized in terms of myriad subtle and superimposed interrelationships. The unifying theme of this book deals with how the human, that is, behavioral and social, subsystems affect and are affected by the nonhuman, that is, the technological, subsystem, and how these subsystems collectively in turn affect and are affected by the usually dynamic social and natural environments in which the larger system is enmeshed.

We shall deal minimally with individual human behavior, say, at the clinical level or at the level of the man-machine interface. Rather we shall be concerned with those features of behavior, perceptual, motivational, decisional, attitudinal, and so on, manifested by people collectively. No fine distinction will be made between the "behavioral" and "social" features of human beings. These grade into one another. Likewise, "technology" involves the collective body of scientific concept, experimentation, and analysis; engineering design; industrial production; hardware and gadgets; and consumer utilization. We are, accordingly, not concerned with say, the design and usage, of a specific aircraft, with specific personnel policies, or with automobile safety, except insofar as they may be representative of a body of technology.

3

In the most general sense, a system can be thought of as being a number or set of constituents or elements in active organized interaction as a bounded[1] entity, such as to achieve a common whole or purpose which transcends that of the constituents in isolation. It is a temporarily autonomous thing. This simple concept must be qualified in terms of the systems dealt with in this book. First, the constituents will almost always include both similar and dissimilar members. Second, organization exists at several or many different levels. Third, the systems possess both considerable inertia and considerable momentum. Thus, changes may be difficult to make, or once made to control, and cause-effect relationships exceedingly difficult to decipher. Fourth, almost all these systems themselves consist of lower-level systems which may possess considerable complexity. And fifth, it is almost impossible to treat these systems without considering interactions and repercussions throughout the complex macro-systems of societies and nations.

The term, *sociotechnical system,* defines the type system with which we are concerned; systems possessing the above and other attributes will be discussed later. Our sociotechnical systems are hierarchically much more complex than those, first bearing the name, which were studied in British coal mines and Indian automatic looms. Likewise, whereas the earlier emphasis was upon the effect of automation and other technology upon the worker in an industrial production setting, our emphasis is upon the interactions of massive technology and technological change upon today's and tomorrow's societies, both advanced and not so advanced.

Stated in another way, *sociotechnical* as used in this book includes systems concepts, hierarchically above, but equivalent to, *man-machine systems.* In addition, the term describes a location on a continuum from *automatic* to *social.* As with man-machine systems, we can speak of the sociotechnical interface, recognizing that this interface or boundary is dynamic, flexible, and permeable. There is a good analogy to the man-machine control loop. This book stresses the highest hierarchical level involving cities, regions, societies, and nations. Lower levels involve man-machine systems and the industrial-organizational socio-technical systems of Trist and Emery, whose pioneering works are discussed in detail later in this chapter.

It should be recognized that an element can be a member of more than one system at a given time and a member of one system at one time and another system at a later time. Accordingly, we can speak of a *transportation system, an urban system, a health services system, an anti-crime and violence system,* etc. We shall discuss problems and cases in each of these systems in detail in Part III.

Although the term, *sociotechnical system,* is relatively new, the problems of

---

[1] In many ways the boundary around a system may be a dynamic region more than a line.

the interaction of technology with society and with patterns of life and work has been with us in force since the Industrial Revolution and even before. Indeed, anthropologists have long been concerned with the interaction, over all of human evolution, between man and his tools. Likewise, the considerable body of material in human factors, industrial engineering, social change, and managerial psychology can be considered complementary to the present emerging field. What is new is the belated recognition of the immense complexity of systems and the rise of the systems approach to theory and to practice in considering wholes and interrelations, repercussions, and impacts. Yet, as in the field of systems science as an entity, there is still no all-encompassing theory and little integration of theory and practice. Indeed, practice itself is largely in the groping, trial-and-error stage.

A FURTHER LOOK INTO OUR
SCOPE AND LIMITATIONS

We shall stress the need for integrating themes in tying together an immense amount of material from myriad sources, disciplines, degrees of aggregation, extents of cohesiveness, and hierarchical levels. These themes are basically behavioral, at least by implication capable of being expressed in terms of perception, self-concept, motivation, decision, value and attitude, action, etc. At the same time we shall attempt to express these psychological dimensions as aggregate behaviors of different levels in our culture, to express them in a form consistent with general theories of human behavior, and to express them as dynamic forces within society. In a similar manner we shall deal with the main technological forces (e.g., automation and technological change), economic forces (e.g., growth), and environmental consequences (e.g., saturation and extinction). Throughout, we shall emphasize dynamics rather than statics, feedback relationships, interactions, impacts, and subtle or complicated responses.

There is an immense amount of extant material in the field which requires assembly, collation, and integration; the requirement for advancing the theory to provide structure and predictive capability to this mass of knowledge is even greater. Until now this material has not been subsumed under the sociotechnical theme.

Unfortunately, data and facts do not usually exist in forms amenable to the above behavioral, technological, and environmental interpretations. Problems of translation, therefore, are among our most formidable. Nevertheless, we are not forced to start from scratch, and a considerable body of approaches and knowledge now is available for guidance. For example, we can extrapolate considerably from our experience designing aerospace and weapons systems and our knowledge of man-machine systems, that is, concepts of man-machine interface, interactions, and symbiosis. This is true even though there has seldom been theory to guide our practice.

We infer that our emergent expertise should be valid and applicable at all levels of sociotechnical hierarchy, from small organizations to the macrosystems of world society. In this regard, our theories will have to explain systems behavior in hierarchical terms in addition to stratum-limited input-throughput-output terms. For example, theory should tie together such hithertofore unrelated areas as the effects of technology on alienation, the effects of automation on the needs for people of various skill levels, the effects of computerization on management structure, the role of new computer-related communications devices on the need for people to meet together personally, and the role of information systems on policy-making and decision-making. Equally critically important will be the identification of major subsystems within society (e.g., transporation, health, power-generation, urban), their description and illustration by cases, and their interrelating by both correlative (regression) and dynamic (computer simulation) models.

Environmental Features
Encouraging the Structuring of Systems

Prerequisite to the description, analysis, measurement, data collection, and interpretation within a given science is the simple recognition of events or phenomena that contribute to the identification of the scope of that science. And prerequisite to the solution of problems of both design and management is a basic awareness and a definition of those problems. In this section we shall permit our perceptions to wander along a broad spectrum of events, phenomena, and problems, which might appear unrelated to the superficial observer, but which collectively, we believe, force us to take a systems approach both to these events of nature and society and to the systems field itself.

Accordingly, a glance at the world about us may reveal a picture of impermanence, loss of purpose, even chaos. Perhaps we might summarize our observations and ask questions somewhat as follows. In the course of this book we shall attempt to provide at least partial interpretations of these observations and answers to the questions.

1. When the public, and by extension society's policy-makers, learn about a problem it is often too late effectively to do much about it, because of the operation of time lag and of latent forces. Thought and practice tend to lag far behind systems dynamics. Public awareness can be examined in terms of words printed, dollars spent, etc., relative to such areas as "pollution," "systems," "the environment," "ecology," "racial equality," etc. Contrariwise, a practice once initiated may be quite difficult to dampen. It is probably not unfair to state that most U.S.

"social" thought and policy is still either largely economic and rooted in the problems of the Great Depression, or based on the belated recognition of racial injustice stemming from civil rights movements of the 1950s and 1960s.

2. What is economic growth? social system growth? Can they be equated to biological and organic growth in general? For example, are such concepts as surface/volume ratio, heat production and loss, the limits to size of completely terrestrial animals, gravity, the ability of birds and other organisms to fly, and animal control and coordination mechanisms of general systems theoretic value? Are the concepts, from astronomy, of a star's collapse under its own weight of value here? How useful are the mathematical laws of growth? Are there organic limitations applicable to an economy? Certainly it is plausible to assume that unlimited economic growth is contrary to Nature.

3. Society and technology tend to reinforce one another in a positive feedback manner, which is not always desirable. At the same time there is often a loss of negative feedback and self-regulation. In cybernetic terms, there may be no comparator because of the diminution of absolutes and other values.

4. What sorts of R & D should be encouraged and for what purposes in our time of rapidly changing thought? How is funding to be allocated? How do we evaluation return on R & D investments?

5. Introduction of a new technology may reduce costs, but may disrupt an existing organization and social structure, perhaps dangerously and irreversibly.

6. Social and technological systems may be asynchronous or out of phase. Cultural lags occur. The rates of change of the two systems may be different. This situation is particularly dangerous today with our flamboyant technology and anachronistic or frontier-age attitudes of simplification and near veneration of the positive value of bigness, newness, fastness, change, and growth.

7. Have we reached a plateau beyond which further "improvements" may be impossible, at least without major breakthroughs? For example, life expectancy has not changed appreciably since the 1950s. And there is plentiful evidence from industry (the C-5A aircraft or the entire Lockheed Aircraft Corporation), from the military (Southeast Asia), and society (urban decay) that we live in a time of big failures or at least starkly curtailed successes.

8. With regard to the management of society, considered in detail in the last chapter of this book, we must consider the contact, coalescence, or even collision of three major forces: massive technology, the recognition of myriad social and ecological problems, and decision-making and other processes in government. Which should or indeed can be viewed as the forcing function?

9. How do subsystems, originally informal and loosely structured, grow more and more together and intertwined until society finds itself "out on

a limb" and must face the necessity of cutting off that limb when it realizes where it is? A salient example involves the role of automobile production as a percentage of the economy and of the GNP and as an employer on the one hand, and as a source of vast, automobile-created pollution, congestion, blight, and decline problems on the other. Is there a Principle of Malevolent Adaptation: in complex societies people become specialized and adapted to non-essential gadgets; then everything seems to become intertwined and later, when some feature or subsystem is lost, people can no longer adapt and the whole system is shaken? In other ways technology "forces" changes in perceptions, motivations, and attitudes. How modifiable or immodifiable are such changes?

10. How much can technology stress society and government before they break? This implies that new concepts for the management of society are of paramount importance. How are the main functions of management of society now changing? These transcend such concepts as *democracy, free enterprise, capitalism, communism,* and *socialism.* In a related sense, with regard to the concept of *equifinality,* and alluding to the management of society, we could infer that because of technology the U.S., U.S.S.R., Western Europe, and Japan will all, within a matter of a couple of decades, end up with essentially the same social structure.

11. To what extent does the (more dynamic?) infraculture of blacks, youth, drug users, and hippies force change in the majority? Or is this even the right way to phrase the question? Are not these groups themselves under some control?

12. Many social entities are potentially a system or an incipient system, even though at a given time they may be fragmented, behave at cross purposes, and possess structure that is not coincident with function. We might call such entities *quasi systems.*

13. In dealing with human population problems, it is advantageous to develop the concept of a *personal envelope* which surrounds each person. Thus, population numbers and concentrations can be conceptualized and to some extent quantified in terms of proxemics (Hall, 1968); psychopathology; amounts of food, water, and air; transportation; scarce natural resources; recreation; etc. The envelope, or course, is dynamic and flexible.

14. Sociotechnical systems, like man-MACHINE systems, tend really to be socio-TECHNICAL systems. Decision-makers typically look for a simple technological fix to complex problems. For example, urban transportation problems are usually thought to involve more busses, freeways, and so forth instead of changes in school zones, tax laws, blight, etc., as incentives to encouraging moves back to the cities. And as time goes by, and, say, cities become dominated socially and politically by "newcomers," the patterns will become fixed and the trends irreversible. Another example involves tradeoffs between quick fixes for the automobile (more padding or smog control devices, for example) and development of an integrated transportation system. Often the quick fix

operates at cross purposes to the long-term solution. It appears that attention to a minor need satisfies the major need to attack more serious and profound problems. This appears consonant with the theory that people are "satisficers."

15. There is evidence of disillusionment with the solution: more technology to solve sociotechnical problems. Halting development of the supersonic transport and perhaps the trans-Alaska oil pipeline represent prime examples.

16. A glimpse of almost any eastern North American city suggests chaos, clutter, and superposition of incongruous elements. Most urban redevelopments, being counter to the real and dominant themes, forces, functions and dynamics, seem doomed to failure. Such "islands" are perhaps analogous to a new hat perched atop the head of a slatternly bawd. Yet, if the real structure and function of society and of a city can be determined, it is important not to work against the real dynamics. Continuing these thoughts, we must ask what are the historic purposes of cities: protection, exchange of goods, exchange of ideas, coordination or control and governance? Cities are no longer necessary to fulfill these purposes. Further, what basic human needs, originally fulfilled by cities, are now being frustrated? Urban redevelopment and elaborate transportation schemes may be really incidental at best and harmful at most. This point stresses again the urgent need for the integrated transportation system planning and integrated regional planning highlighted in the next to last chapter of this book. Even so, can we abandon our cities as was done at Tikal and Angkor, because, in our case, of the near impossibility of preserving the cities against the natural ecology of slums and decay. Slums can serve needs not being met elsewhere.

Continuing these same thoughts, do U.S. and Canadian cities which represent a junkpile of bridges, oil and gas tanks, warehouses, freeways, railroad tracks, churches, dwellings and businesses in various states of preservation and decay, and ostentatious high rise, really represent a nightmarish and garish yet vital pattern, a pattern, however ugly, which has evolved to fit the needs represented by decades or even by a couple of centuries? Is it possible that the latest spurt of change, represented by the freeways and high rise, is destroying or has destroyed this pattern?

17. A city, an "environment," a person's clothing, and an organizational structure may be viewed as a projection or extension of the self, modifying and being modified by the individual in terms of positive and negative feedback loops. Accordingly, if the individual does not care about himself by virtue of poverty, apathy, lack of education, or pathology, how can he care about (public) housing or the environment (for example, consider the thousands of junked cars along the roads and in the streams of eastern Kentucky)? Further, aggression, perhaps felt toward the self, becomes directed against the environment; hence, the starkly evident increase in vandalism today.

18. The technological impact of television most likely includes subtle effects,

say, relative to the increased spread and popularity of drugs. Thus, years of constantly being "turned on," "tuned in," and overstimulated reduce the capacity for quiet meditation and reduce the boredom threshold. Further, passive adaptations are strengthened over active ones.

19. It is easier to look for the source of difficulties outside the self or society rather than inside; hence, the ploy, as old as history, to direct attention to foreign "isms."

20. The present times may be characterized, paradoxically, by the increased hopes and expectations of the lower classes on the one hand and the death of hope of the middle classes on the other. Thus, we miss crucial points when we compare only medical, economic, and technological changes.

21. Once a system reaches a given hierarchical level, it can never reverse itself and return to a simpler level without fragmenting. Thus, because of increased mobility, all-pervasive communications, and changing values, we can never return, however much we should like to, to simpler concepts, say, of family structure, morality, or "law and order." A system under stress cannot adapt by regression, although decision-makers can break the positive feedback loops at a given level.

22. Of special importance in the development of sociotechnical systems theory, we must consider how systems: (a) impact on one another and on the environment(s); (b) collide; (c) conflict; and (d) may be irreconcilable regardless of our best intents and efforts; that is, they may possess unmalleable or irreducible properties. All these items must be considered in the context of developing a theory of sociotechnical macrosystems. Similarly, we must concern ourselves with the growth, and differential growth, of subsystems. Subsystems tend to outgrow their allotted "growing space." Results may involve: (a) coalescence; (b) conflict; (c) emergence of the stronger with elimination of the weaker; (d) establishing new liaisons; and (e) increased dependence of the total system upon the new pattern, so that loss or weakening of a subsystem precipitates a major crisis.

23. The effects of the technological subsystem upon the social subsystem and upon the environment are more often than not delayed, subtle, or secondary, tertiary, and so forth. Consider two examples. Industries, such as steel and petroleum refining, are mostly automatized and must now rely on (stimulating) growing *demand* and upon better plant utilization to reduce unit costs. Strict controls on air pollution have led to over-exploitation of low-sulfur-content coals in the western U.S., in turn leading to abusive strip mining.

In summary, many of the features considered alone can be further conceptualized in terms of the *interactions* among the subsystems of society as depicted in Figure 1-1. Note that certain variables can be considered dominant. This is a simple example of block- and flow-diagram modeling, an important step

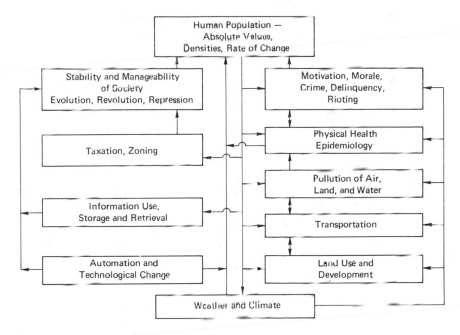

FIGURE 1-1
Representative interactions in a complex sociotechnical macrosystem.

in going from unorganized observations and impressions to loose mental models to logically consistent models amenable to treatment by the methods of systems science. We shall say a lot more about modeling later in the text. What other diagrammatic models could you construct to bring order to the above list of observations?

Lack of All-Purpose Theory
or Methodology

Before one can attend to the above points and others and develop a meaningful relationship between theory and practice of sociotechnical systems, it is first necessary to examine the nature of theory. Such examination reveals a fairly dismal picture. This is associated with the fragmented, nonsystematized nature of behavioral and social science theory, in turn related to the unfortunate disciplinary specialization of our times. Also, most of our techniques in systems engineering are based on systems with definite boundaries which can be easily isolated for study. With the complex systems of concern to us in this book we do not know the state variables or how many dimensions there are. Theory in this over-all field is still generally incipient. For example, there is no real population theory that deals with interactions, thresholds, etc., as opposed to numbers and concentrations. A start might begin with the analogy of cells becoming tissues.

A number of workers have commented on deficiencies in theory, methodology, practice, or emphasis within speciality areas: for example Albee (1970) on clinical psychology, Lockard (1971) on comparative psychology, Baron (1971) on experimental psychology, and Argyris (1969) and Silverman (1971) on social psychology. J. G. Miller (1955) and Grinker (1967) exemplify attempts to develop unified theories of behavioral science.

Similarly, Broady (1969) comments on the insignificance of much sociological study purportedly bearing on planning problems, and on the inability of academic sociologists to adapt to the demands of planning practice. Such failures are due especially to sociologists and urban planners having very different views of time. The academician is reluctant to predict on the basis of limited evidence; the planner must commit himself now on whatever evidence he has. We can add to this the inability of the academician to understand enough of his system to be able to study problems now that will be significant in the future.

The role of the sociologist is often grossly oversimplified. He is viewed as something of a market researcher—survey and establish the facts that will tell the planner exactly how to achieve the social goals. Ignored is the significant point that *between fact-finding and action lies theory.* And the last 20 years have involved too much simple fact-finding and too little theory.

Some Attempts at Integrating Systems, Organization, and Management Theories

The picture is hopeful, however. Today we possess a wealth of theory, practice, and findings, which properly synthesized, will prove invaluable to managers of sociotechnical systems. A coalescence of systems, organization, and management theories is of especial importance in designing new institutions. The success of organizations, and the managers which go with them, is a function of time and place. Thus, some organizations are most adapted to a climate of innovation and rapid change, others to maintaining a status quo, and still others to a climate of environmental change. Wrong combinations of organization, management, and environment thus make for failure. It is probably rare that any one organization possesses the adaptability necessary to succeed at all stages. This may be most typically witnessed in the behavior of bureaucracies which function in terms of past goals and objectives, or ostensible goals and objectives, and whose major function often seems to be offering employment to bureaucrats. One of the most important features for designing new organizations and institutions to cope with the problems of the seventies and beyond may thus be a self-regulatory, even a self-destruct mechanism. This will serve to evaluate constantly organization-environment interrelationships, to revise goals and objectives in the light of this relationship, and to phase the organization out of existence when dissonance exists. Balanced theory, involving cybernetic and other concepts, could help in just such designs.

This book in toto may be viewed as an attempt to develop a description and a theory of sociotechnical systems. As such it transcends a synthesis of extant theories. Nevertheless, it will be of value here to summarize other attempts at integration or synthesis, which at our level of emphasis are mostly at the sub-system level. For example, Hilgert (1964) has reviewed organization theory as applied to business management, and Hughes and Mann (1969) the convergence of systems theory and planning theory. Hilgert concludes that in most cases the applications of organization theory to actual planning may be small. Most organizational planners lack a theoretical understanding, as we emphasized above.

In looking at an organization as a "whole" or "system," one must recognize that a description of functions (marketing, production, etc.), or an organization chart, gives a partial and biased impression. An organization is more realistically a many dimensioned system of interdependent factors, including individuals, groups, attitudes, motives, formal structure, interactions, goals, status, and authority. The environment includes social, cultural, legal, physical, technical, and economic factors.

Alfred North Whitehead, as long ago as 1925, applied the concept of organism to the modern factory, emphasizing the need to comprehend such an organism in all its completeness. Extending this view, present emphases are of organizations as complex and dynamic structures interacting symbiotically with elements in their environments.

A number of models of organizations, some elaborate, have since been formulated. Bakke's comprehensive (1959) model involves *bonds*, which represent the ongoing activities identifying the organization, giving it purpose and direction, and maintaining it in an evolving state. These bonds are:

1. *Identification bonds* which include the functions and objectives which develop and legitimize an organization.
2. *Perpetuation bonds* which provide and perpetuate basic resources.
3. *Work-flow bonds* which produce a service or product.
4. *Control bonds* which control and coordinate operations and behavior.
5. *Homeostatic bonds* which provide a state of evolving dynamic equilibrium.

Somewhat related is Whyte's (1959) interactional approach which views the organization as a total system in which individual and group interactions, activities, and (even) sentiments are mutually dependent upon each other.

Mathematical approaches to the theory of organizational behavior tend to stress problem-solving and decision-making. Some studies have dealt with quantifications of information flow. Simon's book, *Models of Man* (1957), is a collection of essays on mathematical models of group and organizational processes. Interactions, activities, and sentiments are dealt with.

Another step has involved the development of "revisionist concepts in personnel management." This involves an attempt to reconcile and integrate the classical scientific management theory, popular early in the 20th century, which viewed the needs of the workers as secondary to those of the assembly line, with the human relations theory, which emphasized that workers could be motivated to work more productively if the work situation offered gratification of psychological and social needs. "Revisionist" organizational theories emphasize that the goals of the organization and of the individual are not usually in harmony, and indeed, may actually conflict. We shall return to integrative attempts in some detail below.

Cyert and March (1959) conceptualized that a business organization is made up of coalitions and subcoalitions such as managers, workers, and stockholders. Each makes demands on the organization and these must be integrated. Through a process of intra- and intergroup bargaining, organizational objectives are defined and organizational decisions reached.

Argyris (1960) has theorized that industrial organizations are formalized and structured with objectives that are basically in conflict with the needs of individuals. People adapt by creating an informal employee culture. Thus, the total behavioral system is a composite of: (1) behavior resulting from formal organizational demands; (2) behavior resulting from demands of the employee culture; (3) behavior resulting from each individual's attempt to fulfill his own needs; and (4) behavior resulting from a patterning of the first three in each organization.

Organizational and systems theory have made some contribution to the area of planning. Haire (1959) has compared organizational growth to the growth of organisms. Dubin (1959) has theorized that organizational stability can be best achieved by minimizing the number of linkages between elements. Dror (1968) emphasizes the application of qualitative ideas to public policy-making, and he implies elements of extra-rationality and creativity in public decision-making. Thorstein Veblen (1953) states that institutions are adapted to past circumstances and, hence, never in full accord with present requirements. Thus, we might think of groups and organizations as being in part reactions to stress, and, hence, always *ex post facto*. Argyris and McGregor (Argyris, 1957) believe job enlargement, i.e., expanding the nature of job responsibilities as opposed to the further division of labor, can be an important means of integrating individual and organizational goals. Often organizational decentralization of decision-making and responsibility is stressed. This bridges theory and reality and enables some reconciling of achievement of the organization's objectives and fulfillment of individual needs.

To formal social organizations governed by public policy, the concepts of wholeness, hierarchical differentiation, orderliness, open systems, interdependence, and steady-state behavior appear to be particularly appropriate. Program Planning and Budgeting System (PPBS)[2] can be thought of as a general theory of planning, appropriate to nearly every type of organization. PPBS includes programs designed around long-range goals which are broken down into measurable objectives. It is a process whereby objectives and resources (ends-means) and their interrelationships are combined to produce a comprehensive program of action for an organization conceived as a whole. However, it has its limitations, associated with political elements, lack of systems analytic procedures for solving problems of social change, poor assumptions and data, emphasis on a personally demeaning centralization, inadequate government staffing, and emphasis on measuring only what is easy (or popular) to measure. Perhaps prematurely, it has spread widely throughout the federal and some local governments. We shall return to these problems in Parts II and III.

Pugh (1969) has looked at developments leading to the conceptualization of the emerging field of organizational behavior, a theoretical-research-oriented field which attempts to understand the behavior of men in organizations, a study in its own right. Several types of theorists have participated, including management and administrative theorists, structural theorists, group theorists, individual theorists, a heterogeneous assortment of technology theorists, and economic theorists.

Contributions have been made to the understanding of reactions to stress, decision-making under conditions of uncertainty, social learning and conformity, creativity, and adult human motivation.

From the theoretical emphasis stems the need to choose scientific problems for study rather than managerial ones. Too pragmatic an approach may simply cloud the issue. Further, the study of organizational behavior should involve both the clinical-processual and the statistical-factorial approaches. Cross-sectional surveys and logitudinal studies must supplement each other if we are to develop relevant theories. Further, one should be cautious of over-reliance on managerial philosophies, such as the "human-relations movement." Terms like *democratic* and *authoritarian* leadership, with gross connotations of good and bad, are not loosely used in the newer approach to organizational behavior.

A number of authors have couched theory and problems of organization and management within the framework of general systems theory. See, for example, Rubin (1971).

Roberts (1970) has reviewed cross-cultural factors in organizations. Lichtman and Hunt (1971) have summarized the relationship between personality and

----

[2]Often referred to as Planning, Programming and Budgeting System or by a similar variation.

organization theory. Both articles provide good summaries of contributions to organization theory.

Lichtman and Hunt (1971), stressing that a theory of organization[3] can be no stronger than the assumptions made about the human personality, after a thorough literature review conclude that normative theories are much less useful in understanding organizational behavior than are theories that recognize situational contingencies (that is systems-environment theories).

How one does relate persons and organizations involves just one, albeit important, area in the total sociotechnical context of this book. Organization theories have variously emphasized social structure, human personality, and other attributes, the requirements and functions of the organization, and systems-level integration of the foregoing.

Lichtman and Hunt employ a fourfold classification. A summary of their classification with representative theories follows (see Lichtman and Hunt [1971] for detailed literature references).

1. *Traditional structural theorists* (**classical organization theories**) generalize that man is lazy, untrustworthy, and works only for money; hence, organizational design typically results in bureaucracy, and motivation is interpreted solely and rationally in economic terms.
   a. *Marx:* Man is influenced entirely by society, thus, the only way to change man is through changing society.
   b. *Durkheim:* Man can be characterized as a function of the structure of society, once a division of labor has been established.
   c. *Taylor* (**scientific management**) and the *Gilbreths*: Man is an extension of the job, performance on which can be made more efficient through time, time and motion, and method studies. Organizations can be designed and specified in terms of organization charts and job specifications. Motivation, except in terms of economic emolument and duty, and the worker's life away from the job, are unimportant.
   d. *Gulick and Urwich* (**administrative management**): Organizational efficiency can be increased through task specialization and the grouping of similar tasks into separate departments for production, personnel, supply, etc. (N.B. Not only do the last two approaches ignore the organization's boundary and environment, but they remain strong today, wearing the modern dress of computer-based exercises in model building, operations research, and cost-effectiveness.)
   e. *Bureaucracy:* The individual human being is essentially unimportant and can be made compliant through the proper use of rules, procedures, rewards, and punishments. Organizational efficiency is enhanced through providing offices according to jurisdiction and hierarchical

---

[3]Organizations, following Scott (1964—see references at the end of the primary reference) are defined (p.488) as "collectivities . . . established for the pursuit of relatively specific objectives on a more or less continuous basis."

structure or authority and staffing these offices with experts controlled as above. The resulting behavior typically is static, rigidly inappropriate, and depersonalizing Byproducts are wasted time, higher costs, low morale, lower-quality work, figure "fudging," etc. However, in effect, organizations tend to be differentially bureaucratized.

2. *Modern structural theorists* generalize that man is self-actualizing; hence, organizational design should result in a looser, more decentralized structure than bureaucracy.

   a. *Merton:* **Anomie** arises from conflict between the goals of a society, e.g., attainment of wealth and stature and the means of attainment, e.g., hard work and devotion to duty. Similarly, to other authors, the structure of an organization itself interferes with the realization of individual human needs.

   b. *Maslow:* Human needs can be expressed in an ascending hierarchy, as physiological needs, survival and safety needs, social needs, ego needs, autonomy needs, and self-actualization needs. A higher-level need cannot be satisfied until lower-level needs are met. All human activity reflects an attempt to work upward through this hierarchy. (This concept provides one major unifying theme for this book; see also Chapter 2, Motivational Factors.)

   c. *Argyris:* Organizational structure, to achieve efficiently its objectives, should provide increasing opportunity for self-esteem and at the same time reduce compulsive, defensive behavior associated with low morale, feelings of insecurity, etc.

   d. *McGregor* (**Theory X** and **Theory Y**): Man is either lazy, unwilling to work unless driven, uncooperative, and requiring management control to get the job done (X), or the opposite (Y). It is up to management to determine best how to utilize human resources.

   Accordingly, in view of all the above, emphasis of these theorists is upon participative decision-making ("participatory democracy"), job enrichment, increased responsibility, mutual confidence between employee and supervisor, and so forth.

   However, there may be many ("assembly line") job situations in which power-equalization and perhaps "job-enrichment" techniques may be more expensive than they are held to be worth. The controversy as to if and how jobs can be enriched or otherwise made satisfying, and what substitutes (e.g., use of leisure) are possible, remains active. Undoubtedly, "human relations" theories are as much oversimplifications as are the classical theories against which they express reactions. A total systems approach would require consideration of, at least, organizational size, organizational level, subunit size, line and staff hierarchies, hierarchical steepness, degree of centralization or decentralization, and span of control.

3. *Personalistic theorists* emphasize individual differences in human cognition, emotion, experience, and so forth. Emphasis is thus at the level of the individual or small group (the psychological level) rather than at the sociological level of organizational structure.

a. *Lewin* (**field theory**) (by extension of his ideas): Man reacts to an organization on the basis of his perceptions of it and the perceptions in turn are based on man's needs, motives, values, and attitudes. Hence, to change an organization one must alter the perceptions of people (by the group-dynamics-based T-group approach, for example).

b. *Mayo and the Hawthorne studies:* Friendship patterns or human relations provide the essential, if informal, structure of an organization. Management's interest can best be served by changing people's perceptions toward work and toward the organization as it is. "Participative management" thus turns out to be manipulative.

c. *Likert:* An organization functions best when its major functioning elements are not individuals but groups with high work-performance goals. The groups should be overlapping in both the hierarchical and horizontal senses, in order to enhance employee participation in decision-making.

d. *Maslow:* Work itself is a primitive need, quite apart from its social- or ego-need symbolism, and can be intrinsically interesting.

e. *Herzberg:* The only true job satisfaction comes from the work itself. "Hygiene" (good working conditions) and friendship on the job can make the job only tolerable.

We shall return to the theories of Lewin later in this chapter and in Chapter 2, those of Maslow in Chapters 2 and 9, and those of Herzberg in Chapter 9.

There is no clear separation between Lichtman's and Hunt's modern structural theorists and personalistic theorists. Individuals such as Maslow appear in both groups. However, all three groups so far have the deviciency of failing to take a total systems approach. Thus, any comprehensive organization theory must incorporate considerations of the formal structure of the organization, the functions of informal groups, individual human functions, and the environment in which the organization is enmeshed.

4. *Integrative organization theories* attempt to synthesize the above. A number of approaches have been made to the synthesis of the immense number of organizational variables.

a. *Katzell's framework for determining organizational policies and practices:* Organizational size, degree of interaction and interdependence, personalities of organization members, degree of congruence or disparity between organizational and member goals (degree of goal internalization by employees), and which person(s) take action to further organizational abilities.

b. *Social systems:*

(1) *Homans:* A social system consists of a mutually dependent external system and an internal (less formal) system, operating as human activities, interactions, and sentiments, in an environment of three parts, viz., physical, cultural, and technological.

(2) *Katz and Kahn* and the extension of **open systems theory**. We shall

return later in this chapter to a further examination of Katz and Kahn's work.

(3) *The Tavistock Institute* and the sociotechnical system extension of open-systems theory and the importance of interactions between the organization and the environment. We shall examine the Tavistock work in considerable detail later in this chapter.

(4) *Role theory:* Role provides the basic major building block of social systems as a link between the individual with his personalistic charac- teristics and the organization. Yet this idea, under another term, has long been recognized by the U.S. Air Force; cf. the Air Force Specialty Code (AFSC). Role permits a merging of social and individual phenomena, previously treated separately.

(5) *Role Conflict:* Role conflict can arise from disparities between expectation and performance within the role system. Role conflict varies as a function of a number of specific organizational and personal characteristics. Job satisfaction and emotional health are associated with role conflict.

Roberts (1970) follows Blau's (1968) definition of an organization (p. 298): An organization is "the existence of procedures for mobilizing and coordinating the efforts of various, usually specialized subgroups in the pursuit of joint objectives." After a large review of the cross-cultural literature, she concluded we are far from comprehensive theories about behavior in organizations, because of disciplinary specializations, lack of methodology, use of isolated cases, lack of replicability of studies, etc. Little is known about how organizations arise in cultures, develop, and interact with one another. Most work is on individual behavior in organizations and organizations are rarely viewed as parts of their environments.

Greene (1971) stresses an ahistorical approach to systems structure and systems environment. He considers knowing the past of the system useless information.

Finally, much can be learned from success or failure stories of actual complex organizations studied as a whole. For example, permanent or temporary cor- porate failures involving Penn Central, Rolls Royce, and Lockheed Aircraft Corporation, Douglas Aircraft Corporation (now part of McDonnell-Douglas), Pan American World Airways, and Litton Ships Division should be carefully dissected in terms of both theory and practice. Our present ignorance is due partially to our being encouraged to study organizations only at a subsystem level (e.g., worker morale) or as requested by the top management who them- selves may have been a large part of the problem. The Penn Central case, representing an especially egregious misuse of corporate power by the chief financial officers of the U.S.'s sixth largest corporation and largest transporta- tion corporation, ended with the loss of four million dollars and the collapse of the railroad on June 21, 1970.

INTERDISCIPLINARY APPROACH
AND CONTRIBUTING FIELDS

The field of sociotechnical systems as a whole is new. However, as seen above, it possesses historical antecedents in many areas and can also be thought of as a framework applicable to most any discipline which deals with complex problems. Contributing fields and fields of application include engineering, psychology, sociology and demography, medicine and public health, ecology, meteorology, mathematics and statistics, operations research and management science, economics, and political science and public administration. It is assumed you are familiar with each of these, at least at the level of definition and general scope. We shall examine problems and cases from each of these fields throughout this book.

The relative value, in public thinking and in policy-making, of the above fields differs greatly, however, Biderman (1970) has reviewed five social science books (Beals, 1969; Lyons, 1969; National Academy of Sciences, 1968; National Academy of Sciences, and Social Science Research Council, 1969; and National Science Foundation, 1969). Three of the books are committee reports and the two written by individual authors were also based on inquiries undertaken by organizations. In some ways the reports are already archaic, because of rapid social change. Some of the reports find the social sciences to be poorly equipped, poorly motivated, poorly organized, poorly situated, and just poor.

In a somewhat opposite vein, Deutsch, Platt, and Senghaas (1971) have analyzed 62 "social science" advances since 1900, and conclude that most come from a few centers and have rapid effects and are accepted as soon as technological advances; they are as clearly defined and operational as technological developments. However, their definition of "advances in social science" is extremely broad, including areas as diverse as information theory, cybernetics, and computers on the one hand, and the theories of Lenin and Mao on the other. Yet they are arbitrarily selective and exclude areas such as television and the achievement motivation of D. McClelland.

According to the authors, the advances appear to indicate a definite cumulative growth in this century. Theory, metholology, and empirical results form "one production cycle of knowledge." Advances appear to have occurred at the rate of approximately one per year. Interdisciplinary teams of social scientists, with appreciable funding, at specific centers of intellectual activity appear to have been favored over "lone wolf" investigations in isolation. Quantitative topics have assumed greater and greater importance. Practical demands stimulated about three-fourths of the work.

SYSTEMS CONCEPTS

In this section we shall examine the major concepts applicable to the study of all larger complex systems, some of the properties of such systems, and examples, representing especially salient problems of our times, which typify failure to think in systems terms.

Milsum (1968) provides a useful framework for an overview of interlocking systems problems. The approach is flavored by his background in control systems engineering. Processes are classified in terms of geosphere, biosphere, technosphere, and sociosphere. Various cyclic and circulation phenomena in the geosphere and biosphere provide examples, e.g., of moisture-trapped energy, carbon, and oxygen. Natural selection, competition, and adaptation in evolution represent a positive-feedback unstable process. Organization of an ever-increasing higher order is produced, in contrast to the usual situation, prescribed by the second law of thermodynamics, of degradation to a uniformly lower order. This emergence of an ever-higher order occurs because living organisms are *open* to the sun. Predator-prey relationships and self-regulation, both within ecologies, exist in order to ensure some balance or stability between animal and food supply, not only in the short range but also taking statistical fluctuations into account. In this context, the entire September, 1970, issue of *Scientific American* on the biosphere, which treats the above-referenced cycles, should be reviewed.

Technological advances have occurred much faster than man's or society's capability of adapting to them. The time constants of technological change are probably at least one order of magnitude greater than that of social change. Further, societal problems, solutions to these problems, codification, resistance to the establishment, etc. may occur in discrete jumps with thresholds and crumbling of resistance (a form of relaxation oscillation). The magnitude of threshold for system change separates evolution from revolution

Both in biology and society rates of change appear to be more important than absolute values. Similarly, comparison and derivation of an "error signal" is important with regard to evaluating performance.

There are fundamental incompatibilities simultaneously held, say, with regard to accidents, safety, and the value of life itself, between public and private, and conscious and unconscious attitudes about society. Further, because societies possess so much positive feedback, plans and prophecies may become self-fulfilling. The managers of society must bear this in mind.

Based partially on Milsum (1968) and Lamb (1968), the most important phenomena of complex systems can be considered to be as follows.

Growth and Positive Feedback;
Regulation and Negative Feedback

Concepts of positive and negative feedback, especially alternating or coupled positive and negative feedback, are important in determining reaching, overshooting, undershooting, or oscillations about some goal level.

Examples here derive from biology, the city, and the interrelationship between technology and demand for goods and services. Negative feedback is associated with self-regulation and goal-direction, positive feedback with growth and decay. Endocrine control in mammals provides an example of both negative and positive feedback. The growth of cells and organisms represents positive feedback. Of most concern to us in the present book are the interrelated feedback mechanisms of organizations, cities, and societies. This is especially true of the positive loops involving population growth, economic growth, the growth of knowledge and technology, advertising, and technology and consumer demand.

Positive feedback is fundamental to all growth processes in both living and nonliving systems. Exponential or logistic (S-shaped) curves may apply. Examples include fire, organisms, knowledge, capital, fads and fashions, mob violence, and political bandwagons. Because of elimination of competition through purpose or accident, laws, beliefs, practices, and systems may be carried on by their own momentum after performance has fallen below the level of superiority originally necessary, and people have become satisfied.

Interactions and Rate Processes at
Subsystem Boundaries

Predictive power for processes of system change depend on understanding of interactions and of rate processes at the boundaries of subsystems. Anticipatory control is dependent on better understanding, say, of the increase in information energy due to education, communications, and so on. Thus, driving forces (goods/gap ratios) such as aspirations/achievement or expectations/perceptions, related respectively to political "goods" and societal "goods," are societal energies transformed from information energies.

Lamb (1968) suggests that that fraction of the populace with information energy above a threshold energy of activation can originate change in a societal system. Thus, the exponential rates of change and growths of population, electronic communications, publications, speed of airplanes, gross national products, education, etc. appear to be largely due to just such a fraction. We just don't understand well the rate of change processes.

Oscillations and Damping

The biological world provides many examples of oscillations, fluctuations, and periodicities, usually associated with damping efforts to restore an equilibrium or steady state. Circadian and other biorhythms and vertebrate homeostatic mechanisms will be familiar to most readers. From ecology, the population explosions of lemmings, voles, mice, and rats are of interest. Society provides examples of economic business cycles, and indeed the confusing mixture of inflation and recession characteristic of our times.

Oscillations occur especially where there is mutual interaction, especially in the younger stages of maturity of ecologies and organizations. Yet the normal state of organisms is one of continual cycling.

Unidirectionality, Asymmetry, and Convergence of Forces

Unidirectionality is examplified by the firing pattern of stimulatory or inhibitory neurons and by the contraction pattern of agonist or antagonist muscles in animals. This results in a balanced, integrated, or steady-state condition. In society and in the ecosystem, forces may converge producing either balance or synergesis and instability. A contemporaneously important example involves the apparent "cancelling effect" of increased CO_2 and increased particulate matter, both due largely to man's activities, on global temperature.

Atwater (1970), for example, looks at changes in the planetary albedo, i.e., the proportion of incoming solar energy reflected back to space by earth and its atmosphere. Changes, associated with pollutants, may affect the temperature of the earth.

It is generally believed that an increase in carbon dioxide is contributing to an increase in mean annual world-wide temperature. Atwater believes, however, that the ratio of absorption to backscattering of solar radiation and the surface or lower cloud layer albedo are the most important determinants of climatic change. Combinations of factors are important. Aerosols play a role. Thus, if solar radiation were the only thermal process, the present urban aerosol-surface albedo would produce a warming trend, whereas the desert or prairie aerosol-albedo combination would produce a cooling trend.

Although, as we have just seen, there are still unknowns in our understanding of the myriad interrelated factors determining and influencing global climate and weather, it is better to be cautious than optimistic in dealing with the consequences of man's activities. The effects of human-induced pollution could be dire, indeed. Thus Rasool and Schneider (1971), using the theory of multiple scattering, have calculated that, for aerosols, the net effect of increase in density is to reduce the surface temperature of earth. Because of exponential[4] effects on backscattering, the rate of temperature decrease is actually augmented with increasing aerosol content. An increase in global aerosol background concentration by only a factor of 4 (only twice the estimated increase from 1910 to

---

[4]We shall consider many examples of such exponential growth or decay in the course of our treatment of complex systems.

1970) could reduce the surface temperature by 3.5° K, which, if sustained globally for several years, could induce a new ice age!

Clearly, the forces that can produce a climatic steady state are functions of both natural and human activities. It may not always be possible to detect incipient but potentially dangerous anthropogenic changes against a "noise spectrum" of natural fluctuations. The need for a worldwide monitoring system to determine the effects of aerosol, CO_2 and thermal pollution is thus urgent (Landsberg, 1970). The unplanned effects of human activities on local temperature, wind field, and perhaps rainfall have already been demonstrated. We shall discuss this further in Chapter 8 under the topic, The Urban Heat Island.

That control over pollution itself must reflect a balance of forces is demonstrated by a study of the San Francisco Bay Area (Burton, 1971). Pollution derived from transportation was considered to be the major source. Although some improvement in air quality might be expected over the next few years because of stricter automobile pollution controls, in the long run these improvements will be negated by a rapidly increasing human and automobile population. It would appear that an alternative low-pollution transportation system to shift emphasis away from the automobile is greatly needed. However, see the discussion in Chapter 8 of Bay Area transportation developments.

Man-Machine-Medium-Mission-Management Interaction

Borrowing the 5-M concept from human factors, we see that when we analyze or design, or otherwise study, systems, we must consider the human or social subsystem as it interrelates with the machine or technology subsystem in a given medium or environment, functioning in terms of a given mission reflecting the goals or purposes of users or management. Often actual system performance is much different from optimum performance based on abstracted concepts.

For example, automation of some functions within an organization may have over-all effects on:

1. Ability and skill levels secondarily affecting personnel manning and training policies.
2. Tolerance for acoustic noise levels with implications of hearing damage and lawsuits.
3. Monotony and boredom leading to decreased vigilance, increased tension, frustration, hostility, and alienation and therefore to increased errors, decreased productivity, absences, vandalism, etc.
4. Disturbances of work-rest-recreation cycles.
5. Decreased organizational loyalty.

6. Displacement upward or laterally of policy-making and decision-making, following the major sources of and control over information.

In our studies we must never lose sight of the capabilities and limitations of man the constituent of our systems. Often the relationships are subtle. For example, possible hearing loss in a computer operator who must work around many mechanical printers, tape drives, etc. is straightforward. The effects of computer equipment on one's feelings of adequacy are not.

Degree of Closedness or Openness

The closedness or openness of a system is, of course, a relative thing. Thus, the Earth can be viewed as a closed system in terms of the loss of nonrenewable resources such as fossil fuels and atmosphere. There is no interchange of atmospheric particles with space; for this reason, Earth's moon and the planet, Mars, are regarded as essentially dead bodies. On the other hand, in terms of the interchange of energy with space, Earth must be regarded as an open system. The same concept can be extended downward to nations, states, cities, homes, and vehicles. Because of expanding demands on fixed resources, and because of the deleterious side effects of industrial processes, it is necessary to design more and more closed systems within society. These range from recycling sewage and other wastes to use as fertilizer or fuel, to the extension of closed-system space-craft design concepts, to the "experimental cities" of Spilhaus (1968). A good example of these practices is the recent use of Chicago's copious amounts of sewage sludge to fertilize corn fields planted on land in southern Illinois which had been ravaged by strip-mining for coal.

Nations, states, and cities as open systems. The city is not a self-sufficient or wholly independent entity; it is dependent, for example, on rural areas for food, fiber, metal, and men. The city, in turn, provides direction, control, coordination, and integration. Further, there is interdependence within cities as well as between cities and between city and countryside. However, many of these points are ignored in Forrester's "urban dynamics" modeling to which we shall return in detail later in this chapter and in Chapter 8.

Points of analogy between the city and an organism include: (1) The elements of the city, the individual human beings, like many cells of the organism, are replaceable and interchangeable; and (2) the city may grow. Fast and slow growing cities are different structurally.

In our time, cities are multiplying in number and are growing larger in area and in population size; they are containing progressively larger proportions of mankind all over the world. Yet actually we know relatively little about cities. Some questions we might ask are (Schnore, 1966): What is the general impact of the city on the individual? Is there a distinctly urban personality? Just how and why do particular patterns of growth occur?

Hierarchy

Hierarchy is evident everywhere in Nature and society. Examples include the chemical, cytological, and histological arrangements within the living organism; functions and tasks within a job; the parts, units, components, etc. in a piece of electronic equipment; and the company organization chart.

In true hierarchy, the constituents at each level combine so as to produce a new whole, and different properties emerge at the next hierarchical level. Hierarchy is discussed in greater detail later in this chapter.

Miscellaneous

Other phenomena could include:

1. *Minimal principles and optimality.* These involve minimizing certain costs, say of surface for a given volume or metabolism for a given organ function in biology.
2. *Extreme value statistics.* This can be defined as an expected value or cost, as equal to the probability of an event times the value or cost of the event should it occur.

Need for Whole Systems Approach: Critical Examples

In this section we consider two salient examples of incorrect, undesirable, or deleterious results consequent to selecting a subsystem, even a subsystem at a high level of complexity, out of total systems context. These examples involve economic growth, a philosophical pillar of all modern nations, and the use of pesticides, a basis for the world's present "standard of living."

Need for pattern rather than discrete element emphasis. Economic growth as independent variable taken out of context: some limitations to economic growth. General systems theory can be used to explain the principles of growth—including limitations to growth—of all systems. These principles place limits on economic growth and on technology, which at best can produce a temporary and unstable state beyond these limits and the likelihood of catastrophe when a stable condition is restored.

A system can be regarded as an organization for increasing order or negentropy (negative entropy). System order increases as long as the increase in order of (low-order) input converted to output exceeds the order reduced in conversion of input to waste.

Bonds, such as in the atom, the cell, or the human family, hold together the elements of a system at any hierarchical level. Economic growth weakens the bonds of human society by increasing mobility and results in people's being treated as units of labor to be shifted around to meet the demands of industry. Likewise, it places stress upon the system by encouraging, like cancer, the differential growth of some elements. Growth of elements no longer satisfies the requirements of the system as a whole. Growth occurs by multiplication rather than by the differentiation required to meet environmental demands. Goldsmith (1971), examining systems theoretic limits to growth, exemplifies this with the production by our educational institutions of vast numbers of persons with specialized knowledge in obscure areas for which there is unlikely to be any demand. Education is foisted on people in a totally indiscriminate way quite aside from individual intellectual or personal characteristics. Thus, Goldsmith stresses, the basic mechanism of environmental selection is breaking down more and more. A further limit to economic growth must be set by the increasing chaos associated with the uncontrolled proliferation of culturally undifferentiated people all over the world. Similarly, Goldsmith believes, society will disintegrate when the cultural constraints which control the behavior of differentiated elements of society are eroded away.

Unfortunately, we know little about what constitutes a proper environment for human beings, beyond the simple creature comforts usually touted as the "standard of living." A look at such abysmal human and economic failures as the Pruitt-Igoe public housing project in St. Louis should make this manifestly clear. In addition, outside forces reduce self regualtion at any system level and increase dependence of the elements of that subsystem on these external agencies.

Though hunter-gatherer societies lived off the interest rather than off the capital, advanced societies increasingly do the opposite. When resources are exhausted, the economic system will grind to a halt. When collapse does occur, it will be dramatic, Goldsmith prophesizes.

Global waste disposal provides a further limit to economic growth, by virtue of converting elements of the larger ecosystem into random elements, that is, with a march toward total entropy.

The simplification or reduction in variety of the modern world renders it much more vulnerable to unpredicted stresses. Such a reduction in stability is characteristic of plant monocultures and of the increased human homogeneity.

In Nature, systems are adaptive to a number of conflicting environmental requirements. We tend to stress solving problems one at a time, thereby creating other problems. Technology, especially, introduces positive feedback into the increasingly unstable world system.

In another very perceptive article, Wagar (1970) argues that our widespread acceptance of unlimited growth is not consistent with survival on our finite planet. In economics and other fields, past experience provides the major basis for current decisions, even though changing times may have reduced the appropriateness of such decision-making. Thus, growth was important in the less-populated past; today it may still increase material wealth but there are vast undesirable side effects.

Wagar believes too few people have recognized the relationship between uncontrolled growth and environmental woes. Because of rising levels of pollution, congestion, and social and biological disorder much of what passes as progress is really illusory. More and more energy must be expended to offset these problems of growth—one must run faster and faster on a treadmill just to inch forward. While we charge forward with frontier-day attitudes, the runaway growth creates such physical and social side effects as to threaten the very quality of life.

In the short run, growth offers a deceivingly simple solution to problems of distribution of wealth, debt, population growth, unemployment, and international competition. For example, only growth provides the means for bringing the "Have-nots" up without bringing the "Haves" down. In our society, production is closely related to consumption and we stress consumption stimulated by dissatisfaction with last year's model. The standard of living is increased by increasing waste. Inadequate demand would mean recession, it is feared. Many feel, for example Myrdal (1963), that economic growth, coupled with a massive retraining program, is the only way to bring the increasingly structured underclasses into the main stream of American society.

The typical growth pattern starts slowly because an adequate base is required. Then it proceeds at a compound rate, accelerating as the base increases. Eventually it is stopped by limiting factors, such as lack of space, exhaustion of resources, predation, disease, parasitism, social or psychological disorganization, and concentration of waste products.

The growth of the U.S. economy fits this general growth model. However, the end of growth is inevitable. In a finite environment no pattern of growth can continue forever. When and how will population and economic growth halt? How much time do we have? These are salient questions to which we shall return later in this book.

The problems we hope to solve derive from growth. By stimulating more growth, we may be intensifying the causes. Perhaps, as Boulding (1966) suggests, we have one chance to convert our environmental capital into knowledge such that we can henceforth live without a rich natural environment.

However, the U.S. is not alone, and must experience increasing competition for influence and raw materials and markets in a world of rising nationalism and aspirations. The U.S. with 6% of the world's population consumes about 40% of the world's annual production. There will be tension and antagonism exacerbated by rapid communications. It is well to remember Britain's economic woes since she lost her colonies, Wagar points out.

These are external forces, but there are also internal forces that could slow down our rate of growth. These could include decreased demand for goods as people become more frustrated with environmental problems. They could include labor resistance to automation and the increasingly disruptive power of strikes (or airplane hijackings). They could include the rising number of permanently unemployed and unemployable people who threaten our domestic tranquility. They could involve a decreased expenditure on defense now contributing to growth. They could involve an increased expenditure of energy to extract resources, such that the costs of extraction exceed those resulting from production and sales. They could result from the very complexity of modern organizations such that one failure starts a chain reaction leading to collapse.

Interdependencies and interactions: example of biomagnification of insecticides. DDT and related organochlorine insecticides have been widely associated with increased crop yields and reduction of insect-borne disease, yet there is mounting evidence of undesirable, subtle, even fatal, side effects within the biosphere. As a managerial problem, with implications of risk versus return to man and to the total ecosystem, this problem transcends even the tragic effects of DDT on bird life. The management of today and tomorrow requires much better awareness of the indirect and long-range consequences of its decisions.

Cox (1970) analyzed phytoplankton samples collected in Monterey Bay, California, from 1955 to 1969 for DDT and related compounds. Concentrations were approximately three times greater in the later samples.

Annual use of DDT in the United States has declined in the last 10 years, yet there is recent evidence of abnormally high concentrations in marine fish and pelagic birds. Phytoplankton are important because they represent the first link in pelagic food chains. DDT uptake by phytoplankton is rapid and essentially irreversible, so concentrations can be considered to represent environmental DDT. The importance of time is evident here. Thus, DDT residues may be increasing in the primary stages of the pelagic food chains in spite of a decline in the domestic use of DDT. This appears to be associated with processes of nondecomposition and dispersal.

Harrison, *et al.,* (1970), have constructed diagrammatic and mathematical models (based on flows of matter) of DDT transport throughout the "food web" and as a function of trophic (nutritional) level. The models describe how DDT concentration varies with time and trophic level, and how population size in any trophic level depends upon population in adjacent levels. Using the models, it is possible to predict population changes attributable to DDT. The results suggest that even if no more DDT is ever added to the biosphere, the concentrations of the insecticide at or near the top of the trophic hierarchy could continue to rise for years (See Figure 1-2). Thus, additional species may decline or disappear resulting in secondary effects upon prey populations.

The combination of high solubility in fat (but not in water) and high stability allows the magnification of DDT concentration proceeding from lower to higher trophic levels within the ecosystem. For example, in a Lake Michigan ecosystem

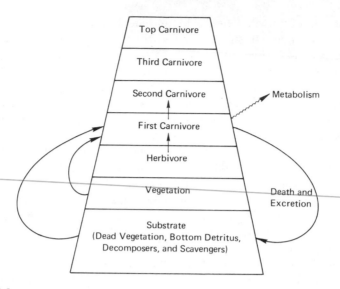

FIGURE 1-2

Trophic structure in the biosphere. Arrows indicate DDT flows. For purposes of simplification, all interactions are not shown.[5]

the concentration of DDT in the herring gull is 7,000 times that of bottom muds (See Table 1-1). It should be emphasized that only a few parts DDT per 10^9 parts water reduce photosynthesis in a number of species of phytoplankton. These microscopic floating plants account for about 70% of earth's annually produced oxygen supply. Likewise, DDT has been shown to be fatally toxic to invertebrate species in concentrations as low as one part DDT per billion parts water.

Mathematical modeling, utilizing as time constants the life spans of carnivorous birds, which may be up to 100 years in the cases of falcon, osprey, and eagle, indicated major ecosystem time lags. The authors suggest that ecosystems with such long-lived members may not even yet have felt the full impact of the original use of DDT in the 1940s. Further calculations indicate that a sudden sustained increase of DDT at one trophic level yields an exponential increase in concentration at the level immediately above. Each trophic level requires approximately four life spans to reach equilibrium in response to changes in DDT concentration in the level below.

Modeling also examined the impact on the ecosystem of elimination or decline of predator species. Oscillatory responses were produced that qualitatively represented actual population fluctuations. Significant variations in

[5]From H.L. Harrison, et al., "Systems Studies of DDT Transport," *Science,* Vol. 170, pp. 503-08, 30 October 1970. Copyright 1970 by the American Association for the Advancement of Science.

TABLE 1 - 1
Biomagnification of DDT.*

Tropic Level	Concentration of DDT (parts per 10^9)
Bottom muds	14
Amphipod crustaceans	410
Fish	3000-6000
Herring gulls	99,000

*Adapted from H.L. Harrison, et al., "Systems Studies of DDT Transport," *Science*, Vol. 170, pp. 503-08, 30 October 1970. Copyright 1970 by the American Association for the Advancement of Science.

predator populations might result in widespread disruptions throughout the entire ecosystem and out-of-control conditions.

This modeling has made it possible to predict the consequences of adding DDT to the environment, based on transport, concentration, accumulation, and impact information. Accordingly, even if adding DDT to the environment were halted today, widespread effects could still occur. This is especially true because the "top carnivores" which play major roles in stabilizing the ecosystem may take a long time to respond to DDT input. It is obvious that the over-all consequences of contemporary widespread use of DDT will not become apparent for many years.

Finally, it should be noted that the situation could be even worse. For example, Woodwell, *et al.*, (1971, p. 1106) report, on the basis of a global model, that "mere good fortune has protected man and the rest of the biota from much higher concentrations" of DDT than have in reality been absorbed. The total amount of DDT circulating in the biosphere is estimated as being many times greater than that necessary to eliminate many animals; however, most organisms appear to absorb only a small part of the DDT available.

REVIEW OF RELEVANT THEORIES

To be meaningful, theory must be capable of explaining the main properties of systems described in the last section, and also the behavioral-social dynamics discussed in Chapter 2. In addition, it should provide a predictive capability prerequisite as a substrate to the management concepts considered in Chapters 3 and 9. This book represents an attempt to synthesize the main theoretical approaches to complex sociotechnical systems. As such, it can be thought of as third-generation theory encompassing such second-generation theories as the sociotechnical theory of the Tavistock Institute School and the systems dynamics of Forrester. First-generation theories are exemplified by the open-systems theory of von Bertalanffy and the cybernetics theories of Wiener and of Ashby. Tangential theories which early or late have also contributed threads for our pattern are also briefly discussed here or were considered earlier in our discussion of attempts at integration of systems, organization, and management theories.

First-Generation Theories

First-generation theories laid the groundwork for presently widely accepted concepts of equilibrium and steady state, openness and closedness with respect to the environment, and feedback and cybernetics.

Equilibrium and steady state. Köhler (1938), who to some extent has recognized the need for a systems theory since the 1920s, objects to use of the simple term, *equilibrium,* as applied to organisms. Organisms are not closed systems, because they absorb and emit energy. Thus, from the viewpoint of physics, it is impossible to state that transformations in organisms occur in the direction of motionless equilibria. For example, many mammals stand while at rest, whereas in a state of physical equilibrium the center of gravity should be lowered as far as possible. These organisms thus set up processes which prevent the attainment of equilibrium.

Köhler thus emphasizes that the "standard state" of an organism cannot be a state of equilibrium and that an equilibrium theory of organic homeostasis is not compatible with biological knowledge. *Equilibrium* is viewed as an outworn general term. The standard state, unlike an equilibrium, contains a maximum of potential energy.

The individual and the realworld environment. The understanding of complex systems requires a conceptualization of the interrelationship between an individual and his real-world environment and the treatment of those variables characteristic of behavior in natural situations. Unfortunately, much of behavioral and social science has, over the years, represented—and still represents—a fatuous quantification of minutiae. A real strength of such scientists as Freud and Lewin lies in that they provide us with a framework for studying not easily quantifiable things such as unconscious motivations, personality adaptations to frustration and conflict, aspirations and expectations, and social environments. The approaches of Freud and Lewin embody the scientific study of a wide spectrum of human behavior and experience in *natural* settings, as opposed to formal theory building based on highly constrained laboratory situations. These approaches promise a maximum possible reinforcement of theory and observation.

Let us consider briefly the contributions of Lewin. Lewin did not believe in the creation of a single, formally elegant theory apart from the slow accumulation of empirical data (Cartright, 1959). Rather, Lewin developed a number of *quasi-constructs,* which could be synthesized or replaced as observations provided more data. Collectively, Lewin's broad contributions to psychology are best subsumed under the term, *field theory.* Field theory, with its roots in theoretical physics, holds that behavior at any given time is a function of the *total* field of forces at that time only—that is, of the field of forces both internal to the person and external to the person as he perceives and evaluates the situation. Psychological forces, like those in physics, can be quantified by use of vectors. For example, this enables us to study conflict situations involving goals of different strengths. For a detailed discussion of field theory, see Lewin, (1951).

A particularly felicitous construct of field theory is that of *life space,* that is, the totality of interdependent factors characterizing the person and his psychological environment (the world as it exists for the given individual). Thus, any meaningful explanation of behavior must take into consideration the social—and by our extension sociotechnical—environments.

We must stress here that there is usually no simple one-to-one relationship between these environments and the physical environment. This is one feature underlying the *counterintuitive* behavior of social systems which we shall discuss later in this chapter.

Field theory can be thought of as one example of a "general systems theory" (see the next section below). It has been applied to the explanation of phenomena of learning, perception, motivation, personality, development, and social behavior. Through utilization of the mathematical concepts of vectors and topology, it provides a framework for treating both obviously quantifiable and "soft" or "messy" variables. Through its emphasis on interdependence and total situations, it provides an antidote to the unfortunate increasing fragmentation and specialization within science.

We shall return to the specific motivational theories of Freud and Lewin in Chapter 2 under the section entitled Motivational Factors.

General systems theory. Von Bertalanffy (1968) has summarized in one place the main aspects of general system(s) theory of which he is a major founder. Many of his theories appear to represent arguments against the (long-dead) issues, important in the 1920s, of vitalism, mechanism, reductionism, and simple physical science.

Major aims of general systems theory include the integration of sciences, developing unifying theories applicable to all sciences, and integration of scientific education. General systems theory, providing laws of similar structure for different fields, makes possible the use of simpler or better known models in more complicated or less controllable situations. This should also reduce replication of effort in different speciality subjects. General systems theory, by indicating exact criteria, should help guard against superficial analogies. Certain general principles apply to systems, irrespective of their nature.

Unity of science is to be accomplished, not through reduction to physics and chemistry—or to biology—but by structural uniformities applicable to all the various levels of reality. General systems theory had its roots in the organismic concepts of biology. In psychiatry the work of Goldstein, Menninger, and Grinker represents the systems viewpoint. So do Gestalt psychology and the field theory of Lewin.

There are, of course, many varieties of systems theories, not just the general systems theory of von Bertalanffy. Examples are "classical" system theory, which applies classical mathematics (calculus) and aims to state principles which apply, for example, to open and closed systems; computerization and simulation; compartment theory; set theory; graph theory; topology; factor analysis; net theory; cybernetics; information theory; theory of automata; game theory; decision theory; and queuing theory.

The concept of information, in information theory, is defined by an expression isomorphic to the negative entropy of thermodynamics, suggesting a common approach to the two theories. Some people have thus suggested that information could be used as a measure of organization.

However, most of these systems theories have limitations; all may not be applicable to the same situation. For example, information theory has proved disappointing in biology, psychology, and sociology (see, for example, Johnson, 1970). Game theory has not improved political decision-making and the state of the world. Models of equilibrium and homeostasis explain the maintenance of systems but are inadequate relative to change, differentiation, evolution, negentropy, prediction of improbable states, creativity, self-realization, etc. The theory of open systems applies to many phenomena in technology and biology, but von Bertalanffy cautions against its "expansion to fields for which its concepts are not made (von Bertalanffy, 1968, p. 23)." Accordingly, it may have been overstressed in the theories of sociotechnical and social systems.

General systems theory emphasizes there are models, principles, and laws that apply irrespective of the particular kind of system, the nature of the elements, and relations among the elements. For example, the exponential law of growth, of which we say a great deal in this book, applies to certain bacterial cells, to populations of bacteria, to populations of animals and people, and to numbers of publications in science, even though both the entities and causal mechanisms are different. A similar condition obtains with regard to conflict among plants, animals, or nations. The mathematical laws are the same, and the entities can be considered to be systems.

Biological and social systems are characterized first by a dynamic interaction of elements followed by fixed constraints which make the system and elements more efficient but also eventually abolish equipotentiality. In organisms and societies, adaptiveness, purposiveness, goal-seeking, and self-maintenance are of particular significance. Models of importance here are equifinality and feedback, or the homeostatic maintenance of a state or seeking of a goal.

Characteristics of organization are of particular concern to us. These include wholeness, growth, differentiation, hierarchical order, dominance, control, and competition. There may be certain laws of organizations such as a Malthusian law, a law of maximum size, and a law of instability associated with interactions among subsystems.

Progress in a system is associated with differentiation of elements, but these elements become fixed. Progressive segregation thus means progressive mechanization with less regulability. When the system is a unitary whole, disturbances are followed by a new steady state because of subsystem interactions. This self-regulation is lost if the system is split into independent causal chains, and processes in the subsystems go on irrespective of each other. The more elements are specialized, the more irreplaceable they become and loss may lead to total system breakdown. This appears to be what is happening in today's socio-technical macrosystem.

A general theory of hierarchical order, connected with concepts of organization, differentiation, and evolution, is especially important to general systems theory.

Hierarchical order involves the superposition of systems. Each level is characterized by wholeness, summativity, progressive mechanization, centralization, finality, stationary states, approach to steady states, growth in time, relative growth, equifinality, competition, and differentiation.

General systems theory stresses multivariable interaction. "Classical science," on the other hand, emphasized two-variable problems (or just a few variables), linear causal trains, and one cause and one effect. However, even in mechanics, von Bertalanffy maintains, the three (celestial or atomic particle)-body problem is insoluble in principle and can be approached only by approximations. We shall comment on this point later when we discuss simulation. Finally, general systems theory has evolved over the years. Not every worker, for example, believes that "system" can or should always be defined. And there has been a shift in thinking of some authors away from the older emphasis on isomorphy to one involving a systems "spectrum." A general systems "spectrum" focuses on similarities *and* differences and on a continuum between hard and soft sciences.

Open-systems theory. Von Bertalanffy regards the theory of open systems an important generalization of physical theory, kinetics, and thermodynamics. Conventional physics dealt only with closed systems, that is, systems considered to be isolated from their environment. The thermodynamic laws apply to closed systems. The second law states the quantity called entropy, representing complete disorder or the most probable distribution, must increase to a maximum with the process's eventually coming to a stop in a state of equilibrium.

"An open system is defined as a system in exchange of matter with its environment, presenting import and export, building-up and breaking-down of its material components (von Bertalanffy, 1968, p. 141)." Open systems are never in a state of chemical or thermodynamic equilibrium, but are rather maintained in a *steady state*. This is the essence of metabolism and other cellular processes.

The steady state in open systems is viewed as being maintained at a distance from true equilibrium and thus is capable of doing work. The system remains constant in composition in spite of continuous irreversible processes. "If a steady state is reached in an open system, it is independent of the initial conditions, and determined only by the system parameters, . . . (von Bertalanffy, 1968, p. 142)."

In terms of thermodynamics, the open systems can maintain themselves in a state of high statistical improbability, that is, of organization or order. According to the second law of thermodynamics, physical processes trend toward increasing entropy or states of increasing probability and decreasing order. At the present time there is no thermodynamic criterion to define the steady state in open systems similar to the definition of equilibrium as maximum entropy in closed systems.

Von Bertalanffy recognizes there may be systems in equilibrium within the organism but states the organism itself cannot be considered an equilibrium system. However, the true equilibria in closed systems and "stationary equilibria" in open systems may be similar in appearance. But the underlying situation is fundamentally different. Chemical equilibria in closed systems are based on reversible reactions. In open systems the steady state is not reversible as a whole. The second principle of thermodynamics, by definition, applies only to closed systems and does not define a steady state. In summary, apart from some individual processes, living systems are not closed systems in true equilibrium but open systems in a steady state. These features play a fundamental role in metabolism, for example.

Of course, no real natural system can be closed; it is necessary, instead, to speak of a system's being relatively closed. For the type of systems we deal with in this book we can contrast open and closed systems as follows.

Open systems are those with a continuous flow of energy, information, or materials from environment to system and return. For an open system to survive, it must move against a tendency toward entropy (maximum disorganization). It is often said that such systems must acquire negative entropy; open systems thus develop a steady state of "negentropy" by taking in as inputs a higher level of complexity than that output. Stated in another way, open systems import matter that contains free energy which compensates for the increase in entropy associated with irreversible processes within the system. The stability in a time-independent steady state is quite necessary for adaptation to changing environments. Living systems both adapt to their environments and affect and modify these environments. Open systems move toward differentiation and elaboration, with increased specialization of functions. The reintegration of differentiated elements is of paramount importance to organisms and organizations. Open systems can spontaneously reorganize toward states of greater heterogeneity and complexity and can achieve a steady state while still doing work. Growth is by processes of internal elaboration. Additionally, open systems are selective and to some extent self-regulating.

Closed systems, on the other hand, grow to maximum homogeneity of the elements so that a steady state can be achieved only through a cessation of all activity. A closed system uses up all its energy in throughput and becomes simpler in time with entropic processes.

In irreversible processes, entropy increases and the change in entropy in closed systems is always positive with the continual destruction or order.

A much stressed additional property of open systems is that of *equifinality*. This states that a system can reach the same final state from differing initial conditions and along a variety of paths. The amount of equifinality is reduced as more control mechanisms come into play. Open systems as they attain a steady state must show equifinality.

Finally, it is of value to note von Bertalanffy's contrasting of two of the important approaches to systems, the open-systems model and the cybernetic model. The open-systems model emphasizes the dynamic interaction of system elements, the cybernetic model emphasizes the feedback cycle by which a value is maintained or a target reached. The open-systems model does not talk about information; the feedback system is closed and has no metabolism. In a closed feedback situation, information can only decrease, never increase; that is, information can be transformed into noise but not vice versa.

The open system actively tends toward a higher level of organization owing to conditions in the system; the feedback mechanism reactively does the same because of learning or of information fed into the system. In summary, the feedback approach seems more applicable to secondary regulations. Primary regulations must accrue from the dynamics in an open system. Feedback mechanisms become more important later in development. Both concepts are, of course, quite important to the systems we are considering in this book.

Feedback systems and homeostatic control, regarded as just a special yet admittedly significant class of self-regulation and of the means of adaptation, can be characterized as follows: (1) regulation is based upon structural pre-establishments; (2) causal trains are linear and unidirectional; the feedback loop is regarded as a simple extension of the classical stimulus-response scheme; and (3) phenomena are open with respect to matter and energy. In this sense Forrester may be right in his use of "closed system." As a result of the feedback concepts of homeostasis, ". . . American biology, . . . under the influence of cybernetic concepts, . . . has returned to the machine concept of the cell and organism. . . ." (von Bertalanffy, 1968, p. 160). See the discussion below of models of man.

Extensions and consequences of systems theories: theoretical bias in problem solving. The results and value of our systems studies will depend on our concept of system, the model utilized, and the amount of abstraction and oversimplification involved. Several points follow from the above discussion. There are two different ways of looking at situations: (1) the summative characteristics of an element are the same within and outside a complex and may be obtained by summation of the behavior of the elements known in isolation; and (2) constitutive[6] characteristics, which are dependent on the specific relationships within the complex, and the understanding of which requires knowledge of both the elements and the relationships, are not explainable by the behavior of isolated elements.

Von Bertalanffy contrasts two further approaches to systems study: (1) *empirico-intuitive approach,* represented by von Bertalanffy himself, involving studying many different kinds of systems; and (2) *deductive approach* represented by Ashby, involving considering all conceivable systems and then reducing the set to a more reasonable size. Von Bertalanffy believes this approach may be a gross oversimplification. Thus, the most important types of self-organizing systems may have no place in Ashby's approach, namely, those systems organizing themselves by progressive differentiation and evolving from states of lower to higher complexity. Self-differentiating systems evolving toward higher complexity (decreasing entropy) are possible only as open systems. Accordingly, the living organism and social systems are not an Ashby machine because they evolve toward increasing differentiation.

As we have seen, a system in the simplest sense can be defined as a number of elements in interaction. Only in simpler constrained cases (where Q indicates some measure of an element p) can a system be represented by simultaneous differential equations of the form (von Bertalanffy, 1968, p. 56):

$$\frac{dQ_1}{dt} = f_1 (Q_1, Q_2, \ldots \ldots Q_n)$$

$$\frac{dQ_2}{dt} = f_2 (Q_1, Q_2, \ldots \ldots Q_n)$$

$$\ldots \ldots \ldots \ldots \ldots \ldots$$

$$\frac{dQ_n}{dt} = f_n (Q_1, Q_2, \ldots \ldots Q_n)$$

Systems of equations of relevance here have three different kinds of solution: (1) asymptotic assumption of a steady state; (2) never the attainment of a steady state; and (3) periodic oscillations. One could also look for "aiming" at a future steady state, distance from an equilibrium state, or dependence on a future state.

What is or is not considered a system structures the method of problem solution. Thus application of the above analytic approach depends on: (1) interaction between elements being non-existent, or so weak it can be ignored in scientific study; (2) relations describing behavior of the elements being linear, that is, the equation describing the behavior of the total is in the same form as

---

[6]Elsewhere De Greene (1970) has argued use of the word *constituent* to describe the most general system element as opposed to such terms as *component, unit,* or *part.*

the equations for the parts. In the case of systems, that is, elements in interaction, the above is seldom true. Sets of differential equations may be difficult or impossible to solve; in such cases computer simulations may be of advantage. We shall return to this important distinction many times in this book. The problem of equation difficulty is summarized in Table 1-2.

TABLE 1-2
Difficulty of solution of mathematical problems by analytic methods.*

	Linear Equations			Nonlinear Equations		
	One Equation	Several Equation	Many Equations	One Equation	Several Equations	Many Equations
Algebraic	Trivial	Easy	Essentially impossible	Very difficult	Very difficult	Impossible
Ordinary differential	Easy	Difficult	Essentially impossible	Very difficult	Impossible	Impossible
Partial differential	Difficult	Essentially impossible	Impossible	Impossible	Impossible	Impossible

*From R. G. E. Franks, *Mathematical Modeling in Chemical Engineering,* published by John Wiley & Sons, Inc., Publishers, 1967. And modified from original data from Electronic Associates, Inc.

As we have already pointed out, there are isomorphies between biological systems and "epiorganisms" such as animal communities and human societies. Yet to what extent are generalizations possible and to what extent does transfer lead rather to dangerous fallacies? Can society be regarded as a system? Can history?

Science is *nomothetic,* that is, it establishes laws based on repeatable events in nature. History is *idiographic,* that is, it describes events that occurred only once. However, it appears there have been a limited number of cultures in history, each of which presents sort of a life cycle suggestive of that of businesses and ideas in science and art. Von Bertalanffy (1968, p. 204) thus states, ".... the differences between West and East probably will, one way or the other, become insignificant because the similarity of material culture in the long run will prove stronger than ideological differences." We add, perhaps there is now something wrong with human thought processes, with our emphasis on mass technological civilization.

Extensions and consequences of systems theories: models of man. The model(s) of man an individual, say a manager, holds in his mind determines that individual's attitudes and behavior toward his fellows. The model(s) of man held collectively by a society determines the management practices of that society. We have already referred to a number of models of man. Theory X and Theory Y, man the self-actualizer, the quantitative problem-solving and decision-making models (Simon, 1957), and the phenomenological and behavioristic models (summarized in Hitt, 1969) provide examples.

Von Bertalanffy (1967) writes of a *robot model* of man, which he believes has led to an unsatisfactory situation in psychological theory. Von Bertalanffy argues psychological theories share an image of man which originated in the physical-technological universe; this is the "robot model of human behavior." Von Bertalanffy believes this applies to such apparently divergent fields as Skinnerian behaviorism, psychoanalysis, cybernetic concepts in neurophysiology, industrial and consumer psychology, and computer models of cognitive processes. This has helped to make psychology the handmaiden of pecuniary and political interests. The robot image closely corresponds to the worship of mass society, glorification of the machine, and utilization of the profit motive as a sole measure of progress.

The robot concept of man is thus both an expression of, and a powerful motivating force in, our industrialized mass society. This is reflected in behavioral engineering, advertising, and in commercial, economic, and political areas. There is thus a large-scale manipulative psychology.

Von Bertalanffy argues the mechanistic view, the robot model of man, the glorification of physical technology has led to the catastrophes of our time. We unfortunately lack a knowledge of the laws of human society, a "sociological technology." Scientific control of society is no highway to Utopia. These views, of course, are diametrically opposed to those of Skinner, discussed in Chapter 9 of this book.

The living organism maintains the steady state of an open system and is capable of spontaneous activity. The robot model, with its overemphasis on homeostasis, deals with responses to stimuli, reduction in tensions, reestablishment of an equilibrium disturbed by outside factors, and adjustment to the environment. This robot image appears to be eroding away, as reflected by the motivation theories of Maslow and personality theories of G. Allport. Further, developmental psychology has a holistic orientation and views the organism as being primarily active as opposed to reactive. The new image of man is held to replace the robot image with that of system and emphasizes *immanent activity* rather than *outer-directed reactivity*. The new image emphasizes the specifity of human culture as compared to (constrained) animal behavior.

In the context of philosophies underlying the management of society, we shall return to humanistic and robot models in Chapter 9.

Feedback and cybernetics. Cybernetics in its important modern form, involving the integration of concepts of information (communication), feedback, and control, stems from the work of Norbert Wiener (1948). The concepts are general purpose and apply to animals, machines, human organizations, and societies. Basically, cybernetics involves the transfer of information (communication) between the system and its environment, and control through feedback of system function in relation to the environment. Etymologically, "cybernetics" and "governor" have the same Greek origin.

The cyberneticist views an organized, adaptive system as a goal-seeking ensemble which can sense its relationship to an objective and modify its behavior in order to approach that objective more closely. This is illustrated in Figure 1-3.

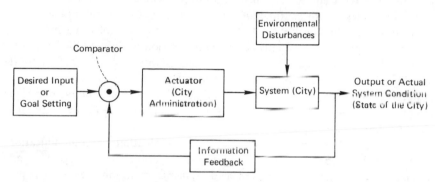

FIGURE 1-3
A cybernetic model of sociotechnical and social systems showing basic elements. [7]

The desired system condition is selected by a goal-setting process, entered into a comparator, and then tested against the actual condition which is observed and reported by means of information feedback. Discrepancy between the two conditions causes the actuator to act on the system to reduce the discrepancy. The dynamic nature of the process is associated with external environmental forces necessitating control to counteract their effects.

The theory and applications of cybernetics, particularly with reference to the biological sciences, have been advanced by Ashby (1956, 1960). For example, Ashby designed an adaptive brainlike machine, the "homeostat." This model involves step functions which, having reached a critical value, step to a new family of differential equations, and the system starts on a new way of behavior. The system adapts through trial and error by means of these step functions. Eventually, when there are no more critical conflicts with environmental values, the system settles down.

Cybernetic concepts have been applied to the study of the dynamic

[7] Adapted from E.S. Savas, "Cybernetics in City Hall," *Science,* Vol. 168, pp. 1066-71, 29 May 1970. Copyright 1970 by the American Association for the Advancement of Science.

properties of organizations since at least the 1950s (see, for example, Wilcox, 1962). Feedback is utilized for continuous measurement of the *actual* performance of the design and fabrication in an engineering organization, and actual performance is *compared* to job *requirements*. Management *control* involves corrective action to reduce the *disparity* between actual and desired performance.

In the case of engineering design or industrial production organizations, a measure of performance for a given output can be the relationship of progressive accomplishment, expressed for example as degree of completion, man-months of effort, or dollar costs, versus time, expressed in weeks or months. A combination of block diagrams and subsystem (for example, engineering, drafting, fabrication, and sales) transfer functions provides a mathematical model of the organization in this likening of the organization to a complex machine. Feedback is all-important, and fundamental consideration is given to the application of time lags, dead time, lead compensation, adaptive control, sampled data, stability, linearity, and nonlinearity—concepts of great importance in control systems engineering. These features can be of significance in organizational design and operation, for instance, by sampling performance on a weekly rather than a monthly basis.

In short, this approach holds that the combination of communications, control, and computers will provide the foundations for management as a science. The organization is viewed as a dynamic multi-loop feedback control system. It is analyzed by reducing it to the least element necessary for required detail, and each element is viewed as having dynamic characteristics which may be mathematically represented by transfer functions. The term "transfer function" comes from servo-mechanism theory. An example of an organizational transfer function could be a quadratic S-curve response of total cumulative effort versus time. Others could be time lag of accomplishment, time lead of anticipation, delayed action, proportion, integration, and rate operation. All these are expressed in terms of system or subsystem inputs and outputs, and the ever-lessening disparity between input and output. The block diagrams indicate the output of one block representing the input to the next, as a process is transferred through the organization from one functional group to the next.

Wilcox's case histories include viewing an engineering group as having the three major functions of preliminary design, development, and test; each can be represented by a linear transfer function. Often transfer functions can most expeditiously be obtained by curve fittings.

This approach can be of value to management, for example, by reducing transfer delays from one group to the next, as between engineering and drafting.

In the block diagrams, blocks represent the functional activities and their transfer functions; interconnecting signal lines indicate information or product output of the preceding operation. For example, the drafting operation has as an input the documents, sketches, and verbal information from engineering, and transfers this engineering output into drawings. Detrimentally, a slow response by any one functional group results in a delay (dead time) in passing information to the next operation. Dead time may result in a phase shift which, in turn, results in an unstable organization; the gain of the system then has to be reduced to maintain stability. Cost increases, in the form of overruns or undershoots of the program. Similarly, infrequent data sampling can cause instability in the program, because costs are out of control or management is not having the desired technical results.

In summary this approach involves:

1. Design of the organizational process using work flow charts and block diagrams of the functional groups.
2. Development of performance response curves from case histories based on past performance.
3. Development of the mathematical model(s).
4. Use of control systems techniques to improve performance. This may involve feedback and feedforward features. Improvement could involve procedures and standards. Feedforward might mean bypassing certain operations for a time and then bringing them in later to refine the product output.

Extensions of such cybernetic and control systems concepts, basic to the "systems dynamics" models of Forrester, are discussed much more fully below.

Second-Generation Theories

This section includes mainly the sociotechnical systems theory of Tavistock Institute scholars and the systems dynamics theories of Forrester.

The Tavistock Institute approach. Tavistock personnel were influenced by the thinking of von Bertalanffy and others on general systems theory,[8] especially with relation to *open-systems theory.* Their effort represented one of the first applications of open-systems concepts to social science. Emphasis was placed upon studying the (production) system as a whole, rather than in terms of isolated functions, such as assembly-line operations, as had hithertofore been the case with behavioral and social scientific research. Special stress was placed upon the interrelatedness of all aspects, both social and technical, of the system. Thus, the social and the psychological could be understood only in terms of detailed engineering facts and of the behavior of the technological system as a whole within the given environment. Organizations were considered open sociotechnical systems interacting with their environments.

The Tavistock concept of sociotechnical systems is closely related to ideas about work organization. Original work dealt with the study of industrial and commercial enterprises. Concepts have been tested in coal mining, manufacturing, textile mills, building, bus operations, power plants, on shipboard, and

[8]For reasons discussed elsewhere (De Greene, 1970), the terms *systems* theory, *systems* science, *systems* analysis, etc., will be used instead of system theory, science, analysis, etc., even though the original literature may have followed the latter usage.

in other operations involving different degrees of mechanization and automation and rates of technological change. The researchers have studied ways in which groups can be organized relative to size, skill, status, roles, and "task"9 structure. Responsible autonomy of subgroups was deemed especially important in the design of work systems. Tavistock personnel have performed studies in the area of industrial democracy, particularly with reference to the alienation of worker groups, to the transfer of managerial power to employees, and to job redesign more in keeping with modern concepts of job satisfaction.

The Tavistock approach differs from most social systems research that deals with closed systems. Although the closed-system approach was originally fruitful in industrial studies, it has tended to overemphasize social structure and neglect social change. At Tavistock, attempts were made to take a total systems approach to such areas as human engineering, job evaluation, selection, incentive schemes, group organization, supervision, and management organization. Concepts of sociotechnical systems emerged from the studies of the above enterprises, and relevant findings in experimental social psychology, clinical psychology, and sociology.

Understanding of a production system thus requires consideration of both the technological and social elements. It is impossible to understand these systems simply in terms of some arbitrarily selected technological feature, such as the repetitive nature of the work, the fragmented nature of the tasks, or the coerciveness of the conveyor belt. Contrariwise, the "human relations" emphasis on the social and psychological situation of men at work is incomplete. Thus, work group autonomy should not be maximized in all production settings, nor should one assume that the basic psychological needs met by workers' groupings are those of friendship on the job, as "human relations" advocates often insist. Rather, workers should be related in terms of task requirements and task interdependence leading to development of mutually supportive roles in the face of stress.

The approach stresses that the organization is constrained by the environment, with regard both to inputs in terms of raw materials, labor, and money, and to outputs by the state of the economy, consumer preference, and government regulations. Moreover, human capacities, perferences, and expectations, which further constrain the organization, need not be personalistic but may be derived from organizational structure. Human behavior in organizations results from the interaction between formal role requirements, a function of design, and the nature of people, a function of selection.

It should be emphasized that the usefulness of the open-systems concept is related to what the system does in achieving a steady state in the face of environmental influences. Important are: (1) the variation in output that can be

---

9 See also De Greene (1970) relative to limitations in usage of the word *task*.

tolerated without structural change; in an enterprise this is a function of the technical production apparatus; and (2) the tolerable variation of the input, itself a function of the technological element. However, there is no simple one-to-one relationship between variations in inputs and outputs, because different combinations of inputs may result, depending on the technological system, in similar outputs and different products may result from similar inputs. Further, the technological system, in converting inputs to outputs, is a major determinant of the self-regulating properties of the system.

The mediating boundary conditions must be represented among the open-systems constants which define how the steady state is achieved. The technological system plays such a mediating role; hence the open-systems concept must be referred to the sociotechnical system of the enterprise, not just to the social system.

Often a given organization can be maintained in a steady state only by the constant large effort of management, whereas a reorganization based on sociotechnical analysis is inherently stable and self-correcting, freeing management for more important work. Thus, the "primary task" of management is to relate the total system to its environment, and not internal regulation.

Considering "enterprises" as open sociotechnical systems helps picture how they are both influenced by and influence their environment. Management is concerned with managing both an internal system and an external environment. To view the enterprise as a closed system and emphasize managing the "internal enterprise" would expose it to the full impact of vagaries of the environment.

Over the years the Tavistock Institute has contributed to both the development of sociotechnical theory and the empirical work in validation of such theory. A summary of this work is given by Emery (1959), Emery and Trist (1960), Bucklow (1969), and Cooper and Foster (1971).

The term *sociotechnical system* was first employed in 1951 by Trist and Bamforth of the Tavistock Institute of Human Relations, London (Trist and Bamforth, 1951). The formal origin of sociotechnical theory can be traced back to studies by these authors relative to the effects of technological change in a British deep-seam coal mine. The traditional method of mining involved small, almost autonomous groups of miners; the two or three members of each group worked closely together. Control over the work was internal to the group, each miner performed a variety of tasks, jobs were more or less interchangeable among the workers, and there was considerable satisfaction in perceiving and completing the entire "task." Sociotechnically, the social-psychological and task requirements were *congruent*. Technological change involved replacing this costly manual method with the mechanical coal-cutters and conveyors representative of mass-production technology. No longer restricted to working a short face of coal, miners could now extract coal from a long wall. However, the new *longwall method* required a different type of individual and group work organization. Shifts of 10 to 20 men were required and workers were restricted to narrowly defined and unvaried tasks. There was now a high degree of interrelationship among the tasks of the three shifts of a coal-extraction cycle. Problems at one stage tended to be carried forward to later stages and to hold up work at later stages. The complex and rigid system was extremely sensitive to both social and production disruptions. Low production, absenteeism, and intragroup rivalry became common.

Later, in studies of other coal mines (Trist, Higgin, Murray, and Pollock, 1963), this conventional longwall method was compared with a composite longwall method utilizing a combination of the new technology and features of the old social-psychological work structure. This involved greater independence of the strict cycle imposed by technology, a greater variety of skills for the worker, and self-selection of team members. Table 1-3 indicates two measures of

TABLE 1-3

Two measures of system effectiveness under conditions of two different sociotechnical designs.*

Productivity Index	Longwall	
	Conventional	Composite
Productivity (% of coal face potential)	78	95
State of cycle progress		
In advance	0	22
Normal	31	73
Behind	69	5
Absence rates (% of possible shifts)		
No reason given	4.3	.4
Sickness and other	8.9	4.6
Accident	6.8	3.2
Total	20.0	8.2

*From E. L. Trist *et al., Organizational Choice,* published by Tavistock Publications Ltd. Copyright 1963 by Associated Book Publishers Ltd.

system effectiveness under conditions of two different sociotechnical designs. Similar results were obtained by Rice (1958) in a redesign of the work-relationship structure of a textile mill at Ahmedabad, India. Even though equipment layout and work loads had initially been studied by engineers, productivity was low and damage to equipment and materials high. Before Rice's redesign, work groups had been organized on the basis of role similarity and not task interdependence. After redesign, bringing together workers whose tasks were interdependent, and also redesigning supervisory roles, productivity rose and damage dropped.

In their detailed studies of coal-mining operations, Emery and Trist (1960) found that different social systems and different work organizations can apply to the same technology and same environment. One social system can be found superior in terms of task performance, productivity, personal requirements of the workers, and personal and interpersonal reactions to crises and other stresses.

Emery and Trist found that two very different forms of worker and supervisor organization both operated economically within the same coal seam and with the identical technology. It is seldom that only one work relationship structure fits the given tasks. However, these studies, comparing a complex rather rigid organizational structure with simple work rules on the one hand, with a simple more flexible organizational structure with complex work rules on the other, found the latter superior in terms of production, costs, and stress indices.

Thus the technological system sets requirements on its social system and the effectiveness of total production will depend on how adequately the social system copes with these requirements.

Emery and Trist clearly differentiated between (relatively) open and closed systems.

Enterprises[10] thus grow by processes of internal elaboration and achieve an equilibrium with a continuous throughput in spite of a range of external environmental changes. The ability of an enterprise to maintain a steady state is a function of the "technological component's" ability to deal with variations in the input and output markets. The system as a whole may remain constant with a continuous throughput in spite of external changes. There is no simple one-to-one relationship between inputs and outputs, and the technological component in converting inputs into outputs contributes preeminently to the self-regulating features of the system. Emery and Trist consider that the technological component functions as one of the major boundary conditions of the social system by mediating between the enterprise and the external environment. For this last reason the term *sociotechnical system* was coined; *social system* was deemed insufficient.

---

[10] Emery (1959) defines an enterprise as "an organization of men and materials about some human endeavor."

According to Emery (1959), in the development of sociotechnical theory, there are two poles of forces determining the internal elaboration of the social system of an enterprise, i.e., its structure, norms, and values. These poles are the work-relationship structures and the solidarity of management about the mission of the enterprise.

As we have seen, apparently identical technologies rarely, if ever, have identical social systems. Differences arise from unique historical, cultural, and environmental factors. This should be borne in mind when dealing with the effects of mechanization and automation. Thus, in determining what is required of management under conditions of increased automation, the analyst must be aware of changes in both the internal and external environment, especially the latter. Internal changes seem to shorten the chain of command leading to a simple, single-command management. However, this may be negated by the proliferation of information and associated intermediate staff roles. External changes appear to act in the opposite direction requiring group decisions on the part of management. It may be that the executive element of management tends to become simpler (with the aid of computers), while the policy-making element becomes more complex and requires a higher order of managerial and social skills.

Sociotechnical theory must deal with additional areas including: (1) job satisfaction, especially perhaps with relation to *alienation;* (2) recalcitrance of individuals and social groups in the face of over-all requirements by the enterprise; and (3) emergence within the enterprise of purposes other than those of the enterprise. It can be seen that sociotechnical systems analysis must draw upon other areas of behavioral and social science for findings and concepts related to these problems. For example, there is much to be learned from a worker's perception of his job as "libidinal" or (as is usually the case) "nonlibidinal," and his reactions to his job in terms of fatigue, "dull contentment," neurotic satisfaction, etc.

In summary, the concept of sociotechnical systems used in this sense refers to *production* systems, and stresses that any such production system requires both a *technology* consisting of machinery, plant facilities, and raw materials, and a *work-relationship structure* which relates the human workers to both the technology and each other. The technology stresses and delimits the possible work structure and the work structure is possessed of psychological and social properties which generate their own requirements as to how the job is to be accomplished.

The interfacing of human and technological elements in an industrial production system is given in Figure 1-4. The basic elements of such a system are operations performed on materials by men and machines. These basic elements combine, and at each level of combination different interactions result. One can thus visualize hierarchically first- and second-order sociotechnical "units" and eventually the complete sociotechnical system (Cooper and Foster, 1971). An

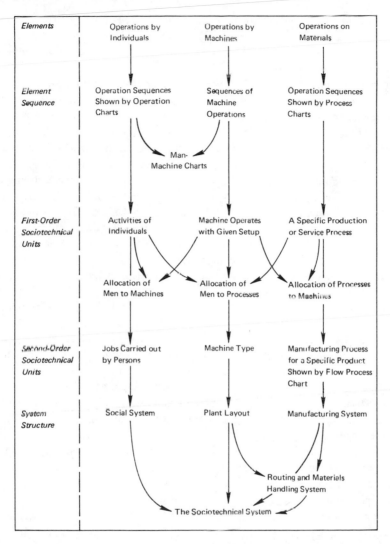

FIGURE 1-4
The sociotechnical framework of a typical industrial production system. [11]

example for the first-order sociotechnical unit, of an activity or completed sequence of operations by a person is assembling a piece of equipment, of a set of operations performed by a machine is trimming and cutting metal sheets, of production and service processes is welding, inspecting, and storing. Interaction of the first-order sociotechnical units leads to various allocations: (1) of men to

[12]From Herbst, 1959.

machines *in order to minimize idle machine time and satisfy production schedules and process sequences;* (2) of processes to machines in order to accomplish a given machine setup; and (3) of men to processes as determined by job selection and training.

It can be seen from the above, and especially from the italicized words, that the driving force or "leading edge" of technology is emphasized in this thinking. This seems to be at considerable variance from the, at least ostensibly joint, man-machine functions allocations of classical human factors. In fact, considerable symbiotic reward should accrue from better amalgamation of the two approaches, as attempted in this book. For our purposes here we might stress that human factors is much more precise in examining human perceptual-motor, and to some extent cognitive, capabilities and limitations, in recognizing the interactions among equipment design, staffing, and training, and in the analysis of tasks; however, human factors has essentially ignored the motivational and morale problems and social stresses ensuing from given system designs, points thoroughly considered in sociotechnical theory.

Second-order sociotechnical units can be defined in terms of description of jobs carried out by persons, a given type of machine (e.g., joining or materials moving), and a given manufacturing process and end units, thus emphasizing relationships between a given individual and his equipment and tools. Here Cooper and Foster (1971) suggest the term "psychotechnical units" is preferable; indeed many production technologies require a work-relationship structure centering on the individual and not on the social group.

Total systems structure of the factory now emerges as: (1) the *social system* involving the total set of individuals, their activities, and interrelationships; (2) the *plant layout,* that is, all the machines and their immediate surroundings; and (3) the *manufacturing system* of processes and interrelationships. The social system is determined to a considerable extent by both the plant layout and the materials handling system. The *sociotechnical system* itself results from the interaction of the social and technical systems.

Cooper and Foster (1971) urge against equating human and machine functions, except possibly at the physiological level. Psychologically, man is a self-realizing creature who can achieve much given the right environment, but who becomes refractory in a dependency relationship and forced to function at a slight level of his ability. Man performs best when he can control environmental contingencies; otherwise performance is degraded. Man does not willingly assume responsibility for machine or other operations unless these responsibilities are clearly defined and he can exercise effective control over them. Motivation must derive from the task itself, a difficult thing in systems designed so man must do the least or must function, without challenge, like a machine.

An environment can be analyzed in terms of supports and constraints to behavior; this determines the particular social and psychological factors of the production system. The level of *mechanization* appears to be the single most important technological determinant of the social system. Technology deter-

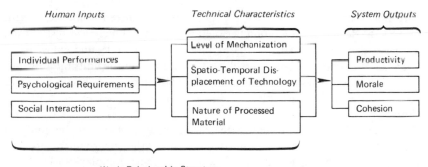

FIGURE 1-5
An input-conversion-output model of a sociotechnical system.[12]

mines the *spatial* and *temporal* features of the social system, as well as how little (in mass production) or much (in automated flow) control the worker has over it. In automobile assembly, workers are separated spatially, in flow technology, temporal factors are more important, and in electric power generation, technology is highly integrated in time. Thus, different operators on the same shift are better integrated than the same-type operators on different shifts. Spatial differences are apparently emphasized by slow throughput and temporal differences by rapid throughput. The physical nature of the throughput can also be an important technologically determined variable. These technological features help shape dimensions of the work-relationship structure as follows: (1) role differentiation, that is, the degree of task variety, complexity, and, by implication, challenge in a given individual or group job; (2) task dependence, as determined typically by two or more persons working together; and (3) goal dependence which may be independent or mutual.

When the system becomes increasingly differentiated and segmented, external coordination and control is required which reduces system autonomy.

Thus, in terms of sociotechnical design there is frequently considerable choice in determining work structures and, in turn, this choice is a function of the interdependence of the social and technical systems. This interdependence, of course, is a function of the particular type of production system. Effectiveness of a given design as measured by such factors as productivity and morale is indicated in Figure 1-5. The outputs are in balance, so if productivity, for example, is overemphasized either by technology or management, morale and cohesion will suffer. The question, say, relative to the production of automobiles, is whether the gains in productivity are worth the costs in employee

[12]From Robert Cooper and Michael Foster, "Sociotechnical Systems," as adapted from R. M. Stogdill, 1959, *Individual Behavior and Group Achievement,* in *American Psychologist,* 26(5), 1971, 467-74. Copyright 1971 by the American Psychological Association, and reproduced by permission.

apathy and absence. In most cases, though, it appears there is some latitude for improving the degree of integration between the social and technical systems and accordingly the state of balance among productivity, morale, and cohesion. In sociotechnical systems design, controlling variance within the units by providing unit self-regulation is also important. Thus, management's role becomes one of support to the unit, particularly with reference to interactions with the environment.

Emery and Trist (1965) emphasize that a main problem in the study of organizational change derives from the fact that the environment itself is changing, at an increasing rate and toward increasing complexity. Thus, the characteristics of organizational environments *per se* warrant study. Although the properties of open systems discussed earlier facilitate understanding of interchanges between organism or organization and environment, they do not deal with processes of the environment itself. Hence, the additional term, *causal texture,* is utilized (the term was used by the psychologists Tolman and Brunswik in other contexts in the 1930s).

A comprehensive understanding of organizational behavior requires knowledge of: (1) processes within the organization, or internal interdependencies and interrelationships; (2) exchanges of energy and resources both ways and interrelationships between the organization and its environment, emphasizing one or the other as more active; and (3) processes through which elements of the environment become interrelated. Causal texture refers to the third situation. Most work has been in the first category, although there is increasing interest in Category 2-type studies, the main emphasis of the present book.

Often events outside an organization become connected to one another so as to lead to irreversible general change, and this changed texture of the environment will not be recognized until it is too late. Such problems have been observed in industry, political organizations, educational organizations, hospitals, and prisons. Emery and Trist identify four types of causal texture which form a series in which the degree of causal texturing is increased:

Step 1.   *The placid, randomized environment* in which goals and noxiants ("goods" and "bads") are relatively unchanging in themselves and are randomly distributed.

Step 2.   *The placid, clustered environment* in which goals and noxiants hang together in certain ways. Survival becomes critically linked to what an organization knows of its environment, and *strategy* emerges as distinct from *tactics.* Organizations require a concentration of resources, subordination to the main plan, and a "distinctive competence;" hence, they grow in size and become hierarchical with a tendency toward centralized control and coordination.

Environmental Types 1 and 2 are *static*.

Step 3.   *The disturbed-reactive environment* in which the existence of a number of similar organizations becomes the dominant feature of the environmental field. *Operations,* a level of organizational response intermediate between tactics and strategy, emerge. An operation consists of a planned series of tactical acts, calculated reactions by others, and counteractions. The required flexibility encourages decentralization and decision-making at peripheral points. This is a *dynamic* environment.

Step 4. *The turbulent-field environment* is also dynamic. The dynamic quality of the field is derived from the interdependence of economic and other features of society, the increased reliance on research and development to meet competitive challenge, and persistent effects of organizations on their environments. For organizations this means a great increase in uncertainty.

Environmental changes may thus confront an organization with problems it is poorly adapted to meet. It now becomes necessary to perform *parallel analyses* of the organization and its environment. Redefinition of identity, reversal of basic values, and redesigning the organization—all quite difficult—may be required. Preservation of organizational stability becomes a prime problem. *Values* emerge, which have significance to all members of the field; these are coping mechanisms making possible the dealing with uncertainty. However, the establishment of a new set of values may take a generation or more, unless social science can help develop new means. And so far very little systematic work has been done in this area. We shall return to this all-important topic in Chapter 9 of this book.

Thus, we see there has been a movement, since the early formulations, toward a *general open sociotechnical theory to be used in the design of total systems.* Basic concepts have been developed (for example, the *activity*), which permit the simultaneous analysis into both behavioral and technical elements. Especially, emphasis is now placed on systematically dealing with the environment. Attempts have been made to determine elements of analysis, the relationship between social and technical dimensions, and the optimization of the relationship between these dimensions. Also, the basic element for sociotechnical systems analysis must itself be a sociotechnical element having the characteristics of an open system. Further, there is no simple one-to-one relationship between the social and the technical. Cybernetic modeling of the organization as an interrelated interacting series of open sociotechnical elements has been attempted. Organizations are held to exist in changing and demanding environments to which they must constantly adapt. Organizations further can be thought of as open systems with inputs, internal make-up, outputs, and corrective feedback mechanisms.

According to Cooper and Foster (1971), further extensions of sociotechnical thinking will require much more serious consideration of the relationship between man and machine because organizations will be increasingly structured around their work technology. And "as technology becomes more complex so does human nature (page 473)." Affluence in modern countries has been accompanied by changes in human values. This is particularly true in the shift away from adequacy and security of income to greater individual autonomy and self-expression. These values, sustained by education, will become increasingly felt and will require a new psychology to complement technology.

As yet, however, there is no established discipline for the study of large complex *socio-economic-technological systems,* although progress is being made.[13]

In summary, the Tavistock Institute of Human Relations emphasizes the following points:

1. Organizations are open systems.
2. Organizations are defined by a "primary task," that is, the "task" the organization was created to perform; however, it is most difficult to treat an organization as if it had a single goal or task.
3. Organizations encounter boundary conditions which may change the characteristics of the organization.
4. There are multiple channels of interaction among individuals, groups, organizations, and the environment.
5. Territory, technology, and time are important dimensions.
6. An organization can be used for purposes for which it is not designed.

The Tavistock concept and theory of sociotechnical systems tends to regard the technological subsystem as given and essentially fixed, the social subsystem as given but modifiable within limits. The present book accepts no such limitations; it is an outgrowth of the theory of *ideal* man-machine systems wherein functions are assigned to men and machines simultaneously.

Nevertheless, the Tavistock approach represents a sizable step forward in systems integration, in viewing the working group neither as a social system (as by the group dynamicists) nor as a technical system (as by engineers), but as an interdependent sociotechnical system. Data at different levels of analysis—individual, group, organization, and environment—can be interrelated within this framework and empirical approach. Regarding the organization as a self-maintaining organism, rather than a mechanism designed and redesigned to meet needs, seems most promising.

The systems dynamics approach. "Systems dynamics," a body of modeling and computer simulation techniques and associated theories applicable to the study of large and complex social systems had its origins in cybernetics and control systems engineering (feedback systems and servomechanism theory). The term, originally "industrial dynamics," has come to include "urban dynamics"

---

[13] Emery (1967) (cited in Chapter 7), considers this term misleading, "A society is composed of socio-psychological organizations and sociotechnical organizations, and at the same time is a population or aggregate of individuals. There are economic, political, and affective *aspects* to all organizations (p. 209)."

and "world dynamics." It is held to be a new way to analyze social systems which permits the design of revised policies. Industrial dynamics was originally defined (Forrester, 1961, p. 13):

> Industrial dynamics is the study of the information-feedback characteristics of industrial activity to show how organizational structure, amplification (in policies), and time delays (in decisions and actions) interact to influence the success of the enterprise. It treats the interactions between the flows of information, money, orders, materials, personnel, and capital equipment in a company, an industry, or a national economy.
>
> Industrial dynamics provides a single framework for integrating the functional areas of management—marketing, production, accounting, research and development, and capital investment. It is a quantitative and experimental approach for relating organizational structure and corporate policy to industrial growth and stability.

Industrial dynamics as a practical approach (Forrester, 1961), to use the original term, begins with the recognition of some problem in system functioning and ends with changes in system structure or policy to remedy the problem. Recognition of the problem is followed by the identification of the system structure that produces the problem. Next, a formal model of the system can be constructed and run on a computer equipped with the DYNAMO compiler. Then experiments can be conducted in the model and their effects over time studied. Successful experiments may then be implemented in the realworld system. The approach does not relate an observed system behavior to a simple cause, but emphasizes the multiple and circular interactions among system variables. Time periods dealt with may range from minutes to years. However, once a time period has been selected, only those factors capable of changing within the time interval are dealt with. Many potentially important factors may not change within the time period of a given model and, hence, do not influence behavior that does vary during that time. Model validity is not accomplished in terms of statistical significance, but in terms of asking what are realistic alternative explanations. In model building, reliance is on existing data sources in records and on the estimates of experts. New data may be developed by questionnaires and other methods, as required.

The industrial dynamics model is usually constructed at the highest level of aggregation that preserves the essential features of the system and the given problem under study. The model can be expressed as a flow diagram or as a list of equations; one form can be readily translated to the other form. Levels and rates are the elements of the model. Levels are variables that accumulate various flows, and rates indicate the rapidity with which the quantity in the level is increasing or decreasing at a given instant. An industrial dynamics study begins with a look for the network of causal factors (the system) that produces a symptom, condition, or problem of interest. Many potentially relevant factors must be considered and discarded before those to be included in the model are determined. Determination to include a factor does not depend on formal organization charts or formal boundaries, but upon causal linkages to other system factors. Factors are interrelated as causal loops, the positive and negative feedback loops. Only those factors are included within the system boundary which influence one or more other factors and are in turn influenced by one or more other factors. The approach is deterministic, although there is a random-signal-generating capability in the DYNAMO compiler.

Industrial dynamics has received rather wide exposure with mixed conclusions as to its efficacy. See, for example, Forrester (1968a), Ansoff and Slevin (1968), and Forrester (1968b).

Forrester's industrial and urban writings tend to be difficult to understand. This is partially remedied in his combined text-programmed workbook (Forrester, 1968c) which presents in easy-to-follow form, his concepts of systems structure and dynamics, but *not* his assumptions as to how to use basic and empirical scientific data. This book introduces the reader to the techniques of numerically simulating dynamic systems behavior. Emphasis is upon numerical solutions to systems models.

Our poor grasp of the basic nature, concepts, and principles of systems is held to be due to a general absence of structure or theory to tie together unrelated facts and observations. The concept of *feedback* systems which behave in a time-varying or dynamic manner is used as such a long-sought basis for structuring our observations about social, economic, and managerial systems. Social sciences should be easier to teach if based on principles common to all systems, human or technical.

Forrester classifies systems as *open* systems or *feedback* systems. He uses "open" in a manner that would be found objectionable in the original sense of open-systems theory and sociotechnical systems theory. Actually he means *open-loop* and in places uses "open" and "open-loop" interchangeably.

He deals with both *negative feedback* systems, which seek a goal and respond as a result of failing to achieve the goal, and *positive feedback* systems, which generate growth processes wherein action builds a result that generates still greater action. Thus, feedback systems control action based on the results of previous action. Classification of a system as open-loop or feedback is relative to the apparent purpose of the system, and changes with hierarchical level. One looks to positive feedback structure to find the forces of growth or decline, to negative feedback or goal-seeking to find causes of perhaps wild fluctuation and instability. *Nonlinear coupling* may result in the shift in dominance from one type feedback loop to another.

The following curves, illustrated in Figure 1-6, show these factors.

The simplest system structure is provided by the feedback loop in which a single rate controls the input to one system level or state. This is a *first-order* system because there is only one level variable. Each level variable is assigned an

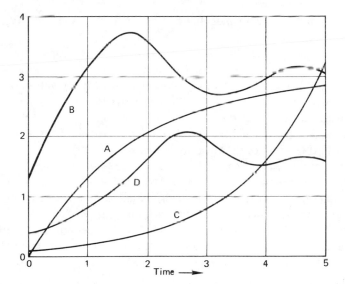

Curve A represents the simplest kind of feedback system in which the variable rises at a decreasing rate toward a final value (here a value of 3). This simple approach to equilibrium might be illustrated by the increase in an employee group as hiring expands the group toward an authorized level.

Curve B is a more complicated approach to the final value wherein the system overshoots this value, then falls below in trying to recover from the earlier overshoot. This curve can result from excessive time delays in the feedback loop or from efforts to correct a discrepancy between apparent system level and system goal. Such fluctuation can be observed in the rise and fall of industrial production seen in economic cycles.

Curve C shows growth where there is, in each succeeding time interval, the same fractional increase in the variable. Here the vertical value doubles in each unit of time. Such "exponential" growth is seen in cell division, in the sales of a product wherein salesmen sell more to provide more revenue to hire more salesmen, in the chain reaction of an atomic explosion, and in the increase in many animal populations.

Curve D indicates an initial section of exponential growth like Curve C followed by a leveling out. It is a composite of the exponential section and a later section having the characteristics of Curve B (the later section could of course be as in Curve A with no overshoot beyond the final value). A curve without overshoot beyond the final value can represent the growth of an animal which at first is increasingly rapid and then slows in its approach to final size. Both type curves might also represent an animal population that rises rapidly to the point where the food supply is overtaxed and no more animals can be supported.

FIGURE 1-6
Positive and negative feedback systems. [14]

[14]Adapted from Jay W. Forrester, *Principles of Systems.* Copyright 1968 by Wright-Allen Press, Cambridge, Massachusetts 02142.

initial value in the system model. An "exponential" response is typical of a first-order, negative-feedback loop.

A *second-order* system has two level variables, for example, inventory and goods on order. In such a system oscillation can be clearly demonstrated.

A negative-feedback loop seeks a goal introduced from outside the loop; a positive loop diverges from the "goal." The negative loop shows a reversal in sign in traversing the loop; in the positive loop, action increases the discrepancy between the system level and the "goal" or reference point. Thus, there is a basic difference in the nature of the "decision process."

Complex systems possess the attributes of *coupled nonlinear feedback loops,* in which dominance shifts from positive to negative loops. For example, there may be rapid growth at first until systems dynamics interact to inhibit growth. Fluctuations may then occur, associated with time delays.

Relatively simple structures produce much of the complex behavior of realworld systems. System structure can be represented in many layers or hierarchies of substructure in outline form as follows:

I. The "closed" (i.e., closed-loop) system generating behavior that is created within the system *boundary* and is not dependent on outside inputs.
   A. The feedback loop or sequence of alternating levels and rates as the basic element generating dynamic behavior from which systems are assembled.
      1. The level or state variable.
      2. The rate or policy variable which tells how a "decision-stream" or "action stream" is generated.
      a. The goal as an element of rate.
      b. The apparent condition to which the goal is compared.
      c. The discrepancy between goal and apparent condition.
      d. Action resulting from this discrepancy.

Forrester stresses that nothing flows across the system boundary (except perhaps disturbances for exciting the system). Thinking in terms of such an isolated system forces one to construct within the boundary of the model those relationships which *create* behavior. Here Forrester appears to use "closed" in the "open-systems theory" sense. Perhaps here is a major weakness in his theorizing: "Any interaction which is essential to the behavior mode being investigated must be included inside the system boundary." (1968c, p. 4-2)

The feedback loop couples decision, action, level, and information with a return to the decision point. Forrester uses "decision" in a much broader sense than human decision-making. It can be, indeed, a human decision—or a valve in a chemical plant or the governing processes in biological development. Decision processes are usually easy to determine, even though the associated feedback loops may not be.

Any dynamic system is formed by interconnecting feedback loops. Within each loop, level and rate variables are both necessary and sufficient elements of substructure. Level variables describe the condition of the system at any particular time; they are integrations in the mathematical sense and accumulate the rates of flow or results of action within the system. Levels integrate the net difference between inflow and outflow rates. Computation of a level does not involve the values of any other level variables; level variables are independent of one another.

In summary, the integration of a flow rate with respect to time gives a system level. First-order difference equations of state variables are called rate equations; equations resulting from application of an Euler integration scheme to the rate equations are termed level equations, in the sense of modern control theory. A path through the system encounters alternating level and rate variables.

Rate variables tell how fast the levels are changing, that is, they determine the slope or change per unit time of the level variables. Rates are action variables which cease when action stops. Rates do not control other rates without an intervening level variable; no rate variable depends directly on any other rate variable. A rate equation is a pure algebraic expression; it is not time dependent.

Only the values of levels are needed to describe fully the condition of the system; rate variables can be computed from the levels. All level equations must be given initial values at the beginning of the simulation.

A level equation represents an accumulation of the rates of flow that increase or decrease this accumulation. Any number of rates can be involved.

As an example of Forrester's use of flow diagramming and equations in model building and simulation, consider the following figure (Figure 1-7). Two equations describe this simple system.

Forrester believes integration creates the dynamic behavior in systems, because it occurs naturally in both the physical and biological worlds. However,

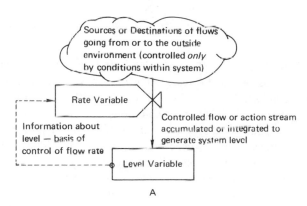

A

FIGURE 1-7(a)
Simplest possible feedback loop.[15]

[15]Adapted from Jay W. Forrester, *Principles of Systems.* Copyright 1968 by Wright-Allen Press, Cambridge, Massachusetts 02142.

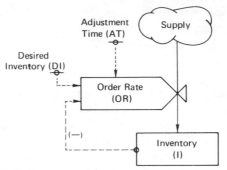

First-order negative feedback loop with inventory delay = AT.

Two equations describe this simple system: the rate equation stating the policy for order rate and the level equation to generate the inventory.

$$OR.KL = \frac{1}{AT} (DI - I.K) \qquad \text{Rate Equation}$$

$$AT = 1 \qquad \qquad \text{Constant}$$
$$DI = 1 \qquad \qquad \text{Constant}$$
$$I.K = I.J + (DT) (OR.JK) \qquad \text{Level Equation}$$
$$I = 0 \qquad \qquad \text{Initial Value}$$

where

OR—Order rate (units/week)
AT—Adjustment time (weeks)
DI—Desired inventory (units)
I—Inventory (units)
DT—Solution interval (weeks)
I, J, K—Times
JK, KL—Time invervals

B

FIGURE 1-7(b)
Two equations describe this simple system. The figure shows the structure of the loop.[16]

most of the mathematics of physical science and engineering is expressed as differential equations, which Forrester believes is misleading and leaves people without a strong linkage between the real world and the world of mathematics. Presentation in the form of differential equations may create feelings of reversed cause and effect. Thus, one typically thinks of changing position as causing velocity rather than vice versa. Nowhere in natural processes does differentiation occur. Even the "differential analyzer" is built of integrators and requires that the differential equations first be converted to integral equations.

Forrester makes extensive use of flow diagrams to show level, rate, and auxiliary equations and their interconnections. This nomenclature is summarized

[16]Adapted from Jay W. Forrester, *Principles of Systems.* Copyright 1968 by Wright-Allen Press, Cambridge, Massachusetts 02142.

in the above and below figures (Figures 1-7 and 1-8). Forrester views a "parameter" as a value which is constant during a simulation run.

Forrester's simulations utilize the DYNAMO II compiler, although other compilers could be used instead. DYNAMO is a computer program which accepts the system equations and produces simulation results as graphical plots and numerical tables. DYNAMO accepts a model written as level, rate, and associated equations. DYNAMO can be used as part of a time-sharing system utilizing a remote typewriter terminal for model entry and editing.

DYNAMO has some useful special capabilities, for example, to generate random sequences, "noise," and first-order exponential decay.

Forrester contrasts between information and rates. Information about a level can be taken as an input to a rate without affecting that level. Information is not depleted by use. Information provides the only input to rate equations. Information may be distorted in that the "true" and apparent system levels may not coincide. Information can be delayed or distorted by random error or biased. It can be subject to "cross-talk" in which apparent source is changed.

The dynamic behavior of the system arises from the process of integration, which can on occasion produce a variable with a time-shape and time-position different from those of the input flow rate. For example, integration can produce successively straight lines, a parabola, and a cubic curve. But is there some shape or curve not altered by integration and therefore capable of recirculating in a closed loop containing integration? The answer is, of course, the exponential family of simple exponential functions and complex exponentials, that is, sine and cosine functions. *All* positive feedback loops and the first-order negative feedback loop generate their time response in a simple exponential shape. Higher-order negative loops can generate sinusoidal curves.

Forrester, extending his concepts from industry to the city (1969), looks further at complex systems. A "complex" system is a high-order, multiple-loop, nonlinear feedback structure, and Forrester believes all social systems, including urban, corporation management, national government, international trade, and economic process systems, to be in this category. High-order refers to the number of level equations (integrations or states) in the system description. A system greater than fourth or fifth order can be considered complex. Social systems tend to be tenth to hundredth order; his "urban dynamics" system is twentieth order.

The system is characterized by an interlocking structure of feedback loops. The interplay of three or four interacting loops of shifting dominance is held to give a complex system much of its character. Both positive and negative feedback loops are present. Positive feedback generates growth or decay processes, and is goal divergent; negative loops are associated with goal-seeking and equilibrium. Most engineering work has dealt only with negative feedback.

Modern mathematics deals almost exclusively with linear processes. Yet in

$$I.K = I.J + (DT)(RR.JK - SR.JK) \qquad \text{Eq. 7-1, Level Equation}$$

Flow Rate In (RR) ⟶ | Inventory (I)   7-1 | ⟶ Flow Rate Out (SR)

(a)   Level equation (integration of difference in flow rates) and rectangle representing it.

$$SR.KL = \frac{BL.K}{DD} (IA.K) \qquad \text{Eq. 7-2, Rate Equation}$$

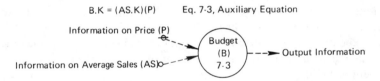

Information on Delivery Delay (DD)

Information on Backlog (BL) ⟶ Sales Rate (SR)   7-2

Information on Actual Inventory (IA) ⟶

(b)   Rate equation (policy statement) controlling rate of flow and valve symbol representing equation.

$$B.K = (AS.K)(P) \qquad \text{Eq. 7-3, Auxiliary Equation}$$

Information on Price (P)

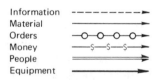

Budget (B) 7-3 ⟶ Output Information

Information on Average Sales (AS) ⟶

(c)   Auxiliary equation, part of a rate equation, and circle representing it.

Information   -----------▶
Material   ───────────▶
Orders   ─o─o─o─o─▶
Money   ─s─s─s─▶
People   ══════════▶
Equipment   ───────────▶

(d)   Flow lines used to connect main symbols.

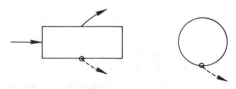

(e)   Information take-off lines indicated by small circles to distinguish from lines indicating content flow. This symbol can be used redundantly at the beginning of all information lines.

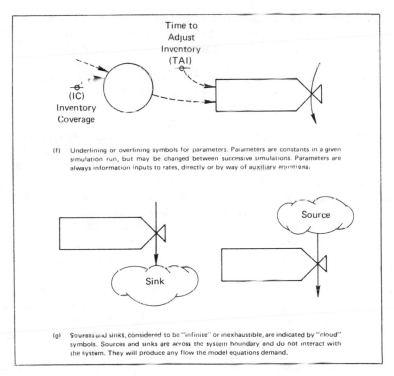

(f) Underlining or overlining symbols for parameters. Parameters are constants in a given simulation run, but may be changed between successive simulations. Parameters are always information inputs to rates, directly or by way of auxiliary equations.

(g) Sources and sinks, considered to be "infinite" or inexhaustible, are indicated by "cloud" symbols. Sources and sinks are across the system boundary and do not interact with the system. They will produce any flow the model equations demand.

FIGURE 1-8

Flow diagrams showing level, rate, and auxiliary equations and their interconnections.[17]

biological and social systems nonlinear coupling permits one feedback loop to dominate the system for a while, followed by the shifting of dominance to another part of the system in which behavior may be so vastly different as to appear unrelated. This multiloop realignment makes the system very insensitive to most system parameters and to attempts to change its behavior. However, nonlinearity is easy to handle by the simulation as opposed to the analytic modeling approach. Emphasis should be upon system structure as opposed to measuring parameters.

Forrester sees the following as especially important characteristics of complex systems:

1. *Counterintuitive behavior.* Urban growth, aging, and population movement result in urban decay; however, program solutions may make matters even worse. Hence, policy changes in the exact opposite of most present ones

[17]From Jay W. Forrester, *Principles of Systems.* Copyright 1968 by Wright-Allen Press, Cambridge, Massachusetts 02142.

are what are really needed if the decaying inner city is to be revived. Intuition and judgment, based on simple, first-order, negative feedback loops (such as warming one's hands by a stove) having a single important level variable result in misleading expectations and perceptions. In complex systems, cause and effect are not closely related either in time or in space, yet coincident events often suggest simple cause and effect. The cause of a difficulty may lie far back in time from a symptom, but if one searches for a "cause" near in time and space, one usually finds it but is really dealing only with coincident events. Almost all variables in complex systems are highly correlated and much statistical and correlation work is therefore futile. Intuitive solutions to problems of complex systems are, thus, wrong most of the time.

2. *Insensitivity to changes in system parameters* (constants in the equations). Changes of as much as sevenfold have little effect, because social systems are dominanted by psychological or biological factors that change very little across societies and historic times.

3. *Resistance to policy changes.* This results from the first two features above.

4. *Influential pressure points occurring in unexpected places.* The system is sensitive to changes in some parameters (the converse of item 2), but sensitivity or lack thereof is not immediately evident, and policy changes may result in pressures unexpectedly radiating throughout the system from obscure points.

5. *Corrective programs counteracted by the system's behavior.* These may shift the system balance so that natural processes encounter more resistance. Emphasis should rather be on system modifications resulting in changed internal incentives.

6. *Reactions to policy changes different in the long run from short-run reactions.* Voter pressure and political expediency favor short-term solutions leading to long-term deterioration.

7. *Drift to low performance.* Counterintuitive behavior and long-term opposition lead to detrimental design changes. A solution is tried leading to a little improvement; more of the solution is attempted lowering long-term performance.

A simulation model, to Forrester, is a theory which describes the structure and interrelationships of a system. The correct concepts of structure must guide model-building. The simulation model differs from a simple conceptual or verbal model in being logically complete. The basic assumptions of the model can be checked against available experience and data.

Forrester's model, as we have seen, is a *closed* model, not dependent for its behavior on variables transmitted across the boundary from the external world. "Troubles" are not imposed on the system from the outside, but are generated by internal processes. The first step in modeling is to generate a model that creates the problem. Only if we understand the processes giving rise to the system's troubles can we restructure the system so as to get different results.

Thus the model must contain all the interacting relationships leading the system into trouble. In contrast to the RAND approach to systems analysis and to modeling and simulation discussed in Chapters 4 and 5, there is not such a deliberate comparison of alternatives, but rather more emphasis on the understanding of basic processes.

The concept of closed boundary emphasizes that the simulation model has within it all the generating mechanisms for the problem; this concept is held to be essential to the realistic study of complex systems.

In social sciences, the failure to understand systems is often held to be due to inadequate data. However, Forrester believes the impasse is not due to lack of data but rather to deficiency in existing theories of structure. Conventional data-gathering, thus, seldom produces new insights into the details of system structure. When structure is properly represented, parametric values are of secondary importance. The real barrier derives from a lack of ability or willingness to organize already existing information into a structure representing the real world.

The basic flow diagrams indicated above can be extended in great detail. Model equations are developed for each rate, each level, and for numerous processes intermediate between rate and level. The intermediate processes may represent attractiveness factors (for example, for migration), perception time lags (e.g., it may take one generation 20 years to become aware of changing social conditions), other time values, normal values (which may be modulated as necessary), public expenditures, etc.

With regard to parameters of the simulation model, ultimate equilibrium values are mostly independent of the starting point. Parameters are defined as constants or table functions describing relationships within the system. Parameter sensitivity can be tested by asking: (1) Does the parameter affect the growth, stability, or equilibrium of the system? (2) Can the parameter be changed or controlled? (3) Does change in the parameter affect the selection or use of other parameters or structural modifications to improve the system?

Forrester (1970), in summarizing his philosophy, stresses that his methods form a bridge between engineering and social sciences. They are felt to be quite general purpose. He believes it is relatively easy to include psychological variables, attitudes, and human reactions, if they can be described.

Forrester believes identical structures recur in apparently dissimilar fields. Examples could be a simple swinging pendulum, a chemical plant, the processes of management, economics, power politics, internal medicine, and psychiatry. In a sense, therefore, he is here contributing to general systems theory. Unfortunately, he is not more explicit in stating what these systems have in common other than feedback loops. He states that a universal approach to time-varying systems, now emerging, seems capable of application to systems of any complexity. The student has only to master the principles and practice of dynamic analysis. Forrester believes there are no professional schools in this area. Educational materials are still being developed, and learning is by apprenticeship and trial and error. Also needed are theory, laboratory, and case studies at least as extensive as those in the established professions.

Although Forrester pays lip service to quality of life, his emphasis is still upon economic and technical variables at a high degree of aggregation. For example, he believes the aging of buildings is central to the urban decline process. Although he believes his theories are as equally applicable to "New York, Calcutta, a gold rush camp, or West Berlin," he does not appear to appreciate that buildings can be built for beauty and permanence. Thus, incentives to demolish old buildings and clear the land for new development may be as bad as present tax laws and regulations which offer incentives to keep old buildings in place. In this sense, his suggestions may produce bad systems management. Indeed, he appears to be operating at a very abstracted subsystem level, just another variation of the sterile, "optimizing" operations research approach to complex problems. Worst of all, by neglecting subtle factors associated with esthetics, identification, and permanence in a city, he is violating his own principles and is counterintuitive!

Numerous criticisms of Forrester's approach have been made, for example, by Ansoff and Slevin (1968), Hester (1969), Averch and Levine (1970), and Gray, Pessel, and Varaiya (1971). We shall return to the criticisms of the urban model in Chapter 8. Among the salient points to be considered are the following which we have summarized from the perceptive analysis of Ansoff and Slevin (1968).

1. It is not a general systems theory about the behavior of organizations; it is, indeed, not a well circumscribed body of theory. Thus, it lacks *predictability, verifications of validity,* and *transferability.*

2. The simulation must be completely quantitative, eliminating rank ordering of alternatives and human participation in the simulation runs.

3. There is overemphasis on interview techniques in determining from managers and other experts the decision rules employed in the real world. The rules the managers verbalize may not be the ones actually used from one time to another. Systems dynamics is very closely associated with judgments of particular practitioners.

4. The models are overly related to verbal descriptions and observations.

5. The DYNAMO compiler may exert a Procrustean influence with its highly stylized structure and system of notation.

6. Model emphasis is upon reproducing the nature of the system with little concern for forecasting the condition of the system at some future time. The failure to predict outcomes seriously limits the value of the model.

7. Validation is associated with reproducing the behavior characteristics of the system, such as stability, oscillation, and growth. Validation ignores correspondence between predicted and realworld behavior and ignores time-phased behavior. There are real and difficult problems with validation.

8. Paradoxically, Forrester insists on reduction of model content to fully quantitative terms but accepts qualitative and subjective validation.

9. Too simple analogies are made to wind-tunnel tests in aerodynamics and to chemical processing on the one hand, and computer simulation models of social and economic systems on the other.

10. Systems dynamics is not unique but shares many deficiencies with management science and operations research in general. *Nonrepeatability of an analysis* is a common occurrence.

11. Validations, using historical data, are minimal.

12. There is slight chance of two or more systems dynamicists coming to the same recommendation when faced with the same problem.

13. The table function provided by DYNAMO permits including any arbitrary function, but may also encourage the inclusion of hidden arbitrary assumptions.

14. The complex political and social variables which influence decision-making are probably oversimplified and fitted into quantitative formulae.

15. Forrester fails to formalize his processes of abstraction of data from managers and other experts or to provide tests of validity of information obtained.

16. Applications of systems dynamics differ as a function of the degree of quantification. For example, production and inventory control are more amenable to this approach than are marketing or research and development.

17. All aspects of complex systems need not best be studied in terms of information feedback. It may be an oversimplification that a relatively few easily discernible factors interact, resulting in the feedback loops felt to dominate system behavior. The cybernetic concept, generally true, may be inapplicable to specifics.

18. In terms of costs and benefits, construction of the models requires considerable effort, for example, in terms of information collection on operations. Acceptance by management may be slight.

19. As with all systems analysis techniques, flow-chart modeling may be of great benefit. In fact it may not be desirable most of the time to proceed with the actual simulation which is much more costly.

20. Qualitative validation makes it impossible to state that systems dynamics is any more valuable than any other method.

21. Forrester's main contribution may be on his greater emphasis on the system as a whole. The main value may be in terms of generalizations which stimulate others to validate and to find specifics.

Gray, Pessel, and Varaiya (1971) report that a greatly simplified version of Forrester's original urban model exhibited essentially the same behavior.

Miscellaneous Second-Generation Theories

Some approaches to hierarchy. Classifications of systems levels or hierarchy have been made, for example, that of Boulding. Theoretical models are most successfully developed at the static and simple dynamic levels. Work at the cybernetic and open-systems levels is also improving. Boulding's (1956) rather anthropocentric classification, somewhat simplified, follows:

1. Static structure; e.g., the anatomy of the universe.
2. Simple dynamic structure; e.g., clockworks with predetermined motions.
3. Cybernetic systems; e.g., thermostats.
4. Open systems; e.g., living organisms.
5. Genetic-societal systems; e.g., division of labor among cells.
6. Animal systems; e.g., goal-directed behavior and self-awareness.
7. Human systems; e.g., the individual human being.
8. Social systems; e.g., human organizations.
9   Transcendental systems; e.g., ultimates and absolutes.

Simon (1969), stressing the importance of hierarchy, has explored some of the concepts underlying a science of design. Among other things, this would involve the separability of the outer and inner environments in studying an artificial or adaptive system. Often we can predict behavior from knowledge of the system's goals and its outer environment, with minimal assumptions about the inner environment. Contrariwise, quite different inner environments may accomplish similar goals in similar outer enrivonments (analogies in biology, for example). Partial independence of the outer environment may be accomplished through passive insulation, negative feedback, predictive adaptation, etc.

In simulation, Simon maintains, we need not comprehend all the internal structure, but only that crucial to the abstraction from detail. Likewise, in design with unreliable elements, unreliability can be coped with only by our manner of organization.[18] There is no need in either case for having a micro-theory of the lowest hierarchical level, say at the physical or neurophysiological level. Thus, Simon views human (goal-directed or cognitive but perhaps not motivational-emotional) behavior as quite simple, with the apparent complexity over time being largely a reflection of the complexity of the environment. Goals are attained by adapting the inner to the outer environments. The inner environment can be defined by describing its *functions* without detailed specification of its *mechanisms.*

Complex systems are constructed within a hierarchy of levels. The ideas expressed above refer successively to each hierarchical sublevel. Design involves

[18]I suggest the same idea applies to the organizat.on of basically reliable operations research and other subsystem techniques.

discovering ways to *decompose* the complex system into semi-independent constituents corresponding to the many functional elements. The design of each constituent can then be carried out somewhat independently of the design of others, since each will affect the other largely through its functions and apart from basic mechanisms. Perhaps our present woes, say with pollution, might provide counter-arguments here.

Simon thus stresses that system complexity frequently takes the form of hierarchy, and hierarchical systems have some special properties independent of their specific content. For example, hierarchical systems will evolve much more quickly than nonhierarchical systems of comparable size. In social hierarchies interaction is as important as spatial arrangement.

As we have seen, biological (and social) systems absorb free energy (e.g., from the sun); hence, the complex system has a smaller entropy than do the elements. Likewise, from thermodynamic considerations, it is possible to estimate the increase in entropy when a complex system decomposes into its elements. However, organisms are not energetically closed systems, so this does not provide a means to deduce the direction or rate of evolution.

Complex systems will evolve from simple systems much more rapidly if there are stable intermediate forms or hierarchies.

Simon speaks of *nearly decomposable* systems with weak, but not negligible interactions among the subsystems. Here the short range behavior of the subsystems is approximately independent of the short-range behavior of the others, and in the long run the behavior of any one of the subsystems depends, in only an aggregate way, on the behavior of the others. The detail of the interaction can be ignored. Simon appears to be assuming similar or identical subsystems, however. Yet he states that in social systems where members of a system communicate with and influence other members, near decomposability is usually prominent. However, as in physical systems there are usually limits to the simultaneous interaction of large numbers of subsystems. Also the higher-frequency dynamics are associated with the subsystems and the lower-frequency dynamics with the system itself. At any rate, hierarchies have the property of near decomposability, with intra-element linkages generally stronger than inter-element linkages.

Most hierarchic systems possess considerable redundancy; most are made up of only a few kinds of subsystems like the chemical elements or amino acids. Thus, system descriptions can be enormously simplified, perhaps at risk of cries of "reductionism."

Simon contrasts *state description* (pictures, diagrams, and chemical structural formulae) with *process description* (recipes, differential equations, and equations for chemical reactions). Problem-solving requires continual translation between the two descriptions of the same complex reality.

Simon concludes that a theory of hierarchy provides one means of constructing a *nontrivial* theory of complex systems.

In evaluating these concepts, we must stress the importance of not ignoring the *externalities;* i.e., the inter-subsystem linkages in the study of ecological and sociotechnical systems. Any theory of coordination in government must consider this. There is grave danger in thinking of the external environment as composed of independent or loosely linked subsystems. Such concepts seem most appropriate to simpler, lower-hierarchical-level, less rapidly changing systems than those of modern society and environment. Using Simon's extension of *span of control* (how many subordinates in an organizational report to a single boss) to system span, sociotechnical systems are characterized by a very wide span at the level of important subsystems.

This line of thinking has been paralleled by Platt (1970), who looks especially at *sudden changes* in structure or *hierarchical jumps,* represented by evolutionary jumps, social revolutions, capturing of a population by a philosophy, personal insights, etc. Little attention has been paid until recently to the sudden formation of larger integrated systems from conflicting or malfunctioning subsystems.

This concept of hierarchy stresses not the static structure of the watchmaker, but of flow patterns in which the "things" are invariant, self-maintaining, or self-repeating features of the flow. Thus, a waterfall, a flame, and a cloud have a characteristic, self-maintaining form even though subject to flows of water, air, and other gases. Here we can speak of a *flow hierarchy* involving structures that are self-maintaining, even though matter, energy, and information are continually flowing through them. Such flow systems can undergo sudden transitions to new self-maintaining organizations which, in turn, will be stable for a long time. The "quantum jump" of an electron from one steady state of an atom to another steady state provides a familiar example.

Also, restructuring to larger hierarchical patterns occurs with growth over time. Growth may be non-uniform and by successive small jumps.

Hierarchical growth by restructuring to a higher level of organization can occur when subsystems having different properties come into contact. Patterns may be initially unstable at a given hierarchical level *i* until a resolution through conflict or cooperation results either in breaking apart the old system or reorganization to a new level *i + 1* with a new stable pattern involving the larger experience of the larger system.

Predicting the future—social or technological—is rendered exceedingly difficult because of such jumps. The jumps from the Ptolemaic to the Copernican systems in astronomy and from classical mechanics to quantum mechanics in physics, both within two or three decades, represent well-known examples. Likewise, atomic energy, space travel, and television were not reliably predictable in advance, although in retrospect they were almost inevitable consequences of an earlier scientific revolution.

This *self*-restructuring of a system is very different from assembly by an external designer. Especially in the area of social evolution, we see sudden collective restructurings such as occurred in the Reformation, Industrial Revolution, American Revolution, and Russian Revolution. Whole populations were united in creating change at every level. We are now in the incipient stages of a world reorganization, as a sudden collective change in awareness sinks in.

Platt states these common characteristics of self-generated jumps in a hierarchical organization:

1. A cognitive dissonance, or recognition of a disparity between old theories, practices, and assumptions and new data, experiences or observations. Or there can be realization that practices do not even fit the system's own goals or images of itself. This applies alike to personality change, scientific revolutions, and social reconstitutions. Pathological resistance to awareness of cognitive dissonance is a common response and is reflected in the paranoid delusions of individuals and states; so is alienation.

2. The dissonance is expressed in many-faceted symptoms and the later transformation in many-faceted effects.

3. The restructuring, when it arrives, is strikingly sudden, because the change has been prepared for everywhere at once. The individual elements of reform may seem weak, but when they reach a certain critical density they begin to join forces. The new patterns are self-reinforcing and mutually reinforcing as soon as they touch, because they form a better integrated system Sudden insights, heightened by modern communications, have occurred. The old system is overwhelmed from without and betrayed from within from sources it never expected.

4. A move toward greater simplification in ordering or understanding occurs.

5. Interactions jump up over the old system level i from the old subsystems $i - 1$ to the emerging supersystem $i + 1$. This is because of self-maintenance and resistance to change (or to stress that precedes hierarchical jump!) at level i. Build-up of any one(s) of the conflicting elements or a restatement of old premises just doesn't work. Thus, a design principle for sociotechnical systems and for society must recognize that the largest well-functioning subsystems must be fitted into the larger integrative supersystem within which conflict must be resolved. The still healthy subsystems must not be allowed to "go down the drain."

Platt concludes it is not clear that self-structuring hierarchical jumps can be either anticipated or guided. This has serious implications for both future forecasting and the management of society, topics considered in detail later in this book. Our present transition to a new world system is thus the outcome of personal and unpredictable events over the centuries. (Contrast this view with that of Greene [1971] already mentioned earlier in the chapter, that there is no such thing as a trend and that history is unimportant in describing the state of a system.) Certainly this concept of hierarchical jumps complicates the picture of simple exponential growth.

The prospects for understanding of and control over hierarchical jumps may be dim indeed. One candidate for special consideration in this discussion is the Maslow hierarchy of motivation, as people move upward through it with resulting changes in goals, aspirations, and expectations.

Mesarović, *et al.* (1970), partly utilizing Simon's ideas in an application of the mathematical general systems theory of multilevel systems, look at hierarchical systems in terms of levels of abstraction (in modeling), levels of complexity of decision-making, and levels of priority of action. Large-scale systems are considered to consist of a family of hierarchically arranged decision-making subsystems. Of special significance is coordination for which a mathematical theory is developed. This involves a two-level system with n decision or control elements on the first level and one decision element on the second level. Coordination is considered to be decision involving the second-level element with the objective of influencing the first level so as to promote a total-system goal. The relationship between the elements on different levels is considered the main issue; to deal with it the decision problems of the subsystems are greatly oversimplified.

Examples of automation from the steel processing, petrochemical, and electric power industries are presented. Problems in manual systems include the disparity between a plan prepared in advance and its actual execution, increased emphasis on profitability in the face of competition, and the sheer size and diversity of operations. For example, automation in the steel industry involves linking information processing and control functions into a single system, from customer orders to plant motor and temperature control. An integrated steelwork can be illustrated as a multilevel system with an organizational hierarchy. The three main functions of production planning, scheduling and coordination of operations, and process control provide a framework for a hierarchical arrangement of subsystems. Coordination, especially of production activities, is a major problem.

In these industries bulk capacity and continuity of production mean that even small improvements in operations result in considerable financial savings. The decline in steel industry sales from 1959 to 1964 highlights the need for such improvements. Unfortunately, the side effects on people and on society are seldom considered in mechanistic treatises such as this! One might, indeed, ask: What actual and symbolic power is given to theorists and managers by virtue of control, especially computer control, over complex systems? Thus, relative to the gap between planning and operation we must learn (Mesarović, *et al.*, 1970, p. 7):

> . . . In between these two levels, human operators are using manual supervision and control, a rather *outdated* mode of operation. It is only *natural* to close this gap using modern decision-making and information-processing procedures [emphasis added].

Electric power systems have grown by a stepwise process of interconnecting existing systems into larger pools, which have appeared to offer economic gains with no major technical or operational problems. The resulting tightly coupled systems of enormous power and complexity have experienced some dramatic failures, however (see for example, De Greene, 1970). A multilevel approach offers an attractive alternative. Say, in a two-level (power pool and n areas) organizational hierarchy, the problem is in finding an optimum allocation of power generation in each area, and power exchange through the lines such that the cost of power generation is at a minimum. Computers are placed in each area (representing a different company) and at a central power pool; and the tasks of the individual computers must be designated.

An organization also can be viewed as a family of interacting, hierarchically arranged, decision-making elements.

Mesarović, *et al.* inform us that "today's managers need all the help they can get to do their job properly (p. 15)." Yet little is known, they say, about organization theory or about organizations, partly because of complexity but partly because of the scarcity of workers in the field. Hence, their research was motivated toward making systems theory more directly relevant to the theory of organizations. Tragically, these well-intentioned but in many ways naive people may develop a big following through overwhelming—or inspiring—with mathematical detail.

Another insight as to the dangers of regarding systems science an unmixed blessing is provided on p. 16 of the above reference:

> ... managers ... are men responsible for the well-being of an organization ... who ... *need instructions* on how to affect the organization from within so as to improve its operation [emphasis added].

Mesarović, *et al.,* feel they are taking a definite step toward a *normative* theory of organization. They question the applicability to organizations of *single-level,* although dynamic, multivariable, input-output, feedback control systems. The limitations to such "industrial dynamics" approaches, they say, occur because of discrepancies between the structures of an input-output model and the organization itself.

The analysis of Mesarović, *et al.* of the limitations to organizational theory of classical (structural), behavioral (personalistic or motivation), and systems ("systems dynamic") theories are more meaningful. Contrast is made in terms of how the individual members of the organization are viewed, how organizational structure is represented, and the methodology or tools used. For example, some of Simon's work is held not to differentiate between hypothetical multilayer hierarchies and more realistic multi-echelon hierarchies in organizations.[19] Or behavioral theories emphasize personality without regard to a person's role and position in a hierarchy. Mesarović, *et al.* thus argue that multilevel systems

---

[19] *Level* is used as a general term; specific terms used, respectively, are as follows: *strata* to apply to level of description or abstraction, *layers* to apply to level of decision complexity, and *echelons* to apply to organizational level.

theory cuts across all three of the above theory categories by: (1) emphasizing hierarchical structure of decision-making elements in the sense of organization charts; (2) viewing the person as a decision-maker or goal-seeker, with recognition of levels of satisfaction and discrepancies between actual and operational goals; and (3) recognizing that an organization consists of an interconnection of decision-making subsystems. The decision-maker is viewed more a satisficer than an optimizer; thus variations in level of aspiration can be included. Other ideas, based on Simon's concepts of organization, are also included in their modeling, for example, analytical conflict resolution by either problem-solving or persuasion.

Because of the large size of modern organizations and the new use of computers and information-processing, which aids the logic capability of the decision-maker, the general mathematical theory of multilevel systems is proposed. The theory, they feel, is structural, formal, and independent of the field of specialization. However, to use multilevel analysis, the methods of study and analysis on individual levels must be perfected. Determining the relationship between or among the levels, perhaps one level above and one below the given level, is particularly important. A simple two-level model may involve a coordinating element as a second level; this decides which of, say, two first-level control modes will be used and how. In biology, for example, there may also be widespread applications, especially in explaining integration.

Figure 1-9 illustrates the interaction among levels in a hierarchical system.

In summary, the theory of Mesarović, *et al.* on organization-type systems with multilevel decision-making has stemmed from several sources: (1) from the area of automation and control of complex industrial systems and multivariable control theory; (2) from the von Neumann-Morgenstern theory of games concerned with competitive situations and the more recent Marshak-Radner theory of teams concerned with cooperative situations; (3) from problems of communications and control; and (4) from organizational models of hierarchy and decision-making.

For a summary of the points of view on hierarchy of other authors from many diciplines, see the discussion by Wilson (1969), who categorizes hierarchy as a concept, hierarchy in nature, and hierarchy in artifacts such as language and computers.

Further extensions of general systems and open-systems theory. Katz and Kahn (1966), in developing a social psychology of organizations, take their model of an energic input-output system from the open systems theory of von Bertalanffy. This permits the stability or recurrence of activities in a system to be stated in terms of the energic input into the system, the transformation of energies in the system, and the resulting product or energic output.

Katz and Kahn believe it is better theoretically not to start the study of organizations with trying to identify the rational purposes of the designers and then trying to correct for them when they are not fulfilled. Rather, theory

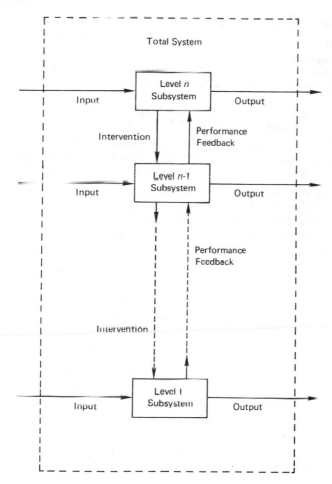

FIGURE 1-9
Interaction among levels in a hierarchical system.[20]

should begin with input, output, and functioning of the organization as a system in terms of the above model.

Katz and Kahn suggest the following nine attributes define all open systems and provide a meaningful framework for the study of organizations:

1. Importation of energy from the environment.
2. A throughput process.
3. Output into the environment of a product.

[20]From M.D. Mesarović *et al., Theory of Hierarchal, Multilevel Systems.* Copyright 1970 by Academic Press, Inc.

4. Cyclic nature of energy exchange, particularly with regard to feedback.

5. Negative entropy, achieved by importing more energy from the environment than expended and then storing this energy to counter entropic processes. The entropic process can be viewed as a universal law of nature in which all forms of organization move toward disorganization or death. Social organizations can resist the process better than can biological ones, yet many of the former fail each year. How does this concept relate to "valence," "cohesiveness," etc.?

6. Information input and coding and negative feedback. When the system's negative feedback stops, the steady state disappears, and the system terminates.

7. Steady state and dynamic homeostasis (not a motionless equilibrium). This eventually can be traced to the principles of Le Chatelier in chemistry. The steady state incorporates, at different levels, homeostasis and the preservation of the character of the system through growth and expansion.

8. Differentiation and specialization over time.

9. Equifinality. The system can reach the same final state in spite of different initial conditions and a variety of pathways. In a related sense there does not have to be one single method for reaching an objective.

J. G. Miller (1965a, 1965b, 1965c, 1965d) subsumes his system theories, of particular relevance to biology, under the term "living systems." Living systems: (1) are open systems; (2) maintain a steady level negentropy even though entropic changes (homeostasis) occur within them; (3) are more than minimally complex; (4) contain genetic material of DNA; (5) are composed largely of protoplasm; (6) possess a critical control subsystem; (7) possess other critical subsystems in symbiotic relationships, and integrate subsystems to form actively self-regulating, developing, reproducing unitary systems with goals and purposes; and (8) can exist only in a certain environment. Negative feedback plays a particularly important role. When it disappears, the steady state disappears, and the system ends.

B. Gross has contributed greatly to advances in social systems theory and has been a leading advocate of the concept of social indicators to which we shall return in Chapter 9 of this book.

There is now quite a bit of useful theory, modeling, and data at the constituent level, but little either in the way of integrating this or relating it to the real world of political policy-making and decision-making. Systems theory can provide a basis for the synthesis of available useful material. However, there must be no simple dependence on "hard-system" methods or mathematical finesse abstracted from the environment. Social systems are greatly differentiated internally and interrelated hierarchically and polyarchically with divergent purposes and conflicts. Every social system is an open system with numerous activities cutting across its boundaries with the social, biological, and physical environment. Gross (1966), in presenting a social systems model at the national level, sees several kinds of boundary-crossing activities; for example, (1) entries and exits of people into groups and organizations; (2) multiple membership in groups and organizations; (3) acquisition of resource inputs and delivery of outputs; and (4) influence across a boundary. The various elements and dimensions of system and subsystem, of course, change at differential, and differentially changing, rates.

Gross also argues theories of equilibrium are poorly suited to deal with the dynamics of social systems. Rather they are more useful to describe temporary states of small elements of the systems. The dynamics of system change far transcend classic equilibrium. Cybernetics and feedback are now more important bases in such systems concepts. This is especially true in the recognition of multiple feedback loops, coupled feedback among cooperating-competing systems, and feedforward loops which provide information on reciprocal expectations of future behavior. Models must be designed not only in terms of goal-seeking feedback, but also of goal changing and multiple, conflicting goals.

Gross states that models, even in natural science, are mainly probabilistic rather than deterministic. A social system model must be even looser; thus, a change in one part of the system does not necessarily mean a corresponding change elsewhere. Social systems display considerable slack and inertia. Gross thus regards a social system as being an "unsystematic" system.

Gross's concept of system structure is derived from concepts of differentiated subsystems, internal relations, and external relations. Thus, after extension to include other features, he states (p. 183):

> The structure of any social system consists of (1) people and (2) non-human resources (3) grouped together into subsystems that (4) interrelate among themselves and (5) with the external environment, and are subject to (6) certain values and (7) a central guidance system that may help provide the capacity for future performance.

Each element of structure has both spatial and temporal dimensions.

Analysis of system performance begins with the input-output concept, expressed as acquiring inputs, producing outputs for external use, and investing in the system's future performance. Thus, after extension to include other features, he states (p. 184):

> The performance of any social system consists of activities (1) to satisfy the interests of various "interesteds" by (2) producing various kinds, qualities, and quantities of output, (3) investing in the system's capacity for future output, (4) using inputs efficiently, (5) acquiring inputs, and doing all the above in a manner that conforms with (6) various codes of behavior and (7) varying conceptions of technical and administrative (or guidance) rationality.

Through combining various elements of structure and performance, an infinite number of permutations can result. However, a complete system-state analysis, probably impossible, is not necessary and a selected number of cross-sectional abstracts can be utilized.

Berrien (1968) and Buckley (1967) provide additional examples of social systems theories and models developed as extensions of general systems, cybernetics, and information theories. Buckley, in particular, is also a good source for review and synthesis of other social systems models to that time.

CRITIQUES OF THE SYSTEMS APPROACH

Churchman (1968), using a "debating of opponents" approach, examines the systems approach from four different perspectives, namely, from the viewpoint of the advocates of:

1. *Efficiency expertise,* in which the emphasis is upon identifying waste and high costs.
2. *Management science,* in which the emphasis is upon looking at the system objectively and building a model; the major emphasis of this book is here.
3. *Humanism,* in which the emphasis is upon looking at the human values of freedom, dignity, and privacy and upon the avoiding of imposition of plans.
4. *Anti-planning,* in which emphasis is upon living with systems and reacting in terms of one's own experiences and not building grandiose plans.

Each approach above involves deception of the opponent, a continual process of perception and deception and reviewing of the world.

Churchman views the systems approach as resulting in confusion as well as enlightenment; for it includes seeing the world through the eyes of another; discovery that every world view is terribly restricted; and recognition that there are *no experts* in the systems approach.

Boguslaw (1965) believes the present utopian renaissance derives from man's desire to master nature; the result may be the extension of man's control over man. Boguslaw's treatise has been welcomed as a dampener of the ardor of over-reliance on purely technocratic systems approaches. Philosophically, it represents the same line of thinking as our own, expressed above, in our reservations about the approach of Mesarović, *et al.*

Boguslaw argues that social theory has remained an after-the-physical fact. The "New Utopians," impatient with "human error" are most concerned with people substitutes. Physical reality is the constant, and social theory must adapt. There is an unquestioning acceptance of the technological status quo: "Contemporary and future populations will be wagged increasingly by their technological tails (p. 4)."

Boguslaw distinguishes four types of systems design used by both the classical and the new utopians:

1. The *formalist approach*. This is characterized by the explicit or implicit use of mathematical and other models. This approach is the most fashionable and easily quantifiable.
2. The *heuristic approach*. This uses principles to provide guides for action.
3. The *operating-unit approach*. This begins with carefully selected people or machines specially tooled with regard to certain performance characteristics.
4. The *ad hoc approach*. This views present reality as the only "given."

The present crisis in society cannot be attributed to a dearth of planning. If anything there is too much planning—by hardware designers, systems designers, operations researchers, etc. The humanistic orientation has been lost. Large numbers of workers and students and even middle managers, excluded from any real possibility of participating in the new order, feel alienated. The scientists, engineers, and top managers (*until recently!*) are the real producers, with others going along for the ride. Many segments of society, thus, represent a powerless form of alienation. One answer to this problem, Boguslaw suggests, could be better education programs, involving essentially every specialty, for familiarization with the implications of large-scale systems design. It follows that variables such as retraining costs for displaced workers, costs for dislocation of communities, and mental health costs must also be considered in design.

Finally, Boguslaw emphasizes, any method, whether logical, mathematical, experimental or what, can be used as a substitute for problem-solving. In such cases the purpose is to impress rather than to inform. And when truth alone becomes an end in human existence, humanity may lose out. "The spawn of truth is efficiency (p. 98)." Truth and efficiency ignore the value of human beings.

A view of the rational man. The great debates of our time frequently express the position that one group of opponents (social reformers, peace advocates, "humanists," "ecologists," conservationists, safety advocates, consumer advocates) is emotional and irrational as contrasted to a group whose cognitive processes, unbiased by emotion, reflect rational, usually economic choice. The concept of rational choice underlies many exercises in game theory and in decision theory, which have not produced the practical results for which we might have hoped. It appears questionable that any person or group can be considered as purely rational, except perhaps in the most constrained situations.

Simon (1956), for example, has looked at "rational choice" and the theory of decision-making, areas which seemed to interface psychological and economic theory. Economic theories appeared to postulate a much larger capacity in the organism for obtaining and processing information than did the psychological learning theories. However, the learning theories appeared to account better for observed behavior. See Chapter 2 for more on limitations of economic theory.

Thus, Simon has attempted to learn more about rational decision-making by considering capacity limitations of the organism, and that psychological environments to which the organism must adapt have properties which further simplify the choice mechanisms. His paper tries to look at fundamental structural characteristics of the environment which might lead to clues as to the approximating mechanisms used in decision-making. Next, he works through a mathematical model of a hypothetical organism in a situation involving choice among multiple goals. He found that blocks of the organism's time could be allocated to activities associated with individual needs (separate means-end chains) without requiring over-all allocation, coordination, or a general utility function. He did not apply his model to human behavior. However, he does state we should be skeptical in postulating for any organism elaborate mechanisms for choosing among diverse needs.

Simon, in concluding his analysis, casts serious doubts on the usefulness of current economic and statistical theories of rational behavior as applied to actual animal or human behavior. Rather, approaches more related to psychological theories of perception and cognition appear to be more promising.

SUMMARY AND CONCLUSIONS

Early in this chapter we made observations and asked questions relative to problems in the world about us. Underlying these questions and problems are recurrent themes of lack of order, incongruence, asynchronization, saturation, growth and decline, collision and impact, competition, unexpected results, unexpected and baffling complexity, and lack of apparent cause-effect relationship. The concept of *system* promises a means of organization and explanation of these difficulties. More specifically, the concept of a *sociotechnical system* provides a framework for interrelating and study of problems which may be loosely, and perhaps arbitrarily, classified as problems of the social subsystem, problems of the technological subsystem, and problems of the natural and social environments.

Over the years, particularly in the last two or three decades, a sizable body of systems, organization, and management theory has evolved. Many classifications of these theories have been offered, and we have mentioned examples of such classifications. For our purposes here, the following additional classification is useful:

1. Theories of the individual
2. Theories of the group
3. Theories of the individual and group within the organization
4. Theories of structure or processes within the organization
5. Theories of organization-environment interactions
6. Aggregative theories of environment, including theories of society, economic theories, and ecological theories

7. Generalizable systems theories including, but not limited to, general systems theory

We have summarized, or at least mentioned, representative examples from each of these categories. We shall be minimally concerned with the first four categories which are well represented in the literature. On the other hand, we have reviewed in fairly great detail several approaches which appear to be particularly general-purpose and adaptable to the complex (in terms of number of variables), upper-hierarchy level of problems. These theoretical approaches are: (1) general systems theory; (2) the open-systems theory extension of general systems theory, particularly as represented by the pioneering Tavistock Institute sociotechnical work; and (3) the systems dynamics of Forrester. Additionally, we have examined a number of systems concepts and properties, illustrating these with realworld problems. From a synthesis of these and miscellaneous theoretical approaches, a fourth body of theory emerges.

In conclusion, it would perhaps be premature to state that we have developed the final, all-encompassing theory of sociotechnical systems. Nevertheless, we venture the point that the synthesis and extension of extant theory and of observations on realworld phenomena given below *does* represent a step forward in understanding and predicting the behavior of the forces confronting us and a basis for improved management of organizations and of society.

Sociotechnical systems, thus:

1. Are open systems with the properties summarized by von Bertalanffy, the Tavistock workers, J. G. Miller, and Katz and Kahn.
2. Can be specified in terms of a recognizable technological subsystem and social subsystem which nevertheless interact with one another.
3. Have measurable impacts on their environments.
4. Do not remain static in changing environments, and must be understood in terms of (reciprocal) responses to a changing environment.
5. Possess the properties, highlighted by Forrester, of being counter-intuitive, resistant to change and to policy-making, and of showing differential short-term and long-term behavior, unpredictable response to attempts at change, and drift to low performance.
6. Are typically nonlinear.
7. Are characterized by interlocking positive and negative feedback loops, with frequent and unexpected shifts in dominance of growth, steady state, and decline.
8. Are hierarchically complex, whether expressed in terms of order (levels of integration), or moving toward saturation at one level and sudden, unexpected jumps to a higher level.
9. Are characterized by tension, competition, conflict, and loss of steady state when new subsystems come together; the result may be fragmentation or integration at a new system level.

10. Over the long range evolve toward a balance of (unidirectional, temporarily asymmetry-producing) forces.

11. Over the short range show frequent oscillations, which may be misunderstood and exacerbated by policy makers.

REFERENCES

Albee, George W., 1970, The Uncertain Future of Clinical Psychology, *American Psychologist,* 25 (12), 1071-1080, December.

Ansoff, H. Igor, and Dennis P. Slevin, 1968. An Appreciation of Industrial Dynamics, *Management Science,* 14(7), 383-97, March.

Argyris, Chris, 1957, *Personality and Organization.* New York: Harper, pp. 177-87.

———, 1960, *Understanding Organizational Behavior.* Homewood, Illinois: Dorsey Press, p. 24.

———, 1969, The Incompleteness of Social-Psychological Theory: Examples from Small Group, Cognitive Consistency, and Attribution Research, *American Psychologist,* 24(10), 893-908, October.

Ashby, W. Ross, 1956, *An Introduction to Cybernetics.* London: Chapman and Hall.

——— 1960, *Design for a Brain,* 2nd ed. New York: Wiley.

Atwater, Marshall A., 1970, Planetary Albedo Changes Due to Aerosols, *Science,* 170(3953), 64-6, 2 October.

Averch, Harvey A., and Robert A. Levine, 1970. *Two Models of the Urban Crisis: an Analytical Essay on Banfield and Forrester,* RM-6366-RC, Santa Monica, California: The RAND Corporation, September.

Bakke, E. Wright, 1959, Concept of the Social Organization. In M. Haire (ed.), *Modern Organization Theory,* p. 72, New York: Wiley.

Baron, Jonathan, 1971, Is Experimental Psychology Relevant?, *American Psychologist,* 26(8), 713-16, August.

Beals, Ralph L., 1969, *Politics of Social Research.* Chicago: Aldine.

Berrien, F. Kenneth, 1968, *General and Social Systems.* New Brunswick, N.J.: Rutgers Univ. Press.

Biderman, A. D., 1970, Self-Portrayal, *Science,* 169(3950), 1064-7, 11 September.

Blau, P. M., 1968, Organizations: Theories. In D. L. Sills (ed.), *International Encyclopedia of Social Sciences,* New York: Macmillan.

Boguslaw, Robert, 1965, *The New Utopians: A Study of System Design and Social Change.* Englewood Cliffs, N.J.: Prentice-Hall.

Boulding, Kenneth E., 1956, General Systems Theory—the Skeleton of Science, *General Systems,* 1, 11-17.

———, 1966, Environmental Quality in a Growing Economy, In H. Jarrett (ed.),

Environmental Quality in a Growing Economy; Essays from the Sixth RFF Forum, pp. 9-10. Baltimore: John Hopkins Press.

Broady, Maurice, 1969, The Social Context of Urban Planning, *Urban Affairs Quarterly*, 4(3), 355-78, March.

Buckley, Walter, 1967, *Sociology and Modern Systems Theory*. Englewood Cliffs, N.J.: Prentice Hall.

Bucklow, Maxine, 1969, *Readings in Socio-Technical Systems*. London: Tavistock Institute of Human Relations, HRC 279, October.

Burton, Robert W., 1971, On Affecting the Long-Term Air Quality in the San Francisco Bay Area, *IEEE Transactions on Systems, Man and Cybernetics*, SMC-1 (4), 307-13, October.

Cartright, Dorwin, 1959, Lewinian Theory as a Contemporary Systematic Framework. In Sigmund Koch, (ed.), *Psychology: A Study of a Science*, Vol. 2, *General Systematic Formulations, Learning, and Special Processes*, 7-91. New York: McGraw-Hill.

Churchman, C. West, 1968, *The Systems Approach*. New York: Dell.

Cooper, Robert, and Michael Foster, 1971, Sociotechnical Systems, *American Psychologist*, 26(5), 467-74.

Cox, James L., 1970, DDT Residues in Marine Phytoplankton: Increase from 1955 to 1969, *Science*, 170(3953), 71-3, 2 October.

Cyert, R. M., and J. G. March, 1959, A Behavioral Theory of Organizational Objectives. In M. Haire (ed.), *Modern Organization Theory*. New York: Wiley.

De Greene, Kenyon B., 1970, *Systems Psychology*. New York: McGraw-Hill.

Deutsch, Karl W., John Platt, and Dieter Senghaas, 1971, Conditions Favoring Major Advances in Social Science, *Science*, 171(3970), 450-9, 5 February.

Dror, Yehezekel, 1968, *Public Policymaking Reexamined*. San Francisco: Chandler.

Dubin, Robert, 1959, Stability of Human Organizations. In M. Haire (ed.), *Modern Organization Theory*, p. 225. New York: Wiley.

Emery, F. E., 1959, *Characteristics of Socio-Technical Systems*. London: Tavistock Institute of Human Relations, HRC 527, January.

Emery, F. E., and E. L. Trist, 1960, Socio-Technical Systems. In C. W. Churchman and M. Verhulst (eds.), *Management Sciences, Models and Techniques*, Vol. 2, pp. 83-97. London: Pergamon Press.

———, 1965, The Causal Texture of Organizational Environments, *Human Relations*, 18(1), 21-32, February.

Forrester, Jay W., 1961, *Industrial Dynamics*. Cambridge, Mass.: The M.I.T. Press.

———, 1968a, Industrial Dynamics—After the First Decade, *Management Science*, 14(7), 398-415, March.

———, 1968b, Industrial Dynamics—A Reply to Ansoff and Slevin, *Management Science*, 14(9), 601-18, May.

——, 1968c, *Principles of Systems.* Cambridge, Mass.: Wright-Allen Press.

——, 1969, *Urban Dynamics.* Cambridge, Mass.: The M.I.T. Press.

——, 1970, Systems Analysis as a Tool for Urban Planning, *IEEE Transactions on Systems Science and Cybernetics,* SSC-6(4), 258-65.

Franks, R. G. E., 1967, *Mathematical Modeling in Chemical Engineering.* New York: Wiley.

Goldsmith, Edward, 1971, The Limits of Growth in Natural Systems, *General Systems,* 16, 69-75.

Gray, J., D. Pessel, and P. Varaiya, 1971, *A Critique of Forrester's Model of an Urban Area,* unpublished paper, Berkeley, California: University of California, Department of Computer Sciences.

Greene, Richard M., Jr., 1971, *New Horizons in Application of System Sciences to Management,* Anaheim, California: paper given at Joint ORSA-IEEE Conference on Major Systems, October.

Grinker, R. R. (ed.), 1967, *Toward a Unified Theory of Human Behavior,* 2nd ed. New York: Basic Books.

Gross, Bertram S., 1966, The State of the Nation: Social Systems Accounting, in Raymond A. Bauer (ed.), *Social Indicators,* Cambridge, Mass.: The M.I.T. Press.

Haire, Mason, 1959, Biological Models and Empirical Histories of the Growth of Organizations. In M. Haire (ed.). *Modern Organization Theory,* pp. 272-305. New York: Wiley.

Hall, Edward T., 1968, Proxemics, *Current Anthropology,* 9(2-3), 83-108, April-June.

Harrison, H. L., O. L. Loucks, J. W. Mitchell, D. F. Parkhurst, C. R. Tracy, D. G. Watts, and V. J. Yannacone, Jr., 1970, System Studies of DDT Transport, *Science,* 170(3957), 503-8, 30 October.

Herbst, P. G., 1959, *Task Structure and Work Relations,* London: Tavistock Institute of Human Relations, TIHR Doc. No. 528.

Hester, James, Jr., 1969, *Systems Models of Urban Growth and Development.* Cambridge, Mass.: M.I.T., Urban Systems Lab., 1 November.

Hilgert, Raymond, 1964, Modern Organization Theory and Business Management Thought, *The American Behavioral Scientist,* 8(2), 25-9, October.

Hitt, William D., 1969, Two Models of Man, *American Psychologist,* 24(7), 651-58.

Howland, D., 1968, *Toward a Community Health System Model,* paper presented at the Symposium for Systems and Medical Care; Cambridge, Mass.: Harvard University, September.

Hughes, James, and Lawrence Mann, 1969, Systems and Planning Theory, *Journal of the American Institute of Planners,* 35(5), 330-33, September.

Johnson, Horton A., 1970, Information Theory in Biology after 18 Years, *Science,* 168(3939), 1545-1550, 26 June.

Katz, D., and R. L. Kahn, 1966, *The Social Psychology of Organizations*, New York: Wiley.

Köhler, W., 1938, Closed and Open Systems. Excerpted in F. E. Emery, 1969, *Systems Thinking*, 59-69 Harmondsworth, Middlesex, England: Penguin Books.

Krendel, Ezra S., 1970, A Case Study of Citizen Complaints as Social Indicators, *IEEE Transactions on Systems Science and Cybernetics*, SSC-6(4), 265-72, October.

Lamb, George C., 1968, Engineering Concepts and the Behavioral Sciences, *General Systems*, 13, 165-9.

Landsberg, Helmut E., 1970, Man-Made Climate Changes, *Science*, 170(3964), 1265-74, 18 December.

Lewin, Kurt, 1951, *Field Theory in Social Science*. New York: Harper.

Lichtman, Cary M., and Raymond G. Hunt, 1971, Personality and Organization Theory: A Review of Some Conceptual Literature, *Psychological Bulletin*, 76(4), 271-94, October.

Lockhard, Robert B., 1971, Reflections on the Fall of Comparative Psychology: Is There a Message for All of Us?, *American Psychologist*, 26(2), 168-79.

Lyons, Gene M., 1969, *The Uneasy Partnership (Social Science and the Federal Government in the Twentieth Century)*. New York: Russell Sage Foundation.

Mesarović, M. D., D. Macko, and Y. Takahara, 1970, *Theory of Hierarchical, Multilevel Systems*. New York: Academic Press.

Miller, James G., 1955, Toward A General Theory for the Behavioral Sciences, *American Psychologist*, 10(9), 513-31.

——, 1965a, Living Systems: Basic Concepts, *Behavioral Scientist*, 10(3), 193-237., July.

——, 1965b, Living Systems: Structure and Process, *Behavioral Scientist*, 10(4), 337-79, October.

——, 1965c, Living Systems: Cross-Level Hypotheses, *Behavioral Scientist*, 10(4), 380-411, October.

——, 1965d, The Organization of Life, *Perspectives in Biology and Medicine*, 107-25, 8(2), Autumn.

Milsum, J. H., 1968, Technosphere, Biosphere, and Sociosphere: An Approach to Systems Modeling and Optimization, *General Systems*, 13, 37-48.

Myrdal, G., 1963, *Challenge to Affluence*. New York: Pantheon.

National Academy of Sciences, 1968, *The Behavioral Sciences and the Federal Government*. Washington, D.C.: NAS Publication 1680.

National Academy of Sciences, and Social Science Research Council, 1969, *The Behavioral and Social Sciences*. Englewood Cliffs, N.J.: Prentice-Hall.

National Science Foundation, 1969, *Knowledge into Action*. Washington, D.C.: U.S. Government Printing Office.

Platt, John, 1970, Hierarchical Restructuring, *General Systems,* 15, 49-54.

Pugh, D. S., 1969, Organization Behavior: An Approach from Psychology, *Human Relations,* 22(4), 345-54, August.

Rasool, S. I. and S. H. Schneider, 1971, Atmospheric Carbon Dioxide and Aerosols: Effects of Large Increases on Global Climate, *Science,* 173(3992), 138-41, 9 July.

Rice, A. K., 1958, *Productivity and Social Organization: The Ahmedabad Experiment.* London: Tavistock Publications.

Roberts, Karlene H., 1970, On Looking at an Elephant: An Evaluation of Cross-Cultural Research Related to Organizations, *Psychological Bulletin,* 74(5), 327-50, November.

Rubin, Milton D., (ed.), 1971, *Man in Systems.* New York: Gordon and Breach.

Savas, E. S., 1970, Cybernetics in City Hall, *Science,* 168(3935), 1066-71, 29 May.

Schnore, Leo R., 1966, The City as a Social Organism, *Urban Affairs Quarterly,* 1(3), 58-69, March.

Scott, W. R., 1964, Theory of Organizations, in R.E.L. Farris, (ed.), *Handbook of Modern Sociology.* Chicago: Rand-McNally.

Silverman, Irwin, 1971, Crisis in Social Psychology: The Relevance of Relevance, *American Psychologist,* 26(6), 583-84, June.

Simon, Herbert A., 1956, Rational Choice and the Structure of the Environment, *Psychological Review,* 63, 129-38.

——, 1957, *Models of Man.* New York: Wiley.

——, 1969, *The Sciences of the Artificial.* Cambridge, Mass.: The M.I.T. Press.

Spilhaus, Athelstan, 1968, The Experimental City, *Science,* 159(3816), 710-15, 16 February.

Stogdill, R. M., 1959, *Individual Behavior and Group Achievement.* New York: Oxford University Press.

Trist, E. L., and K. W. Bamforth, 1951, Some Social and Psychological Consequences of the Longwall Method of Coal-Getting, *Human Relations,* 4, 3-38.

Trist, E. L., G. W. Higgin, H. Murray, and A. B. Pollock, 1963, *Organizational Choice: Capabilities of Groups at the Coal Face Under Changing Technologies.* London: Tavistock Publications.

Veblen, Thorstein, 1953, *The Theory of the Leisure Class,* New York: The New American Library.

Von Bertalanffy, Ludwig, 1967, *Robots, Men, and Minds: Psychology in the Modern World,* New York: Braziller.

——, 1968, *General System Theory: Foundations, Development, Applications.* New York: Braziler.

Wagar, J. Alan, 1970, Growth versus the Quality of Life, *Science,* 168(3936), 1179-84, 5 June.

Whitehead, Alfred North, 1925, *Science and the Modern World.* New York: Macmillan.

Whyte, William F., 1959, *Man and Organization.* Homewood, Ill.: Richard D. Irwin.

Wiener, Norbert, 1948, *Cybernetics or Control and Communication in the Animal and the Machine,* New York: Wiley.

Wilcox, Robert B., 1962, Analysis and Synthesis of Dynamic Performance of Industrial Organizations—The Application of Feedback Control Techniques to Organizational Systems. *IRE Transactions on Automatic Control,* AC-7, 55-67, March.

Wilson, Donna, 1969, Forms of Hierarchy: A Selected Bibliography, *General Systems,* 14, 3-15.

Woodwell, George M., Paul P. Craig, and Horton A. Johnson, 1971, DDT in the Biosphere: Where Does It Go?, *Science,* 174(4014), 1101-1107, 10 December.

2

Behavioral-Social Dynamics

In the first chapter, we examined the main observed structural-functional properties of complex sociotechnical systems and theoretical attempts to explain these properties. In this chapter, we look at the behavioral-social dynamics which may crosscut the above. These are the driving forces of the modern world, without an understanding of which rational management of either technology or society is impossible. These forces are complexly interrelated. They are also "interdisciplinary" and involve considerations of ecology, engineering, economics, medicine, and so on, in addition to behavioral features, such as perception and motivation.

In this chapter, we shall be concerned with many problems of growth, steady state, feedback, movement, change, stress, saturation, impact, hierarchy, and adaptation.

These are stormy times. It is typical to be buffeted and cast about by the waves, to be drawn hither by the first swell only to be returned by the next. Yet underlying mechanisms remain obscure. Permit us to make another natural metaphor. In October 1871, many small fires, mostly started by woodsmen, were burning in eastern Wisconsin; on October 8 (the same day as the great Chicago fire!), environmental conditions became propitious and the fires united and emerged as the Peshtigo fire which killed several thousand people and became, after the Galveston hurricane and Johnstown, Pennsylvania, flood, the greatest natural catastrophe in terms of loss of life in U.S. history.

The sparks of many ideas lead to a few small fires, which may burn themselves out or quietly continue to burn until times and places become propitious or the opportunity arises to join with other small fires yielding a force capable of generating its own favorable environment. The fire storm explodes, but literary license permits us to switch ourselves to the now relative quiet of the hurricane.

The present coalition and expansion of a number of previously obscure trends and movements provides a case. These include conservation, consumer protection, anti war feelings, the youth movement, the quest for a simpler life, concern with pollution and other destroyers of the pleasant environment, and so on. What are the basic forces here? Why these trends whose time has now come? Are these representative of permanent evolutionary changes, or are they oscillations—fads? These questions must be answered in terms of the behavioral factors of motivational level, satiation, frustration, redirection of behavior and of educational level on the one hand, and in terms of legal, recent historical, and political factors on the other.

The last several years have witnessed the passage of a number of environmental protection laws in the political atmosphere of 1966 to the early 1970s. Legal advocacy has become the weapon of the times, and lawyers have gained control of leading conservation and consumer efforts or have spearheaded opposition of established industrial and governmental practices through the courts. This may be all well and good, as long as these activities are consistent with the underlying behavioral and social dynamics. There is evidence the future may be less felicitous to the furtherance of ideas and policies not firmly rooted to basic forces. Automation and chronic unemployment, for instance, continue as direct threats. Hence, short-range flamboyance could do the conservation, environmental protection, and consumer protection movements irreperable damage. By being in the focus of perception, they could represent obstructionist obstacles to "the good life."

With regard to sociotechnical change, there are at all times early-warning indicators of things to come. Sensing and integrating these provides one of the major challenges to our field. Some individuals are more sensitive to early warning signs than are others. These include persons who superficially seem to be poles apart. Yet there must be personality and cognitive reasons why such diverse groups as youth, minority groups, hippies, academicians, and conservationists question the status quo and reject conformity. For different Maslovian reasons, they have nothing to lose by questioning and rejecting. Eventually the underlying trends reach a level where they become self-sustaining; others more timid now jump on the band wagon. The trends may coalesce or conflict. What signs exist *now* of significance to the next decade(s)?

In considering further the different properties of the social and technological subsystems and sociotechnical systems, it is well to remember that there are different perspectives of what technology is. Also for our purposes these subsystems have meaning only in relationship to one another. And our problem continues to be one of exploding contact or coalescence.

Let us now add to the body of structure and theory of sociotechnical systems from Chapter 1, the following postulates as to basic or dynamic forces:

1. A "growth force" with interrelated elements of population growth, economic growth, knowledge growth, and technology growth. Today there is a belated recognition of the problems of interrelated exponential growth forces, the growing rates of growth, the disparities between certain rates of growth, the reinforcing effects of still other types of growth on each other, the diminishing returns of growth, and growth as it exacerbates the absolute gap between Haves and Have-Nots. A particularly enlightening study of such problems is that sponsored by the Club of Rome. It employs the systems dynamics approach (Meadows *et al.*, 1972). The study involves the modeling and computer simulation of five interacting forms of exponential growth: population, agricultural production, consumption of natural resources, industrial production, and pollution. We shall return to the results of this study and its implications for the management of society in Chapters 8 and 9. Within these broad fields of growth are subpatterns that must not be neglected. Nor may we overlook the disparities between the rates of growth of different elements. Thus, science has for several decades maintained a percent-per-annum growth rate much larger than that of society as a whole or of most other elements of society (Martino, 1969). Yet eventually science must come into equilibrium with society. Policies toward stabilizing such growth will have widespread repercussions if enacted today. Nevertheless, consequences could be dire indeed, if the needed policy making is postponed by even a few years. Likewise the rate of increase of Ph.Ds must receive our closest attention regarding possible, even probable, reversal (see Wolfle and Kidd, 1971). We shall mention here only one other example to dramatize the pervasiveness of rampant growth. All measures of growth—population, GNP, waste load, recreation—suggest that demands on U.S. river resources are increasing at a rate which exceeds the rate of installation of facilities for waste treatment. Yet rivers have finite waste assimilative or carrying capacities. Once given thresholds are exceeded irreversible changes may occur. To make matters worse, our present measures of water quality may give us a very unrealistic picture of a serious and deteriorating situation (Wolman, 1971).

2. An "automation and technological change saturation force." Human capabilities and limitations are potentially fixed, assuming no genetic, surgical, pharmacological or other modification, and, furthermore, natural organic evolution does not keep pace with sociotechnological change. The limit to these capabilities is fast being reached; that is, a saturation point is being approached. Machines increasingly stress man; technology increasingly stresses society. See Harrison (1971) for a bibliography of further readings in the immensely large and complex area of automation and technological change. We shall provide other particularly important references later in this chapter.

3. A "motivational force" with elements of need satisfaction, hierarchical jump, cognitive dissonance, frustration, apathy, alienation, fantasy and escape, hostility and aggression, etc.

4. A "value force" expressed as attitudes or other behaviors.

5. A "reactive-compensatory force" of a control subsystem in society to maintain equilibrium or steady state in the face of ongoing stress.

We thus see that systems can be described, and hopefully, measured, in terms of structure, function, and the basic forces which crosscut, integrate, and interrelate structure and function. These basic functions may be thought of as genotypic and underlying many apparently dissimilar phenotypic behaviors. This framework not only describes complex systems, but also provides a new hope that systems science can indeed attack the formidable problems of our age. The deficiencies of present mathematics and operations research are pointed out elsewhere in this book. It may be that the science of complexity itself now requires the quantum jump we discussed in Chapter 1.

It should be emphasized here that we are not attempting to express behavioral and social variables in engineering terms. This has been attempted in human factors with little success. Rather, it is important that a common language be used for social, behavioral, technological, and environmental variables.

A further word of warning is in order here. Complex biological, social, ecological, and sociotechnical systems are characterized, as we have seen, by multiple levels of integration and by multiple interlocking positive and negative feedback loops. This makes the determination of simple cause-effect relationships essentially nonsense. There are numerous examples from our everyday efforts to build a healthier and safer society. What really is the *cause* of death from a stroke: high blood pressure, emotional problems, psychosomatic disease, overweight, smoking, heredity, poor childhood stress-tolerance development? What is the *cause* of the typical automobile accident: faulty road design, poor vehicle condition, poor driver skills, another motorist, drugs, emotional tension, weather? And so on. It is quite evident that we must view our world in terms of *patterns* of interacting forces, rather than in terms of *simple linear chains*. Further insightful examples are provided by Arthur Koestler (1956) relative to capital punishment, and by Scheuch (1968) relative to the teratology apparently induced by thalidomide.

Finally, a most crucial thing is to provide a basis in knowledge for working toward evolving policies. This would involve, for example, the integration of problems and policies associated with employment, power production, and pollution. A *pattern* of causes may underlie thousands of recognized and unrecognized problems. For example, the "California Tomorrow Plan" (Heller, 1972), discussed further in Chapter 9, has identified as major patterns for the state of California: (1) a damaging pattern of population distribution; (2) damaging patterns of consumption; (3) lack of individual economic strength; and (4) lack of individual political strength.

We shall now turn our attention to the major forces defined above. Population growth, including factors associated with the interrelationship of population growth, economic growth, and technological growth; effects of automation and

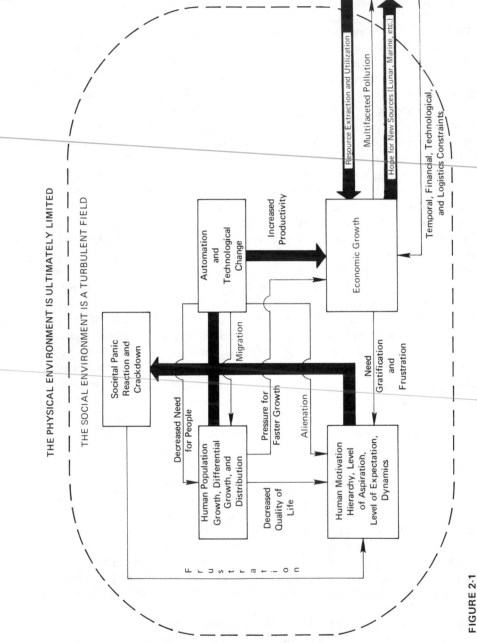

FIGURE 2-1

Sociotechnical Macrosystem (society). Heavy arrows represent main societal reactions to system stress.

other technology; and motivational dynamics will receive our greatest attention. We shall also note salient features of other areas. The major forces or subsystems and dynamics of the sociotechnical macrosystem are shown in Figure 2-1.

POPULATION GROWTH

Our world today is one of growth toward chaos. And although all the other growths—economic, technological, education, expectation—are vitally important, human population growth is singled out by many thinkers as *the most dangerous* form that we must understand and manage today. The following section reviews major problems and interpretations. We shall consider, in turn, growth curves, behavioral and social factors contributing to population growth and stability, sociotechnical impacts of large absolute numbers and rates of increase of people, the effect of high density and crowding, and means of controlling human population growth and its impacts.

Growth Curves

The processes of growth are of immense complexity, and a large number of formulas may represent observed data and curves. However, curve fitting by itself may be misleading and approximations of empirical data do not necessarily verify a given equation. The latter occurs only when parameters can be confirmed by independent experiment and predictions can be made.

Yet the main growth laws or equations are often considered quite general. For example, the *logistic* or *sigmoid* law in which growth is limited by some restricting conditions, as in autocatalysis, may find application in railroad growth. The *allometric* law, expressing competition, which may take the shape of a parabola, may express the growth of cities in comparison to the rural population. Also, this may be true of the growth of staff as compared to the total number of employees in a company (von Bertalanffy, 1968). Also, there is evidence that the rate of cultural change is not exponential or compound interest but is, rather, log-log or super-acceleration. Simple growth laws, thus, seemingly apply to urbanization, division of labor, companies, and society.

Austin and Brewer (1970), in an exceptionally fine article, reflecting development of a new course in "sociotechnological system analysis—societal engineering," provide data related to population growth, in a format specifically designed for the technologist. This article, we might note, has been received with controversy.

The concept that world conditions are directly influenced by human population levels was introduced in 1798 by Thomas Malthus, who stated that population increases geometrically and food supply only arithmetically. Population would eventually thus far outstrip food supply. However, disaster did not occur because Malthus did not anticipate the development of technology or the possibilities of widespread migration. Unfortunately, some people still base their thinking—and their policies—on the spurious argument that this deficiency proves the invalidity of attempting to predict population levels and future world conditions.

Over the years a number of attempts to predict population growth have been made (Austin and Brewer, 1970).

1.   *The exponential (Malthusian or compound interest) law.* If a small population is introduced into a virgin environment, growth occurs initially at a rate directly proportional to the current population:

$$\frac{dN}{dt} = (b - d)N = rN \tag{1}$$

where N = population size, b = birth rate, d = death rate, and r = fertility rate. With a small population, the fertility rate is constant and:

$$N = N_0 e^{r(t - t_0)} \tag{2}$$

where N_0 is the population at some initial time t_0. This can be checked experimentally in *closed* systems for various species and found to be valid for *low* populations. However, the second equation has been used to calculate the time to double even a high population. This is done by letting N/N_0 = 2 and solving for the doubling time, $(t_2 - t_0)$ = 0.693/r. Assuming a present world fertility rate of about 1.9%, gives a population doubling time of 37 years.

2. *The logistic (or sigmoid) growth law.*   After a certain period of growth, the population has increased to a level high enough to affect food supply and other resources and also probably other (psychophysiological) factors. During the later stages of growth, population size is limited to an upper bound, with environmental resistance as a dominant growth inhibitor. Pearl and Reed (1924), in studies of fruit flies in a *closed* ecological system, observed that population growth followed an S-shaped curve. On this basis they postulated the logistics growth law:

$$\frac{dN}{dt} = rN\left(1 - \frac{N}{M}\right) \tag{3}$$

where r is *constant,* M is the upper bound on population, and the term in parentheses represents environmental resistance, or as $N{\rightarrow}M$, the growth rate approaches zero. Solution to the above gives:

$$\frac{N}{N_0} = \frac{e^{r(t - t_0)}}{1 - (N_0/M)[1 - e^{r(t - t_0)}]} \tag{4}$$

which gives the familiar S-shape when plotted.

Differentiating Equation (3) with respect to time and equating the result to zero shows the maximum slope occurs when N/M = ½. This implies the upper bound can be predicted from current growth rates. That is, when the population growth rate passes through a maximum, the upper bound is found by doubling the population at that time.

Pearl and Reed attempted to predict human population growth by curve-fitting Equation (4) to 1924 population data. In retrospect, the logistics law is grossly in error. For example, the predicted upper bound for world population was only 2 billion.

3. *The coalition law.* The deficiencies of the above two suggest that, for large population sizes, human population growth differs greatly from that of any other plant or animal. Accordingly, von Foerster, *et al.* (1960) in 1958 postulated that human beings, possessing an effective system of communications, form coalitions until all elements are strongly linked. This coalition continues until the population as a whole acts as a single element engaged in a gigantic game with Nature the opponent. This process is abetted by urbanization, medical technology, industrialization, etc. As a result, death rates have decreased faster than birth rates and the fertility rate r is, therefore, not constant but is rather a slowly increasing function of N:

$$r = aN^{1/k} \qquad k \leq 1 \qquad (5)$$

Substituting this factor into Equation (1), the coalition law becomes:

$$\frac{dN}{dt} = aN^{(1+1/k)} \qquad (6)$$

Integration from N_0, t_0 to N, t gives:

$$N = N_0 \left[\frac{t_d - t_0}{t_d - t} \right]^k \qquad (7)$$

where

$$t_d = \frac{k}{a} N_0^{-1/k} + t_0$$

This t_d was called "doom time" when world population with growth unbounded approaches infinity. Doom time can be calculated from a measure of a, k, N_0, t_0. Thus, a least-squares fit of Equation (7) to world population data was made, and estimates made of world population data from zero A.D. to 1958. The results were a $t_d = 2027 \pm 5$ years (when world population will approach infinity!) with a $k = 0.990 \pm 0.009$, and $N_0 = 10^8$ at $t_0 = 0$. Yet bad as this may seem, one is horrified to find that when post-1958 data are plotted on the curve generated by Equation (7), the actual population is shown growing slightly faster than predicted!

However, physiologically there is an upper limit to the possible birth rate, set by the gestation period, and there must be some lower bound to the death rate. Thus, the fertility rate cannot grow indefinitely and must stabilize eventually.

But the question is: when and how will such stabilization occur? Austin and Brewer (1970) believe the coalition law will remain valid for the next 20 years or so, but eventually environmental resistance will change the fertility rate substantially.

4. *The modified coalition law.* As a result of the above arguments, Austin and Brewer have modified the coalition law. They indicate population growth rate can be characterized in the form of a series:

$$\frac{dN}{dt} = a_1 N + a_2 N^2 + a_3 N^3 + \cdots + a_i N^i$$

where the coefficients a_i might be obtained by fitting historical data. Yet this does not facilitate the physical meaning of each coefficient. Hence, it is preferable to construct a law as a composite of individual phenomena affecting human population growth.

Recognizing an upper limit to fertility rate, Austin and Brewer modify Equation (5) as follows:

$$r = A\left[1 - \exp\left(-\frac{a}{A} N^{1/k}\right)\right] \tag{8}$$

A Taylor series expansion reveals this approximates Equation (5) at low values of N. For high values of N, it implies the fertility rate approaches the upper bound A.

Further, the logistics law must be implicit in any realistic prediction. Thus, a combination of Equations (3) and (8) gives a growth equation accounting for both environmental resistance and the coalition characteristic of human behavior:

$$\frac{dN}{dt} = A\left[1 - \exp\left(-\frac{a}{N} N^{1/k}\right)\right]\left[1 - \frac{N}{M}\right] N \tag{9}$$

This equation cannot be integrated for any arbitrary values of the constants and, therefore, numerical methods with machine computation were used to carry out the integration. The constants were obtained by curve-fitting the results to past data. Accurate population data from 1900 are available from the *Statistical Data Book* of the United Nations (1967), but uncertainty exists as to earlier periods. Using data from various sources for the period prior to 1900, Austin and Brewer composed the following table (Table 2-1).

These data were then used to fit Equation (9) and to determine values of the constants. Plotted as follows the curves compare the solutions of Equations (6) and (9) and fertility rates given by Equations (5) and (8). Data points are also plotted. (See Figure 2-2)

A sensitivity analysis of Equation (9) was made to determine the effect of variations in the parameters A, a, k, and M. Changes in A and a were found to produce only a lateral shift in time, but a 1% variation in k led to a 20% variation in the upper bound M. Hence, accurate predictions depend upon the accuracy of existing data and k must be carefully determined.

A look at Figure 2-2 thus suggests that *if human population growth is not limited by effective artificial means, in a relatively short time we will reach the upper bound and environmental resistance will become the dominant mechanism*

TABLE 2-1

Estimates of population and data for curve fitting.*

1. Estimates of population vs. time (millions), based on five original sources

Date, A.D.	Source				
	1	*2*	*3*	*4*	*5*
0	300			< 200	100
200	325				
400	340			220	
600	355				
800	390			240	
1000	430				200
1200	460			300	
1400	550				
1600	650			900	
1650		545			460
1700					
1750	791	728		694	
1800	978	906			
1850	1262	1171		1091	
1900	1650	1608		1550	
1920	1860		1834		
1930	2069		2070		
1940	2295		2295		
1950	2515		2517	2545	
1960	2998		3005		

TABLE 2-1 (con'd.)

II. Selected population data for curve fitting (millions)

Date, A.D.	Data	Table 2-1 Source
0	100	5
200		
400		
600		
800		
1000	200	5
1200		
1400		
1600		
1650	545	2
1700		
1750	728	2
1800	906	2
1850	1171	2
1900	1608	2
1920	1834	3
1930	2070	3
1940	2295	3
1950	2517	3
1960	3005	3

*Adapted from Arthur L. Austin and John W. Brewer, "World Population Growth and Related Technical Problems," *IEEE Spectrum,* December 1970.

limiting growth. The precise value of M is uncertain because of its sensitivity to $k;$ nevertheless the upper bound is estimated at between 40 and 60 billion people! And in spite of attempts at birth control and the effects of World War II and other catastrophes, population continues to rise. The chances of lessening future population growth seem slight. Further, some estimates, based upon the amount of arable land and the assumptions of a life style like that in an industrialized state, suggest an upper bound of 34 billion.

Accepting the predictions from Figure 2-2, it becomes evident that in about 100 years a population of 40 billion will be reached, requiring ten times the existing facilities just to maintain the present quality of life. Such growth may be impossible for "underdeveloped" nations.

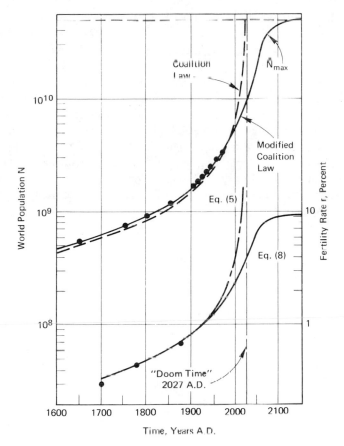

FIGURE 2-2
World population since 1600 A.D.[1]

Behavioral and Social Factors Contributing to Population Growth and Stability

The growth laws just considered, in dealing with aggregate situations, present only part of the picture. The differential age composition of a population, accident or intent in conception, *machismo*, industrialization, religion, race, education, and health advances and practices all contribute to a demographic

[1]From Arthur L. Austin and John W. Brewer, "World Population Growth and Related Technical Problems," *IEEE Spectrum*, December 1970.

situation that continues to be murky. For this reason, we urge a policy of extreme caution in assuming that human population problems are either being handled effectively, or—worse—are handling themselves. We should be especially wary of taking solace from what may be merely minor inflections on the growth curves. Decreased birth rates in the United States, characteristic of the early 1970s, may represent such beguiling inflections. Better to assume the worst with resources left over, than to continue to pursue policies of demographic brinks-manship. Thus, population estimates and predictions change as a function of the time of estimate. This is illustrated in Figure 2-3.

Frejka (1968), for example, examined a number of circumstances which may eventually lead to a stationary U.S. population. Emphasis was upon the main factors of *age-specific* mortality rates, fertility rates, and reproduction rates for the female population.

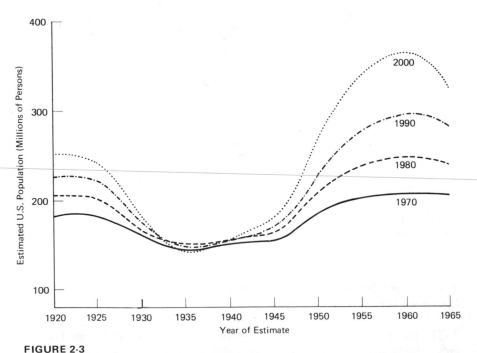

FIGURE 2-3

Comparison of population estimates for the United States. Curves for the four terminal years indicated are generated by connecting points predicted on the assumption of simple constancy of trends, starting from the years indicated on the horizontal axis. Births are adjusted for underregistration.[2]

[2]From *Resources and Man: A Study and Recommendations* by the Committee on Resources and Man of the Division of Earth Sciences, National Academy of Sciences–National Research Council with the cooperation of the Division of Biology and Agriculture. W.H. Freeman and Company. Copyright 1969.

A distinctive feature for all measures of population growth toward a fixed total number was that, when plotted against time, the graph assumed a sinus-oidal shape with gradually damped oscillations. Measures of population growth other than crude birth rate, for example net reproduction rate, gross repro-duction rate, and total fertility rate, were found related to the age groups of childbearing women. These had much greater effect on the amplitudes of the sinusoids than did crude birth rate. This is one more specific example of the oscillations of complex systems considered throughout this book.

Over-all the results of Frejka's studies indicate that an immediate constancy in the total number of people is not realistically possible.

A number of studies were also made assuming the decline of period of fertility to a level where the net reproduction rate equals 1.000 (that is, a two-child family) and remains constant thereafter. A purpose was to determine how the total size of the U.S. population would change under changing fertility conditions. Thus, because of age structure and mortality conditions, even if a net reproduction rate of 1.000 were achieved at once, total population of females by 2035 would be about 136 million, an increase of 37.6%. These and similar findings from 11 projections of population are summarized in Table 2-2. The

TABLE 2-2

Eleven Projections of Final Size of United States Female Population.*

Projection	Years of fertility decline period	NRR= 1.000 from the year	Peak is reached in	Period from 1st NRR= 1.000 to peak	Size of female population (in millions)	% of 1965 population
1	0	1965	2035	70	135.9	137.6
2	5	1970	2040	70	141.9	143.9
3	10	1975	2040	65	147.1	149.0
4	15	1980	2045	65	152.7	154.6
5	20	1985	2055	70	158.8	160.8
6	25	1990	2060	70	165.0	167.1
7	30	1995	2060	65	171.1	173.3
8	35	2000	2065	65	177.9	180.2
9	40	2005	2070	65	184.4	186.7
10	45	2010	2080	70	192.3	194.7
11	50	2015	2085	70	198.9	201.4

*From Tomas Frejka, "Reflections on the Demographic Conditions Needed to Establish a U.S. Stationary Population Growth," *Population Studies,* Vol. XXII (November 1968).

period of at least 65 to 70 years is the time required for the crude birth rate and age structure to stabilize at values indicative of a population with given properties of mortality and net reproduction rate. If Projection 1 were to be implemented as soon as possible, it would be necessary for women on the average to have no more than 2.1 children. This, in turn, would require an immediate and major change in fertility behavior among women of all ages. However, most estimates indicate that women will bear about three children each by the end of their reproductive periods.

Frejka next performed studies assuming changing cohort fertility. For example, it can be assumed women just entering childbearing ages will only replace themselves, that is, the net reproduction rate of this birth cohort, or group of women, will be equal to 1.000. Some 30 to 35 birth cohorts of women who had earlier started childbearing would, of course, also affect the over-all period fertility rates. Results, based on census data, are shown in Table 2-3, which indicates *minimum* limits to U.S. population growth in the next 50 to 100 years. This dramatizes both the inertia in fertility behavior of women already in childbearing ages and the large weight contributed by young age groups. Most importantly, the results indicate that by the year 2000 the U.S. population will have grown by at least 30% and that by the year 2050 the U.S. population is likely to have increased to one and one-half times its present size, excluding the effects of immigration.

In summary, a zero-growth rate for the United States could not be achieved for over 60 years, by which time the population would number 280 to 300 million. This is because it takes some time for the effects of past fertility on the age structure to wear off, and there is such a large percentage of the population today in childbearing or soon-to-be-childbearing age ranges. If women entering the childbearing years between 1965 and 1970, 1970 and 1975, and so on, were

TABLE 2-3

Projections of total female population based on cohort fertility assumptions, 1965-2065 (in millions). *

Projection	1965	1975	1990	2005	2020	2035	2050	2065
A	98.8	109.4	122.8	135.0	145.2	150.4	150.8	150.9
B	98.8	108.3	121.3	132.6	142.1	146.7	146.9	147.1
C	98.8	107.3	119.9	130.4	139.2	143.1	143.1	143.4
D	98.8	106.6	118.9	128.7	137.1	140.6	140.4	140.7

*Adapted from Thomas Frejka, "Reflections on the Demographic Conditions Needed to Establish a U.S. Stationary Population Growth," *Population Studies,* Vol. XXII (November 1968).

to achieve a fertility of exact replacement, the population would still continue to grow until at least the year 2035 with an increase in size of 40 to 50%!

Bumpass and Westoff (1970) have inferred the desired number of children by subtracting the number of unwanted births from the total number of births. This procedure resulted in considerably lower estimates of the number actually desired than by simply asking a woman how many children she would like to have. It was found that nearly 20% of all recent U.S. births were unwanted. These values were about one-fifth for whites; about one-third of black births in the sample years of 1960-1965 were unwanted. Eliminating these unwanted births through various "perfect contraceptive" policies and devices could contribute substantially to reducing the future U.S. population growth rate.

Of course this is only part of the story. In addition to eliminating unwanted births, policy must include the necessity of changing the number of children couples want, which might shift dangerously upward again in the future.

We have stated that there are baffling fluctuations in human population, indicating that it is better to be cautious than optimistic with regard to human population dynamics. Clear cause-effect relationships are rare. Consider, for example, Livi Bacci (1971), who establishes that Portuguese fertility was on a decline even before the advent of industrialization. Further, during the time of study, fertility was 16% higher in the industrial north than in the more illiterate agricultural south. It is clear that changing patterns of occupation and education do not, by themselves, offer hope for solving the problems of overpopulation. Fertility may shift downward or surge upward for still undetermined *patterns* of reasons.

In a complementary sense, it is best not to rely too heavily upon promised technological means of mitigating the woes of overpopulation. These means, even if possessed of demonstrable success on a limited scale, may prove infeasible in the long run because of limitations or unpredictability of resources, questions of palatability or religious restriction, production or cost difficulties, or undesirable environmental or social side effects. For example, see Holden, 1971, on the difficulties associated with production of fish protein concentrate; and Meadows, *et al.,* 1972, on the side effects of the "Green Revolution".

Considering all these factors, it is tragic when a technologically advanced country like Japan, which has manifested considerable success during the last two decades in reducing its population growth rate, decides during the euphoria of a fantastic economic boom (see Kahn, 1970) to increase its birthrate (Boffey, 1970).

Sociotechnical Impacts
of Large and Growing Populations

Population must be used as a multiplier for a vast array of technological and environmental data. Austin and Brewer (1970), looking at the problems of maintaining a massive population through the process of industrialization, consider energy, pollution, and food supply. Energy consumption per capita is suggested the best index of "quality of life."

Changing compositions of world population are indicated in Figure 2-4, and of world energy consumption in Figure 2-5. Per capita energy consumption is also given in Table 2-4.

Figure 2-5 indicates that if population grows as predicted, world energy requirements will increase rapidly beyond year 2000. Energy from fossil fuels will not be easily obtainable after 2020 if consumption continues at the present rate. Further, there is the serious problem of pollution and environmental degradation associated with the use of fossil fuels. Hence, other energy sources must soon be developed for large-scale use. Hydroelectric sources provide only a small percentage of energy and earth-bound solar-energy conversion schemes need large collection areas and, furthermore, efficient methods do not presently

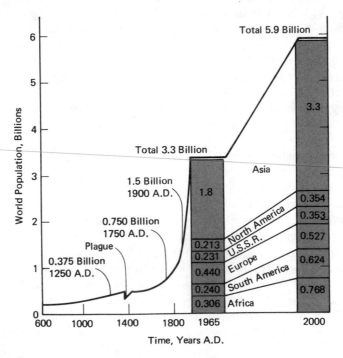

FIGURE 2-4
Expected world population distribution.[3]

TABLE 2-4

Per-capita energy consumption* (kilograms of hard-coal equivalent**).

Region	1958	1966	% Increase
World	1287	1648	128
Africa	250	289	115
North America	7422	9436	127
Other Americas	1274	1574	124
West Asia	318	539	170
East and South Asia	202	339	168
Western Europe	2388	3131	131
Oceania	2744	3747	137
Mainland China, U.S.S.R. East Europe, North Vietnam, North Korea, Mongolia	1106	1510	137

*From Arthur L. Austin and John W. Brewer, "World Population Growth and Related Technical Problems," *IEEE Spectrum,* December 1970.

*1 kg = 27,300 Btu.

exist. Thus, nuclear energy seems the only reliable future source, but this will require the imminent development of fast breeder reactors and ultimately the development of controlled fusion reactors. However, there is the problem of releasing vast quantities of energy over a short time, for example, the problem of waste heat discussed further below. We shall return to the problems of energy generation in considerable detail in Chapter 8.

Austin and Brewer consider air pollution to be a technically solvable short-range problem. They believe the harmful products of combustion can be technically eliminated, but that this will not occur until public pressure becomes great enough and the costs and legislation are accepted. However, this still leaves carbon dioxide which will continue to increase in the atmosphere.

The thermal energy exchange in the biosphere is greatly dependent upon concentrations of CO_2 and water vapor. The "greenhouse effect" occurs because the fundamental absorption band of the CO_2 molecule lies in the infrared range; hence, CO_2 acts as a shield against long-wave thermal radiation back into space. We already touched briefly on this problem in Chapter 1.

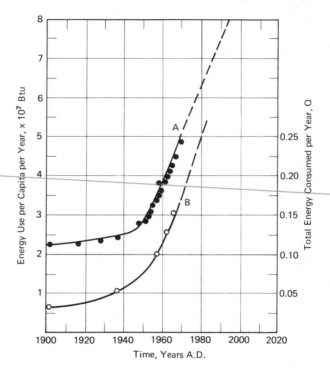

FIGURE 2-5
World energy consumption since 1960. Curve A measures the energy use per capita per year; Curve B the total energy consumed per year.[4]

Figures 2-6 and 2-7 show world energy use since 1960 and world CO_2 production.

The nature of the greenhouse effect is still not well understood, and arguments as to its danger are contradictory. Increased use of nuclear fuels and of fossil raw materials for chemical synthesis of commodities may eventually slow CO_2 production greatly. This is summarized in Figure 2-8.

These problems demonstrate the lack of our understanding of earth as a system, and of man's impact as increasingly global; they demonstrate the need for global models, including a large-scale energy model to control and optimize long-range development of energy usage. Such a model, to maximize benefits and minimize undesirable effects, would involve at least fuel types, conversion processes, distribution, rates of consumption, and undesirable by-products. It could be a basis for developing more realistic design criteria. We shall return to energy modeling in Chapter 8.

[4]From Austin and Brewer, 1970, based on *World Energy Supplies,* 1965-1968, Statistical Papers, Series J, No. 11 of the United Nations, New York.

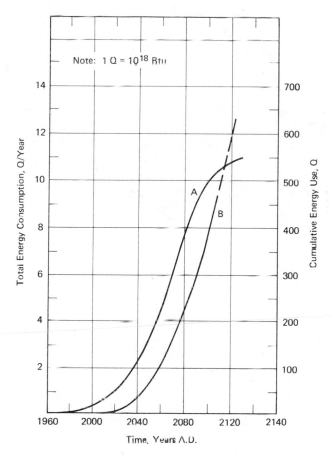

Note: 1 Q = 10^{18} Btu

FIGURE 2-6

World energy use since 1960. Curve A measures total energy consumption, and curve B indicates the cumulative energy use.[5]

The use of nuclear energy presents serious problems with regard to radionuclide production, radioactive waste disposal, safety, and the misuse of radioactive material. These problems emphasize that we have reached the point where we must realistically distinguish between energy *needs* and energy *demands;* we shall return to this point later in the chapter.

As mentioned above, any energy conversion system/presents the problem of rejected energy (thermal pollution), inescapable as a consequence of the second law of thermodynamics. With increased energy demand, this problem becomes increasingly important. Thus, at present, industry uses about 50% of the water

[5]From Arthur L. Austin and John W. Brewer, "World Population Growth and Related Technical Problems," *IEEE Spectrum,* December 1970.

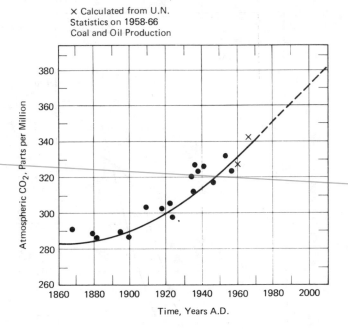

× Calculated from U.N.
Statistics on 1958-66
Coal and Oil Production

Time, Years A.D.

FIGURE 2-7
World carbon dioxide production from combustion of fossil fuels.[6]

consumed in the U.S., and 90% of this is used for cooling. The electrical power industry uses about 70% of the industrial cooling water. It is estimated that the actual amount of 19 billion m³ per year will be doubled by the year 2000.

Such use results in an increasing problem of localized heating of waterways. The cumulative effects of thermal pollution may have a profound effect on aquatic life. The usual suggestions to remedy this situation involve placing large reactors on artificial islands or on barges in the ocean with high-voltage transmission to land, and placing the reactors in colder regions and using the waste heat. These, and the use of cooling towers which are expensive and contribute to fogging, can be only stop-gap measures. What many authors believe is needed is controlled nuclear fusion with direct conversion of thermal to electrical energy.

Austin and Brewer define as an additional index of the quality of life in an industrial society the per capita production of garbage! (See also the formula for

[6]From Arthur L. Austin and John W. Brewer, 'World Population Growth and Related Technical Problems," (based originally on data from G. S. Callender, "On the Amount of Carbon Dioxide in the Atmosphere," *Tellus*, 1958) *IEEE Spectrum*, December 1970.

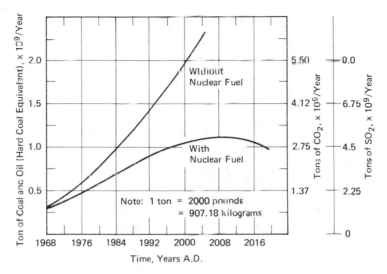

FIGURE 2-8
Projected CO_2 and SO_2 production by the U.S. power industry.[7]

quality of life discussed in Chapter 9.) Figure 2-9 shows the relationship between refuse production and energy consumption. The efficiency of energy use is continually decreasing. Thus, there must be a point of diminishing return if energy use continues to be associated with increasing quantities of thermal and solid wastes. Waste disposal *must* be replaced with waste conversion, a costly path to follow. Man-made systems must be made closed, in the sense that natural systems involve the use of all by-products of each element by other elements. This will not be easy technologically, economically, or managerially, especially in the sense of balancing short-range gains (and accompanying vested interest, misuse of the communications media, and advertising pressure) against long-range losses which are hard to define. This will require greater understanding of the interaction of man, technology, and environment, and a change in the basic attitudes of everyone. We shall return to these important issues in Chapters 3 and 9.

Further quantitative indications of the close relationship between population and standard of living on the one hand and use of raw materials on the other are

---

[7]From Arthur L. Austin and John W. Brewer, "World Population Growth and Related Technical Problems," (adapted from material from Milton Shaw's testimony before Congress on "Environmental Effects of Producing Electric Power," 1969), *IEEE Spectrum*, December 1970.

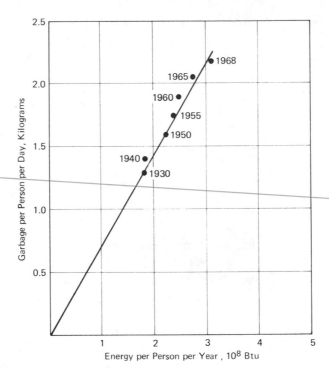

FIGURE 2-9
United States per-capita refuse production as a function of per-capita consumption.[8]

provided by Gough (1970). The "developed" countries are more and more dependent upon the "underdeveloped" nations to supply materials. For example, about one-third the total weight of a U.S.-made automobile consists of foreign metal. In the case of aluminum, 89% comes from foreign sources. The political and military implications here are clear.

If the present population of the world had the U.S. standard of living, depletion of many indispensable minerals would occur within a few years to a few decades. This is shown in Figure 2-10.

Each person in the U.S. is now responsible for over 10 pounds of waste per day, of which 7 pounds are household, commercial, and municipal wastes and 3 pounds are industrial wastes (Black, *et al.*, 1968); these figures do not include agricultural wastes. The composition of municipal waste is summarized in Table 2-5. Inspection of Table 2-5 should be in terms of the misuse of forest products and of the necessity to develop means of recovering metals and other materials.

[8]From Arthur L. Austin and John W. Brewer, "World Population Growth and Related Technical Problems," *IEEE Spectrum*, December 1970.

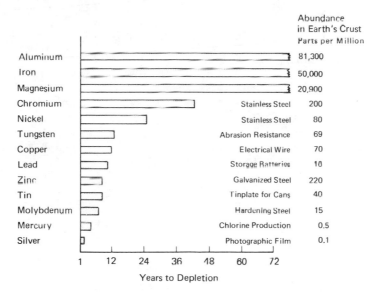

FIGURE 2-10
Depletion of world reserves of commercial grade ores if world population had U.S. living standard.[9]

Shortage of food, of course, provides the most direct, most written about form of environmental resistance to overpopulation. The food capacity of the earth can be estimated using the method of Watt (1968), based on the premises of required conversion of solar energy to chemical energy, available solar energy per surface area, the total available arable land, and human caloric requirements. Table 2-6 summarizes the food capacity of the earth. However, this estimate does not include the need for proteins, vitamins, and minerals.

It is estimated that about 2250 m^2 are required for support at the 3000-kcal/day/man level. Based on approximately two crops per year, arable land area limits population to about 34 billion using existing agricultural methods. If algae could be used productively, say by devoting 50 million acres of level tropical land to algal culture, it might be technically possible to double world food supplies. Fortunately, this harebrained concept requires large investment; the side effects of such a scheme could be most depressing. It seems there is no limit to those whose managerial schemes are rooted at the lowest level of Maslow's hierarchy of motives. In the same vein, a look at Figure 2-11

[9]From William C. Gough, as based on data from the Division of Mines (1969), *Commodity Statements,* and Robert C. Weast (1969-70), *Handbook of Chemistry and Physics.*

TABLE 2-5

Average composition of municipal refuse (percentage by weight).*

Rubbish (64%)

Paper, all kinds	42
Wood and bark	2.4
Grass	4.0
Brush	1.5
Cuttings, green	1.5
Leaves, dry	5.0
Leather goods	0.3
Rubber	0.6
Plastics	0.7
Oils, paint	0.8
Linoleum	0.1
Rags	0.6
Street refuse	3.0
Dirt, household	1.0
Unclassified	0.5

Food Wastes (12%)

Garbage	10.0
Fats	2.0

Non Combustibles (24%)

Metals	8.0
Glass and Ceramics	6.0
Ashes	10.0
	100.0

*From William C. Gough, based on data from Civil Defense Research Project, "New Utility Concepts for New Cities," 1968.

can suggest the use of marine food is low and might be expanded to meet future needs. However, it should be noted that this survey of the field, done in 1968-69, was prior to recognition of the 1969 *absolute decrease* in the yield of fisheries.

TABLE 2-6

Food capacity of the earth.*

Crop	Efficiency of Conversion of Solar to Chemical Energy, percent	Approximate Area to Produce 10^6 kcal/yr to Feed One Man, km^2	World Population Supportable by Terrestrial Resources Alone
Algae	12.5	13	9.1×10^{12}
Potatoes	0.1	1 550	7.5×10^{10}
Grain	0.05	3 100	3.8×10^{10}
Milk	0.04	3 900	3.0×10^{10}
Pork	0.02	10 400	1.2×10^{10}

*From Arthur L. Austin and Jay W. Brewer, "World Population Growth and Technical Problems," *IEEE Spectrum,* December 1970.

Figure 2-12 indicates that per capita food production has remained almost constant since 1962. Further, much of the world's population exists on as little as 2100 kcal/day/man.

In the face of these problems there have been suggestions to harvest sea plants as well as sea animals, especially as a source of protein. However, low-density algae make up much of sea-plant life (1 m^3 of sea water contains about 1 cm^3 of algae), and there are so far no efficient ways of harvesting algae. Likewise, there are no extant means of making such food palatable and of storing and distributing it, and little research and development in the area. Means of synthesizing protein economically would seem to this writer to be both more promising and more desirable.

Figure 2-13 indicates that, even given that over-all food production is increasing, the per-capita food production of underdeveloped countries is actually decreasing.

Austin and Brewer believe wheat, the only well-rounded bulk food requiring few changes in dietary habits which can be produced and distributed on a large scale, will continue to be the basic food. This means that the U.S. and Canada must provide wheat to underdeveloped countries until these sources are exhausted, with consequent political games of favoritism and manipulation.

The results of the "Green Revolution," in producing high-yield varieties of grain, remain to be seen. There is evidence that a whole new set of problems

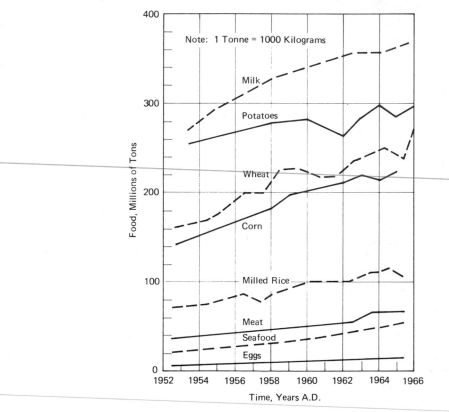

FIGURE 2-11
World production of major foods (except curve for seafood, data do not include mainland China).[10]

must now be solved, and even with the best of results massive famine may be delayed only a few decades at most. The predicted upper bound of 50 billion people assumes *all* necessary developments without major setbacks.

Coale (1970) believes that economic factors are even more important than population growth in threatening the quality of American life.

He suggests that the way our economy is organized is the essential cause of pollution, trash accumulation, and concentration of pesticides in animals. Such harmful practices derive from disregard of what economists call *externalities*, i.e., consequences (good or bad) which do not enter the calculations of gain or

[10]From Arthur L. Austin and John W. Brewer, "World Population Growth and Related Technical Problems," *IEEE Spectrum*, December 1970.

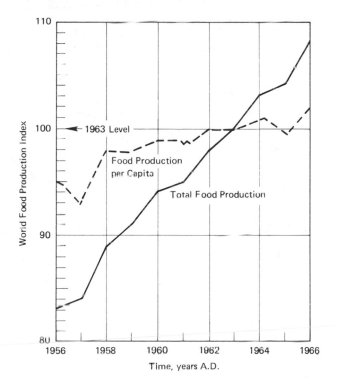

FIGURE 2-12
Total and per-capita world food production (excluding mainland China).[11]

loss. Air pollution caused by an industrial plant provides a good example of an externality. The basic economic factor resulting in degrading the environment is that we have permitted economic activities without assessing individuals or institutions for adverse effects or externalities. Pure air, pure water, and waste disposal can no longer be treated as free in a modern, urban, industrial society.

To counter the above, various taxes could be proposed, e.g., to minimize the use of disposable, nondeteriorating cans and bottles; or users of flowing water could perhaps be required to take in the water downstream of their operation and discharge it upstream.

Coale, commenting on the rapid and rising rate of extraction of raw materials, states that the distinction between renewable and nonrenewable resources is not

[11]From Arthur L. Austin and John W. Brewer, "World Population Growth and Related Technical Problems," *IEEE Spectrum*, December 1970.

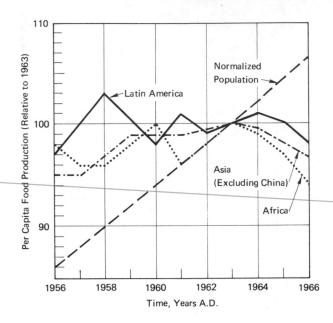

FIGURE 2-13
Per-capita food production by world area.[12]

always clear. Fossil fuels are examples of nonrenewable resources; metals, examples of renewable ones. The energy we use is lost but the minerals we use are still with us. However, at the moment it does not pay to recycle these materials. With added taxation on mines that despoil the environment, there could be more incentive to improve methods of recycling.

Coale suggests the connection between the current growth of our population and deterioration of our environment is largely indirect, that is, per capita increase in production is more important than population growth. For example, since 1940 population has increased by about 50%, but per capita use of electricity has been multiplied several times and attendance in national parks has increased by more than 400%. Thus, a wealthy industrial nation of 100 million could have most of the pollution problems we do. Contrariwise, Coale reasons even with 300 million, given "the will and intelligence to devise and apply proper policies (p. 135)," we could improve our environment.

Ehrlich and Holdren (1971), in a very fine article, propose five theories countering the notion that population growth in advanced industrial nations such as the United States is a minor factor. The theories are:

[12]From Arthur L. Austin and John W. Brewer, "World Population Growth and Related Technical Problems," *IEEE Spectrum*, December 1970.

1. Population growth causes a disproportionate negative impact on the enviornment.
2. Population control alone is not a panacea but must be considered on a global basis in interaction with resource utilization and depletion, and environmental deterioration.
3. Population density is a poor sole measure of population pressure, and population redistribution is a pseudosolution.
4. "Environment" must include the physical environment of urban ghettoes, the behavioral environment, and the epidemiological environment.
5. The usual technological solutions are often not solutions at all.

Population size and per capita impact are not independent of one another. Indeed, there are many complex interactions. In looking at power-consumption increases, for example, it is misleading to consider electrical power utilization out of the over-all context. Thus, total energy use increased 140% from 1940 to 1969, even though electricity consumption increased 760% in the same time period. Similarly aluminum consumption increased over 1400% since 1940, but much of this was due to substitution of aluminum for steel. The combined consumption of aluminum and steel has increased only 117% since 1940.

Thus, per capita consumption of energy and resources and associated per capita impact on the environment are themselves functions of population size. *Impact can increase greater than linearly with population.*

Further, in exploitation of resources we are reaching points of *diminishing returns,* for example, relative to mineral extraction, water use, growing food, and fishing. Diminishing returns are also recognized in rectifying damage to the environment, for example, in secondary treatment of sewage and in air pollution control. Thus, the cost of secondary treatment of sewage runs to two to four times the cost of primary treatment. It appears recycling will also be no panacea.

Other ways in which population size influences per capita impact are associated with transportation and communication links—the number of links increases much more rapidly than the number of people. There are interesting effects, such as the *threshold effect;* for example, below a certain level trees can survive in smog or a lake can cleanse itself of sewage, yet a small increase results in death of the trees or eutrophication of the lake. Here are other examples of the ubiquitous hierarchical jumps we discussed in Chapter 1. Another factor is *synergism,* the effects of which are little studied.

World population is growing by about 70 million people each year; at the same time 10 to 20 million starve to death annually. Yet attempts to increase food production are bound to have unpredictable, positive-*and*-negative-feedback effects and to have tremendous effects on the environment. For example, the Food and Agriculture Organization of the United Nations reported that in 1969 the world experienced the first absolute decline in the yield of fisheries since 1950. Ehrlich and Holdren attribute this to agricultural pollution and overexploitation of fisheries.

The United States alone uses some 30% of the world's (non)renewable resources which are consumed each year, for example, 37% of the energy and 28% of the tin. This is quite inconsistent with America's statements about developing the "Third World." Thus, Ehrlich and Holdren maintain, because of consumption and the negative impact on the environment, population growth in the advanced countries must be regarded as the most serious. Even if population growth were halted and consumption remained the same or increased, the world could be destroyed.

Comparing the United States as "uncrowded" to countries like the Netherlands as "crowded" also makes no sense, because the latter requires, through importation, vast areas of land to support it. For example, Holland must import essentially all its minerals and cotton, 63% of its cereals, and 77% of its wool. Likewise, the carrying capacity of vast lands, such as the deserts of Australia, North Africa, and the American West, is associated with many factors other than acreage, and these lands can be settled only at great expense.

Economist Joseph Spengler (1964) has estimated that 4% of national income goes to support the 1% per annum of population growth characteristic of the U.S. Hence, the faster we grow, the less able we will be to rectify the situation. In the same sense, we must consider the huge costs of education and welfare devoted to nonproductive portions of our population.

Technological fixes are limited by lead time, cost, and scale. Desalination of sea water for agriculture, high-protein diet supplements, and so forth prove inadequate in practice. Even worse, these "solutions" often create further problems, as attested to by the synthetic organic pesticides and inorganic nitrogen fertilizers. Often "solutions" such as electric automobiles simply shift the environmental burden from highways to electric power plants. In each case, all such alternatives should be weighed against the costs. Each solution should be just that and not an excuse for satisfying or placating the public. The elements of our crisis, none of which can be either ignored or treated in isolation, are social, technological, ecological, economic, and behavioral.

Effects of Crowding and of Increased Frequency of Contact with Others

We have examined the "big picture" of population problems. Now let's turn our attention to factors, even more subtle and perhaps potentially even more disastrous, accruing from high densities of individuals, crowding, and increased frequency of contact with others. Relating these factors to human behavior, health, and cultural rise or decline continues to represent an area of tragic and abysmal ignorance. Variables are difficult to conceive, let alone to measure; among the most important variables, undoubtedly, are perceptual and behavioral mechanisms, whereby people and other animals space themselves and define personal space or territory, and psychophysiological reactions to stress. Particularly intriguing approaches are the *proxemics* of Hall (1968) and the *personal space* of Sommer (1969).

Many dramatic and enlightening observations have been made on animal behavior in crowded situations. These include laboratory studies, especially the work of Calhoun (1963, 1968) and the field studies to which we shall shortly turn our attention. For example, in the laboratory, rats may withdraw socially, display cannibalism or homosexual behavior, or even increase their voluntary intake of alcohol, normally avoided. You may wish to review the pros and cons as to the validity of generalizing human and other animal behavior. Calhoun (1968) and Lockard (1971, referenced in Chapter 1) should be reviewed in the context. We believe that much is to be learned from observing animal behavior, particularly under field conditions, as long as too literal interspecific translations are not made.

Christian (1970) suggests that social behavior is a major force in the evolution of mammals. Social organization may be based on hierarchies of social rank consisting of dominance-subordination relationships between individuals, families, and groups. Individual aggressiveness against members of the same or other species is an important feature of competitive social behavior. Social hierarchies also constitute an important mechanism for dispersion. Low-ranking individuals are generally forced to emigrate from their birthplaces. Similarly, weak individual human beings, or tribes are forced to migrate to peripheral or undesirable areas. In the past, this was southern Africa, America, the Antipodes, and inaccessible highlands; today it is the urban slums.

Christian suggests there is an optimum degree of aggressiveness for a given species, and extreme aggressiveness and high reproductive rates may be incompatible. Applying this concept to man leads to mixed conclusions.

Most of the results Christian summarizes come from the studies of small mammals, particularly rodents. In the breeding season in a year of high population density of the meadow vole, *Microtus pennsylvanicus,* all mature males were scarred from fighting but the immature males were unscarred. Thus, excessive density and aggressiveness could interfere with reproduction. Population density together with intraspecific competition is a major force toward dispersal. When densities are high the proportion of individuals who disperse is greater.

Density of populations may fluctuate greatly, both inter- and intra-annually, but this differs among species. Most dispersed animals, usually the young, fail to survive. However, the raw material for speciation is held to be the occasional subordinate which, because of mutation, survives in the new environment. Relatively nonaggressive species are not thought to evolve so rapidly and to exploit new environments so fully.

Species may differ in their survival characteristics. Thus, the meadow vole may have survived because it did not develop a negative feedback control of population size, the deermouse, *Peromyscus maniculatus,* may have survived because it did so and thereby avoided overexploiting the environment. Between these rodents are the house mouse and Norway rat which are potentially, but not regularly, irruptive.

In the case of the microtines and other irruptive mammals, there is a high reproductive potential and the ability to realize it rapidly. However, reproduction is progressively inhibited as density increases and may be totally suppressed if density becomes high enough. This is part of a density-dependent endocrine mechanism that may involve the adrenal cortex. It is believed to operate through social intolerance and aggressiveness related to increased numbers. This seems particularly true of species which have evolved in discontinuous habitats (e.g., patches of meadow in a forest). Colonization of extensive continuous habitats which do not require regular dispersal and exploitation of new sites may have resulted as reactions against this social intolerance and adrenocortical response.

Terman (1971) looks further at the population-regulating behavior of the deermouse, viz., the prairie deermouse, *Peromyscus maniculatus bairdii.* The rodents (1) show marked numerical variability at population asymptote under identical laboratory environments including surplus food, water, and harborage; (2) control their population growth through social interaction other than overt aggression; and (3) control population either through complete cessation of reproduction or by failure of the young to survive. Reproductive failure is associated with an inhibition of maturation; as a result 90-95% of females born into the populations and 80% of all females 90 days of age or older do not reproduce. In contrast, 80% of control females produce young by a similar age. Accordingly, *crowdedness is a relative term and deleterious effects may occur at low densities.* Likewise, *the absolute amount of space may not be so significant as the social system developed therein.*

The effects of high density and overcrowding on human populations are still poorly understood, although they are presumably deleterious. Studies are beginning on the effects of crowding stress in urban environments on psychophysiological, cognitive, and social processes, and on the adaptive mechanisms among the confined dense populations on remote Pacific atolls.

Schmitt (1966) has attempted to answer the question: Which measure is more closely identified with social disorganization, *high density* defined in terms of population or housing units per net acre, or *overcrowding* expressed in terms of persons per room? Few researchers hithertofore had attempted to isolate the separate effects of density and overcrowding. Simple, multiple, and partial correlation analysis was performed on data for the 42 census tracts comprising the Honolulu Standard Metropolitan Statistical Area.

Nine health and disorganization measures were analyzed. These were on data about 15 years old, which represents a typical difficulty in studies of this sort. For example, rates were expressed as average annual civilian deaths by suicide, 1948-1952, per 1000 civilian population 14 years of age or more, 1950. The nine rate measures were: (1) death rate, all causes; (2) infant death rate; (3)

suicide rate; (4) tuberculosis rate; (5) venereal disease rate; (6) mental hospital first admission rate; (7) illigitimate birth rate; (8) juvenile delinquency rate; and (9) prison admission rate.

The above were correlated with three measures of overcrowding and two of density: (1) dwelling units with 1.01 or more persons per room (as a percentage of all occupied units); (2) population per net residential acre; (3) households with four or more members; (4) married couples without their own household; and (5) dwelling units in structures with two or more units. All referred to 1950.

Two control variables were used: (1) population 25 years of age or more with 12 years or more of schooling; and (2) families with incomes of $3,000 or more per annum.

Results cast doubt on the thesis that overcrowding is much more associated with health and social disorganization than is high density and that high density may, indeed, be desirable. In Honolulu, at least, population per net residential acre revealed a close association with morbidity, mortality, and social break-down, when overcrowding, as measured by percentage of occupied units with 1.01 inhabitants per room, was held constant. However, with net density kept constant, correlations between overcrowding and the nine variables approached zero.

Means of Controlling Human Population and Its Impacts

Attitudes about the population problem and willingness to work toward policies aimed at rectifying this problem represent one of the most important changes in social thought of our times. Only a few short years ago, most people apparently considered any mention of population problems to be heresy. The leaders of great nations now speak out against the dangers of overpopulation. The United States has presidential and congressional advisory commissions, e.g., the Commission on Population Growth and the American Future (see the Final Report, 1972). Without an understanding of the underlying dynamics stressed in this book, this would seem quite remarkable considering the 175 years or so of somnolence since Thomas Malthus, and considering that Margaret Sanger was jailed in the 1920s for advocating the supply of birth-control information. Nevertheless, there is still a long way to go, and we can expect additional, even more fundamental, changes in attitudes and practices. But time is running out and many recommendations, such as those of the above-referenced comission, tend to be neither forceful nor particularly imaginative.

Control of human population growth and its impacts must be within a total systems context. Isolated methods, such as setting up local clinics to distribute birth-control pills and intrauterine devices and to perform vasectomies will not, by themselves, be sufficient. A total systems package should involve at least the following (based partly on Austin and Brewer, 1970; Coale, 1970; and Singer, 1970):

1. About 20% of births in the U.S. are unwanted; equivalent percentages for other nations remain to be determined. Elimination of unwanted births could reduce fertility greatly. Policies should reflect education and provision of clinical services for contraception and abortion.

2. At least at certain times and places, people want too many children. Science must determine why, and policies and educational programs must be instituted which influence downward the number of children people want.

3. Strictly voluntary birth control will not be achieved worldwide in time to yield the luxury of a choice between a quality of life and a quantity of life. Hence, in many parts of the world death rates will increase until fertility rates are zero or negative. Strong national goals must reflect these realities.

4. A better distribution of population is needed. At the present rate of U.S. growth of about 2.5 million people per year, a new city the size of Tulsa or Dayton would have to be added every month. Most additions occur in already crowded metropolitan areas on the coasts. Thus, we could: (a) spread population by generating growth to sparsely populated rural areas; (b) stimulate the growth of presently existing small cities; and (c) build new cities. The last is the most intellectually stimulating from the point of view of design and management, but probably would be the poorest solution in the long run.

5. There should be a redirection of all growth in terms of real personal welfare and quality of life, rather than simply using the Gross National Product (GNP) as an index. This would involve how to reorient and shift consumption goals and growth goals away from things that consume large amounts of raw materials like water, fuels, and metals. A shift could be toward things that do not consume raw materials and which do not have an unfavorable impact on the environment, things like marked improvements in health and education services. How do we, then, develop such new life styles? We shall return to these issues in the last chapter.

6. Techniques for conversion of waste products and pollution into useful substances should be developed, for example, through recycling junk automobiles and sewage sludge, extracting sulfur from fuels, use of some waste heat from electric power plants, and extracting valuable materials from refuse. Indeed, as we have pointed out, Chicago sewage sludge is now being used experimentally to convert land in southern Illinois, ravaged by strip mining for coal, into productive corn fields.

7. Industrial practices should be revised. At this time of coalescing systems, we must be willing to pay the penalty for past prodigality.

8. Taxes for waste of resources, abuse of the environment, use of the "commons," and so forth should be initiated.

9. A central agency for control of energy and natural resources and for development of a rational basis for national policies of growth and development should be established.

10. Acceptance of pseudo-solutions, such as the "Green Revolution," "farming the sea," or "making the desert bloom" that substitute one problem for another and, at best, postpone by several decades the day of reckoning, should be refused. We must resist the temptation to accept population growth, or *any* growth for that matter, as inevitable. The best way to fight the population problem is to refuse to recognize it as always the "leading edge" and to recognize that technological "fixes" must not be implemented under many circumstances. For example, the promise that "farming the sea" is just around the corner will make any attitude-changing program and the management of society just that much harder.

11. Development of more efficient methods of energy conversion is necessary, particularly direct thermal-to-electric, an area now lagging; and also new fuels are needed to replace fossil fuels in all forms of transportation. Should these not now become our national—or better, world—goals, parallel to the manned-space program of the 1960s? Must the "enemy" against whom or which the goal is directed always be an outsider, a cultural heritage of the past?

12. Development of national and international centers for intensive systems studies in the areas highlighted in this brief review is essential.

IMPACT OF ADVANCED TECHNOLOGY

A major purpose of this book is to dramatize the interrelationships of the social, technological, and economic subsystems with their environments. The complexities ensuing from these interrelationships make it exceedingly difficult to extrapolate a simple evolution of society, such as from production-oriented or industrial to post-industrial and on to post-service-oriented.

In Chapter 1, we considered sociotechnical interactions, mainly involving mechanization and industrial organization. Earlier in this chapter we considered the effects of population multiplied by advanced technology, on the physical and biological environment. In this section we shall highlight some of the ways advanced technology, especially the computerization or rationalization aspects of automation, is reshaping how people do their jobs, how they perceive themselves, whether their jobs are needed, and how management must change—indeed, how the very structure of society is being reshaped.

Of course, by definition of a system, "shaping" is reciprocal. Sometimes things backfire, and our predictions of a smooth leisured future fall by the wayside. Consider the interactions involving aerospace technology and industry. Military, political, and commercial "demand" stimulated a remarkable growth of aerospace for almost three decades between the early 1940s and late 1960s. For example, in 1967 aerospace and related industries employed over 500,000 persons or 43½% of manufacturing employment and 11% of total civilian employment in ten southern California counties. In 1971 employment had dwindled to about 344,000, that is, with a loss of about 156,000 persons. Similar declines obtained for percentage of total Department of Defense prime contract awards (Parry, 1971).

The industry was thus vulnerable. Among other things, a reversal in the business cycle coincided with cutbacks in government expenditures which had previously provided a damping effect on large economic fluctuations.

The future picture of this industry may not be good, for the following reasons of special importance to the theme of this book:

1. There is no *easy* transferability of education and skills to the solution of problems of pollution, crime, urban design, and oceanology. Indeed, where attempts have been made ot retrain displaced aerospace engineers in environmental engineering, job offers have been limited.

2. The aerospace industry and local governments mutually lack the expertise to deal with one another.

3. Both the aerospace industry and airlines are particularly culpable for adhering to a policy of growth for growth's (and short-range profit's) sake. Thus, the release of the wide-bodied or jumbo jets while first-generation jets were still flying with numerous unfilled seats on many runs, during an economic recession curtailing business and other flying, resulted in an over-capacity with average passenger seat-occupancy below 50%. DC-8s and Boeing 707s fly almost empty on many runs. In retrospect, the need for the jumbo jets seems to have been superficial and ill-thought-out, indeed. Here we witness a combination of limited philosophical imagination and foresight, an unwillingness or inability to consider alternative sociotechnical futures, and a failure of economic and perhaps technological forecasting.

Shef (1968) has indicated technological growth has been generally exponential in the 20th century, doubling every 20 years in advanced nations. Assessing the parallel social growth and social cost is much more difficult.

Advanced technological societies are pressed with critical problems, because, as we have seen, a technological subsystem once enmeshed within the political, economic, and behavioral framework of a society is difficult to reverse or eradicate. Thus, even though *engineering solutions* to social and environmental problems may be possible, implementation of these solutions in terms of economic readjustment, political jurisdiction, and restructure of social behavior may be impossible. It may take decades to implement presently known technological solutions, and then it may be too late. In addition, the time from conception to implementation of a technological idea has, contrary to popular belief, not been shortened by modern management techniques. It is still long, with the length of time related to the complexity of the development. However, what has changed is the time from first use to widespread integration into the social system. Widespread use of a new technological development may occur before its social impact may be properly assessed. Hence, predictive technological assessments are an urgent social need, and this will require a scale of relative social values.

Starr (1969) suggests readily available historical data on accidents and health provide a point of departure. This is based on the assumption that society has (subconsciously) performed tradeoffs and essentially optimum sets of values achieved. From these analyses, government regulatory agencies could establish performance design objectives for the safety of the public. Starr views societal activities as being either voluntary, e.g., a citizen's decision to move from the city center to the suburbs as a result of performing tradeoffs on transportation, education, crime, etc., or involuntary, as in the case of war where there is an operational separation of the decision-makers from those most affected. Use of electric power and the automobile also are essentially involuntary today. The rationale of these concepts is that the statistical pattern for a large social group may be a meaningful realtime indicator of societal tradeoffs and values.

Gross (1967) has looked at the realities of fast-paced, worldwide change and the need for social indicators and social accounting. Many works pay great attention to the acceleration of science and technology, particularly to "mobiletics," the movement of information, mass, and energy, but little to the social changes reciprocally related to the technological changes.

The most important changes are *system changes* which Gross divides into the three areas of the uneven transformation of many agricultural societies to the first stages of industrialism, with a decline in the percentage of the population involved in agriculture and with rises in agricultural output; the uneven transformation of the United States and Western Europe to post-industrial societies, with a decline in the proportion of people in manufacturing and an increase in the proportion producing services; and the painful emergence of a world society of interdependent nations.

How do we understand the emerging world society? The world society is made up of myriad subsystems locked in conflict-cooperation relationships. It tends to submerge national characteristics and values in a homogenizing flood of goods and styles; nevertheless, it includes severe conflicts of values. Gross sees the following in terms of "social time"; changes in generations occurring much more quickly than ever before, with, in some contexts, the intermingling of several active human or machine generations; life and activity expectancies increasing, several careers over a lifetime, and a blurring of the distinction between work, education, and leisure; and millions of persons in learning programs outside the formally recognized educational enrollments.

Finally, the role of communications presents a classical area of how the technological subsystem impacts on the social subsystem. Massive, rapid, pervasive, and multi-medium modern communications produce both an almost instantaneous uniformity of behavior and an impetus to change that behavior. We might argue, for example, that the widesparead use of drugs among youth today has been aided and abetted by the decade-long or more, pre-narcotic environment of being passively tuned-in, tuned-out, and turned-on by television.

An excellent recent look at massive communications and their effect on world society is provided by Cherry (1971).

Automation

Using the term, *sociotechnical,* in the broad sense of this book, it is probably fair to state that studies of automation have provided the largest array of sociotechnical studies, exceeding even those of communications. Yet this is an emotionally charged area, and at the societal as opposed to the industrial level, the picture remains clouded.

A wealth of material has been produced in recent years by both government agencies and the private sector. Recommended analyses and evaluations include the numerous research summaries and literature reviews on specific topics provided between 1964 and 1972 by the ill-fated Harvard University *Program on Technology and Society;* the reports of the *National Commission on Technology, Automation, and Economic Progress* (1966); and the reports of the annual *Georgia-Reliance* symposia (Scott and Bolz, 1969, 1970).

Part of the problem of determining the effects of automation lies in just how the term is defined and used. For example, some workers (cf. Bates, 1969) differentiating between mechanization and automation, conclude that the former has already had profound social effects but the latter has had negligible effect so far, but probably will have great effects on society some decades in the future. In this book, we consider automation to involve mechanization, continuous process or mass production, automatic (usually cybernetic) control, and rationalization; however, in keeping with the hierarchical level defined earlier, we are most concerned with the last. Another part of the problem of determining the effects of automation is associated with just what is being studied. We know a lot more about the effects of automatizing certain industries than we know about the effects on society as a whole.

The problems associated with automation are multifarious. Only in passing, we might include costs of automation, effects on specific jobs, labor relations, how automation is introduced and managed, changes in productivity, needs for training or retraining, displacement of workers, and use of leisure and other free time.

What we know of the effects of automation in industrial and military facilities is well summarized by Emery and Marek (1962), who have reviewed a series of case studies involving the introduction of more highly automated equipment into power plants.

The equipment was introduced with smoothness and the staff adjusted to their new jobs. Disputes, labor stoppages, and deterioration of management-labor relations were not observed, even though union representation was high. Success appeared to be a function of stability in the external economic environment, stability in the internal environment, and staff confidence in management's past handling of technological change. However, the critical factor appeared to be management's belief that technical and economic considerations alone were not sufficient grounds for introducing major technological change.

Emery and Marek emphasize that, in selecting cases for study, organizations with poor management or management-employee relations should be avoided. These would only compromise the effects of automation which could become the focal point for past grievances.

The magnitude of changes is, of course, a function of what is automatized. In the case of the power plants, fine motor operations were not extensively required. Human participation was mainly required in control operations involving perceptual skills (sensing, measuring, judging), conceptual skills (abstracting, calculating, inferring), and feedback actions (rejecting, rectifying, or resetting tools or equipment). Other forms of automation, e.g., transfer automation, usually require changes in the degree of human participation in transfer and production operations requiring fine motor skills.

Automation of the power plant was accompanied by increased capacity and pressure, but also increased complexity in terms of the number of steps involved, decreased tolerance for disturbances, and increased separation of operators from the process (the operator now monitored and controlled the automatic controls required by the rigorous new system). Nevertheless, there were compensating satisfactions in that centralized indicator panels gave operators a greater integrated knowledge of the total process than was hithertofore possible.

These technological changes affected all the operators almost equally. There was not the increased heterogeneity often characteristic of mechanization. However, the operators had to be concerned with a much greater number of things than previously. There was much less opportunity to develop a personal map of the operations through moving about, adjusting valves, checking gauges, etc. Rather, the operator had to tolerate periods of waiting, while absorbing redundant information and responding immediately to emergencies by activating more complex controls. Some individuals could not adapt to this stress. Thus, there were more potential crisis points which had to be brought under control almost immediately by the operator using his own resources. Further, the operator's knowledge was now second hand, because of the greater separation from the productive process, i.e., information was obtained from an imperfect medium.

The supervisory roles were also affected, in that the supervisor could make the operator's job as easy as possible by minimizing disruptions of the "steady state," i.e., controlling over-all inputs and outputs, checking on maintenance and repairs, etc. The operator's role became unified and the supervisor's job extended in time. The key functions of operators were now performed only in crises and could not be subjected to routine supervision. Only peripheral tasks, e.g., log-keeping, remained subject to routine supervision.

Boguslaw (1965) emphasizes that computers take their place within existing social systems, but this significantly redefines system arrangements and leads to redesigns. Lateral, hierarchical, and organizational structures are changed, as are flow of information and work structure.

The lowest-skilled people, eliminated by automation, are not at the bottom of the status and reward ladder—they are removed from it. However, the middle- and high-level managers are also affected, and the demanding positions become those related to the computer. Former key decision-makers are so no longer. The exercise of power now becomes mediated through computer technology. And at the same time internal dissension is usually poorly prepared for, even though the society may be prepared to meet external threats.

Differences in system designs may really involve more and more how power is allocated differently. Do the elements of society remain together by virtue of coercion or consensus? Power in large systems resides in differing degrees, differing in the extent that they can understand and specify decision requirements, with the user, hardware designer, and computer programmer. If the user is unable or unwilling to understand the detailed operations of the system, *de facto* power shifts to the designers. Enshrouding decisions in technical language may deprive the masses of power as surely as despotism or bureaucratic mass. In each case, democracy is eroded. Values are debased through technological necessity and value structures change.

Michael (1966), in a particularly thought-provoking article, has looked at the implications for human behavior in organizations involving computerization. People will be drawn increasingly, because of sheer size and complexity factors, toward a *rationalized* society in which the computer plays a powerful role. However, there are counterforces related to the inability of institutions to change as fast as their role in society requires and to the needs of professionals whose abilities are displaceable by computers. Michael does not see a stalemate, but rather an increasing separation between rationalized and nonrationalized individuals and organizations. "Rationalization" here refers to activities and attitudes applied to the systematic implementation of efficiency and effectiveness. (See also Boguslaw, 1965, and Churchman, 1968.) The computer becomes the core element of rationalization methods.

Increasingly, solutions to social problems will be statistical, because of the aggregate needs of large societies and because of the nature of problem definition by social technicians to fit their computers. These will be the people turned to for problem definition and solution. Already, administrators and planners are beginning to value most those aspects with which the computer can best deal.

Large-scale cannot be turned on and off easily. Interlocking vested interests produce an inertia of formidable proportions. There is a great need for rationalized methods for long-range planning, for assigning program priorities, for evaluating program progress, and for modifying or terminating programs when they are no longer useful or of high priority.

There will be a persistent shortage of qualified professionals and managers to guide our ever more complex society; not many of these are turned out because we don't know how. Even now we are short of topflight personnel to guide socially desirable programs. We shall return to this problem in Chapter 9.

Many professionals will be heavily burdened. Human technical aides, as well as computers, will be required to lighten this burden, especially at the higher levels. Developing such aide roles will require a careful breakdown of the essentials and non-essentials of skills and tasks. Michael thus sees the professional's job as being more rationalized and precise with a more rationalized state of mind accompanying it.

These, then, are pushes toward rationalization; there are also pulls. There will be, for example, enormous increases in the knowledge needed to understand and manipulate society. The computer provides the behavioral and social scientist with the means of complex modeling, combining large numbers of variables needed to simulate the behavior of men and institutions. It also provides the capability for storing and processing huge amounts of near-realtime data which can be used, among other things, to test and refine the theoretical models. It is to be expected that organizations will rearrange their missions to take advantage of such powerful techniques.

It is to be expected that more scientists and technologists will become involved in policy-making to which they will bring their rationalized modes of thinking. In addition, planners who are frustrated by present bureaucracies will tend to gravitate to rationalized centers.

Michael looks at some implications for upper and lower management of increased rationalization. There will, of course, be differences among organizations and among levels of management. However, many agree that the quality of management in government and industry will change. Managers will need more flexibility, imagination, and fundamental intelligence. There will be much less need for people to do routine decision-making. Computers will do much of the routine "thinking" now performed by middle managers. It is believed that a single decision-maker will be responsible for tasks now allocated among many individuals; that there will be much greater centralization of control in political and economic organizations; that fewer managers will be making decisions that affect more individuals; that the checks and balances on the manager will be reduced. Subordinates will not have access to the computers and the complex problems comprehended by centralized management. Hence, they will be in a much weaker position than they are in today.

Cybernated organizations will not require so many managers. Many middle-level managers and technologists will explicitly have to be fired. These jobs do not "turnover" rapidly. Such processes will generate cynicism, disillusionment, and deteriorated interpersonal relationships among the potential victims of rationalization. Indeed, some organizations may recruit managers just for their hard-headed abilities to fire their fellow workers. Contrariwise, other organizations may practice featherbedding. Or there may be a major attempt to discover and reallocate to live middle-level professionals tasks that cannot be computerized.

These forces will have great effects upon personal involvement in and loyalty toward an organization. Persons lacking loyalty and security will be less inclined to work overtime in order to enmesh themselves in the higher echelons of the organization. There will thus be greater mobility. There may be a new breed of middle manager, aggressive and not concerned with security. The professional will be forced into lifelong learning and relearning. To all the other insecurities of suburban, indebted, status-conscious, upper-middle-class life will be added the new threat of being dispossessed from it by failing to pass the new tests of professional advancement, tests which reflect a person's own intellectual abilities. People with quantitative skills will be in especial demand.

Management will thus become highly competitive, intellectual, and political, with a high proportion of washouts. Organizations and individuals will have a hard time selecting and fitting persons to meet the ever-changing requirements, even though there may be a flowering of aptitude testing techniques. There will be a lessening sense in the individual that he can make of the world what he wishes. There may be profound changes in values about the individual and about freedom.

There are of course counterpressures to rationalization leading to internal organizational strife. Management might accordingly delay computerization, initiate featherbedding, or sabotage the computerization. However, Michael feels computerization will in the end win out.

Another ploy might be to assume the form without the substance of rationalization. Social-welfare programs are cited as an example—the systems approach at the federal level diffuses downward into the political mire of local vested interests.

Another pressure militating against rationalization derives from the need of society to find a meaningful role for the mass-produced average managers, engineers, teachers, etc. This could involve inventing and paying for jobs, say, in social welfare. Michael states that paying well for mediocre service has precedents in our present practices both of paying well for mediocre material goods and paying for mediocre research and development. Much that passes for scientific and technological research is trivial and second rate. In the government, overlapping research and demonstration programs indicate poor relationship to any systematic set of goals. Programs, like the poverty program, become means in themselves rather than means to another end.

Behavior will change accordingly. There may be more emphasis on interpersonal relations, on reinforcing roles not replaceable by a machine. There will be more inventions of protest behavior to give personal meaning in a world too complex to permit personal identification. These processes will manifest a new intensity. Further, there will be greater self-indulgence. Novelty and sensation-seeking will increase and more people will try to enlarge their sense of self. This will, of course, involve increased use of drugs, perhaps eventually government sanctioned, to give the "best of two worlds."

Michael concludes that we must develop wise men who understand the limits of human knowledge and can resist the pressures to value most those things which can be computerized. The public will be a poor arbiter, insofar as knowing what policy best meets its long-term interests—the problems will be too complex and the techniques for defining and coping with them too esoteric, especially in the mathematical sense. Finally, computerization will eliminate the "out" that managers are not responsible for their actions, because they know so little of the interactions and indirect effects.

The interpretations of Bates (1969), less flamboyantly written, are more or less consistent with those of Gross, Boguslaw, and Michael, with regard to changes in amount of time spent on and off work and how this time is spent, changes in power structure, and emergence of even larger organizations and networks. However, Bates, contrasting automation with mechanization, believes the former is moving slowly with a presently small impact and will not have a major effect for 75 to 100 years. (See also Weizenbaum, 1972.)

Finally, for another flamboyant but highly interesting presentation of the effects of computer equipment, data processing, and systems on society, including the misuse of these things, see Martin and Norman (1970).

MOTIVATIONAL FACTORS

If we were to state that motivational factors were the most important in understanding "human nature," we should expect to be soundly criticized for doing so. But state it we do, and our motivational factors involve the basic theoretical frameworks of Maslow on hierarchy of motives, of Lewin on level of aspiration, of Freud on ego-defense mechanisms, of Dollard on frustration and aggression, and of Festinger on cognitive dissonance, and extensions thereof. These present unifying themes throughout this book. In these terms we shall examine the "revolution of rising expectations" and satisfactions available to various racial, socioeconomic, and consumer groups. Through education and dogma we are led to expect that all our needs will be met through hard work, and belief and faith in the "establishment." Yet we are witnessing the emergence of a meritocracy with severely limited "room at the top."

Because of the special importance of the motivational theories of Freud, Lewin, and Maslow, we shall summarize salient aspects of each at this point.

The motivational theories of Freud are extensive and include concepts of basic drive, unconscious processes, derived motives, frustration and conflict, and defense mechanisms. Our emphasis here is upon those processes which help us understand the irrational—or even more important, the plausibly rational—behavior of managers, leaders, pressure groups, and consumers—in short, those individuals and groups which most influence the design, operation, and management of complex systems. In this context, see also the section, A View of the Rational Man in Chapter 1.

The concept of unconscious motivation holds that behavior may be driven by forces below the level of awareness; that is, that a person may do things for reasons other than those most apparent either to him or to others. Further, frustration of motives and conflict between motives can also take place at the unconscious level. Some motives produce conflict so hurtful to the individual's concept of himself that the form of these motives is changed. The resulting so-called ego-defense mechanisms involve various aggressive, withdrawal, and substitute reactions. We emphasize here that, although much of Freudian theory originally stemmed from observations of clinical patients, unconscious processes and ego-defense mechanisms are very much a part of everybody's personality makeup and, therefore, influence everyone's perceptions, thoughts, problem identifications and solutions, and decisions.

As examples of ego-defense mechanisms of importance in explaining behavior in complex systems we can mention *displacement of aggression,* illustrated by a frustrated youth, whose hostility toward the environment manifests itself as vandalism; the "alternative lifestyle" *withdrawal* from an establishment perceived as both frustrating and sterile; the excessive drive of the manager or politician as *overcompensation* for some real or imagined inferiority; and the *rationalization* by policy makers that destruction of the environment is necessary for progress or for preserving an ideology.

Lewin has recognized that what a person considers success or failure does not depend on the achievement *per se,* but upon the relationships between that achievement and the person's expectation. The amount of success or failure the person experiences depends on whether the achievement is above or below the momentary *level of aspiration.* Further, the level of aspiration itself can be changed by success or failure, with a greater tendency to raise the level of aspiration following success than to lower it after failure. The progressive rise in the level of aspiration (and of expectancy, which we shall discuss later in this section) coupled with an at least partially innate need for change and activity ("work"), provide one of the major driving forces in complex systems. This rise is associated with an apparent insatiability of human needs, with a continuous emergence of new fields to conquer and new environments to master and exploit, and with the insurrectional consequences of a marked disparity between aspiration or expectation on the one hand and actual achievement on the other.

Maslow has conceptualized that human needs can be arranged in a five-level hierarchy of prepotency. The emergence of a given need usually depends on the previous satisfaction of a more demanding need. Thus, man is perpetually wanting.

Maslow's need-hierarchy concept formulates the following overlapping categories from most to least "basic": physiological, safety, love or social, esteem or ego, and self-actualization or self-fulfillment. The most prepotent goal monopolizes consciousness and organizes behavior. Less prepotent needs are minimized or may even be forgotten. Most people are characterized by partial fulfillment and partial nonfulfillment of a wide variety of needs. There are of course wide differences in capabilities for need satisfaction both between societies and within societies. In addition, the more basic needs can be gratified by material means, the higher needs cannot, except symbolically. This truism underlies such behaviors as the demands of underprivileged groups for more consumer goods, the alienation of middle-class youth in technologically advanced societies, and the concern for the environment of affluent members of the professions.

Because of the diffuseness of motivational theory and the many uses of the term, a formidable problem remains in measuring motivation and its effects at different levels of aggregation. The Maslow and other motivational theories, further, must be modified in the context of present complex sociotechnical systems. Emphasis must be not only on the changes of level as perceived and modified by the person motivated, but also on the fact that the hierarchical structure itself and the means of reaching a goal are themselves dynamic and may be changed by the time a person moves to another level. This is what makes the present so awfully frustrating. There are no anchor points; for example, a person perceives an automobile or a freeway as meeting a certain need for comfort or status, but there is a delay involved, say in paying off the automobile or completing the freeway, and by the time the goal is reached it no longer satisfies the original needs. Further, a person cannot count on a permanency of goals or of need-satisfaction. The means of realizing a goal become so complicated and enmeshed with other factors that they may no longer represent a realistic route to the goal.

Reactions to ambiguity-induced frustration can be considered parallel to the usual ego-defense mechanisms; for example, alienation in the social sense is analogous to individual apathy and withdrawal, communal behavior and "searches for Jesus" analogous to regression, etc.

It must be remembered that "rising expectations" apply as much to goals and political power as to material goods. Here the "revolution of rising expectations" and Maslovian concepts merge. Rise has been spawned as much by education as by economic growth, and blind faith in education is as much the villain. It is social philosophy based on a faulty model of man, with implications paradoxically of both human limit (to need satiation) and human infinity (to human individual or group resourcefulness, and ability and skill level), that makes the present time so tragic, so fraught with danger.

We have seen that the sociotechnical system can be expressed in terms of basic dynamic forces which approach one another, blend and coalesce and merge, or conflict and oppose one another to produce, subtly over shorter or (usually) longer periods of time, an entirely different and unexpected whole of frightening properties and dimensions. These are genotypic explanations to the familiar phenotypic phenomena witnessed by the educated and uneducated layman to behavioral and social science today. These are the forces that must be better described, measured and quantified, and factored into our decision-making models and simulations.

We use the term, *layman,* to include the thousands of persons, most with the best intentions, from engineering and many other fields, who now are turning their attention to "solving" social and environmental problems. These people typically deal with the most superficial phenomena, or layers, of sociotechnical systems (remember we use *sociotechnical systems* to include analytic, transportation, communications, psychological testing, and other expertises as well as machine technology; other workers may speak loosely of *social systems*), and may do much more damage than good. Cluttering the literature is one thing; influencing decision-making because of prestige of past professional accomplishments, because of force of personality or organization, or because, in a vacuum permitted by an effete behavioral and social science, nothing else is available, is quite another thing.

The Forrester systems dynamics approach, discussed in Chapter 1, is one of the best today, by virtue of the scope of and experience with its methodology. Nevertheless, it, too, suffers from being based upon a limited two-dimensional approach. Not only does the closed system preclude real dynamic interaction with the environment, but the ahistorical approach, with no statement as to how the levels got that way, precludes any real comprehension of systems dynamics and behavior, other than at superficial levels and perhaps in incorrect terms. As Forrester points out, the real role of social science is to offer explanation of the underlying forces, not just the collection and correlation of data.

Today, it is Forrester and his followers, not the traditional social scientists, who are exciting the imagination of decision-makers throughout the world. There is the possibility that this may result in the legitimization of a crudely mechanistic view of man in systems. In this context you should review several models of man, such as the phenomenological and behaviorist summarized by Hitt (1969), and the robot of von Bertalanffy (1967).

The implied models of lay workers in social science could become "cast in concrete" and a self-fulfilling destiny, by virtue of their common acceptance by decision-makers and implementers of policy. Once again we see that an apparent means of salvation may represent an even greater threat.

Let's now take a look at several studies which, extending the basic theoretical ideas mentioned above, give promise for understanding the basic societal motiva-tion dynamics of our time. We shall include theories and models of revolution.

Davies (1962), synthesizing ideas from de Tocqueville, Marx, Plato, and Aristotle, theorizes that revolutions are most likely when a prolonged era of economic and social improvement is followed by a short period of sharp reversal in which people are apprehensive that progress made at great effort is likely to be lost.

Thus, quite insightfully, de Tocqueville remarked in *L'Ancien Régime,* in 1856:

> Revolutions are not always brought about by a gradual decline from bad to worse. Nations that have endured patiently and almost unconsciously the most overwhelming oppression often burst into rebellion against the yoke the moment it begins to grow lighter. The regime which is destroyed by a revo-lution is almost always an improvement on its immediate prede-cessor. . . . Evils which are patiently endured when they seem inevitable become intolerable when once the idea of escape from them is suggested (p. 214 of the John Bonner translation).

And, antithetically, Marx emphasized that progressive degradation of the proletariat would ultimately reach a point of despair and therefore revolt. Likewise, Plato and Aristotle emphasized the role of poverty.

Davies stresses that during an era of economic and social progress, people came to *expect* a continued ability to satisfy needs which continue to rise. During a short period of reversal, anxiety and frustration emerge when the anticipated world diverges from the real world. *The absolute state of socio-economic development is not nearly so important as the expectation that past progress can and must continue into the future.* It is the feeling of dissatisfaction and frustration that is important in determining revolution, not the absolute values of food supply, material goods, equality, or liberty. These ideas are expressed in Figure 2-14.

We see here important behavioral concepts associated with level of aspira-tion. The hierarchy of needs can similarly be considered. Thus, people in extremely harsh environments of near-starvation, concentration camps, etc. endure evils, deprivations, and injustices, because their energies are totally employed just to stay alive. Prolonged poverty *per se* is not likely to produce revolutionaries. Rather, it enhances concern for the self or for the immediate family, usually associated with resignation and mute despair. It is only when complete preoccupation with mere survival is no longer necessary that revolution becomes possible. Revolutionary thinking involves the dynamic expectation of greater opportunity to satisfy needs, coupled with a threat to need-satisfaction.

Davies meaningfully interprets a number of past revolutions, including the American, French, and Russian, within this framework. In each case real economic and social gains contrasted with indecisiveness and attempts at reaction and repression. It should further be noted, in a total systems sense, that

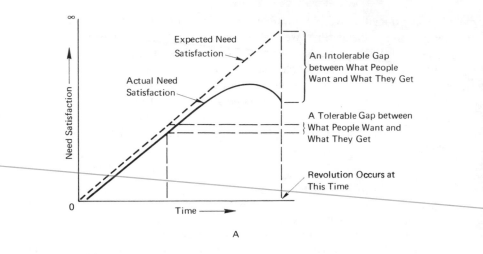

FIGURE 2-14(a)
Factors causing revolutions.[13]

factors outside the control of government, such as poor weather for agriculture and the actions of foreign powers, also entered the picture.

Davies feels it is utterly improbable for a revolution to occur either in a society offering continuing and unimpeded opportunity to satisfy new needs and new expectations, or, contrariwise, in a (static) society offering no hope and no period of rising expectations.

In modern dynamic societies, outside of the use of repressive force, there may be no way to avoid revolution, apart from a continuous and effective response by established governments to the continuously emerging needs of the governed. In this sense, it is beneficial to review events relative to a revolution that did not occur, namely, the Great Depression in the United States. Although many of the formative elements of revolution were present, such as a reversion of many economic indicators to the levels of two decades previous, widespread alienation among the different segments of society was absent, no clear scapegoat was available, and government action was positive.

Davies believes we are not at the point of being able to predict revolution. However, various data, especially longitudinal data, could be better used to sample the tensions, gratifications, and frustrations of society. These could involve not only systematic public opinion analysis, but also data such as incidents of suicide, inept use of force and other restrictive measures, and financial failures of government. We shall return to this concept of paramount importance in Chapter 9.

---

[13]From J.C. Davies, "Toward a Theory of Revolution," *American Sociological Review*, February, 1962, p. 6.

Tanter and Midlarsky (1967) extend the theory of Davies. Several classifications of revolutions are considered, and a number of recent successful and nonsuccessful revolutions are evaluated. Cultural or regional differences, for example between Asian and Latin American revolutions, are noted.

Most of the revolutions considered in this study involve the "underdeveloped nations," and, hence, are probably of limited value in our study of sociotechnical systems. However, further evidence is provided that, in the cases of the 17th-century-English, American, French, and Russian revolutions, all were preceded by general economic improvement.

Tanter and Midlarsky refine several definitions of general importance.

1. *Achievement* and *aspiration* are defined by the rate of change of GNP/CAP (gross national product divided by population) over time.

2. *Expectations* are defined by the drop or reversal of the rate of change of GNP/CAP.

Achievement represents a composite of economic, political, and cultural developments. Expectations are held to be more closely related to an immediate decrease in the production of goods and services, whereas aspirations are more long-range things generated by long term past experience. Aspirations result from the visibility of achievements; the rates of change of the two are positively correlated. *Revolutionary gap,* the disparity between expectation and aspiration, is suggested as a measure of the potentiality for the occurrence of a violent revolution. See Figure 2-14b.

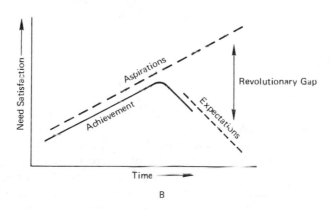

B

FIGURE 2-14(b)
Measuring probable occurrences of revolutions.[14]

[14]This excerpt from "A Theory of Revolution," by Raymond Tanter and Manus Midlarsky is reprinted from *Journal of Conflict Resolution,* Volume II, Number 3 (September 1967), pp. 264-80, by permission of the Publisher, Sage Publications, Inc. Figure was originally based on J.C. Davies, "Toward a Theory of Revolution," 1962.

Stagner (1970), in a similar vein, looks at the problem of satisfactions in the city. (In this context, see also the work of Krendel and of Savas discussed in Chapter 8). Satisfactions, of course, are just part of a sequence involving aspirations which are, in turn, dependent on a person's perceptions of himself, his progress, and his relationship to others. Probably frustration of needs for security, status, recognition, and self-expression contribute much to present-day urban violence. Stagner urges the collection of satisfaction, economic, and other data, perhaps by census tract or smaller area, and testing hypotheses relative to the effects of urban planning and design upon the sequence of above events.

Stagner proposes developing social indicators based on the *psychological* outputs (including also anxieties as well as the above) of the urban system, that is, based on the individual human element of the system. This is because economic statistics are aggregate and often misleading. For example, Keynesian economics led to the view that unemployment could be eliminated by a major increase in aggregate demand. Yet massive increases in demand have led to overtime and moonlighting by skilled workers, but hard-core unemployment has remained. There has been a rising output of automobiles, but no increase in the number of people employed by this industry.

An important principle of behavior is that human motives are essentially nonsatiating. When fundamental needs are gratified, new motives, higher on the hierarchical level, take over to influence behavior. As needs for housing, transportation, and jobs are met, people will turn to demands for higher status, prestige, and self-expression. If these latter needs are frustrated, aggressive behavior of one sort or another is likely to result. These factors at least partially underlie the counterintuitive behavior stressed by Forrester and discussed elsewhere in this book.

Prior achievement, expectation, and aspiration, as we have seen, play major roles in satisfaction and aggression. *Rising* expectations and aspirations are especially critical features. Further examples of this are provided from rural aggression during the Great Depression, and more recent urban black rioting.

We have seen that satisfaction is a function of relative rather than of absolute deprivation. For example, wealthy families depicted on television, or the managerial elite may be the people poor urban blacks use as reference standards.

The social indicators Stagner suggests could be expressed in terms of input-output tables in which outputs of the urban process would include levels of satisfaction or dissatisfaction, comfort or anxiety, security or insecurity, and so on. Psychological inputs would supplement engineering, ecological, demographic, economic, and other inputs.

The Lewinian term, "level of aspiration," defined earlier in this section, has been widely and differently used in psychology, in decision theory, and in economics. In the last two, concepts of risk, certainty, and uncertainty stem largely from the utility model of von Neumann and Morgenstern (1944).

Level of aspiration can, for example, be thought of as maximum expected utility, minimum acceptable outcome, a target or standard, or a liminal achievement dividing the satisfactory from the unsatisfactory and rejecting one *best* solution (Simon's *satisficing*) A binary (success or failure) outcome or a dynamic balance between success and failure or a continuity of outcomes may be variously stressed. Likewise, Cyert and March (1963) view aspiration level as equal to the weighted sum of one's most recent aspiration level, one's most recent experience, and an index of the most recent performance of a reference group of other people. Similarly, the achievement motivation and related motive to avoid failure of McClelland and Atkinson and their co-workers (e.g., McClelland, *et al.*, 1953; Atkinson and Reitman, 1956; and Atkinson, 1957) can be thought of as the product of motive strength, the subjective likelihood of success or failure, and the incentive value of success or failure; there may thus be three different aspiration levels.

Obviously, then, aspiration level is a function not only of one's own success or failure, but also of one's society and culture. Thus, upward drive appears to be ubiquitous in Western European and derivative cultures. This is consistent with the social comparison model of Leon Festinger (1954). However, little is known about changes in reference groups, a feature of paramount importance in today's world.

McWhinney (1965) has attempted to synthesize these many incompatible viewpoints into an eclectic theory. McWhinney's eclectic theory, in the simplest form summarized as Figure 2-15, stresses that all the disparate viewpoints of aspiration level may be correct at one time or another in a person's life. This theory proposes to examine the decision-making environment of goals and prior success and failure and, thus, the referents against which the satisfactoriness of alternatives is tested. It improved over the simple maximum expected-utility model which does not account for how success or failure modify the motivation to succeed and, therefore, the subjective evaluation of the likelihood of success. However, even here, the concept is recognized as sterile compared with the richness of real human motivation. Further theory must explain how aspirations can remain insatiable while satisfaction can be achieved for a particular line of activity. The Maslow hierarchy should be synthesized into the theory here.

Vertinsky (1969), in a similar vein, has looked at mathematial models of political behavior. Two definitions of aspiration-level models are offered: (1) aspiration level as a target outcome; i.e., the decision-maker in an uncertain situation acts in terms of the outcome he prescribes as a target; and (2) aspiration level as a function reconciling the needs to achieve and to avoid failure; i.e., one outcome is desirable and one not.

Both approaches suffer from an inability to define operationally the "target" or "outcomes." Vertinsky believes the two approaches can be reconciled. Thus, the decision-maker can be considered achievement-motivated relevant to some

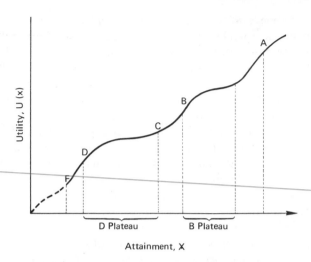

FIGURE 2-15
Aspiration level, a generalized utility function for a society.[16]

regions of the total resources scale, and inclined to avoid failure in other regions. Failure is considered to be a sacrifice of resources beyond a prescribed level. Decision-making is a choice between activities, given a particular level of resources. The resource scale of the decision-maker includes regions where he is a risk-taker (the need to achieve is dominant) and regions where risk-aversion (the need to avoid failure) is dominant. Outcomes that separate these regions are the "prominent" outcomes, in terms of decision-making under uncertainty. The outcome that separates a risk-taking region from a risk-averting region can be considered the "target."

Vertinsky defines a von Neumann-Morgenstern utility function over resources (income) for each individual. Convex-upward segments of the curve represent qualitatively different socioeconomic levels; concave-upward regions represent transitions between such levels. The individual's level of aspiration will be the level of income corresponding to the inflection point of the utility function changing from a concave to a convex zone. The individual whose position is within a concave interval is frustrated and searches for a different position; in doing so, he will accept risky alternatives (he is achievement motivated). Contrariwise, the individual in the convex region of his utility function is satisfied (he is failure-avoidance motivated). The stereotyped model may apply particularly to behavior in highly institutionalized cultures. Examples are given from rioting and fiscal policy-making in a dictatorship.

[15]From W. H. McWhinney, "Aspiration Levels and Utility Theory," *General Systems*, 10, 1965.

In Introducing this section, we referred to the diffuseness of motivational theory and to the importance of measuring motivational forces in complex systems. Not all features of motivation can be so conveniently conceptualized in quantitative or semi-quantitative terms as aspiration level expressed as a utility function can. For example, how should the Maslow hierarchy be further quantified? We are attempting to do this using scaling techniques. We have broken each of the five main levels down into five to ten sublevels which can be expressed in terms of actual gratifications or probabilities of gratification. Gratifications are measured in terms of possession of a car, housing, etc. General gratifications at one level are followed by "stepping" to the next level. The importance of substitute gratifications and of symbolism (what does possession of a car really mean?) is recognized.

Finally, one of the most nebulous concepts in the area of motivation is that of alienation. Yet even here progress is being made. For example, Seeman (1971) has defined alienation in terms of six distinct but interrelated categories: (1) individual powerlessness over his own life; (2) meaningless of one's life; (3) normlessness, cynicism, or *anomie* to the established methods of society; (4) cultural estrangement; (5) self-estrangement, especially as a consequence of performing unfulfilling work; and (6) social isolation or loneliness. Seeman has attempted to measure the first form of alienation using a forced-choice scale reflecting the individual's expectations of personal or external control.

FURTHER EXTENSIONS OF THE BASIC FORCES

We have now examined in considerable detail the basic forces of population, technology, and motivation and their interactions with the physical-biological and social environments. There are, of course, many quite critical extensions of these basic forces to which, in the interests of some brevity, we can pay only lip service. Nevertheless, advancement of sociotechnical theory must include the pushes and pulls, conflicts, and other dynamic patterns included below. Some of the points made below have been made earlier in broader contexts, but are summarized here for convenience.

Push-Pull Forces and Migration

The migration of rural and small-town folk all over the world to the cities presents a serious problem contributing to urban decay, national imbalances, the disappearance of small-scale agriculture, and so forth. Although much has been written, say, relative to the adaptation problems of the migrants (cf. Brody, 1969), little is still known as to the basic perceptional, motivational, and decisional processes involved. At the level of systems analysis we shall return later to the urban dynamics simulations of Forrester and to matrix algebra analyses of migration patterns as they affect California population projections.

Obviously, understanding—and management—requires a consideration of the interplay among the (would-be) migrant, the attracting environment, and the environment to be left. Obviously, both positive and negative incentives at both origin and destination, as perceived through the eyes of the migrant, must be better understood than in such gross terms as "jobs," "welfare," or "civil rights." Cybernetic concepts will be of value here.

Study of patterns of migration, especially to the cities, must involve at least the following: (1) landlord and tenant laws; (2) estimates of numbers of people migrating; (3) analysis of public housing compared to other forms of housing; (4) international cooperation; (5) research into the infrastructure of health services, etc.; (6) possible job openings; (7) educational opportunities; (8) other perceived opportunities for self-improvement; and (9) geographical features, including climate.

Bunge (1971) provides a start at modeling human migration in the form of two deterministic and two simple stochastic models. Further specific attention to the contemporaneously very important topic of human migration is beyond the scope of the present discussion.

Societal Polarizations

Our time is one of increasing polarizations: of Haves and Have-Nots, of rich and poor, of educated and overeducated, of educated and uneducated, of races, of workers and the idle, of workers and managers, of conservationists and exploiters, of younger and older. These are reflections of changes in motivational level, in massive education, in instantaneous communications, and in population, technological, and economic growth. In a sense, then, these are secondary or tertiary manifestations of such primary forces as the forms of growth. Nevertheless, there are no simple causes and effects here, and being polarized as a Have-Not undoubtedly results in greater "demand" for technological output.

There have been polarized societies before. Today, however, the number and degree of change of polarizations is increasing.

Changes in Role and Status

Our changing society brings with it marked changes in role and status. Contrast the "idle rich" of past times with the working elite and disillusionment of the unemployed today. The past three decades have seen the scientist and technologist emerge from retiring, arcane roles to the forefront of society and become the objects of mistrust, suspicion, and derision. Power within organizations has shifted to the controllers of information.

Changes in, and contrasts of, relative status and perception thereof are particularly dangerous to self-concept and personality integrity.

Adaptation and Action-Recruition

Rapid sociotechnical change stresses everybody's capability to adapt. Many cannot or will not do so. This is manifested in opposition to the status quo, by foot dragging, by vandalism and other destruction, by alienation and withdrawal, and by insurrection and revolution.

Changing "Demand" for Products and Services

The concept of "demand," much used in justifications for more electric power, more freeways, more housing, more oil wells, etc., comes from the so-called "law of supply and demand." Demand refers to the quantities of a commodity a consumer will buy at various prices, which are in turn a function of scarcity or availability. Usually, one-to-one relationships between stimuli (say, prices) and responses (demands) are implied; however, demand can be increased by the entry of advertising into the loop, influencing the decision-maker's (buyer's) perceptions. This is, of course, only part of the story. For example, Keynesian economic theory holds that unemployment can be reduced through increasing aggregate demand.

Economic theory tends to be incomplete, and systems-wise economics has not always melded well with other behavioral and social sciences (see, for example, Katona, 1963, and Simon, 1963). In Chapter 1 we referred to limitations to the concept of the rational man. However, for our purposes here, we must stress the increasingly glaring inadequacy of economic theory in assuming almost unlimited sources and sinks. Thus, jobs can be created, industry cranked up, productivity increased, demand increased, GNP increased—all in the name of growth—with no thought to the externalities, the noxious side effects on the environment, and on the structure of society itself. It is quite evident that we must take a hard, critical look at economic theory, and that we must develop a better systems blend of economic, behavioral, social, and ecological theory. Hard as it may be, separating *need* from the artificial demand should be a first step of high priority.

Fortunately, in conjunction with the above-discussed rising level of expectations and changes in the standard of living, we are witnessing changes in management and in the manner of doing business. Among other things, there is some evidence of a breaking effect on the "demand" for products and services. This is associated with the creditable efforts of consumer-protection advocates and conservationists, a lesser allure of Madison Avenue advertising, and increased public disillusionment with shoddy goods with built-in obsolescence. Unfortunately, this skepticism is shown most by persons high on the hierarchy of Maslovian needs. Those in and ascending from the lower levels probably think in entirely different terms, presenting a fundamental and critical societal problem to which we shall return in Chapter 9.

Stress

One of the most pervasive yet nebulous forces acting on individuals, organizations, societies, species, and ecosystems is stress. Stress almost always is both multiple and has cumulative effects, yet we know very little about these effects. Even identification of a stressing agent may be difficult. Our system designs, however, must account for stress and to a considerable extent reduce or eliminate it. For example, a total design of home, work, and commute time-space could markedly reduce the undesirable effects of disturbed biorhythms and of epidemics. There is much to be gained from integrating from many disciplines our knowledge of stress, for instance, the effects of crowding, the effects of climate and weather, and the human-engineered design of environments.

Social organizations, like individuals, can be stressed. If structure is fluid, resilient, or adaptive, the organization may survive. If rigid or constrained it will eventually fail. Providing understanding of the basic stressful forces so as to manage the adaptive capabilities of organizations is perhaps the single greatest challenge presented by this book and to our world. In the absence of understanding, organizations and societies will respond with regression, repression, or other maladaptive behavior.

Political Behavior

The political subsystem cannot be thought of as existing outside of—or above!—the local, urban, national, or world sociotechnical system. It is very much a part of it and must be regarded as one of the major forces to be studied, analyzed, redesigned, and managed.

Several areas emerge as of preeminent importance:

1. The force of vested interests as represented by the interlocking web of large corporations (e.g., oil, automobiles, construction, and land use), advertising and propaganda, and professional lobby groups, and associated policy-makers, decision-makers, and jurists.

2. The means by which politics reflects the tune of the times. This includes how legislation gets enacted, and the all-important question as to how much cultural and temporal lag there is between the world and its governors.

3. The existence of genuine conflicts of interest. Conflict prevention and reduction have received much more study than conflict resolution. Some salient examples today involve as opponents conservationists versus other users of outdoor resources, and advocates of mass transit versus those who urge the continued and expanded use of the private automobile.

SUMMARY AND CONCLUSIONS

The body of sociotechnical structure and theory from Chapter 1 has been extended to include the major dynamic forces of our times. Thus, although our systems can be viewed cross-sectionally and hierarchically, it is also of advantage to view them longitudinally, to examine historical trends. The most critical forces are those of population, automation and technological change, and motivation. These interact with one another and with the physical-biological and social environments with ominous results.

Where we stand today is unique in terms of the magnitude of interacting forces. However, with the remarkable changes in speeds, quantities, sizes, and newness, there have not been parallel changes in quality, personal satisfaction, or our methods of governance. This is a major challenge presented here.

REFERENCES

Atkinson, John W., 1957, Motivational Determinants of Risk-Taking Behavior, *Psychological Review*, 64(6), 359-72.

Atkinson, John W., and W. R. Reitman, 1956, Performance as a Function of Motive Strength and Expectancy of Goal Attainment, *Journal of Abnormal and Social Psychology*, 53, 361-66.

Austin, Arthur L., and John W. Brewer, 1970, World Population Growth and Related Technical Problems, *IEEE Spectrum*, 7(12), 43-54.

Bates, Frederick L., 1969, Impact of Automation on Organization of Society, in Ellis R. Scott and Roger W. Bolz (eds.), *Automation and Society*, 107-48. Athens, Ga.: The Center for the Study of Automation and Society.

Bertalanffy, Ludwig von, 1967, *Robots, Men, and Minds; Psychology in the Modern World.* New York: Braziller.

———, 1968, *General System Theory: Foundations, Development, Applications.* New York: Braziller.

Black, Ralph J., Anton J. Muhich, Albert J. Klee, H. Lanier Hickman, Jr., and Richard D. Vaughn, 1968, *The National Solid Wastes Survey—An Interim Report,* presented at the 1968 Annual Meeting of the Institute for Solid Wastes of the American Public Works Association, Miami Beach, Florida, Oct. 24. Washington, D. C.: U. S. Department of Health, Education, and Welfare, Environmental Control Administration.

Boffey, Philip M., 1970, Japan: A Crowded Nation Wants to Boost Its Birthrate, *Science,* 167(3920), 960-62, 13 February.

Boguslaw, Robert, 1965, *The New Utopians: A Study of System Design and Social Change.* Englewood Cliffs, N.J.: Prentice-Hall.

Broady, Maurice, 1969, The Social Context of Urban Planning, *Urban Affairs Quarterly,* 4(3), 355-78, March.

Brody, Eugene R., (ed.), 1969, Migration and Adaptation, *American Behavioral Scientist,* 13(1), entire issue, September-October.

Bumpass, Larry, and Charles F. Westoff, 1970, The "Perfect Contraceptive" Population, *Science,* 169(3951), 1177-82, 18 September.

Bunge, Mario, 1971, Four Models of Human Migration: An Exercise in Mathematical Sociology, *General Systems,* 16, 87-92.

Bureau of the Census, 1967, *Population Estimates,* Series P-25, Table B-2, September. Washington, D.C.: U.S. Department of Commerce.

Calhoun, John B., 1963, *The Ecology and Sociology of the Norway Rat,* U.S. Department of Health, Education, and Welfare, Public Health Service Publication No. 1008. Washington, D.C.: U.S. Government Printing Office.

———, 1968, *Space and the Strategy of Life,* unpublished paper given at the 135th Annual Meeting of the American Association for the Advancement of Science. Bethesda, Maryland: National Institute of Mental Health, Laboratory of Psychology.

Callendar, G. S., 1958, On the Amount of Carbon Dioxide in the Atmosphere, *Tellus,* 10, 243-48.

Carr-Saunders, A. M., 1936, *World Population.* New York: Barnes & Noble, Inc.

Cherry, Colin, 1971, *World Communication: Threat or Promise? A Socio-Technical Approach.* New York: Wiley.

Christian, John J., 1970, Social Subordination, Population Density, and Mamalian Evolution, *Science,* 168(3927), 84-90, 3 April.

Churchman, C. West, 1968, *The Systems Approach.* New York: Dell.

Civil Defense Research Project—Annual Progress Report, 1968, *New Utility Concepts for New Cities.* ORNL-4284, Part I, pp. 109-23, November.

Coale, Ansley, J., 1970, Man and His Environment, *Science,* 170 (3954), 132-36.

Commission on Population Growth and the American Future, 1972, *Population and the American Future.* Final Report. Washington, D.C.: U.S. Government Printing Office.

Cyert, R. M., and J. G. March, 1963, *A Behavioral Theory of the Firm.* Englewood Cliffs, N.J.: Prentice-Hall.

Davies, James C., 1962, Toward A Theory of Revolution, *American Sociological Review,* 27(1), 5-19, February.

Division of Mines, 1969, *Commodity Statements.* Washington, D.C.: U.S. Department of the Interior, Division of Mines (unpublished data), January.

Durand, J. D., 1968, The Modern Expansion of World Population. In C. B. Nam (ed.), *Population and Society.* Boston: Hougton Mifflin.

Ehrlich, Paul R., and John P. Holdren, 1971, Impact of Population Growth, *Science,* 171(3977), 1212-17, 26 March.

Emery, F. E., and Julius Marek, 1962, Some Socio-Technical Aspects of Automation, *Human Relations*, 15(1), 17-25, February.

Festinger, Leon, 1954, A Theory of Social Comparison Processes, *Human Relations*, 7, 117-40.

Foerster, Heinz von, Patricia M. Mora, and Lawrence W. Amiot, 1960, Doomsday: Friday, 13 November, A.D. 2026, *Science*, 132(3436), 4 November.

Frejka, Tomas, 1968, Reflections on the Demographic Conditions Needed to Establish a U.S. Stationary Population Growth, *Population Studies*, 22(3), 379-97, November.

Gough, William C., 1970, *Why Fusion? Controlled Thermonuclear Research Program*, WASH 1165, UC-20. Washington, D.C.: U.S. Government Printing Office, June.

Gross, Bertram M., 1967, The Coming General Systems Models of Social Systems, *Human Relations*, 20(4), 357-74, November.

Hall, Edward T., 1968, Proxemics, *Current Anthropology*, 9(2-3), 83-108, April-June.

Harrison, Annette, 1971, *Bibliography on Automation and Technological Change and Studies of the Future*, P-3365-4. Santa Monica, California: The RAND Corporation, March.

Heller, Alfred (ed.), 1972, *The California Tomorrow Plan*, revised edition. San Francisco: California Tomorrow.

Hitt, W. D., 1969, Two Models of Man, *American Psychologist*, 24(7), 651-58.

Holden, Constance, 1971, Fish Flour: Protein Supplement Has Yet to Fulfill Its Expectations, *Science*, 173(3995), 410-12, 30 July.

Kahn, Herman, 1970, *The Emerging Japanese Superstate: Challenge and Response*. Englewood Cliffs, N.J.: Prentice-Hall.

Katona, George, 1963, The Relationship Between Psychology and Economics. In Sigmund Koch (ed.), *Psychology: A Study of a Science, Vol. 6, Investigations of Man as Socius: Their Place in Psychology and the Social Sciences*, 639-76. New York: McGraw-Hill.

Koestler, Arthur, 1956, *Reflections on Hanging*. London: Victor Gollancz.

Livi Bacci, Massimo, 1971, *A Century of Portuguese Fertility*, Princeton, N.J.: Princeton University Press.

McClelland, David C., D. C. Atkinson, R. A. Clark, and E. L. Lowell, 1953, *The Achievement Motive*. New York: Appleton-Century-Crofts.

McHale, J., 1969, *The Future of the Future*. New York: Braziller.

McWhinney, W. H., 1965, Aspiration Levels and Utility Theory, *General Systems*, 10, 131-43.

Martin, James and Adrian R. D. Norman, 1970, *The Computerized Society*, Englewood Cliffs, N.J.: Prentice-Hall.

Martino, Joseph P., 1969, Science and Society in Equilibrium, *Science*, 165(3985), 769-72, 22 August.

Meadows, Donella, Dennis L. Meadows, Jorgen Randers, and William W. Behrens, III, 1972, *The Limits to Growth*. New York: Universe Books.

Michael, Donald N., 1966, Some Long-Range Implications of Computer Technology for Human Behavior in Organizations, *The American Behavioral Scientist*, 9(8), 29-35, April.

Mills, H. B., 1959, Presidential Address: The Importance of Being Nourished, *Transactions of the Illinois State Academy of Science*, 52 (1 and 2) 3-12.

National Academy of Sciences—National Research Council, 1969, *Resources and Man, A Study and Recommendations by the Committee on Resources and Man.* San Francisco: W. H. Freeman.

National Commission on Technology, Automation, and Economic Progress, 1966, *Technology and the American Economy*, report and six appendix volumes, Washington, D.C.: U. S. Government Printing Office, February.

Neumann, John von and O. Morgenstern, 1944, *Theory of Games and Economic Behavior*, 1st ed. Princeton, N.J.: Princeton University Press.

Parry, Robert T., 1971, *A Report on the Aerospace Industry of California.* Los Angeles: Security Pacific National Bank.

Pearl, R., and L. J. Reed, 1924, The Growth of Human Population. In R. Pearl (ed.), *Studies in Human Biology.* Baltimore: Williams and Wilkins.

Political and Economic Planning Agency, 1955, *World Population and Resources, a Report.* London: Allen and Unwin.

Scheuch, Erwin K., 1968, Some Methodological and Statistical Problems of Medical Research in Teratology, *General Systems* 13, 129-45.

Schmitt, Robert C., 1966, Density, Health, and Social Disorganization, *Journal of the American Institute of Planners*, 32(1), 38-40.

Scott, Ellis L. and Roger W. Bolz (eds.), 1969, *Automation and Society.* Athens, Ga.: The Center for the Study of Automation and Society.

——, (eds.), 1970, *Automation Management: The Social Perspective.* Athens, Ga.: The Center for the Study of Automation and Society.

Seeman, Melvin, 1971, Alienation: A Map, *Psychology Today*, 5(3), 82-84 and 94-95, August.

Shaw, M., 1969, *Environmental Effects of Producing Electric Power*, Hearings before the Joint Committee on Atomic Energy, 91st U.S. Congress, October, November, 1969, Part 1. Washington, D.C.: U.S. Government Printing Office.

Shef, A. L., 1968, *Socio-Economic Attributes of Our Technological Society*, unpublished paper presented at IEEE Wescon Conference, Los Angeles, August.

Simon, Herbert A., 1963, Economics and Psychology. In Sigmund Koch (ed.), *Psychology: A Study of Science, Vol. 6, Investigations of Man as Socius: Their Place in Psychology and the Social Sciences*, 685-723. New York: McGraw-Hill.

Singer, S. Fred, 1970, Reducing the Environmental Impact of Population, *Science*, 169(3951), 1233, September 18.

Sommer, Robert, 1969, *Personal Space: The Behavioral Basis of Design.* Englewood Cliffs, N.J.: Prentice-Hall.

Spengler, Joseph J., 1964, *Population: The Vital Revolution,* in R. Freedman (ed.), p. 67. New York: Doubleday.

Stagner, Ross, 1970, Perceptions, Aspirations, Frustrations, and Satisfactions: An Approach to Urban Indicators, *The Annals of the American Academy of Political and Social Science,* 388, 59-68, March.

Starr, Chauncey, 1969, Social Benefit versus Technological Risk, *Science,* 165(3899), 1232-38, September 19.

Statistical Office of the United Nations, 1966, *Demographic Yearbook, 1949-50.* New York: United Nations.

Statistical Office of the United Nations, 1967, *Statistical Data Book,* New York.

Statistical Office of the United Nations, *World Energy Supplies 1965-1968,* Statistical Papers, Series J, No. 11, New York.

Tanter, Raymond, and Manus Midlarsky, 1967, A Theory of Revolution, *The Journal of Conflict Resolution,* 11(3), 264-80.

Terman, C. R., 1971, *Population Control, Behavior, and Reproductive Inhibition,* summary of unpublished research. Williamsburg, Va.: College of William and Mary, School of Arts.

Tocqueville, Alexis de, 1856, *The Old Regime and the French Revolution,* trans. John Bonner. New York: Harper & Bros.

Vertinsky, Ilan, 1969, The Use of Aspiration Level Behavior Models in Political Science, *American Behavioral Scientist,* 12(5), NS-9 to NS-12, May-June.

Watt, Kenneth E. F., 1968, *Ecology and Resource Management.* New York: McGraw-Hill.

Weast, Robert C. (ed.), 1969-1970, *Handbook of Chemistry and Physics,* 50th ed. Cleveland, Ohio: The Chemical Rubber Co.

Weizenbaum, Joseph M., 1972, On the Impact of the Computer on Society, *Science,* 176 (4035), 609-14, 12 May.

Wolfle, Dael, and Charles V. Kidd, 1971, The Future Market for Ph.D.'s, *Science,* 173(3999), 784-93, 27 August.

Wolman, M. Gordon, 1971, The Nation's Rivers, *Science,* 174(4012), 905-18, 26 November.

3

Problems of Management
of Sociotechnical Systems

The problems of management of sociotechnical systems can be expected to become more severe, paralleling the explosive changes in the environment and in the times in general, paralleling the vastly increased complexity of the systems themselves, and associated with our ongoing lack of comprehensive understanding of what "good" management is really about. Before examining each of these points in more detail, let's see what they result in, *in toto:*

1. We still lack the techniques to synthesize a major system. Judgments are made by managers, usually on a very intuitive basis, with minimum influence by systems scientists.
2. There is a lack of appreciation of the disparities in knowledge, time, etc. between analysts and planners on the one hand and politicians and consumers on the other. All groups lack understanding of the basic societal forces which must be comprehended in order to be managed.
3. The system itself is rapidly changing and we are paying for past mistakes, yet we lack an early-warning system to alert us of danger signs being ignored now.
4. We need a better conceptualization, expressed as curves, of the differential rate of change of awareness, public opinion, values, managerial and government response, etc.
5. The problems with which we must deal are getting tougher and the funds allocated to their solution more limited. This has a profound meaning for R & D management. The numbers and depths of findings will be limited, and the determination of what is good work and what mediocre

perhaps much more difficult. Research is, after all, always a risky thing. For example, in an evaluation of the effects of operations research studies, we have estimated that 4 to 10% of studies have an immediate effect, 30 to 40% have a possible belated effect, and the remainder have no effect at all.

6. When we look at our present efforts we see vast expenditures of money yielding minuscule returns or even a worsening situation. This is particularly well exemplified in the case of welfare.

7. Criticisms of the social picture are common, but solutions, most usually from the extreme right or radical left, tend to be simplistic and naive.

8. Management will require much more problem-recognition as opposed to problem-solving and decision-making. This is illustrated by Curry's (1970, referenced in Chapter 9) classification of types of problems, and Livingston's (1971) look at successful and unsuccessful managers, and Libby's (1971) compilation of problems.

9. Societal decisions, in spite of industrial propaganda, seldom boil down to polemics such as "jobs versus pollution," "homes versus redwoods," etc. Behind each of these arguments lurk the spectres of oversimplification, obfuscation, and mismanagement. With an increasingly enlightened public, management will have to become more direct and more truthful (including with itself). And that's what this book is all about.

10. Industry has exploited both workers and the people, at least in the perceptions of an increasing number of people. Resistance is seen especially on the part of youth, who concretize an older generation's philosophies and theories and idealistically question gaps between what ought to be and what is. The behavior of youth and of disenfranchised groups should always be viewed by management as an early-warning sign of things to come, of emerging new patterns. This anticipatory behavior is a matter of acuteness of perception *and* selective perception, as well as biological brazenness.

The management of sociotechnical systems, to be successful, is dependent upon the proper recognition of the total system. This means including the "decision-making" political elements and factors as well. The histories of operations research, systems analysis, and human factors are strewn with failures, because of inability to recognize subtle psychological, political, and operational factors. In this latter sense we are talking about not recognizing the political environment in which the technical system is enmeshed. In the former total systems case, the political elements are considered part of the system at a higher hierarchical level; they themselves must be analyzed, modeled, and simulated. In this way, the "real" problems confronting the system should become better manifest. These may involve value changes, reconciling conflicting values or conflicting values and behavior, changes in aspiration level, requirements for education, etc.

In the management of sociotechnical systems of the seventies and future decades, major shifts of emphasis will occur. Management solely within the framework of production and of profits will no longer suffice. Considerations must now be made of deleterious side effects upon the environment, over-exploitation of scarce resources, recycling and closed-cycle processes, employee-need satisfaction, contributions to the betterment of the "underdeveloped" world, and so forth. Accordingly, the goals of organizations must change, and new types of managers encouraged and trained, managers less driven by personal power and greed, however subtly rationalized and expressed.

The management of sociotechnical systems implies their mismanagement. We have said that the decision process in society, and perhaps decision-making in general, are faulty. Is there, then, not something fundamentally wrong with automatizing this faulty process? Accordingly, placing models and simulations and hardware systems in the hands of the biased or corrupt is paving the way for immeasurable damage. Indeed, it may be blessing, or imparting a false dignity to, something awfully corrupt. The impact and other misuse of the systems approach, then, require much more attention. For example, a model for managing the deer herd of Mendocino County, California (Anderson, *et al.,* 1971), contained only the capability of varying the number of deer killed by hunters; natural predation, for example, was totally ignored. In this case the model could become an instrument of a vested-interest pressure group, strengthening the influence of that group with a cloak of phony scientism, and helping reduce the consideration of alternate policies. After all, didn't the model *prove* that large-scale hunting was good for the deer, good for livestock and rangeland, good for the forests, and delightfully good for people—especially the hunters? A model for redwood cutting (Bosch, 1971) has the same weaknesses.

Further, there is danger of using systems methods to justify or rationalize executive decisions already made. McNamara may thus have misused systems analysis in the Department of Defense. This may have led to a disturbance of governmental balance of power, stimulating reprisal.

The problems of management cannot be disassociated from the problems of the individual manager. Management, in spite of decades of education and training in techniques, tends to be a personal thing. It can be thought of in terms of three levels. Level 1 is summarized in Figure 3-1, to which we shall return below. Level 2 involves the familiar "functions" of management: planning, organizing, staffing, coordinating, controlling, evaluating, and so forth. These have the disadvantage of being quite superficial and difficult to relate to under-lying human capabilities and limitations. Level 3 involves the functions and task analysis approach of human factors, and the utilization of basic research in psychology and other sciences. It attempts to identify tasks and psychological, physiological, machine, and environmental variables. Much more research needs to be performed in such areas as decision-making, and problem-recognition, -conceptualization, -formulation, and so on.

Figure 3-1 summarizes some of the main features of the management of sociotechnical systems. Note that the system is both open and closed-loop. Note

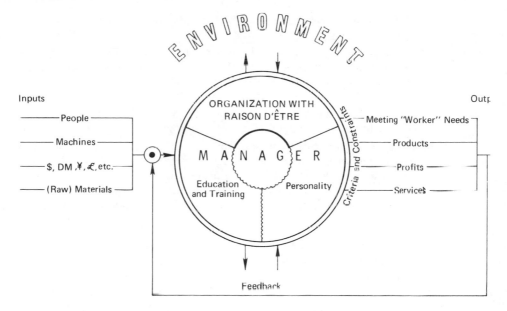

FIGURE 3-1
Basic management diagram.

that output far transcends mere productivity. Note especially that the boundaries between the organization and its goals and purposes for existence, and between the manager as a being and the manager's formal education and training are tenuous and diffuse. Probably one major criterion for "effective" management should always involve the degree to which the manager identifies with and merges into the organization. This is of utmost importance to remember, because many of the problems of the world today are directly associated with management, managers, and their deficiencies. A major goal must be to encourage managers to change their own goals, perceptions, values, and needs, or to find new types of managers more in harmony with changing times.

Finally, in extending our management concepts to the type of situations of interest in this book, it should be noted that years of experience with the management of aerospace systems have taught us:

1. Only 5 to 10% of people can see and pursue a total project. Thus, a team effort is required, but putting together a team representing the correct disciplines and blends of backgrounds and personalities is seldom easy.

2. The evaluation of the usefulness of systems science has been tied to advocacy and helping the customer to devastate his enemy. Accordingly, science itself may not have been so important as sales and keeping the customer happy.

3. There are almost always constraints of budget, time, and contracts.

4. The client or user typically does not really know what his problem is. Therefore, the systems scientist can be of particular help here. Yet we must stress that it is important to produce something with realworld relevance, not something that sells to a journal.

5. The client typically does not know how to use the results of systems science. Therefore, the systems analysis, for example, must be tied to benefits to the user who wants payoff within a year or two.

6. There has been a shift to more in-house work, because outside consultants tend to redefine problems so as to obtain extended work. Contrariwise, many problems internal to an organization are too close to be perceived objectively and require the participation of outside consultants.

7. Change threatens, so many organizations resist the application of systems science.

These experiences may or may not be of direct applicability "from here on out." Nevertheless, they may help preclude our reinventing the wheel.

In this chapter we shall be concerned particularly with use and misuse of natural and human resources, policy and decision processes, establishing long-range goals and objectives, and managing the process of technology itself.

LAND, AIR, WATER, AND LIVING RESOURCES

One of the major shifts today is from a philosophy of unlimited resources, of resource exploitation, of disregard for environmental impact and consequences, and of uncontrolled production and consumption on the one hand to one of recognition of limited, even exhausted, resources, a fragile environment, a need for recycling, and redirected production and consumption on the other.

Limitations and Exhaustions of,
and Competitions for, Resources

The evidence for the limitation and potential exhaustion of resources comes from many sources. Predicted exhaustion of natural gas, petroleum, and uranium is discussed in Chapter 8. The year 1969 witnessed the first absolute decline in the catch of fisheries, in spite of marked improvements in technology. Large and medium-sized whales and mammals and reptiles whose skins are used by the fur and leather trades have been exploited to the brink of extinction. Prime agricultural land in many states is being rapidly lost because of urbanization. If the "underdeveloped" world attempted to exploit raw materials at the same rate as the technologically advanced countries, armed conflicts would most likely result. And so on.

There is the possibility of dangerous thinking here. We might refer to it as the "mañana" attitude, a failure or refusal to take steps now to prevent misuse of resources. The mañana attitude expresses itself in the belief that when one resource is exhausted we simply will have to shift to another. If agricultural land is lost in the lowlands of populous states, technology will find the means to bring water from distant rivers and will provide fertilizers and pesticides so that marginal lands can now be exploited.

We have pointed out above that many resources are finite. Other resources are limited because of the extreme cost of development. Large-scale desalinization of sea water and extraction of petroleum from oil shales are in this category. A third category of resources involves those that remain in some abundance, but the utilization of which involves greater and greater economic costs. These include petroleum in the Arctic, coal and minerals in the Antarctic, and metals on the deep-sea floor. In addition to the economic costs, there must be greater and greater environmental degradation, as marginal, peripheral, and distant lands are exploited. Management policy must reflect the total systems picture, including changing values of the public.

Demands for Goods and Services versus Resource Limitations

In Chapter 2, we mentioned some of the factors that conspire to create an artificial "demand." Galbraith (1958) has also emphasized that the modern affluent consumer is the victim of synthetic desires which are created rather than satisfied by increased production. In a world of subjective and qualitative variables, of uncertainty and impreciseness, and of many false quantitatives, a system tends to rest on very shaky grounds. There is the all-too-common tendency of both analysts and managers and other decision-makers to accept as givens those factors which most emphatically cannot be accepted as given. Economic demand is an especially odious term which, we have pointed out, requires differentiation from need. Both need and demand, however, are complex and must be considered in terms of advertising pressure, hierarchy of needs, age and education, efficient or wasteful use of resources, equipment and system design, symbolic meaning of gadgetry, and so forth. Need and demand are certainly not easy to quantify, except in superficial terms, and estimates based on present practices and projections of trends therefrom are decidedly misleading.

As an example, costs to the consumer strongly influence demand. Thus, the price of electricity makes it almost a free good, because costs only of production, and not also of mining, transportation, pollution, and so on, are considered. The costs of air and water (treated as free dumps) are not considered; yet these are not really free, as our consideration below of the costs of air pollution reveals. Hence, there must be a reevaluation of total costs, including these recently recognized and emphasized additional costs. The producers will have to pay the new costs and some of this price will be passed along to the consumer, resulting in a restructure of demand. And the freedom to choose the cheaper item, e.g., today's choice of cheaper but noisier jackhammers, must be amended. For both producer and consumer, we can expect changed legislation (see a later section of this chapter) amending the tax laws which favor the use of new metal over recycled scrap metal, resource depletion, and so on.

Degradation and Economic Losses: Pollution Examples

The annual cost of air pollution alone has been estimated at about $16 billion per annum, or $80 per person per annum, by the Council on Environmental Quality (MacDonald, 1971). This does not include unknown side effects of pollution. For example, the safe limit for sulfur oxides, insofar as health is concerned, is estimated at .04 p.p.m., yet this is frequently exceeded in today's cities. Similarly, 10 p.p.m. CO dulls mental facilities, yet 50 to 200 p.p.m. can be observed on the streets of Los Angeles, Chicago, and New York. Nor are the "undeveloped countries" free from air pollution. The world's worst offenders are Seoul, Ankara, Taipeh, Mexico City, and Santiago, Chile.

For the United States, the Council on Environmental Quality estimates the costs of clean-up to be, respectively, $25 billion for air pollution, $38 billion for water pollution, and $42 billion for solid wastes. This is about 10% of the GNP and not too much more than the typical yearly defense budget. The costs of clean-up would have effects transcending the direct expenditures. Some required adjustments in industry and loss of some jobs with shifts to different kinds of jobs can be expected.

Although almost everybody agrees that pollution is bad, there is still no consensus as to just how the polluter must pay. Opinions range from those stating the corporate profit and job-loss costs of pollution abatement are too high and any action must be postponed, to those who demand the elimination of pollution immediately. A central position looks to the enactment of legislation, enforcement of standards and restrictions, and control within a reasonable time. What seems "reasonable" of course has the habit of being stretched! Curing pollution is believed to be much harder than preventing it; hence, any future development must be preceded by sound environmental analysis and planning.

Lave and Seskin (1970) have provided a fine assessment of the relationship between air pollution and human health with an estimate of the dollar benefit of pollution abatement. The model utilized was a simple linear regression model (see Chapter 6) in which the mortality or morbidity rate was a linear function of the measured level of pollution, and possibly of an additional socioeconomic variable. This was, of course, an oversimplification, and the linear form probably applied only as an approximation over a limited range. Occupational exposures and personal habits, such as smoking, tend usually to be ignored. Measurement techniques in the past have been crude, with emphasis on a single measurement for a large area and often of a single pollutant.

Lave and Seskin present impressive results from reviewing the literature and performing multiple regression analyses of data extant in the literature. Results are particularly convincing for bronchitis and lung cancer. Air pollution was found to double the bronchitis rates for urban as compared to rural areas.

Their multiple regression analysis involves fitting the following equation to the data:

$$MR_i = a_0 + a_1 P_i + a_2 S_i + e_i$$

where MR_i = the mortality rate for a particular disease in a particular geographic area (e.g., a borough), P_i = pollution in that area, S_i = a measure of socio-economic status in that area, and e_i = the error term with a mean of zero. The coefficients, under the particular assumptions, would be best linear, unbiased estimates. The coefficient of determination (R^2), e.g., of .386, indicated a multiple-correlation coefficient of .62 and indicated 39% of the variation in the death rate was "explained" by the regression. The t-statistic, for a one-tailed test with 23 degrees of freedom, gave a value of 1.71, indicating significance at the .05 level. Coefficients of determination ranged from .3 to .8. Air pollution was a significant explanatory variable in all cases; the socioeconomic variable (population density) in three cases. From these data it was estimated that cleaning the air to the level of the English-Welsh country borough enjoying the best air would bring a 25 to 70% drop in the bronchitis death rate among males. Similar results were found for females, indicating reliability, and suggesting that effect is independent of occupational exposure.

Similar results obtained for lung cancer. If the quality of air for all boroughs were to be improved to that of the best borough, the rate of death from lung cancer would fall by 11 to 44%.

Corrections for smoking yield similar results relative to lung cancer. The urban factor was evident when viewing nonsmokers exclusively, and the smoking factor was evident when viewing rural dwellers exclusively. Similar results obtained when comparing rural and urban postmen holding occupation constant.

The association of other forms of cancer and of cardiovascular disease with pollution, while not conclusive, was certainly suggestive.

Lave and Seskin have collected data for 114 Standard Metropolitan Statistical Areas (SMSAs) and attempted to relate total death rates and infant mortality rates to air pollution and other factors. Socioeconomic data, death rates, and air pollution data were taken from U.S. government publications, e.g., *County and City Data Book, Vital Statistics of the United States,* and *Analysis of Suspended Particles* (see Chapter 6 for a further look at such data sources) for specific years. Regression analysis showed how the total death rate, say in 1960 (there is always a long time lag between events and the availability of data for analysis), varied with air pollution and socioeconomic factors. As the biweekly minimum level of suspended particulates increased, the death rate rose significantly. Also, the death rate increased with: (1) the density of population in the area; (2) the proportion of nonwhites; (3) the proportion of people over age 65; and (4) the proportion of poor families. Eighty percent of the variation in the death rate across the 114 statistical areas was explained by the regression. Other regressions showed that minimum atmospheric concentration of sulfates is a significant explanatory variable relative to infant mortality. Each of these regressions was estimated in alternative ways, viz., by logarithms, by a general quadratic, and by a "piecewise" linear form.

It is difficult to refute these conclusions, applied to various countries, both sexes, various ages, different occupational groups, etc. It is hard to argue that these relationships are spurious because the level of air pollution is correlated with a third factor, the "real" cause (e.g., the pace of city life) of poor health. Thus, the correlation between air pollution and mortality is better within a city (when more factors are held constant) than when comparing urban and rural areas. The body of studies as a whole is particularly impressive.

Having found a quantitative relationship between air pollution and mortality and morbidity, Lave and Seskin next tried to translate this into dollar units. How much is society willing to spend to improve health? This question could be answered by totaling the amount spent on medical care and the value of earnings lost because of death or illness. This is undoubtedly a minimum estimate and ignores psychological and esthetic factors, effects of pollution on vegetation and foodstuffs, accidents, and work efficiency, etc. However, Lave and Seskin knew of no other way to make the estimates. Representative results are that $250 to $500 million per year from bronchitis illness could be saved by a 50% abatement in urban air pollution. Similarly, the savings from reducing all respiratory disease would be about $1.2 billion. For all cancers and cardiovascular disease the total savings could be about $2.1 billion.

Another study relating environmental carbon monoxide to mortality is of interest to us here. Goldsmith and Landaw (1968) report that community air pollution may produce carboxyhemoglobin concentrations in nonsmokers similar to those in smokers, and that there is a correlation between CO pollution and fatality rates of patients with myocardial infarction. In a more thorough study, utilizing linear multiple regression analysis, Hexter and Goldsmith (1971) report a significant association between community CO concentrations and daily mortality in Los Angeles County. However, these results may be suspect because of faulty assumptions and failure to consider properly the contributions of many other atmospheric pollutants (see the letters to *Science*, 173(3997), 576-80, 13 August 1971).

We shall return to related matters under the topic of health in Chapter 8.

Goldman (1970) has reviewed a number of examples of air, water, and land pollution, and erosion of the quality of life in the Soviet Union. Such problems tend to be worldwide and associated with industrialization rather than with free enterprise, socialism, or capitalism *per se.* The motivations of bureaucrats, poorly understood at present in psychological terms, seem the same the world over. Yet differences between communism and capitalism may either mitigate or exacerbate environmental problems, depending on how the governmental frameworks are implemented.

The environmental crisis in the U.S.S.R. is serious, like that almost anywhere else in the world. There have been fish-kill incidents there, as in the U.S. Not only are most rivers polluted or otherwise have lost their "natural" state, but some are officially considered dead or have caught fire as a result of oil slicks. Sewage and industrial pollution are rampant and largely uncontrolled, and some cities have run out of drinking water.

The Aral and Caspian Sea levels have fallen one to several meters in the last decade or two because of diversion of waters for irrigation and hydroelectric power dam-building. Some fear parts of these seas will end up as salt marshes within the next decades. The Aral Sea may disappear. Fish life, particularly that of the sturgeon, has been disturbed; as a result caviar, a major earner of foreign exchange, has fallen in production. Another fish that previously controlled mosquitoes near the mouth of the Volga has begun to disappear; as a result malaria has increased in the newly formed swamps.

The best example of industrial and bureaucratic greed is provided by the despoliation of magnificent Lake Baikal. Despoliation is associated with the building of paper and pulp mills, cutting of trees, rafting of logs which may sink to the bottom and rot, and building of houses. As in the U.S., industrial greed and lobbying circumvent protective measures. Cutting the trees and intrusion of machinery has destroyed an important soil stabilizer, and there is fear the dunes of the Gobi will move into Siberia.

Tbilisi, the capital of Georgia, has smog six months of the year. Near Yasnaya Polyana, the summer estate of Leo Tolstoy, air pollution from a nearby chemical plant is destroying a prime oak forest and threatening a pine forest.

As a result of hauling away pebbles and sand from the Black Sea beaches of Georgia, the beaches have been eroded away by wave action and numerous large buildings have collapsed.

Elsewhere, networks of hydroelectric stations, irrigation reservoirs, and canals have had unanticipated side effects, including water seepage, salination of the soil, disappearance of age-old sources of drinking water, and perhaps restructuring of old climate and moisture patterns.

Unfortunately, the relative impact of environmental disruption everywhere is difficult to measure. Russian industry also has been unable to adjust so as to pay not only the *direct* costs of production for labor, raw materials, and equipment, but also the *social* costs of production arising from dirty air and water. These social costs are difficult to measure and allocate precisely. In Russia, as in the U.S., there are no clear lines of authority and responsibility for enforcing pollution-control regulations. Many agencies have some but not ultimate say.

Violations are flagrant and enforcement minor—it is cheaper to pay repeated small fines than to "clean up" the problem. Obviously they—and we—need a Department of the Environment.

All over the world, air, water, and soil supplies are relatively constant. They can be renewed but not expanded. In this sense Earth is a closed system. A "Doomsday Principle" derived from the Malthusian concept states that with time and pollution we may simply run out of fresh air and water.

There are some reasons for pollution which seem unique to a socialist country. Thus, officials are judged almost entirely on how much they are able to increase their regions' economic growth. Impartial referees are unlikely to be promoted. Further, industrialization has come relatively late to the USSR, and Russians continue to emphasize increases in production. Economic growth has been even more unbalanced than in the U.S. The power of the state is so great it can do immeasurable harm (or good), depending on its perception of relative needs. On the other hand, socialist countries are not yet plagued with the forced-obsolescence consumer idea. Automobiles are not quickly discarded (50,000 were discarded in New York City in 1969); and the junk man can still make a profit collecting junk because labor costs are not so great (Goldman, 1970).

Obviously, considering the world as a whole, better management concepts could lead to less wasteful practices, greater over-all efficiency, and less disastrous impacts on the citizenry and on the environment. Thus, one estimate is that 10% of the electric power of U.S. cities could be generated by burning the trash of those cities. Similarly, California has reduced the demand for more water from northern California and, hence, the pressure to dam three rivers. Throughout the remainder of this book, we shall consider many such examples of improved system designs.

Finally the urgent need to recognize the global ecosystem as a whole as, for example, represented by the June 1972 United Nations Conference on the Human Environment held in Stockholm, is reflected at least in an identification and classification of problems, even though widespread agreement among participating nations as to solutions remains a future goal. For another look at international environmental problems see Russell and Landsberg (1971).

ROLE OF THE PUBLIC AND OF PROFESSIONAL
GROUPS IN DETERMINING POLICIES

In this section we shall examine, from two different perspectives, the role of the public and of professional groups in shaping and determining policies. Both perspectives, however, reflect a common base of changing public attitudes toward science and technology and their practitioners. These attitudes are excellently summarized by Morison (1969), from whom the following points can be stressed:

1. Science and technology are identified in the public mind with the manipulation of the material world, and by extension with the manipulation of the public self.
2. Science and technology are associated with fiendish horrors of war, such as defoliation and napalming, and with abuses against the environment; at the same time there is widespread public questioning of the basic reasons underlying these acts.
3. The wonders brought by science and technology, such as the moon-landing, heart transplants, and even biological cloning, are seen to contrast starkly with poverty, limited progress or even retrogress in the health field, automobile-induced congestion and local transporation system decline, and so forth.
4. Our rationalized systems are seen to have developed a life of their own, a momentum, which carries people, including the practitioners, and whole societies along against their wishes.

In short, although the public is appreciative of science and technology for their more tangible benefits, it is increasingly skeptical about their long-term results, and especially skeptical of rationalized control over the individual.

It can be seen that science and technology can no longer present themselves as being entities apart from society, governed by their own rules, and carried forward by the force of their own processes. Changes in the roles of science and technology will have profound implications for management.

One of the most significant popular movements of our time was unpredicted a decade ago; this is an egregious example of the foibles of forecasting. The movement represents a coalescence of many ideas and small movements, which perhaps analogously to the spread of Christianity in ancient Rome, have been around, but outside the limelight, for a long time. This movement has already had a profound effect upon popular thought and practice, upon education, and upon legislation. It will have a profound effect upon management practice.

The movement involves the amalgamation and *institutionalization* of such previously diverse movements as conservation, environmental protection, consumer protection, participatory democracy, quest for a simpler life-style, anti-war feeling, scientific responsibility, improved public health, etc. In parallel, there has been some shift within industry from resource development to environmental protection. Industrial behavior will be further modified by the recent passage of local, national, and international laws and treaties. The new statutes that require special considerations in relation to decision-making by the federal government are several. Especially important are the National Environmental Policy Act (NEPA) of 1969, the Transportation Act of 1966, the Federal Power Act, the Fish and Wildlife Coordination Act, the Federal Aid to Highways Act, the Urban Mass Transit Act, and the Airport and Airway Development Act of 1970. These acts require consideration of over-all impacts on the environment, air and water quality, wildlife protection, scenic land and historic site protection, and so forth. These features must be considered in development, unless there is no "feasible alternative," regardless of increased economic costs. On the basis of these acts, a number of lawsuits for noncompliance have been entered into by the Sierra Club, a conservationist organization, and by other organizations. Of course, impact is often, at best, hard to measure and may be subtle and unknown. Likewise, feasible alternatives may be difficult to define. All these factors promise to make the management of complex systems increasingly difficult in the years to come.

Let's now look further at a particularly salient example of the new requirement to make environmental impact studies, namely that provided by the controversy over construction of the trans-Alaska oil pipeline and associated facilities. This case also illustrates the murkiness of the vested interest forces behind such developments, the shrill call to shibboliths, the selective utilization or distortion of data, and the close liaison between commercial interests and government agencies which supposedly regulate those interests.

The 48-inch pipeline, sought by a consortium of seven oil companies, would bring petroleum 789 miles from vast new oil fields on the Arctic Ocean to the port of Valdez on the Pacific. Development had been stalled by injunctions granted by a federal court on the basis of motions filed by conservationist and Alaskan native groups.

The preliminary version of the impact study prepared by the Department of the Interior and released in January 1971 was held to be a sorely deficient job (Gillette, 1971). For example, alternative routes or modes of transportation were poorly evaluated. The value of the pipeline in reducing the outflow of dollars, in enhancing national security, in meeting projected "demand," and in reducing dependence upon the "unstable" Near East was much stressed even to the point of oversimplifying issues and distorting or selectively utilizing data. Many aspects of the impact on the natural and socioeconomic environments were superficially evaluated, if at all. Although the final report (United States Department of the Interior, 1972) represents an improvement over the preliminary version, it nevertheless fails to resolve a number of issues of paramount importance. Thus, in the total systems sense there has been no realistic assessment of future societal needs as opposed to crude and selective estimates and projections of "demand," especially in the context of comparison with alternative energy sources. Further, it remains unclear as to just why the oil companies and the Department of the Interior continue to press for the Prudhoe Bay—Valdez route coupled with tanker transport, say, over the alternative all-land route down Canada's MacKenzie Valley to the Midwest. Behind the emphasis lies, many suspect, an intention to sell to Japan.

At the time of this writing it appears the development of the pipeline and associated facilities may proceed. We believe this would be a mistake. The impact study should be corrected for remaining deficiencies and should become an input to a larger scale study involving petroleum-generated pollution, automobile-induced disruptions above and beyond pollution, an integrated program for the development of power supplies, and the need to dampen rampant growth. As important as the impacts of this petroleum mining and transportation scheme are upon the environments of Alaska, the Canadian Arctic, and the northern Pacific, this is merely part of the over-all problem stressed throughout this book. Judicious utilization of natural resources can always take place in the future, following serious evaluations within the context of the world viewed as a system. Postponement—or abandonment—of both drilling and transporation developments could well provide a wonderful opportunity for the exercise of innovative managerial ideas and practices as we shift from the old ethos of blind growth and local interest to the new systems approach.

Other changes in policies we may expect involve preventing violators from selling to the government or obtaining government contracts, and withdrawing of privileges such as the oil-depletion privilege. Effluent charges, or pollution taxes, would provide another approach to protecting the environment; charges would be internalized rather than externalized.

We are thus witnessing a fundamental revolution in human thinking, probably the most important since Marx. What is perhaps especially significant is that it is not the work of any one man or group, and has originated outside the aegis of formal organizations, such as universities. Nevertheless, individuals, such as consumer advocate Ralph Nader, early pollution-warning scientist Rachel Carson, and groups such as the Sierra Club (originally organized for purposes of conservation and outdoor recreation), have had and will continue to have a powerful influence.[1] We may thus be witnessing a shift of decision-making away from formal and usually rather rigid organizations. For an interesting new organization theory applicable to loose networks of different groups with many leaders—"polycephalous, segmentary, and reticulate," yet politically strong networks—see Gerlach (1971). Certainly it is unquestioned that significant changes in company practices and advertising have already occurred. A visit to one's local gasoline station which now provides choices of unleaded and "low-lead" gasoline, in addition to the old kind, amply demonstrates this. And the electric power utilities ply the communications media and the monthly billings, touting the once unquestioned benefits of electricity and urging the construction of more power plants, once built with little concern for public knowledge or opinion. It thus appears we are well on our way to shaping new "motivations" on the part of government and industry.

It is emphasized that there are socioeconomic, racial, and national differences in the recognition of, and participation in, this new revolution, which, in many

[1] For excellent presentations of environmental issues, problems, and programs and conservationist recommendations, see the monthly *Sierra Club Bulletin*. For an excellent summary of the evolving interrelationship between ecology and conservation, see Ripley (1970).

ways, represents a Western middle and upper-middle class phenomenon involving persons high on the Maslow hierarchy. Legitimate conflicts of interest arise and will continue to arise. Nevertheless, there have been some interesting coalitions of unlikely constituents. For example, recently a coalition of conservationists, wealthy land and resort owners, and black fishermen, fearing pollution of the Sound, opposed the development in Beaufort County, South Carolina, of a giant petrochemical plant by the German firm *Badische Anilin und Soda Fabrik* (BASF). The County was considered an economically depressed area, and the plant promised to provide new jobs, including jobs for poor blacks. The jobs-versus-pollution issue stirred considerable controversy over a two-year period, but BASF, sensing the signs of the times, eventually abandoned its plans for the site. Examples of government decision-making that reflect recognition of the new values include the abandonment of plans for California freeways, the decision of Arizona not to continue to recruit polluting industry from outside the state, the abandonment of plans to build the cross-Florida barge canal, and the decision not to go ahead on the development of the supersonic transport aircraft (see below). In each case, considerable money had been spent that could have been saved had the problems been expressed within a broader context of constraints.

In a different vein, we shall now look at the effects of groups of professional experts in shaping policy. Bosch (1971), for example, has attempted to model, using matrix methods, the growth, survival, and harvesting of the California coast redwood *Sequoia sempervirens*. The model involved a matrix relating the reproductive and survival characteristics of different age classes of the trees. A number of assumptions and oversimplifications were made. Dangerously, Bosch concluded that "redwoods can be farmed without driving them to extinction (p. 384)," and that the trees would still "survive and flourish" if lumber companies cut 50% of all redwoods under 800 years old.

This article represents a potentially dangerous misuse of that branch of technology known as modeling, in that policy makers could take it seriously and employ it to give legitimacy to faulty decisions. Indeed, a number of peppery letters to *Science* (174 [4007], 435-36, 22 October 1971) pointed out biological, ecological, logical, and mathematical deficiencies in Bosch's article. These include: (1) faulty concepts of population biology; (2) confusion with classes; (3) overgeneralizations from very limited empirical data; (4) assumptions as to a static forest environment following start of the 50% cutting; and (5) basic conceptual error in attempting to predict future population sizes by iteration of matrices, viz., in assuming that population structure at time $t + 1$ must be completely determined by structure at time t and not also dependent on structure at antecedent times.

An equally limited and potentially dangerous model is that of Anderson, *et al.*, (1971) dealing with management of the deer herd of Mendocino County,

California.[2] In this case, the model is geared exclusively toward hunting interests and neglects the multiple-use concept of natural resource management. For example, the model completely ignores the beneficial effects of predators on deer-herd management. It takes little imagination to recognize that vested interests could use a computer simulation model such as this to provide scientific blessing to their policies of allowing and encouraging hunting of bucks, does, and fawns to the detriment of the total ecosystem.

That systems analysis, modeling and simulation, operations research, and other aspects of systems science possess the capability and potentiality of grievous misuse—perhaps exceeding that of hardware technology—is further highlighted by a recent intramural fracas involving the *Operations Research Society of America* (see the entire Volume 19, Number 5 of *Operations Research,* September 1971). In this case, operations research was used in the adversary process before the U.S. Congress relative to the Safeguard Anti-Ballistic Missile (ABM). For example, consider the following important point (p. 1127):

> When public debate is joined by eminent practitioners of operations research, advocating opposing positions on important issues and offering apparently contradictory testimony (all based, in part, on operation-research methods), the confidence of the public in this approach may be undermined, and the decision makers to whom the testimony is being offered may become confused rather than enlightened.

There were charges of professional misconduct, fabrication of data, using only data biased to substantiate a given argument, using misleading or tenuous kill probabilities, employing biased projections of U.S. and Soviet offensive and defensive capabilities, and so forth. These deficiencies can be summarized as follows:

1. Failure to present assumptions and facilitate discussions among experts.
2. Improper utilization of source materials.
3. Failure to incorporate important features of the system as a whole.
4. Use of limited and inefficient-range strategies and tactics.
5. Suggestion of impractical alternatives.
6. Use of improper criteria.
7. Use of improper costing.
8. Lack of recognition that systems are multifunctional.
9. Failure to recognize lead-time problems.
10. Lack of attention to potential system interactions.

---

[2]Ironically, in the redwood area discussed above. There is a common mentality of resource use in such places.

Although some of the above sins of ommission and commission may be attributable to scientific dishonesty or lack of professional ethics, most indicate a failure to follow a systems approach as long recognized and preached by operations researchers as well as by all other systems scientists.

In summary of this example of misuse of systems science:

The evidence strongly supports the distrubing conclusion that when prominent experts outside the Administration supported their opinions on Safeguard deployment with arguments or results of an operations-research nature, these analyses were often inappropriate, misleading, or factually in error. Moreover, in many instances, elementary standards for proper presentation of results to permit verification and meaningful dialogue were not met. Failure to distinguish properly between the roles of the analyst and the advocate contributed to the lack of complete research to clarify the presentation.

Quite often the misleading nature of an analysis is not apparent on a superficial reading. Because of this, poor analyses can be quite effective in public debate (*Operations Research*, Vol. 19, No. 5, pp. 1176-77).

We shall close this section with these observations. Because of the obtuseness and intransigence of many present institutions, it is likely that more and more groups will attempt to influence policy through routes outside the established channels. Bringing antipollution measures directly to the people, by circumventing the California legislature, during the 1972 elections provides one example. The nomination of South Dakota Senator George McGovern as 1972 U.S. presidential candidate, circumventing the old Democratic party channels, provides a second. The *amicus curiae* lawsuits of the Sierra Club and other conservationist organizations, referred to above, against spoilators of the environment represent a third. The formation of the Club of Rome, an international organization based on the idea that global problems are so interrelated that traditional institutions and policies are useless in dealing with them, provides a fourth. These innovative approaches, operating within legitimate frameworks, are to be encouraged during these times of increasing gap between societal problems and our means of solving them.

MANAGEMENT OF TECHNOLOGY

There is a wealth of literature dealing with the management of technology, an area fraught with uncertainty. Yet there is never a guarantee that scientific discovery or engineering invention will result in industrial payoff or societal fallout. For every transistor, digital computer, jet engine, or laser there are a host of failures. There is about the whole thing both a serendipitous aspect and an aspect of being at the right place at the right time. This makes it extremely difficult to determine which areas of basic research and research and development to pursue. Even when a basic theoretical knowledge is present, translation of this knowledge into action in developing a piece of equipment or a product may present a formidable problem. This is exemplified in the attempt to develop a fast-breeder reactor or controlled-fusion reactor, a problem to which we shall return in Chapter 8.

All the above problems are severely compounded today, because (1) socio-technical and environmental problems are so much more complicated than are hardware problems; and (2) for all problems, including the development of new hardware and consumer items, there is the necessity to antitipate and minimize or even preclude undesirable side effects.

There is today considerable interest in *technology transfer,* that is, the determination of uses other than the original for an extant body of technology. Technology transfer, par excellence, is represented by active attempts on the part of the National Aeronautics and Space Administration (NASA), in conjunction with industry, universities, and private research organizations, to find civil-system uses for products and techniques developed in conjunction with the $35 billion space program. The effort involves multidisciplinary applications teams, data banks and information search, and an attempt to pair problems with technological solutions. Results have been particularly extensive in the biomedical field, but there have also been impressive applications to police and fire operations, mine safety, materials, plastics, and so on.

Space-program benefits or "fallout" can be placed in two categories. "Direct" benefits include various satellites used for communications, broadcasting, weather prediction, navigation and traffic control, and earth-resource monitoring (e.g., for potential infestation of crops). "Derived" benefits are those resulting from technology transfer. Many of these are the results of improvements in materials, microminiaturization, instrumentation, telemetry, and overall equipment reliability, that were necessary for the Apollo moon-landing program.

The NASA Technology Utilization Program was initiated in 1962. A potential application of technology occurs when the NASA Applications Team has identified a solution that the medical researcher, industrial production engineer, representative of local government, etc., feels will solve his problem. The Applications Team serves as a middle-man between the individual(s) who has organized a medical or societal problem and the technological, human, and informational resources of NASA. For further detail on identified problems and applications and the management of the Technology Utilization Program, see the annual review (Technology Application Group, 1971) and Haggerty (1970).

It is difficult to evaluate such programs in technology transfer. NASA cannot afford the effort needed to trace every transfer and to estimate direct economic benefits. There are some estimates of $3 million to $4 million dollars per annum in benefits to industry that have taken advantage of NASA information. No real value can be placed on improvements in health or saving of life. And there is the familiar argument that the vast expenditures for the manned space program could better have been applied directly to health and urban problems. For the purposes of this book, we must emphasize that a total systems approach to these problems seems more meaningful than trying to fit in pieces of technology after the fact. Also the very existence of a massive body of technology may force developments otherwise not desirable.

The effects of technology have long been massive. In addition to the many points made earlier, we can highlight the following. The number of television sets in the United States rose from 100,000 in 1948 to 50 million a decade later, with incalculable effects. Large systems such as airports usually require additional extensive support systems, such as highway access, that typically are not anticipated. The mechanical cotton picker aided by chemical pesticides led to markedly increased productivity, a lowering of the price of cotton cloth, and great wealth to some owners of large plantations, but these technological advances led also to displacement of large numbers of black laborers and the shifting of costs to these unfortunate people and to the cities to which they migrated. The automobile has ramifications throughout society and on the environment, shown in Figure 3-2, which only recently have been fully appreciated.

In keeping with these ideas, there is today much interest in *technology assessment*. A great deal has been written and a number of panels recently convened. A panel convened by the National Academy of Sciences has recommended federal organizations associated with the legislative and executive branches of government. The latter would involve the President's Office of Science and Technology, and from this office most of the work so far has stemmed.

The major points made by the panel of the National Academy of Sciences follow (see National Academy of Sciences, 1969, and Brooks and Bowers, 1970):

1. Assessment of technology is imperative and cannot be long postponed without greatly diminishing the chances of success. Technology holds great promise, but if society persists on its present course, there can be great peril, either from the effects of rampant and uncontrolled technology or from a social and political reaction against technological innovation.

2. An effective means of assessing technology should strengthen, rather than weaken, it; among other things by enabling the nation to choose among many alternate technological paths to the same objective, with a comparison of the social and economic costs of each path.

3. Decision-making should allow the greatest possible latitude for future action. The reversibility of a technological action should be counted as a major benefit, but its irreversibility (as represented, say, by dam-building), must be considered a major cost.

4. There should be limits on the extent to which a major technology is allowed to proliferate without obtaining evidence of possible harmful effects. Automobiles, pesticides, petroleum drilling, and tampering with

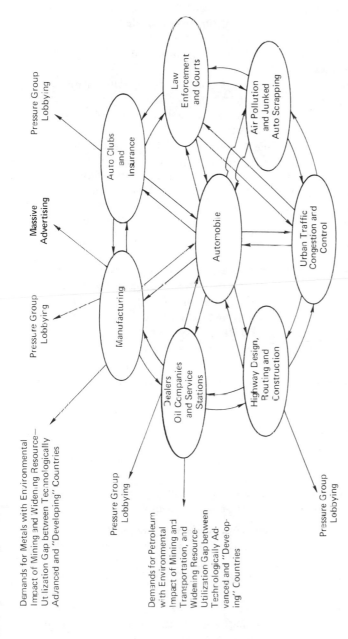

Demands for Metals with Environmental Impact of Mining and Widening Resource-Utilization Gap between Technologically Advanced and "Developing" Countries

Pressure Group Lobbying

Massive Advertising

Pressure Group Lobbying

Pressure Group Lobbying

Demands for Petroleum with Environmental Impact of Mining and Transportation, and Widening Resource-Utilization Gap between Technologically Advanced and "Developing" Countries

Pressure Group Lobbying

Auto Clubs and Insurance

Law Enforcement and Courts

Air Pollution and Junked Auto Scrapping

Manufacturing

Automobile

Urban Traffic Congestion and Control

Dealers Oil Companies and Service Stations

Highway Design, Routing and Construction

Ramifications of technology are exemplified by the automobile, which represents a system of social and technological activities with a combined effect on the environment. The elements of the system also interact, as indicated by the arrows between circles.

FIGURE 3-2

Far-reaching effects of the automobile on society and on the environment.[3]

[3] Adapted from "The Assessment of Technology" by Harvey Brooks and Raymond Bowers. Copyright © 1970 by Scientific American, Inc. All rights reserved.

171

waterways through dam- and canal-building provide relevant examples here.

5. Much more must be done to give all affected interests—not just powerful vested interests—effective representation in crucial decision-making. This would strengthen potentially desirable technologies, such as faster and cheaper building materials and techniques, which could be opposed by powerful construction interests.

6. Up to now, assessment of the costs and benefits of alternative technological approaches has been undertaken by those who hope to exploit these approaches. Social and environmental problems are recognized belatedly, if at all.

7. The recommended federal mechanism should be as neutral as possible, empowered to study and recommend, but not to act; able to evaluate, but not to sponsor or prevent. In this way internal conflicts of interest would be minimized. This contrasts impressively with such organizations as the Atomic Energy Commission which, somewhat contradictorily, is charged with advancing reactor technology while promoting radiation safety; or the Federal Aviation Administration entrusted to further a supersonic transport.

Technology assessment will not be easy, particularly because of the difficulties, discussed in detail in Parts II and III of this book, associated with defining and measuring subjective and qualitative variables, criteria, indirect costs, benefits, and impacts. An attempt, sponsored jointly by the President's Office of Science and Technology and The MITRE Corporation (see Jones, 1971), has been made to develop a methodology which can be applied to many different fields of technology. The methodology must be capable of evaluating impacts and the effectiveness of action options designed to influence these impacts, with regard to as many different criteria as possible. The methodology consists of the following seven basic steps, each of which is extended through the use of checklists for identifying key questions: define the assessment task; describe relevant technologies; develop state-of-society assumptions; identify impact areas; make preliminary impact analysis; identify possible action options; and complete impact analysis.

Five pilot studies have been released, as follows; in each case the area is exemplified by a typical important result, benefit, or impact:

1. Automotive emission controls—small changes in technology and in practices may have large societal impacts in air quality, health, and national welfare.

2. Computer-communications networks—growth may have widespread effects on security and privacy.

3. Industrial enzymes—development of low-cost sugars could have national and international demographic and political consequences, in terms of displacing cane and beet sugar growers and workers.

4. Mariculture—emphasis on it could reduce malnutrition and produce a source of income.
5. Water pollution: domestic wastes—a first step has been laid toward construction of a dynamic interactive model.

Technological assessment will utilize the systems analysis, computer modeling and simulation, operations research, cost-effectiveness, benefit-cost, Program Planning and Budgeting System, and other techniques discussed in Parts II and III of this book.

In summary, the picture, then, is much more than the solution of societal and environmental problems through technology. Rather, in most cases technology (including, as pointed out earlier, analytic, software, and managerial expertise as well as machines and products), poorly managed, can be considered to exacerbate the situation. The effective management of technology, therefore, implies restraints on technology.

It is important to consider the harnessing of technology to meet a national goal. We must be careful, however, how we define that goal. Wiping out poverty or reversing urban decay would be impossible goals for technology. Eliminating pollution; developing a national integrated transportation system, including replacement of the private automobile powered by the internal-combustion engine; or developing an integrated power-supply system, including perhaps development of a practical fast-breeder reactor, would be more realizable goals.

ESTABLISHING LONG-RANGE GOALS AND OBJECTIVES

Long-range goals and objectives must be defined within the context in which the organization or system will exist. At a time of explosive, almost chaotic, change this is probably impossible for a rigid system. The job, then, is to build as much adaptability and flexibility into the system structure, function, and behavior as possible. At the same time, the job becomes even more complicated by virtue of: (1) demands for short-range benefits; and (2) the fact that industrial managers and political decision-makers tend to perceive problems and goals in relation to their terms in office; they are rewarded by accomplishing things today, not by having set the stage for a better organization or world tomorrow. There is thus the very real danger of near-range overexploitation of resources, resulting in greatly increased long-range costs to pay for short-range benefits.

The building of hydroelectric and water-control dams provides a good example here. Perhaps the most egregious is the Aswān High Dam. Long-range effects can be seen in terms of the spread of schistosomiasis and other disease, decreased fertility in the lower Nile Valley, and decreased catch of fisheries in the eastern Mediterranean due to diminished discharge of nutrients from the

Nile. This case is especially tragic because Egypt's population increases have more than made up for the land newly irrigated as a result of constructing the dam. Once again, the foibles of not having followed a systems approach are manifest.

Because of the above factors and other factors discussed elsewhere in this book, long-range planning and even insuring the continued existence of an organization, whether it be industrial, political, or educational, will continue to be most challenging activities, with no certain guarantee of success.

Gross (1965) has looked at the vital role of objectives in the managing of organizations. Any serious discussion of planning by any organization deals with objectives. Yet objectives have been difficult to pinpoint accurately. For this reason, Gross proposes a general systems model for formulating the performance and structural objectives of any organization. Traditionally, objectives have been defined in grossly oversimplified terms, such as "profitability" or "efficiency." Objectives tend to be much more complex and to entail human and organizational as well as budgetary assets.

Gross's general systems model of a business or governmental organization is based on the following attributes of a formal organization, namely, its being:

1. A man-resource system in space and time
2. An open system
3. A system characterized by internal and external conflict as well as cooperation
4. A system for developing and using power within and without and with varying degrees of authority and responsibility
5. A feedback system
6. A changing system, with static concepts derived from dynamic ones
7. A complex system, containing many subsystems; and its being a subsystem of a larger system, and being one of many overlapping systems
8. A system with loose control and coordination over many elements
9. A system only partially knowable with many qualitative variables
10. A system subject to considerable present and future uncertainty

The starting point of systems analysis here is the input-output concept, with the flow of inputs and outputs portraying the system's performance. Two kinds of organizational performance can be recognized: producing outputs of goods and services, and satisfying interests. There are three types of inputs: acquiring resources, using inputs for investment in the system, and making efficient use of resources. In addition, organizational performance includes attempts to conform with behavior codes and concepts of technical and administrative rationality.

Gross uses matrix algebra to bring together system performance and system structure into a 2×1 nested (each consists of seven elements) vector. The model starts with the dynamic action, i.e., performance, and works back to structure. Structure and performance are, of course, intricately interrelated. Many managers make the mistake of planning for only one or the other. Gross emphasizes that the first elements of both structure and performance are people—financial and technological elements are merely ways of thinking about people and their behavior. Hence, an organization's plans for the future are always made by people for people.

Gross next deals with the elements of system performance as performance objectives and of structure as structure objectives. Each of the seven elements in each case is broken down into subelements, or "goals," which are formulated more specifically as "norms." For example, "members" could be one group whose "interests" are "served" as a performance objective; the corresponding goal is "higher morale" and the norm is "reducing labor turnover to 6%." A structural objective could be "types" of "people;" the corresponding goal would be "fewer blue-collars" and the norm "specific manning tables." Rather detailed ideas along these lines are presented in tabular form as the major categories of objectives.

Gross emphasizes that "the essence of planning is the *selection of strategic objectives in the form of specific sequences of action to be taken in the organization* (p. 213)." Such critical variables must be selected in terms of: (1) interest satisfactions promised to obtain internal and external support; (2) contingencies; (3) impacts on other events; and (4) long-range implications of action. Within this framework, many elements of performance and structure may be detailed in subsystem plans. However, there may be a profaning of this approach through concern with documentary minutiae. Also, strategic objectives can be selected rationally only if there is some awareness of the broad spectrum of possible objectives. Otherwise, the result is routine, arbitrary, and superficial.

In a typical organization, there are many groups—top managers, members, stockholders, charter-writers, specialized planners—who possess conflicting objectives. Thus, an organization's objectives tend to be those widely accepted by most of its members. The entire organizational structure is involved *de facto* in the daily formulation, and in winning commitment for future performance and structure. Here, planning is not just an application of technical rationality, but is much more an exercise in conflict management. However, technical calculations may narrow areas of conflict and reveal possibilities for resolution.

The planner must pay attention to power for and against given plans. Persuasion and pressure can be used for conflict resolution. The most common means of conflict resolution is compromise; much more difficult is integration, wherein all gain and none lose.

THE DECISION PROCESS IN SOCIETY

The decision process in society is faulty, to the point of guaranteeing destruction of society. Because much of this book is concerned with this issue, we shall present only a recapitulation here:

1. Goals, criteria, and alternatives are difficult to define quantitatively or so as to insure agreement.
2. There is the need to collect, assemble, and integrate data from many sources, but it may be impossible to identify the data base. Data typically are obsolete, out of phase, scattered, biased, contradictory, spotty, and in the wrong form.
3. Postulates are stated and data exist in such forms as to encourage almost unlimited numbers of "experts" of opposing camps. Each expert can produce substantiating evidence for his point of view.
4. "Experts" offer themselves for hire. The main reason for many "impartial" or "objective" or "scientific" studies is to provide muscle for the appropriate adversary position. The recent controversy, with implications of scientific dishonesty, involving the Safeguard Anti-Ballistic Missile (ABM) System (*Operations Research*, September 1971) discussed above, is an excellent example of this.
5. Decision-makers are rewarded by easily perceivable, short-term results related to their tenure in office, not by solving "real" problems.
6. Decision-makers are rewarded by powerful interests that insure maintaining a status quo rewarding to those interests. This makes political decision-making basically corrupt. Industrial donations to the major political parties and associated tax and zoning benefits awarded industry by the winner provide a perfect case in point. Such industry-government liaison acts as a buttress amidst the swirling currents of change, perhaps contributing by its ridigity to a harder eventual downfall.
7. Society presents many genuine conflicts of interest. Resolution of these presents a much more formidable problem than does simple backing up of one pressure group.
8. There is an almost unlimited number of potential decision-makers, involving all levels and branches of government from neighborhood to international. Jurisdictions and responsibilities overlap, but paradoxically, it is typically impossible to ferret out *the* responsible decision-maker. In many cases, in our changing world, there is none.
9. There is no simple way to determine priorities. All problems are of severe magnitude, all are interlocking, and all have unknown ramifications and side effects. However, let's look at this last feature in a little more detail below.
10. Managerial decision-making is greatly influenced by the highly perceptible systems oscillations that exist at a given time. Managers panic in the face of these extremes. The steady-state value, being obscure, rarely affects policy.

Determining Priorities

Frederickson (1969) has examined the ordering of urban priorities, necessary because of scarce resources, the great decentralization in local government, and the increasing involvement of higher echelons of government. Any ordering tends to enhance some groups and to act to the disadvantage of others. However, there is little understanding of how priorities serve particular interests. Frederickson, using general survey techniques, first determined how people feel about priorities; then he contrasted these attitudes with real urban priorities, as measured by public spending. A stratified random sample of 1036 was held representative of the population of the Syracuse Standard Metropolitan Statistical Area. Each of the 1036 persons responded to an interview (to obtain a complete response) based on a highly structured (to avoid the possibility of interviewer bias) one-page questionnaire. The respondees were asked to rate, on a scale of 1 (most important) to 3, ten urban problem areas such as education, police protection, and water pollution. Results were reported in percentages of respondees who ranked each functional area as most important. Differences in attitudes were found by age and sex. There tended to be general agreement as to the importance of education and police protection; however, middle-level priorities did differ on the basis of income, education, and place of residence. Therefore, it is not possible to generalize about the set of urban priority preferences. When the priority preferences were contrasted with actual spending priorities, it was found that the priority attached to education was being met by the ratio of total spending attached thereto. However, there were disparities for the other functional areas; for example, all groups indicated a strong priority for law enforcement, yet actual spending for this function was well down the list. Higher socioeconomic groups tended to give greater support to issues designed to aid the entire community, but nevertheless attached higher priority to those programs most directly in their own interests, such as water-pollution control.

Bower (1969) describes social decisions and relates systems analysis to the solution of social problems. Systems analysis reflects a confidence in human reason and in the capacity of a nation to solve problems through the use of reason. Thus, the problem of order in society, once thought of as the responsibility of God or kings and ministers, can now be thought of as the field of endeavor of a new kind of engineer.

Bower first looks at the nature of social decisions i.e., those "taken by individuals or groups that have material effects on individuals other than those involved in making the decision (p. 929)." In modern technological societies this is more and more the case as a web of interconnection bonds one person to another. To use the economist's term, these are *decisions with external effects*. Thus, each part of the urban problem—pollution, education, housing, welfare, transportation—represents a problem of external effects. There are two kinds of social decisions. First, there are those which technology forces organizations to make. Electric power and transportation are in this category. Second, there are those which individuals have been held responsible for making themselves. Housing, education, and public safety at various times have been placed in this category. Thus, organizations like schools and airports can be thought of as being the results of social decisions—at one time, at least, there were alternatives to these forms and they were means not ends in themselves. For example, there are numerous alternative ways of educating people to lead individually and socially useful lives. Next, resources to be allocated are almost always scarce. Thus, one must decide not only among alternatives within one social choice, such as education, but also among different social choices, such as education, pollution, and transportation.

A major difference between the decision process of society when viewed systematically and traditional methods is that in the latter, policy is an outcome. The assignment of a particular task to a particular organization is often a matter of accident. Institutions once created seldom die and seldom give up their share of society's resources. Decision-making is usually the result of bargaining among the institutions that feel they have an interest in the issue at hand. Hence, the way in which a decision is made determines what policy will be. Bower illustrates this with an example from the health field in which activities represent less a policy designed to cope with a set of preconceived issues than a combined momentum of all the assorted governmental, professional, educational, and commercial agencies. Thus, it is only by accident that particular institutions, developed historically as responsible for a set of tasks, address themselves fully to a new problem facing society. Fragmentation of organizations is the rule, or occasionally (as in foreign education) there is a single, vast, anachronistic monolithic institution. Systems analysis is posed as the alternative to the existing process.

Jurisdictional Overlaps and Conflicts

In dealing with the systems of society, the noncoincidence of the system and its management is widely recognized. For example, myriad private and local, state, federal, and international organizations are concerned with the problems of air pollution. A morass of conflicting goals, objectives, alternatives, criteria, policies, plans, and decisions emerges. It may be impossible to identify *the* decision-maker. For this reason the plausible argument, "if we can send a man to the moon, we can clean up pollution or eliminate poverty or. . . . " totally lacks substance. Recognition of new systems and new problems will bring about new managements; hopefully, new methods of management will also be developed. These will require both centralized and decentralized management; an integrated, holistic approach; flexibility; more functional organization; and more rapid system sensing and response times.

HISTORIC TENDENCY TO OVEREMPHASIZE THE "TECHNICAL" AND UNDERPLAY THE "SOCIO"

The last couple of years have witnessed a number of interrelated events: (1) a disillusionment with war; (2) a disillusionment with science and technology; (3) a questioning of unbridled population growth, economic growth, and associated wasteful consumption; (4) a retrenchment of the aerospace industry; (5) a concern for the environment; (6) a new economic pattern of mixed inflation, recession, and unemployment; and (7) a readjustment of level of aspiration and level of expectation, especially among the educated. These are specifics within the ideational and peaceful revolution of our times.

We have stated before that technology must be a part of the solution of the complex of problems associated with this revolution. However, technology *cannot* offer the only solution. Unfortunately, many persons persist in thinking in these terms: thus, building high-rise or mass-produced cheap housing will cure the problems of the cities, new turbo-trains will cure the transporation problem, better scheduling through operations research will cure the health crisis, etc.

A glance at an engineering journal (or a behavioral or social science journal) or participation in a systems science conference will impress one with the immense interest in, and concern with, social and environmental problems today. An army of devoted researchers and planners is busy at solutions. Unfortunately, there is little evidence that behavioral or social science theory and know-how are proceeding in stride. Although all disciplines seek "relevance" today, one gets the impression these fields are gasping for air at what should be their finest hour.

Example from Transportation

Historically, technological societies have been preoccupied with a mindless change for change's sake, growth for growth's sake, and with a parallel enamoration of gadgetry. The date 24 March 1971 may possibly symbolize the end of an era. On that date, the United States Senate by a vote of 51 to 46 denied additional funding for the supersonic transport (SST) aircraft. The program to build an American SST had been, from the beginning, plagued with confusion as to systems and objectives and alternatives. In many ways it could be thought of as a gadget looking for a system. Thus, we might and should have asked:

1. Are we dealing with a national prestige "system?" If so, a preferable alternative "design" might have been to eliminate poverty and ignorance in the Arab world.
2. Are we dealing with a "system" to provide jobs for aerospace and other workers? If so, a preferable alternative "design" might have been to build a workable ground mass-transportation system.
3. Or are we dealing with a "system" to provide speedy travel? If so, a preferable alternative "design" might have involved short or vertical take-off and landing (STOL, VTOL) aircraft.

Such confusion of basic objectives and alternatives makes other issues, namely, the impact of the SST on the environment and the impact of the current concern over environmental despoliation on the SST program, almost incidental.

In May, 1971, SST pressure groups, working to catch the environmentalists unaware (an effort based on an incorrect sensing of the moods of the changing times) succeeded in getting the SST program partially reactivated in terms of a slight victory in the House of Representatives. However, the measure again failed to pass the Senate.

ASSESSMENT OF RESOURCES TO MEET SOCIOTECHNICAL PROBLEMS

It would not be a dramatic overstatement to assert that the health and viability of our society and world are directly dependent upon our abilities to deal with sociotechnical problems as defined in this book. Yet, because of the sheer complexity of interrelated problems, and especially because of the compression of time, there is no easy path to salvation. We can approach a program, though, by: (1) identifying skills needed and education for these skills; and (2) by determining best how to use and manage existing organizational frameworks.

Figure 3-3 indicates the scientific base supporting U.S. research and development programs. This is a cummulative plot of the dollars the government has spent since 1900. About $200 billion have already been spent with a projection of $500 to $700 billion more during the next 30 years. It is now instructive to ask, what is the behavioral-social science base for solving the formidable problems of today's society?

Skills and Education Needed

The sociotechnical field represents the emergence of a new scientific and professional discipline—or interdiscipline if you prefer. This book identifies the existing contributory disciplines, theories, and techniques. It is a first step to a reorientation in education. However, the organization of curricula utilizing available source materials is still a time-consuming job. The danger is that many problems may be beyond solution by the time sufficient persons are educated and trained to tackle them. Likewise, the skills we develop must be flexible in accordance with rapidly shifting problem bases. As we mentioned in Chapter 2, present experience indicates that training displaced aerospace engineers to fight pollution does not provide a route we wish to follow. We shall return to this topic in Chapter 9.

Management within Existing Organizational Frameworks

We can view the organizations of the future, say, of the period beyond 1985, as arising from two sources: (1) new organizations created in the light of

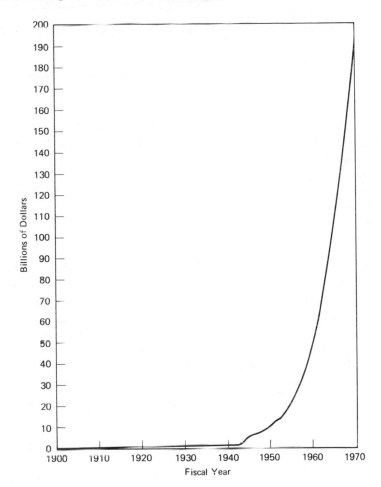

FIGURE 3-3
U.S. Government research and development cumulative expenditures.[4]

problem understanding and solution; and (2) the descendants of today's organizations which have been flexible and adaptive—or lucky—enough to survive. In the last chapter of this book we shall return to the topic of the first type of organization.

Existing organizations will require:

1. Managers who can and will perceive success and personal reward in terms

[4]Adapted from A. Hunter Dupree, 1964, *Science in the Federal Government—A History of Policies and Activities to 1940* and U.S. Government Sources, by William C. Gough in *Why Fusion? Controlled Thermonuclear Research Program*, WASH 1165, UC-20. Washington, D.C.: U.S. Government Printing Office, June 1970.

of the broad scope already discussed, rather than in terms of corporate profit and personal power.

2. Willingness honestly to expend energy and resources in longer-range problem solution, for example, in developing an alternative to the internal-combustion engine.

3. Fairly rapid response to changing public opinion and consumer attitudes.

4. Avoidance of over-reliance on one market or one customer.

5. An ability to discriminate between growth and success. The troubles of the airlines following blind, poorly planned introduction of the Boeing 747 provide an excellent case in point.

6. The ability to resist pointless competition: "If we don't build it, the Russians—or Germans or Japanese—will." "If we don't get in on the lucrative North Atlantic—or Hawaii—route, we'll lose out."

7. Ability to use effectively knowledge and expertise from behavioral and social science, ecology, and other newcomers to management decision-making, as well as the older inputs from economics, business practice, operations research, and engineering.

For another look at managing radical changes in large organizations, see Ansoff and Brandenburg (1971), who emphasize that evolutionary changes in organizations, once satisfactory, are no longer practical. Recognizing a need to integrate often conflicting physical information and behavioral and economic variables, these authors have formulated a language for the design of a purposive organization so as to maximize performance potential for achieving objectives.

Social Choice in Allocation of Resources to Jobs

Present emphasis is upon creating quantities of (new) jobs through economic growth, rather than on building personal rewards into jobs. There is too much emphasis upon the "hygienic factors" of fringe benefits, etc., rather than on satisfying personal needs. This persists in spite of formidable evidence that people are not motivated primarily by economic forces. Without a complete reevaluation of what the job means, it is likely that industry and government will continue to contribute to, rather than rectify, social turmoil.

Thus, for the above as well as the other reasons discussed in this chapter, production can no longer be considered the sole criterion for either industrial or national design, operations, or management. In addition, industrial responsibility toward its workers must transcend considerations of the individual firm, however important this might be. Industry must also consider its social impact on society in terms of displacement of workers, perhaps permanent, by automation.

SUMMARY AND CONCLUSIONS

The management of sociotechnical systems can be expected to become an increasingly formidable job, for a number of reasons. Among these reasons are ubiquitous exponential change characteristic of our times, the vastly expanded involvement of the social and physical environments, and the lack of established principles and guidelines for the management of complex organizations and of societies. Coupled with these are the refusal of many to abandon old philosophies and methods and to recognize the emergence of one of the great historical revolutions in human thought and behavior, and the blatant misuse of systems techniques.

The problems discussed in this chapter are basically worldwide and cannot be either reduced to, or alleviated by, any particular form of present societal structure or government.

The management of technology far transcends the search for products. An integral part of technology development from now on will be technology assessment, the results of which, expressed as impacts, may be used to proscribe an otherwise economically successful technology or product.

Management must be more honest, more flexible and adaptable, and—actually—more realistic. Systems theory and methodology, properly used, promise a major hope in restoring order from chaos.

REFERENCES

Anderson, F. M., G. E. Connolly, A. N. Halter, and W. M. Longhurst, 1971, *Simulation Experiments with a Biomanagement Model of a Deer Herd*, presented at IEEE Systems, Man and Cybernetic Group, Annual Symposium, Anaheim, Calif., 26 October.

Ansoff, H. I. and R. G. Brandenburg, 1971, A Language for Organization Design, *Management Science*, 17(12), B-705 to B-731, August.

Bosch, C. A., 1971, Redwoods: A Population Model, *Science*, 172 (3981), 345-49, 23 April.

Bower, Joseph L., 1969, Systems Analysis for Social Decisions, *Operations Research*, 17(6), 927-40, November-December.

Brooks, Harvey, and Raymond Bowers, 1970, The Assessment of Technology, *Scientific American*, 222(2), 13-21, February.

Dupree, A. Hunter, 1964, *Science in the Federal Government—A History of Policies and Activities to 1940*, New York: Harper and Row.

Frederickson, H. George, 1969, Exploring Urban Priorities: The Case of Syracuse, *Urban Affairs Quarterly*, 5(1), 31-43, September.

Galbraith, John K., 1958, *The Affluent Society*. Boston: Houghton-Mifflin.

Gerlach, Luther P., 1971, Movements of Revolutionary Change: Some Structural Characteristics, *American Behavioral Scientist*, 14(6), 812-36, July-August.

Gillette, Robert, 1971, Trans-Alaska Pipeline: Impact Study Receives Bad Reviews, *Science*, 171(3976), 1130-32, 19 March.

Goldman, Marshall I., 1970, The Convergence of Environmental Disruption, *Science*, 170(3953), 37-42, 2 October.

Goldsmith, John R., and Stephen A. Landaw, 1968, Carbon Monoxide and Human Health, *Science,* 162(3860), 1352-59, 20 December.

Gough, William C., 1970, *Why Fusion? Controlled Thermonuclear Research Program,* WASH 1165, UC-20. Washington, D.C.: U. S. Government Printing Office, June.

Gross, Bertram M., 1965, What Are Your Organization's Objectives? A General-Systems Approach to Planning, *Human Relations,* 18(3), 195-216, August.

Haggerty, James J., 1970, The Giant Harvest from Space—Today and Tomorrow, *Air Force and Space Digest,* 53(2), 30-43, February.

Hexter, Alfred C., and John R. Goldsmith, 1971, Carbon Monoxide: Association of Community Air Pollution with Mortality, *Science,* 172(3980), 265-67, 16 April.

Jones, Martin V., 1971, *A Technology Assessment Methodology: Project Summary,* MTR-6009, Springfield, Va.: U.S. Department of Commerce, National Technical Information Service, June.

Lave, Lester B., and Eugene P. Seskin, 1970, Air Pollution and Human Health, *Science,* 169(3947), 723-33, 21 August.

Libby, L. M., 1971, *Fifty More Timely Problems of the Environment,* P-4589. Santa Monica, Calif.: The RAND Corporation.

Livingston, J. Sterling, 1971, Myth of the Well-Educated Manager, *Harvard Business Review,* 49(1), 79-89, January-February.

MacDonald, Gordon J. F., 1971, *The Global Environmental Crisis,* presented at IEEE Systems, Man and Cybernetics Group, Annual Symposium, Anaheim, Calif., 27 October.

Morison, Robert S., 1969, Science and Social Attitudes, *Science,* 165 (3889), 150-56, 11 July.

National Academy of Sciences, 1965, *Basic Research and National Goals.* A report to the Committee on Science and Astronautics, U.S. House of Representatives, March.

——, 1969, *Technology: Processes of Assessment and Choice,* Washington, D.C.: U.S. Government Printing Office, July.

Ripley, S. Dillon, 1971, Conservation Comes of Age, *American Scientist,* 59(5), 529-31, September-October.

Russell, Clifford S., and Hans H. Landsberg, 1971, International Environmental Problems—A Taxonomy, *Science,* 172(3990), 1307-14, 25 June.

United States Department of the Interior, 1972, *Final Environmental Impact Statement: Proposed Trans-Alaska Pipeline.* In 6 volumes. Washington, D.C.: U.S. Government Printing Office.

United States Government, 1969, *Budget of the United States, Special Analyses, Fiscal Year 1970.* Washington, D.C.: U.S. Government Printing Office.

United States Government, Technology Application Group of the George Washington University Medical Center, 1971, *Applications of Aerospace Technology in the Public Sector.* Annual Review for the Period 1 June 1970-31 May 1971. Washington, D.C.: National Aeronautics and Space Administration.

II

SYSTEMS METHODOLOGY

The analysis, design, and management of sociotechnical systems have at their disposal a wide selection of methodology. However, it must be emphasized that: (1) there is no one all-purpose methodology, and (2) all present methodology possesses at least certain deficiencies where large and complex problems are concerned.

Chapter 4 is an overview of systems analysis in which we examine the nature, use, and limitations of systems analysis, especially the important criterion problem. Chapter 5 continues this discussion with a treatment of modeling and simulation. Chapter 6 examines the important areas of data availability, validity, and reliability, and representative sources of data; the need for improved dynamic and (near) realtime data is especially stressed. Chapter 6 also looks further at specific quantification methods that have received widespread application, and at means of dealing with qualitative data, an area where the development of new methods is of especially critical urgency. This Part concludes with Chapter 7, a consideration of our capabilities and limitations to make future projections and forecasts, and an examination of some specific techniques.

4

Systems Analysis

OVERVIEW AND BASIC NATURE
OF SYSTEMS ANALYSIS

Systems analysis consists of a mixture of logical, quantitative and/or subjective and intuitive processes; this mixture presents varying degrees of formality. Systems analysis possesses a large literature today. Its applications are many, and it shows much promise in furthering our understanding of sociotechnical systems. Its misapplications can also be noted, and like all technology, it can be used by the wrong hands for purposes of mischief.

Because systems analysis far transcends "the scientific method applied to high-level decision-making" or the numerical and analytic solutions of operations research, it is often considered more art than science. It is best understood in terms of case histories, or, better, through actually undertaking a systems analysis.

In the following discussion you should pay particular attention to these features:

1. The ambiguity of terminology and great difficulty in defining "goals," "objectives," "alternatives," "criteria," and so on.
2. The often almost symbiotic relationship between analyst and user.
3. The difficulty in recognizing what *the* system is and where its boundaries lie.
4. The difficulty in recognizing *the* important independent and dependent variables.

5. The frequent paucity or absence of data to verify the assumptions made.

6. The immense difficulty in determining "throughput," "intervening variable," or "transfer function" mechanisms, even when the proper inputs and outputs are recognized and specified.

7. The frequent difficulty in applying the results of even a good analysis.

8. The difficulty in ascertaining the impact of the analysis on future policies and operations, with the corollary deficiency in feedback as to the effects of a good (or bad) analysis.

The problem of the system, the system boundary, and the user are exemplified, say, in "criminal justice" studies. In this case, there are subtle symbiotic relationships between cops, robbers, merchants, and politicians. Similarly, as discussed earlier, the detached and impartial analyses of scientists themselves remain today highly suspect. We might state somewhat flamboyantly: in the sociotechnical macrosystem, the pawns, foot soldiers, and cannon fodder wear the panoplies of game theory and computer data-processing.

The application of systems analysis to sociotechnical problems may be limited by the immense replication of managements in all the fields, and by rigid legal and social restrictions to many experimental studies and pilot implementations. And, unfortunately, the methodology for program evaluation is still weak.

As we have seen, in the most general sense, a system can be considered to be made up of elements which work together toward the over-all objective of the whole. Alternatively, a system can be considered to be a set of elements coordinated to accomplish a set of goals. There are, of course, several systems approaches, not just one, but these have in common the very important property of thinking about total systems and their elements (Churchman, 1968).

Systems analysis may be defined, for example, as (Quade and Boucher, 1968, p. 2):

> A systematic approach to helping a decision-maker choose a course of action by investigating his full problem, searching out objectives and alternatives, and comparing them in the light of their consequences, using an appropriate framework—in so far as possible analytic—to bring expert judgment and intuition to bear on the problem.

Systems analysis emphasizes study of a particular situation, not deduction from well-established theory. In addition, there is heavy dependence upon the judgments of experts, in turn dependent upon construction of and operation within a model.

Theory tends to come late in the development of a field and after many false starts. Theory may lag behind actual events. The absence of basic theory makes it quite difficult to tell a person how to undertake a systems analysis. Further, the steps to be discussed later are more easily stated than followed; selection of objectives, measures of effectiveness, and criteria may be particularly difficult, and, as we have already stressed, even recognition of the problem and the system may present formidable obstacles. Selection of the wrong problem or wrong objectives will lead to trite, or misleading results.

Systems analysis may be considered to have two major uses: (1) to advise in policy-making and decision-making and to sharpen intuition and broaden ability to make judgments; and (2) to advance the scientific understanding of systems.

Systems analysis, of course, cannot stand alone, but is dependent upon numerous antecedent and parallel subsystem studies performed in the laboratory, in the field, by computer, etc. Many additional man-hours must be devoted to these supportive efforts.

A major problem with regard to systems analysis revolves around drawing the line between premature design or policymaking and no analysis on the one hand, and interminable analysis and data gathering on the other.

Models, to which we return in more detail in the next chapter, can be thought of as aiding the organization of thought, thus allowing any qualified person to retrace the steps of the systems analysis. Models of truly complex systems cannot be mathematic or analytic, but must involve simulation, that is, the imitating of a system. There is no universal model. Model-building should begin with the identification of persistent relationships among relevant variables.

The number of variables in a complex system is immense, and the determination of which variables to keep (the key variables) and which to ignore is difficult. Some variables have about the same effect on all the alternatives. This insensitivity often must be found by assigning arbitrary values to variables it is impossible to calculate and then observing the effect on the solution.

Systems analysis can never be completely impartial, because it is imbedded in the politico-social milieu; choice is often thus not among alternatives but among objectives or policies, with their implied conflicts among vested interests. Under these circumstances, it is usually impossible for the analyst himself to remain unbiased.

Objectives exist at different levels of reality. One way to distinguish real from stated objectives is to ask if the system will knowingly sacrifice other goals to achieve any given objective (Churchman, 1968).

The environment of a system deals with things or people that are fixed or given, from the system's point of view, and the system cannot do much about them. This might involve a fixed budget or policy, for example. To be in the environment, these things and people must matter relative to the system objectives. Similarly, resources, money, personnel, equipment, etc., used by the system to do its jobs, are within the system.

In recognizing the system there is always danger if one emphasizes apparent structure, for example, an organization chart, over function. Functions tend to crosscut such superficial structure; thus, measures of effectiveness or cost based on structure may be very misleading. In such cases, the costs of system activities may be unrelated to the true requirements for these activities, making it almost impossible to model the effectiveness of the system.

One stage of a systems approach is to look at the system imbedded in an existing system and to ask what the system would look like if the larger system were radically changed (Churchman, 1968).

Systems performance effectiveness is multidimensional. It is usually impossible to derive a single effectiveness scale broad enough to integrate dissimilar subsystems into an over-all effect.

All systems analysis suffers from the heritage of operations research, with its emphasis on dealing with analytic models and quantitative terms to the greatest possible degree. There may be a common language using such terms as "criterion," "objective," "constraint," "variable," and "optimize," but widely different capabilities to relate these words to things (see also the sections on operations research in Chapter 6). Nevertheless, a major value of subsystem analyses, operations research studies, and the individual cases considered in Chapter 8 lies in deriving recommendations for interface policies at the next, and even higher, hierarchical levels. A major output of a subsystem study must reflect interface and impact problems and how that study can be used in a larger context. Likewise, the "system integrator" must exert pressure on the "subsystem team" for this output.

Apart from the formal definition given above, the term, *systems analysis,* is used in many different ways by different workers in the field. It is probably fair to say that no one comprehensive treatise on systems analysis has yet appeared. Such a treatise would have to cover at least the many types of systems, hierarchical organization of systems, types of system-environment interrelationships, and specific, yet complementary, techniques. These features are considered throughout this book, but not as limited specifically to systems analysis. For our purposes here, we summarize the following techniques which, alone or in combination, represent the practice of systems analysis to different workers:

1. Mathematical modeling
2. Computer modeling and simulation
3. Operations research studies
4. Flow diagramming
5. Data collection through use of files; records; computerized information storage and retrieval systems; bibliographies and literature searches; sampling, surveying, and opinion polling; interviews; and laboratory studies
6. Human factors analyses
7. Behavioral and small-group analyses and simulations
8. Use of scenarios and manual simulations and games
9. Cost-effectiveness analysis
10. Benefit-cost analysis
11. Program planning and budgeting

12. Long-range forecasting studies

13. Utilization of experts, including use of the Delphi judgmental approach

For a general historical review of systems analysis, as presented by RAND Corporation personnel who pioneered many of the methods, see Quade and Boucher (1968). Although most of the cases and examples are taken from a military context, the book is of value in terms of general large-scale systems analysis, planning, and decision-making. For a view of four different philosophies of the "systems approach," see Churchman (1968). For a treatment of systems analysis with a human factors-behavioral science emphasis, see De Greene (1970). And for a short and readable summary of systems analysis geared toward problems of local governments, see Parker (1968).

THE PRACTICE OF SYSTEMS ANALYSIS

In this chapter, we can consider a number of "steps in systems analysis." This cookbook approach must be greatly modified to consider the formidable problems of boundary, system level, real system variables, the user, verifying data, etc. Indeed, extension of these problems provides much of the theme of this book. Nevertheless, guidance such as follows provides a valuable point of departure for analysis of complex systems. For a further discussion of such lists of steps, see Quade and Boucher (1968); Halpert, Horvath and Young (1970); and Forrester (1970).

Systems analysis can be considered to possess the following formal or implicit iterative steps:

1. *Recognition of a problem that can be couched in systems terms and that is amenable to systems analysis.* This involves identifying a system, an environment, and observing system behavior to identify trouble symptoms.

2. *Definition of the problem.* This involves the more detailed identification of subsystems and other system elements, of inputs and outputs as appropriate, of dynamic features such as feedback structures and the rate and level variables of the systems dynamics approach, and of interactions between system and environment. It further involves the recognition, definition, and measurement of total system objectives, of conflicting system or subsystem objectives as appropriate, and of the main decision-makers. Also involved are the recognition and definition of alternative means of achieving the objectives, and establishment of some measures of efficiency of or satisfaction with the alternatives relative to performance, quality, and costs. Unfortunately, such measures have been expressed, either directly or indirectly, almost entirely in terms of easily quantified features of performance, and of money. We should emphasize the dangers

of reliance on oversimplified measures of cost and effectiveness. This represents perhaps one of the grossest misuses of nonhardware technology.

3. *Conceptualization of the realword situation in terms of a model(s).* This involves determining the various independent and dependent variables and trying to establish a functional or mathematical relationship between them. There are three broad categories of formalized (not simply conceptual) models:

   a. *Iconic,* which resembles what it represents, e.g., the scale model of a building.

   b. *Analog,* like a chart, graph, flow diagram, or computer simulation model. These models are of greatest importance in the study of complex systems.

   c. *Analytic or mathematic.* These models are of particular importance in operations research and at the subsystem level.

   We shall return to a fuller discussion of modeling and simulation in the next chapter.

4. *Determination of criteria for ranking alternatives in order of desirability.* This has usually involved weighing costs against effectiveness. The qualitative, subjective, and probabilistic features of complex systems militate agains the use of simple cost-effectiveness measures. The *criterion problem* is a key one in systems analysis, and we shall return to it later in this chapter.

5. *Using the model, derivation of a mathematical solution or a simulation result.*

6. *Testing and modification of the model until it is valid.* This involves determination of isomorphism between the model and the real world. This can be aided by *sensitivity testing,* that is, changing parameters to see how sensitive the model is to incorrect estimates. One should be careful, however, not to reject a fundamentally good model on the basis of incorrect data. The problem of the validation of models of complex systems, discussed in the next chapter, is a formidable one.

7. *Implementation of the solution.* This may be very difficult because of political or economic constraints or changes, organizational resistance to change, or poor working relationships between analyst and user.

8. *Monitoring the effects of change on the operation of the system.* A change in system structure or policy is seldom complete by itself, but should be thought of as one step of an ongoing process.

These guidelines can be extended and embellished, based on Quade's (1968c) principles of good systems analyses:

1. Pay major attention to problem formulation or definition, as opposed to overconcern with detail, early in the analysis.

2. Set forth hypotheses early, and modify the first set of assumptions and first model accordingly.

3. Stress choice of the right objectives what ought to be done. This is crucial. Otherwise, the analysis will be off on the wrong track from the beginning.

4. Keep the analysis systems oriented, expanding the system boundaries as required.

5. Never exclude alternatives arbitrarily, for example, because of "party-line" pressures.

6. Attempt to create, as well as to eliminate, alternatives. New alternatives are often better. This places the analyst also in the role of designer.

7 Be satisfied that a partial analysis is better than none. Partial answers to important questions are more useful than complete answers to trivial questions.

8. Suboptimize with care; criteria for lower-level choices may be inconsistent with those at higher levels. Also, a good new idea may be worth a thousand optimizations.

9. Let the problem, not specific phenomena, determine the model.

10. Emphasize the question, not the model.

11. Avoid overemphasizing mathematics and computing; these are only tools aiding judgment.

12. Analyze the competitor's policies, strategies, and tactics.

13. Remember that estimates of cost, effectiveness, time, state-of-the-art, social acceptability, etc. are essential to a choice among alternatives.

14. Do not select an alternative simply because it is the lowest cost choice within a single contingency.

15. Treat uncertainties explicitly.

16. Postpone detail until later; a rough treatment of many models is better than a detailed treatment of one. The decision-maker can compensate to some extent for uncertainty, for example, by postponing action.

17. Use sensitivity testing or sensitivity analysis, which shows how a system criterion is affected by one or more assumptions or variables influencing its value. This is particularly important because there are no "best" assumptions.

18. Use interdisciplinary teams, which are almost always necessary because a problem looks different to different specialists.

19. Undertake only with extreme caution sponsoring the R & D of a specific system to exist in a very uncertain future.

20. Remember the essence of systems analysis is the efficient use of expert judgment, accomplished by constructing an appropriate model which, by introducing precise structure and terminology, provides a medium for effective communications in a concrete setting.

Finally, we emphasize these guidelines are general, but nevertheless may not cover the analysis requirements of any given system.

SPECIAL CONSIDERATIONS OF SOCIAL
AND SOCIOTECHNICAL SYSTEMS

The problems we have discussed so far may apply to any systems analysis, even to the apparently straightforward development and implementation of simple hardware systems. These problems are heightened markedly when we deal with social and sociotechnical systems. In this section we consider those areas of particular concern to nonmilitary, nonaerospace systems.

Systems analysis can be an invaluable aid to social decision-making by: (1) providing insights to those who must make judgments as to the use of society's resources; and (2) providing the framework both for planning and budgeting and for reorganizing the process of resource allocation. However, there are political, technical, and organizational prerequisites to the successful application of systems analysis. It is almost always necessary for the political leadership to support the analysis and for the analysis to serve objectively the legitimate leadership. Much that the analyst may desire to change is part of the constitutionally based political structure. The results of systems analysis tend to be long-range programs; however, political tenure is much shorter and ongoing planning and funding cannot be guaranteed.

Often, in an entire agency of government there is no one who can or will make use of the analysis. Analysis must be viewed as an opportunity rather than a threat, yet language is often a barrier to communication on the part of both the analyst and the politician or bureaucrat.

Institutions making social decisions often find that society has changed, leaving them less relevant. Evaluations of objectives in planning will help protect an organization from obsolescence. Such examination of prior goals leads to the discovery of the integral relationship between the ends of society and the means of achieving these ends.

It is well to remember that all goals are inconsistent, that some involve unbearable costs, and that resources are inevitably limited. Further, alternative programs must be judged in terms of organizational, social, and environmental consequences, not just in terms of economic costs and performance effectiveness. These consequences may impose severe constraints upon the implementation of policy.

The role of the analyst vis-à-vis the decision-maker is moot. Some writers (e.g., Bower, 1969) believe the analyst should remain in the "how to" capacity and stay out of the "should we" business. Nevertheless, systems analysts historically have exerted strong influence on the shaping of policy. Further, systems analysis *in toto* is undoubtedly an instrument of social change. As such, it may be both a threat to those with formal power and a new source of informal power for those low in, or outside, the bureaucratic hierarchy. Of more long-term significance, implementation of programs based on systems analysis may result in a basic restructuring of organizations and of management (for example, a change from decentralization or centralization of decision-making). See Bower (1969) for a discussion of examples of the effects of systems analysis in an educational project for local government, and in an information storage and retrieval project for state government.

Dealing with uncertainty is a commonly stressed attribute of systems analysis. Uncertainty is used in a general sense to describe an unknown future, and also in a sense, usually in game theory and statistical decision theory, to describe subjective or other unknown probability distributions. Such a situation of uncertainty is usually contrasted with a situation of risk which involves an objective probability distribution.

Systems alternatives exist in an uncertain future associated with social and technological innovations and change and, often, the actions of the opponent. Such a combination of social, technological, and political factors is called a *contingency*. Most systems analyses are applicable only within a given contingency and not across contingencies. In this sense, it is possible to perform suboptimized subsystem studies within each contingency. This approach should not be followed too far, however, because interactions limit the amount of suboptimization within each subsystem and the subsystem studies must eventually be synthesized. A table or matrix relating alternative designs or policies to different effectiveness scales is called a *contingency table*. A similar approach in a Program Planning and Budgeting System can be used to interrelate subprograms to requirements, to costs, to benefits, or to measures of performance. In this context, suboptimization is defined as the operation of one element of a system at its optimum without regard to the operation of the entire system, which may operate at less than its optimum value.

The number of possible futures and, hence, of possible contingencies is immense. Attaway (1968) suggests the following ways of eliminating contingencies:

1. "Best-estimate" analysis, in which the uncertain factors are assumed to coincide with the analyst's best estimate of these factors, a situation which is rarely true.
2. Worst-case analysis, in which the system is designed against the most exacting demands upon it. It is then assumed the system should also work against lesser contingencies.
3. *A fortiori* analysis, in which one alternative is designed as optimistically as possible, and the contingency most favorable to that alternative is selected. If the alternative then performs badly it is discarded and another selected.

Mandansky (1968) adds the following ways to handle uncertainty in systems analysis: Buy time until technology or social or political situation changes; buy information, that is, collect data; buy flexibility in system design; deal with a range of values; and use sensitivity analysis to modify assumptions or eliminate variables.

When purely quantitative techniques are not applicable to systems analysis, that is, when there is major social and political content to the system, four other approaches are possible: (1) computer simulations, discussed in detail elsewhere in this book; (2) scenarios, which are statements of assumptions about the system operating-environment; start with the present state of the world, and, using experts, show step-by-step how the future might evolve; (3) manual or computerized operational games, in which experts play roles in a two-sided confrontation in an economic, management, military, social, or other situation; and (4) the Delphi technique, which has now been computerized (Umpleby, 1969).

More than the first three, Delphi has been considerably used in forecasting the future; in addition, Delphi may be of great value in helping experts arrive at consensus in setting up high-level policies and goals. The Delphi technique is sometimes defined as *cybernetic arbitration,* because deliberation of a group of experts is steered through feedback by a control group over several iterations until consensus is reached (Quade, 1968a). Delphi typically involves the use of successive questionnaires, calculation of median and first and third quartile values, anonymous feedback with documentation of extreme views, and iterative working toward consensus. The Delphi technique, discussed further in Chapters 6 and 7, should be conceptually integrated with classical psychophysical techniques and with the Cooper Rating Scale approach to aircraft evaluation.

The above are ongoing areas of importance. However, the most critical problems of interest to us here stem from the recognition of complex systems as just that—complex. And this requires the recognition and definition of variables, in addition to economic ones. These include a plethora of social and socio-technical indicators, things relating to technology, population growth, human motivational behavior, health, education, scientific knowledge, and so forth, discussed in detail elsewhere in this book.

Beginning in the mid-1960s, there has been a great interest in social accounting, stemming partly from the needs of policy-makers and partly from the activities of social scientists themselves. The Program Planning and Budgeting System, in attempting to determine direct and indirect benefits likely from identifiable inputs (costs) and outputs (services), must answer: "What does this service *mean* to people?" This cannot be done without social indicators and better data. Both at the federal and local levels pressures are arising for more comprehensive planning models, including people as well as land and money, and social as well as economic variables.

Social scientists as well as economists have developed partial-system models. This makes it easier to conceive of larger models integrating economic, political, sociological, and cultural variables into a general systems framework. Some of the work has brought together qualitative and quantitative information. However, much of this work lacks a conceptual framework into which information can be fitted. One ambitious effort to combine model-building with fact collection is provided by *Social Indicators* (Bauer, 1966). This volume deals with an entire set of indicators the authors feel are necessary to answer questions concerning any aspect of a society's past, present, or future.

There are different varieties of social accounting, related partially to the system level involved. According to Gross (1967), a *micro* approach involves identifying inputs that do not occur on the cost accounts of single organizations or proposed projects. In the *macro* case, crude attempts at sensing the social pulse of an entire nation are made. Unfortunately, "social" is often used in the residual sense, i.e., leftover after the economic variables have been dealt with. The term, *social systems analysis,* is preferable because it connotes the entire society, not just residual material. Social systems analysis can be carried out at either a *micro* or *macro* level. An immense amount of conceptual and fact-finding work is, of course, necessary to implement such a system at the national level. We shall return to the all-important topics of "models of society" and the management of society in Chapters 8 and 9.

THE CRITERION PROBLEM

The criterion problem remains one of the thorniest in systems analysis, because without realistic *standards* of effectiveness, worth, costs, value, or benefits it is impossible to assess either the original assumptions or the analysis as a whole.

The luxury of grossly oversimplified quantification must be resisted. When dealing with sociotechnical systems, intangible, subjective, intuitive, and qualitative variables are probably preeminent, even though their effects are tenuous, subtle, and delayed.

A criterion can be considered a rule or standard for ranking alternatives in order of desirability; it provides, for example, a means of weighing cost against performance effectiveness, and hence of determining choice. Criteria, like objectives, are not static, and evolve over a systems analysis. It may be neither desirable nor possible to specify criteria in detail before results of a study are in hand. Likewise, desirable objectives can be identified early but realizable objectives only after study or analysis. There should be evolution of both objectives and criteria with changes in the political picture, in society, and in science and technology.

In social and sociotechnical systems, a wide variety of things may serve as criteria. What represents a criterion in one system or in one situation may not necessarily do so in the next. Representative criteria are time, space, number of users, multiple use, goods or services per capita, standard of living, energy efficiency, quality of life, stress, pollution level, happiness index, esthetic appeal, feasibility, amount of leisure, crimes per capita, errors and accidents, number of mental patients rehabilitated, and so forth. We shall return to examples using these and other criteria in subsequent chapters.

Criteria have been traditionally summarized—and often presented as a "solution" to the user—as benefit/cost and cost/effectiveness ratios. Benefit/cost ratios require the reduction of both benefits and costs to monetary units; cost/effectiveness ratios permit non-economic measures of effectiveness. We shall offer examples of the use of these techniques in Chapter 8. For purposes of completeness, we provide one example here, which represents an insightful way of dealing with the tenuous variables of societal systems.

Benefit/Cost
Assumptions as to User Benefits

Starr (1969) has attempted to develop a methodology for revealing existing social preferences and values, in order to provide insight on social benefits and their costs, relative to national decisions on new technological developments. Incidentally, the methodology helps answer the question: "How safe is safe enough?" Based on certain assumptions, Starr provides calculations pertaining to motor-vehicle fatalities, and fatalities in other transportation (including commercial and general aviation) and voluntary sport activities, disease, etc. Starr attempts to establish relationships between social benefit and justified social cost, in addition to the customary performance-versus-cost relationships which are part of all engineering planning and design. Basically, he tries to establish a quantitative measure of benefit relative to cost for accidental deaths arising from public technological developments.

Analysis is based on the assumptions that historical national accident patterns are relevant for revealing consistent fatality patterns in the public use of technology, and that these patterns are sufficiently enduring to permit prediction. Starr believes that such an empirical approach provides insights into social values relative to personal risk. It should be noted that he does not attempt to determine "what is best for society."

Conventional socioeconomic benefits are health, education, and income; these can ostensibly be related to improvements in the quality of life. If we can understand quantitatively the causal relationships between technological developments and societal values, we will be in a position to guide these developments to achievement of maximum social benefit and minimum social cost. However, such a *predictive systems analysis* has not yet been developed, although we suggest the present book is a step in this direction.

Starr uses as a risk measure the statistical probability of fatalities per hour of exposure of the person to the given activity. These units seem to be associated with the "individual's intuitive processes." The social benefit of each activity is converted into a dollar equivalent as a measure of integrated value to the individual. Starr recognizes the oversimplification, but has no better measure. In the case of voluntary activities, the amount of money spent by a person is assumed proportional to the benefit to him. In the case of involuntary activities, the contribution of the activity to his annual income, or its equivalent, is assumed porportional to the benefit. For example, in the case of transportation, benefits are equated with the sum of the monetary cost to the person, and value of time saved.

Starr arbitrarily defines public awareness of social benefits as the product of the relative level of advertising, the square of the percentage of the population involved in the activity, and the relative usefulness or importance of the activity. He recognizes the negative effects of advertising, as with smoking and its fictitious benefit-risk ratio. Starr concludes that: (1) The acceptability of risk appears to be roughly proportional to the third power of the real or imagined benefits. (2) The acceptable risk is inversely proportional to the number of people participating in the activity. (3) Motor-vehicle risk appears to have leveled off at about 100 fatalities per hour of exposure. Most of the U.S. is involved in this event; hence, this, because of its public visibility, may be of criterion or predictive value relative to social acceptability. And (4) the statistical risk of death from disease appears to be a psychological yardstick for establishing other risk levels.

LIMITATIONS OF SYSTEMS ANALYSIS

The limitations of systems analysis can be classified as those which appear to be intrinsic and those associated with misuse.

Quade (1968b, 1968c) concludes systems analysis will always be deficient in that:

1. Analysis is necessarily incomplete because of limitations in time, money, and manpower, because of the changing nature of the real world, and because of ignorance or uncertainty with regard to intangible and other variables.
2. Measures of effectiveness, and even of cost, may be hard to come by. This is partly due to the fact that system objectives tend to be multiple, conflicting, and ill-defined.
3. There are still severe limitations on our ability to predict the future.
4. Systems analysis may fall short of scientific research. Because of political, social, or military restrictions it may be impossible to verify our models.

We may add further:

5. Systems analysis must function in a dynamic milieu of changing definitions of problems, objectives, alternatives, and criteria; hence, to many people, it is quite frustrating, threatening, and even to be opposed.
6. Systems analysis is very expensive, and cost may preclude its application to small-scale environmental and social problems.

Systems analysis has been frequently misused with regard to (Quade, 1968b, 1968c):

1. Emphasizing what the system can do rather than what it ought to do.
2. Being unduly influenced by dogma ("the party line"), maintaining a rigid position in the face of new evidence, or accepting evidence only from "captive" scientists and engineers.
3. Failing to communicate with other specialists or with decision-makers and policy-makers.
4. Emphasizing suboptimization because the whole to which the part belongs cannot really be completely defined. The analyst should thus accept uncertainty rather than suboptimize.
5. Being overly preoccupied with the model, its details, mathematics, and computations.
6. Misusing the model.
7. Curtailing analysis because of administrative deadlines.
8. Failing to make explicit assumptions and subjective judgments.

This perhaps presents a pessimistic picture. However, there is no choice but to follow a systems approach. Competitive approaches do not provide the capability to let someone else examine the work, evaluate it, and modify it with new information; there is no better way of helping people make decisions in the face of real uncertainty. But this must be in the context of changing times, as stressed throughout this book. The systems analysis of the future will include many qualitative and subjective variables, perhaps emphasize values, and involve participation by large numbers of persons, not just formal "experts."

Finally, it would be advantageous to review the history of the demonstrated usefulness of systems analysis applied to specific policies and decisions, the acceptance or nonacceptance of the methodology, and the education of users and practitioners in the field. Yet, it may still be premature to do this, because of the time lags associated with complex systems. Additionally, our ability to relate analysis to policy to successful implementation of policy is still largely curtailed by the shroud of governmental and industrial secrecy. We can eventually expect the bitter with the sweet—we do have our F-111s, C-5As, and Southeast Asian wars, as well as our successful space programs.

SUMMARY AND CONCLUSIONS

Systems analysis represents a body of interrelated concepts, methods, practices, and experiences. It does not as yet represent a theory of systems, nor is it based on theory. A number of guidelines can be offered to provide an orientation to systems analysis, but these must be greatly extended by experience in performing actual analyses. The really difficult problems derive from system conceptualization, recognition and definition of subtle variables and interactions, and system-environment interrelationships, rather than from the calculation and computation that have usually been emphasized. In the long run, systems analysis, at least as applied to complex social, sociotechnical, and environmental problems, cannot be separated from the theoretical and management concepts applicable to this book as a whole.

REFERENCES

Attaway, L. D., 1968, Criteria and the Measure of Effectiveness. In E. S. Quade and W. I. Boucher (eds.), *Systems Analysis and Policy Planning: Applications in Defense,* pp. 54-80. New York: American Elsevier.

Bauer, Raymond A., (ed.), 1966, *Social Indicators.* Cambridge, Mass.: The M.I.T. Press.

Bower, Joseph L., 1969, Systems Analysis for Social Decisions, *Operations Research,* 17(6), 927-40, November-December.

Churchman, C. West, 1968, *The Systems Approach.* New York: Dell.

De Greene, Kenyon B., 1970, Systems Analysis Techniques. In K. B. De Greene (ed.), *Systems Psychology,* pp. 79-130. New York: McGraw-Hill.

Forrester, Jay W., 1970, Systems Analysis as a Tool for Urban Planning, *IEEE Transactions on Systems Science and Cybernetics,* SSC-6(4), 258-65.

Gross, Bertram M., 1967, The Coming General Systems Models of Social Systems, *Human Relations,* 20(4), 357-74, November.

Halpert, Harold P., William J. Horvath, and John P. Young, 1970, *An Administrator's Handbook on the Application of Operations Research to the Management of Mental Health Systems,* National Clearinghouse for Mental Health Information, Publication No. 1003. Washington, D.C.: U.S. Government Printing Office.

Madansky, Adam, 1968, Uncertainty. In E. S. Quade and W. I. Boucher (eds.), *Systems Analysis and Policy Planning: Applications in Defense,* pp. 81-96. New York: American Elsevier.

Parker, John K., 1968, *Introduction to Systems Analysis,* Report No. 298. Washington, D.C.: International City Managers Association.

Quade, E. S., 1968a, When Quantitative Models Are Inadequate. In E. S. Quade and W. I. Boucher (eds.), *Systems Analysis and Policy Planning: Applications in Defense,* pp. 324-44. New York: American Elsevier.

——, 1968b, Pitfalls and Limitations. In E. S. Quade and W. I. Boucher (eds.), *Systems Analysis and Policy Planning: Applications in Defense,* pp. 345-63. New York: American Elsevier.

——, 1968c, *By Way of Summary.* In E. S. Quade and W. I. Boucher (eds.), *Systems Analysis and Policy Planning: Applications in Defense,* pp. 418-29. New York: American Elsevier.

Quade, E. S., and W. I. Boucher, 1968, *Systems Analysis and Policy Planning: Applications in Defense.* New York: American Elsevier.

Starr, Chauncey, 1969, Social Benefit versus Technological Risk, *Science,* 165(3899), 1232-38, 19 September.

Umpleby, Stuart, 1969, *The Delphi Exploration: A Computer-Based System for Obtaining Subjective Judgments on Alternative Futures, A Progress Report.* Urbana, Ill.: University of Illinois, August.

5

Modeling and Simulation

WHY MODELING?

Although modeling and simulation are integral parts of systems analysis, as we have seen in the last chapter, they are of such profound importance to the study of social and sociotechnical systems that we are devoting a separate chapter to them. Indeed, it would be impossible to disassociate modeling and simulation from the major themes of this book. See, for example, the many specific types of models and simulations discussed in Chapters 1 and 8.

A model in the simplest sense is an abstraction or idealization. Today "model" is an IN-word. What many people call models today would have been called theories or constructs a generation ago. The distinction between models, theories, and simulations is not always clear. For our purposes here, all theories can be considered to be models, but obviously such models as scale models of buildings and flow diagrams are not theories. Theory tends to be vaguer than many models can necessarily be. Likewise, simulations can be viewed as either one form of model or as something one does on or with a model (say, with a computer) once the model has been at least partially formalized. We shall employ both usages of the term *simulation*, but shall stress the latter.

Forrester (1968) has the following to say about modeling and simulation: A model is a substitute for a system. The unaided human mind is not adequate for constructing and interpreting dynamic models of social and technological systems as they change through time. This situation can be improved by converting from mental models or descriptive statements to flow diagrams and equations. Difficulties with purely mental modes are several. First, mental models are ill-defined and based on changing assumptions; they show a high degree of internal contradiction. Second, assumptions are not clearly identified. Third, mental models are not easy to communicate to others; language is imprecise.

Finally, mental models of dynamic systems cannot be manipulated easily. We typically draw conclusions based on analogy to past experience, rather than by tracing interactions. Thus, understanding the behavior of a linear, single-loop, first-order system aids little in anticipating the behavior of a nonlinear, multiloop, several-order system. We cannot manage all features of such complex systems at one time; hence, we fragment the system and draw conclusions separately from the subsystems, yielding little insight as to how the subsystems interact.

CLASSIFICATION OF MODELS

Models can be classified in a number of different ways. There is not always a sharp distinction between different members of a category, and models of truly complex systems possess features of most categories. Our classification of models, meant to be indicative rather than exhaustive, is:

1. By stage of development: (a) conceptual, and (b) postconceptual.
2. By how they are expressed: (a) verbal; (b) block or flow diagram; (c) computer program; and (d) mathematical, e.g., $E = mc^2$, $F = ma$, and the models of operations research.
3. By degree of abstraction, or fidelity, or relationship to the real world: (a) iconic; (b) analytic (also numerical, or symbolic); and (c) simulation. These terms have been defined in the last chapter.
4. By degree to which specific rules can be preprogrammed: (a) algorithmic, and (b) heuristic.
5. By what they urge the planner, policy-maker, or decision-maker to do: (a) descriptive; (b) predictive; and (c) planning.
6. By hierarchical level: (a) system, and (b) subsystem. Or alternatively: (a) macro, and (b) micro.
7. By content: (a) behavioral; (b) social; (c) technological; (d) socio-technical; (e) demographic; (f) economic; and (g) other.
8. As (a) linear, or (b) nonlinear.
9. As (a) discrete, or (b) continuous.
10. As (a) static, or (b) dynamic.
11. As (a) deterministic, or (b) probabilistic.
12. As (a) manual, or (b) automatic.
13. By (a) absence, or (b) presence of conflict.

14. As based on systems theory: (a) open system; (b) closed system; (c) open-loop system; (d) closed-loop system; and (e) other.

Most of the above features should be self-evident, or are defined and discussed elsewhere in this book. However, the models related closely to policy-making and planning warrant a little more attention here.

There are three main classes of such models (Lowry, 1965). *Descriptive models* typically involve computer simulation of features of an existing socio-technical environment or observed process of sociotechnical change. They can tell much about the structure of the environment by reducing complexity to the rigor of mathematical relationships. They dramatize how everything in the system affects everything else. They do not provide information about the future or choice among alternative programs.

Predictive models involve specifying a causal sequence, as opposed to the descriptive statement of covariation (e.g., that variable Y has the value of 5 X). If one can postulate the direction of causation, knowledge of the future value of the "cause" enables prediction of the future value of the "effect." Usually one states the model in the form, "if X occurs, Y will follow" without explicitly indicating the likelihood of X's occurrence. This is conditional prediction.

Planning models are not far developed; they are based on conditional prediction and the outcomes are evaluated in terms of the planner's goals. Alternative programs are specified, predicted, evaluated, and chosen. Most models execute these four steps by means of a linear program. Most important is the problem of making a sequence of choices, with the effects of each choice conditioning the alternatives available for subsequent choices.

The content of a model used, say, for urban planning could be defined as follows[1] (Lowry, 1965):

1. *Technological,* e.g., of traffic flow on a highway as a function of weather, number of lanes, and number of signals.
2. *Institutional,* e.g., of family disposable income as a function of earnings and taxes.
3. *Behavioral,* e.g., housing density level as a function of income, age, and location of work.
4. *Accounting,* e.g., total land use as a sum of residential, retail, and manufacturing use.

---

[1]Note that "institutional" and "accounting" could be placed in the category we earlier called "economic." The model-builder and -user can tailormake such classifications to fit their specific needs.

PROBLEMS OF MODELING LARGE
AND COMPLEX SYSTEMS

The problems of modeling large and complex systems cannot be separated from the other aspects of understanding large and complex systems, especially from the need for a systems theory. These matters have already been treated in Chapters 1 and 2. Nevertheless, we can ferret out certain features that will be instructive to the builders of models of systems characterized by hundreds of thousands of variables and by indistinct boundaries with other systems. These are systems to which widespread experience with smaller systems may not be easily transferable and which present formidable problems of model validation. An excellent evaluation has been provided by Bekey (1971), and although Bekey directs his attention to problems of mathematical modeling, much of what he writes pertains to simulation modeling as well. Among the major difficulties, as seen by Bekey:

1. *Knowledge of the state of the system may be inadequate,* where "state" refers to the minimum number of independent variables, external inputs, and initial conditions, which must be specified in order to make prediction of system behavior possible. For example, it may be impossible to specify precisely the system state at time t or to make measurements on all the relevant variables at the same time.

2. *System identification techniques may be limited* and based on a large number of simplifying assumptions which are difficult to justify. This may lead to quite erroneous values of parameters.

3. *Data to substantiate a large model may be absent or difficult or impossible to obtain.* For example, public agency data may be static and nearly useless in the validation of dynamic models. Cost may prevent gathering of enough data in other cases.

4. *Available data may be "noisy,"* that is, associated with random disturbances within the system itself, arising from inadequate instrumentation and measurement techniques, and associated with the interaction of unknown variables.

5. *Large systems may transcend our ability* ever to obtain a complete and accurate (mathematical) description, at least of the type enabling us to write algorithms for controlling a spacecraft in orbit.

6. *Criterion functions* are hard to obtain. Optimizations are frequently oversimplifications or otherwise inappropriate. There are constraints even to simple engineering criteria such as minimum time, let alone to subjective, qualitative, and contradictory criteria.

7. *Input-output models,* commonly used to express cause-effect relationships in engineering and economic systems, may be grossly misleading. In such cases, controlled input functions are applied and the resulting sys-

tem responses observed. In large systems input and output are intercon-
ted and difficult or impossible to separate.

8. *Decomposition* of a complex system into smaller, more manageable
elements, so that the resulting models can be interconnected, aggregated,
or synthesized to give a realistic representation of the whole system, may
be by no means obvious.

9. *Time scales* may differ greatly over the many hierarchical levels of a large
system.

10. *Physical scales* may differ greatly over the many hierarchical levels of a
large system.

11. *State variables may not have compatible dimensions.* For example, how
does one relate air pollution density to citizen complaints?

Various mathematical and simulation techniques may reduce some of the
above limitations, e.g., changing discrete to continuous systems, transforming
partial differential equations into ordinary differential equations or algebraic
equations through lumping of distributed parameter systems, separating large
systems into subsystems, performing Monte Carlo simulations of extremely large
scale on stochastic phenomena, and synthesizing models to include both the
decision-making features of discrete simulation and the representation of
dynamic processes, as in continuous systems simulation. However, new
developments in computer sizes and speeds and new algorithms will probably be
required to accomplish these ends.

SIMULATION MODELS

Simulation models are of great value because they permit precise, reproducible
study of processes in areas without general theories or analytic descriptions. The
simulation is easier to investigate and manipulate than is the realworld system,
because of the latter's size, complexity, remoteness in time or space, danger, and
lack of control, and because of the need for the analyst to avoid affecting the
system's behavior simply by virtue of studying it.

There is no sharp distinction between analytic and simulation models;
however, the following generalities apply (based partly on Dalkey, 1968):

Simulation Model	*Analytic Model*
Less aggregation	More aggregation
More specific (with a "case-study" quality)	More abstract
Utilizes logical rules more than equations	Utilizes equations

(*cont.*)

Simulation Model	*Analytic Model*
Utilizes heuristics more than algorithms	Utilizes algorithms
Provides a "good" rather than an optimum solution	Attempts solution of equations to yield an optimum
Of particular value used experimentally to generate further detailed studies and data	. . . .

Analytic and simulation models have both been commonly used in systems studies; analytic models relatively more so in the past, at lower hierarchical levels, and at greater degrees of abstraction. In the next chapter we shall return to a fuller consideration of analytic models.

A computer simulation model consists of equations and instructions for step-by-step numerical solutions in time, that is, variables expressed as mathematical or logical formulas, numercial constants or parameters, and the algorithm or program. Simulation models have only recently received widespread attention, as contrasted with solving equations to obtain an analytical solution. For systems of even intermediate complexity, analytical solutions are impossible, and simulation becomes the main—or only—means of analysis. Simulation, unlike the analytical method, does not give the general solution. It gives a one-time history of system operation associated with the coefficients and initial numercial values selected. For behavior based on different conditions, another step-by-step computation of system time response must be made. Simulations require extensive computations, and essentially always a computer. They are very costly in time, money, and manpower, both in terms of the original simulation and in terms of subsequent changes to a large computer program.

One of the particular values of simulation lies in its ability to present a complex pattern of events in time. Also, by formulating a simulation in terms of elementary events it may be possible to synthesize complex interactions.

Strangely, simulation is not new. As Forrester (1968) points out, during the golden age of exploration beginning several hundred years ago it was necessary to know the relative positions of earth, moon, and sun. However, even this relatively simple three-body problem in celestial mechanics was beyond reach, by presently available mathematics, of an analytical solution. But by the seventeenth century men were using simulation to compute navigation tables, a lifetime process of calculation.

We can expect that computer simulation models will become more and more influential in helping solve large-scale sociotechnical, social, and environmental problems. Formal model building by behavioral and social scientists is not yet widespread in spite of the advantages offered. By experimenting with such models it is possible to develop great insights into these systems and to use the results to help improve system performance. We shall return to the use of computer simulation models in planning and policy-making below and in Chapter 8.

A computer simulation model, of course, differs only in complexity, explicitness, and precision from the informal conceptual models characteristic of human thought processes.[2] And some workers, particularly Jay W. Forrester, argue that anything that can be stated about a complex realworld system can be represented in such a laboratory model; unfortunately, there is still a paucity of professional talent to make the statements.

Computer simulation models present a number of advantages to planning and policy-making. As pointed out by Levin, *et al.*, (1971):

1. Modeling requires policy-makers really to understand their problems.
2. In the process of formal model building, the builders discover and resolve contradictions and inconsistencies among assumptions
3. Even a rudimentary running of the model permits rapidly improved embellishments.
4. The outcomes of many policy alternatives can quickly be determined, once model validity is accepted.
5. The model can be realtime and dynamic.
6. Sensitivity analysis reveals which parameters should be pursued further; in much sociotechnical and social work, the true values of parameters may be unknown.

Lowry (1965) has presented a readable overview of computer models as aids to urban planning and administration. Such models are most applicable to situations wherein there are repetitive temporal patterns and fixed spatial relationships. Lowry warns that a client usually accepts from the model-builder a tool of unknown efficiency. Nevertheless, such models, in spite of severe limitations, are better than nothing. If they accomplish only the necessity for framing questions carefully and avoiding sloppy thinking, they are worthwhile.

On Building a Simulation Model

As with systems analysis as a whole, cookbook rules for model building have their limitations. Nevertheless, here again such rules offer a point of departure.

A large-scale digital computer simulation model using heuristic or Monte Carlo techniques should (Packer, 1968):

---

[2] Yet in the opposite vein, the computer simulation models of human cognitive processes may be oversimplifications of the real thing. This is because the simulations are usually dependent on subject verbalizations.

1. Provide a building-block approach allowing development and testing of each submodel before its incorporation into the larger model.
2. Tie together the analytic submodels in a logically consistent manner.
3. Provide means of investigating problems too complicated to be solved mathematically.
4. Accept data descriptive of the realworld system.
5. Provide flexibility in dealing with inputs and outputs.
6. Provide the ability to determine changes over time.
7. Provide a means of analyzing or testing the sensitivity of assumptions, variables, parameters, relations, and data.

Several broad iterative steps are involved in simulation-model building:

1. Establish the objectives of the model, for example, its use in advancing systems theory or its use in planning.
2. Establish the scope of the model, including determination of the boundary encompassing the smallest number of elements within which the system's dynamic behavior is generated.
3. Identify model elements or submodels.
4. Structure model elements through the identification of persistent relationships among variables, of causal sequences, and of a logical framework.
5. Determine data requirements.
6. Acquire and process data after review and selection of appropriate literature, data file, and operational sources.
7. Determine and develop—or utilize "canned"—computer simulation programs and languages, such as DYNAMO, SIMSCRIPT, or GPSS.
8. Fit data to model and establish system parameters.
9. Run simulation on model and compare results with realworld system behavior.
10. Validate model using sensitivity testing, performance testing, and so on.
11. Document or install model into operating organization, as appropriate.

For further general discussions of computer simulation-model building of particular interest to sociotechnical and social systems, see Lowry (1965) and Forrester (1968). For discussions and applications in an exemplary field, the health field, see Levin, *et al.* (1969), Milly and Pocinki (1970), and Levin, *et al.* (1971). For a discussion of simulation programming languages, see Gordon (1969).

Lowry (1965) provides further insight into the actual design of models, particularly as relevant to urban planning.

There are two levels of analysis or aggregation, macro-analysis and micro-analysis. The former is usually associated with urban geography, demography, sociology, and human ecology; the latter with economics and social psychology.

Macro-analysis tends to deal with the statistics of mass behavior; micro-analysis with *market models* in which resources are allocated or events determined by virtue of competitive interaction of optimizing individuals using rational choice. Macro-analysis is often based upon historical trends and may be weak in causal structure. Also, it does not lend itself readily to financial accounting. Micro-analysis is limited by the frequent inability to specify in detail the "rational chooser's" relative values. Also, the number of variables which can be included in market models is quite limited.

Lowry stresses that the way that time is conceived in a model is of especial importance. Choices range from *comparative statics,* through *recursive progression,* to *analytical dynamics.* The method of comparative statics implies that the system is self-equilibrating. The model's parameters are fit from cross-section data and represent equilibrium conditions between independent (exogenous) and dependent (endogenous) variables. The process by which the system moves from its initial to terminal state is unspecified.

Analytical dynamics focuses on the processes of change rather than on the emergent future state of the system. Typically, sets of differential equations are used, some of which include variables whose rates of changes with respect to time are specified. Without self-equilibrating properties, the system may fluctuate cyclically, degenerate, or explode.

Because the statics approach assumes, often unwarranted, equilibria and the analytical approach requires that all variables except time be dependent or endogenous, most analysts compromise with recursive progressions.

An integral part of model design is the algorithm or method of solution. In many cases it is convenient to use iterative methods. In particularly complicated models, weak on mathematical rigor and logical closure, machine simulations (e.g., Monte Carlo) are recommended. These generate exogenous events by random choice from a given frequency distribution of possibilities. Refinements may include man-in-the-loop simulations (games) and the refined judgments of experts.

Fitting variables to the model may be difficult. Few published statistics are exactly what they purport to be from the table headings and descriptions; hence, it is easy to misinterpret either the meaning or the reliability of data.

The fitting of parameters is highly developed. The most common method is regression analysis, the simplest case being the estimation of parameters for a linear function of two variables, $Y = a + bX$. This method can be extended to fit all parameters in a system, even when nonlinearities are recognized (a linear fit is reasoned to be better than none at all). Models fitted in this way are often called "econometric." It is often hard, here, to determine explanations for the values generated for individual parameters. Alternatives to the econometric approach are often called "heuristic," wherein the model is partitioned into smaller systems of equations, some possessing only a single parameter. We shall return to the topics of regression analysis and econometric methods in the next chapter.

Model Validation

Eventually the model builder must ask: Is the model right? Will it work? Is reality well represented by the model? This is the problem of model validation, a topic of great concern to some workers but minimized by others. For example, the systems dynamics approach initiated by Jay W. Forrester dismisses model validity as a relative matter. To these workers the first purpose of a model is to be clear and provide easily communicable precise statements. The important thing is that a model clarifies our knowledge and provides new system insights; we can never know everything about reality. A model should aid us in improving the accuracy of representing reality.

Other workers are a lot less sanguine, and believe that the problems of validating models of complex systems are severe enough to restrict the usefulness of these models. In this context see our discussions in Chapters 1 and 8 of evaluations of systems dynamics models.

Models differ in the extent to which they can be validated. The easiest to validate are simple descriptive models which may apply to only one specific system situation.

Predictive models are difficult to test because of the infeasibility of waiting years into the future, and the usual lack of detailed and consistent data over the years. For most complex models, sensitivity testing is used instead of performance tests. The value of a single parameter or input variable is varied in successive runs of the model and the differences in outcome measured. The model's response should be neither extremely great nor extremely limited; if it is, perhaps the parameter is not really explained or is insignificant.

Let us now examine some of these points in greater detail. Although there are immense practical differences between the validation of models of complex systems on the one hand and the validation of (simpler) scientific hypotheses and experiments, psychological tests, and training simulators on the other, the conceptual bases of all validations are similar. Basically, all validations are performed in an attempt to determine the degree to which measurements in one situation, for example, a computer simulation, are associated with some *criterion* measure. Validation may thus be expressed as the degree to which the variance of a measuring instrument is associated with the variance of the criterion measure.

Specialized forms of validity may be further defined. *Predictive validity*, of particular concern to us, refers to the correspondence between measures on a *predictor* and some future criterion behavior. *Concurrent validity* refers to the degree to which the behavior of the measuring instrument is associated with criterion behavior at approximately the same time. *Consensual validity* indicates that experts agree that a measuring instrument measures what it purports to measure. *Construct validity* indicates the extent to which the behavior of the measuring instrument can be related to psychological, sociological, demographic, economic, urban growth, or other constructs. *Content validity* refers to the extent to which the content of the model or other measuring instrument contains the logical relations and data necessary for representing the real world. *Face validity* reflects the question, Does the measuring instrument *look* as if it is related to criterion performance?

It should be quite obvious that validations can involve a great deal of personal judgment as well as application of statistical techniques. Unfortunately, validations of complex systems have been mainly judgmental. Classical statistical methods for testing the "goodness of fit" of simulation models (for example, analysis of variance, chi square, and regression analysis) are often inapplicable because they assume the existence of independent data or they assume a common variance, normality, statistical independence, linearity, and so on. See Naylor and Finger (1967) for other statistical techniques for testing "goodness of fit" of computer-generated time series to observed historical series.

The extent to which a model describes or predicts the actual performance of a system (criterion behavior, using the above terms) within an acceptable margin of error is dependent on the accuracy of the assumptions, the logical consistency of the internal structure, and the validity and completeness of the input data. However, some workers have considered a model valid if it predicts reasonably well, in spite of deficiencies in the assumptions, internal consistency or data.

From the perspectives of the philosophy of science, economic theory, and statistics, Naylor and Finger (1967) have examined three positions on the validation of computer simulation models, namely, *rationalism, empiricism,* and *positive economics.* They then define a fourth approach, that of *multi-stage verification,* which incorporates the other three, singly necessary but not sufficient, approaches. Three-stage verification involves, in sequence, the formulation of a set of postulates describing the behavior of the system; verification of these postulates subject to the limits of statistical tests; and test of the ability of the model to predict system behavior. Either a historical approach or a forecasting approach can be used for the last, and both present difficulties. Testing the "goodness of fit" between computer-generated simulation time paths and historic or observed time paths can sometimes employ the statistical tests mentioned above. Most systems analysts, however, have utilized simple graphical comparisons involving amplitudes, turning points, etc.

That validation should, indeed, involve a sequence of events is attested by the high costs of constructing, programming, and operating computer simulation models. Testing assumptions is cheaper than testing predictions possibly vitiated by faulty assumptions. These comments emphasize the need for content validity, construct validity, face validity, and so on, in addition to the need for predictive validity. And the more complex the model, in the sense of complex systems defined in Chapter 1, the more important the requirement that attention be paid to the earlier steps of validation.

McKenney (1967) discusses further the validation of complex computer simulation models, adding the importance of *purpose*. A simulation model is a specific theory for a well-defined purpose, and the criteria of successful validation should also include asking, Does the model fulfill its purpose of providing insight into the nature of a process, developing specific policies or plans, or testing and improving system effectiveness?

Schrank and Holt (1967) similarly stress the *usefulness* of the model. Can we rely on the results of the model, apart from concerns with basic truth or falsity, for purposes of application to policy? Is the given model the best available, in spite of contradictions by empirical data? Schrank and Holt further stress the formidable complications to model validation resulting from the introduction of policy decisions and attempting to determine consequent system responses (*conditional forecasting*).

All the above points are pertinent to the validation of models discussed in various parts of the book. But recognition of this fact is just the beginning. Severe deficiencies of data, such as those summarized in the beginning of this chapter and discussed in greater detail in the next chapter, restrict our capabilities both to construct and to validate models of complex systems, especially those dealing with a future years or decades away.

Validation of models of complex systems typically is accomplished by what seems *reasonable* in terms of the judgments of experts. But at least all the above points should be made explicit. Unfortunately, this has not always been the case. See especially our reviews in Chapters 1 and 8 of the systems dynamics models.

For a discussion of computer simulation models of man-machine systems, in which some of these problems of validity are considered further, see Siegel and Wolf (1969).

For a somewhat different look at the question of validity, see Smoker (1969). Smoker writes of *complementary validity* and refuses to accept the real world always as given and the model world only as a means of demonstrating some aspect of reality. Rather, it is possible to view the model world as an ideal world which demonstrates how reality could or should be. The difference between the two worlds could then be rectified by changing the real world through social or political action. This is, of course, just the opposite of the usual attempts at validation wherein the model is altered to narrow any disparity with reality. Yet the two approaches are complementary. Smoker's approach opens the door to the social creation of desired futures. A continual modification of interrelated models and realities could pave the way toward the design of more realistic alternative future worlds.

APPROACHES TO MODELING BEHAVIORAL AND SOCIOTECHNICAL VARIABLES

The techniques discussed so far deal typically with aggregate human behavior. There is also an extensive literature on modeling and simulation of organ subsystems within man, individual human behavior, group behavior, organizational behavior, political behavior, and man-machine interrelationships. By extension, many of these models and simulations can be applicable to the sociotechnical systems of primary concern to us. In this section we consider representative approaches; other examples are covered in Chapter 8.

There has been a proliferation of behavioral and social simulations during the 1960s and early 1970s. Previously, computer simulations of human behavior had been based almost entirely on economic models.[3] Attempts at non-economic modeling of behavioral and social systems gained impetus from such work as the simulations of the 1960 and 1964 U.S. presidential elections (Pool and Abelson, 1961; Pool, *et al.*, 1965), the Inter-Nation Simulation (Guetzkow, *et al.*, 1965), and the simulations of human problem solving (Simon and Newell, 1971). These examples represent on-going research which has continued to evolve over the years. The work by Herbert Simon, Allen Newell, and J. C. Shaw is probably the most thorough to date on the modeling and simulation of individual human behavior. It has reflected a strategy of research extending well over a decade. Research has proceeded along a number of interrelated directions involving study of complex nonnumerical (thinking) tasks; construction of a computer information-processing language; definition of a computer program, written in this language, which is capable of solving problems people find difficult; simulation of a wide variety of human intellectual functions; and utilization of behavioral data to improve the simulations and utilization of the simulations toward better understanding of human problem solving.

Dutton and Starbuck (1971) have provided a comprehensive bibliography of 2034 computer simulation studies of human behavior. They have analyzed and classified the simulation studies as individuals, individuals who interact, individuals who aggregate, and individuals who aggregate and interact. Each study was further classified as to use of data to establish empirical relationships between the model and the real world, and in terms of use of quantitative measurement, use of qualitative measurement, or negligible measurement. Interestingly, 28% of the studies reflected the belief that empirical measurement is not necessary, and another 30% held that the cost of using rigorous measurement exceeds the returns. Relevant human behaviors were learning, perceptual gestalt, choice, and social effects.

The entire July-August 1969 issue of *American Behavioral Scientist* was devoted to social simulations. Page 47 of the issue provides an annotated bibliography of introductory references up to that date.

Chubb (1969) presents an overview of four approaches to man-machine modeling: (1) Describing functions. This is the oldest approach, involving servo-

---

[3]Even today the economic flavor of such large-scale computer simulations as the Bay Area Simulation Study (see Chapter 6) and the systems dynamics efforts (see Chapters 1 and 8) is marked. This is a disadvantage we believe.

theory, and has a long history in control engineering. It is applicable both to man as a whole and to organ subsystems within man. (2) Monte Carlo simulation. (3) Decision-theoretical paradigms. Especially lacking is a composite model of information-gathering and decision-making activities in complex systems. (4) Representational modeling of biomechanical movement. This could be applied to workplace design.

Wolf and Siegel (1969) describe three separate Monte Carlo simulation models developed over a decade by Applied Psychological Services, Wayne, Pennsylvania. These models deal with the simulation of missions and tasks as performed by crews of 1-2, 3-20, and 2-1000 men, respectively. Variables included are stress, proficiency, morale, time, equipment factors, and work-station factors. A recent modification of the first model involves the realtime CRT-console interface of one or two live subjects with the model. In this context simulation is concerned with avoiding man-machine mismatches and preventing design of costly but poorly human-engineered equipment.[4]

All three models were prepared to simulate men operating and maintaining equipment. Task analysis or a mission event sequence form the basic computer input. The models are based on the Monte Carlo approach, in which pseudo-random numbers are repeatedly used to select a number from a statistical distribution. Simulation variables reflect equipment features, the mission itself, and psychological or social variables associated with the operator himself. These last are stress, orientation, proficiency, mental load, and fatigue. Data are generated relative to equipment reliability, working hours, operator failures and data on personnel performance, morale, cohesiveness, goal orientation, and man-machine system efficiency. Output tabulations allow one to predict system performance, personnel overloads, unusual stress periods, and excessive delays. The largest model has been used to predict the performance of a submarine crew on a multi-day mission.

The stimulus-organism-response (S-O-R) paradigm has long been utilized in human factors and in systems psychology (De Greene, 1970). Smith (1969) applied this model to the simulation of residential mobility caused by racial prejudice and to the simulation of the effects of leadership on discipline and disobedience, especially with reference to an army basic training camp, prison riots, and collective disturbances. Stimuli for the simulated behaviors were obtained from social comparison processes in the case of the residential study, and from probability distributions representing climates of perceptions in the case of the leadership study. In Smith's model, a perceptual stimulus was combined with an attitudinal predisposition, resulting in a reaction potential; which, when a threshold value was exceeded, produced a behavioral response. For example, in the residential model an externally caused complaint about a

---

[4]Other uses of Monte Carlo simulation have involved population projections, economic fluctuations, traffic flows, and corporate planning.

neighborhood served as a stimulus. This was combined with a resident's racial prejudice (a predisposition to move) to yield an anxiety about moving (reaction potential). Complaints about the neighborhood arose from comparing a resident's social acceptability (race plus socioeconomic status) with that of his neighbors'. If a resident's social acceptability was greater than that of his neighbor's, he complained about the neighborhood. If his overall complaint score, derived from successive comparisons with randomly selected neighbors, was greater than a threshold, he decided to move. The simulation then proceeded from the decision process to the moving process.

Carter and Ignall (1970) presented a kind of simulation model for the Fire Department of the City of New York. It was designed to compare and evaluate different policies with regard to (1) how many units of each type to send to each incident; (2) which units to send to a given incident; (3) whether and how to relocate units; and (4) where to locate new fire houses.

Even in this situation there were many unknowns. For example, the relationship between deployment of fire-fighting units and loss of life and damage was not known and, hence, was not directly represented in the model. Rather, internal measures of performance, such as response times to incidents and workloads for different units, were substituted for them.

Further, in order to run the model, accurate data were needed on things like the rate of occurrence of various kinds of incidents at various locations, travel times of units, effects of response times on damage and loss of life, and work duration times. These data were not always easy to obtain. Even such a simple thing as time spent traveling to and from incidents had previously not been recorded.

This example illustrates that there is no easy road to applying systems expertise to complex sociotechnical systems. An understanding of the behavior of such systems, even at the gross operational level, will require intensive study. Understanding of more basic dynamics presents the fundamental challenge of the last third of the twentieth century.

SUMMARY AND CONCLUSIONS

Computer modeling and simulation provide a primary tool, probably the primary tool for the study of complex systems. As with systems analysis as a whole, certain guidelines can be offered but these must be greatly tempered by the experiences of building, installing, and using models.

There are serious, but hopefully not insurmountable, problems presently restricting the usefulness of computer simulation models of complex systems. These pertain especially to imperfect system understanding and description; to high, probably unrealistic levels of aggregation; to the nature and availability of data; and to model validation. Of paramount importance is the need to express behavioral and social variables more meaningfully. A major step in this direction could involve a better use of the vast number of submodels of human behavior.

REFERENCES

Bekey, George A., 1971, Mathematical Models of Large Systems, *1971 IEEE Systems, Man and Cybernetics Group Annual Symposium Record.* New York: Institute of Electrical and Electronics Engineers.

Carter, Grace M., and Edward J. Ignall, 1970, A Simulation Model of Fire Department Operations: Design and Preliminary Results, *IEEE Transactions on Systems Science and Cybernetics,* SSC-6(4), 282-93.

Chubb, Gerald P., 1969, *The Use of Computers for Man-Machine Modeling: Status and Plans,* unpublished paper given at the October 1969 meeting in Boston of the Human Factors Society. Santa Monica, Calif.: Human Factors Society.

Dalkey, Norman C., 1968, Simulation. In E. S. Quade and W. I. Boucher (eds.), *Systems Analysis and Policy Planning: Applications in Defense,* pp. 241-54. New York: American Elsevier.

De Greene, Kenyon B., ed., 1970, *Systems Psychology.* New York: McGraw-Hill.

Dutton, John M., and William H. Starbuck, 1971, Computer Simulation Models of Human Behavior: A History of an Intellectual Technology, *IEEE Transactions on Systems, Man, and Cybernetics,* SMC-1(2), 128-71, April.

Forrester, Jay W., 1968, *Principles of Systems.* Cambridge, Mass.: Wright-Allen Press.

Gordon, Geoffrey, 1969, *System Simulation.* Englewood Cliffs, N.J.: Prentice-Hall.

Guetzkow, Harold, F. Alger, R. A. Brody, R. C. Noel, and R. C. Snyder, 1963, *Simulation in International Relations: Developments for Research and Training.* Englewood Cliffs, N.J.: Prentice-Hall.

Levin, Gilbert, Gary Hirsch, Deborah Kligler, and Edward B. Roberts, 1969, *A Model of Interaction Between Patient and Program, and Its Implications for Treatment Drop-Outs Among Severely Disabled Psychiatric Patients,* draft. Bronx, N.Y.: Sound View—Throgs Neck Community Mental Health Center, 7 August.

Levin, Gilbert, Gary Hirsch, and Edward Roberts, 1971, *Narcotics and the Community: A System Simulation,* draft. Bronx, N.Y.: Albert Einstein College of Medicine, February.

Lowry, Ira S., 1965, *A Short Course in Model Design.* Santa Monica, Calif.: The RAND Corporation, April. (Defense Documentation Center [AD 614 413]).

McKenney, James L., 1967, Critique of: "Verification of Computer Simulation Models," *Management Science,* 14(2), B-102 to B-103.

Milly, George H., and Leon S. Pocinki, 1970, *A Computer Simulation Model for Evaluation of the Health Care Delivery System*, Report HRSD-70. Rockville, Md.: U.S. Department of Health, Education and Welfare, June.

Naylor, Thomas H., and J. M. Finger, 1967, Verification of Computer Simulation Models, *Management Science*, 14(2), B-92 to B-100, October.

Packer, A. H., 1968, Applying Cost-Effectiveness Concepts to the Community Health System, *Operations Research*, 16(2), 227-53, March-April.

Pool, Ithiel de Sola, and Robert Abelson, 1961, The Simulamatics Project, *Public Opinion Quarterly* 25(1), 167-83.

Pool, Ithiel de Sola, Robert Abelson, and Samuel L. Popkin, 1965, *Candidates, Issues, and Strategies*, Cambridge, Mass.: MIT Press.

Schrank, William E., and Charles C. Holt, 1967, Critique of: "Verification of Computer Simulation Models," *Management Science*, 14(2), B-104 to B-106.

Siegel, Arthur I., and J. Jay Wolf, 1969, *Man-Machine Simulation Models*. New York: Wiley.

Simon, Herbert A., and Allen Newell, 1971, *Human Problem Solving*. Englewood Cliffs, N.J.: Prentice-Hall.

Smith, Robert B., 1969, Simulation Models for Accounting Schemes, *American Behavioral Scientist*, 12(6), 21-30, July-August.

Smoker, Paul, 1969, Social Research for Social Anticipation, *American Behavioral Scientist*, 12(6), 7-13, July-August.

Wolf, J. J., and Arthur I. Siegel, 1969, *Recent Progress in the Monte Carlo Simulation of Man-Machine Systems*, unpublished paper given at the October 1969 meeting in Boston of the Human Factors Society. Santa Monica, Calif.: Human Factors Society.

6

Systems Data Characteristics
and Treatment

In the last two chapters we pointed out that lack of basic and meaningful data curtail the usefulness of systems analysis in general and of the modeling and simulation of complex systems in particular. We also discussed analytic models briefly, and stressed the increasing importance of dealing with qualitative and subjective data. In this chapter, we first look at the characteristics and limitations of the basic data, then we look at the means of dealing with quantitative and qualitative data in systems.

CHARACTERISTICS AND LIMITATIONS
OF THE BASIC DATA

In this book we have studied and dissected many types of growth, pointing out the desirable and undesirable features of each. The growth of data shows the characteristics highlighted earlier. Accordingly, we are faced with a feast of chaotic, unmanageable, almost unusable data and a famine of meaningful information.

In this chapter several salient features should be borne in mind. First, laboratory experiments—and computer simulation models—may be poorly isomorphic with the real world. Next, the present state of the real world may be so poorly perceived and structured that experiments and models continue to deal with "yesterday's world." Next, bureaucracies and other organizations are busily collecting data, but these data may be useless for either model construction and validation or decision-making. Finally, obtaining needed data may be beyond the state-of-the-art, because of deficiencies in understanding basic processes and because of the absence of the right measuring devices.

A Critical Look at Data Availability, Validity, and Reliability

Problems. The problems and specific areas of data deficiency are myriad and include:

1. *Absence.* For example, when we attempt to study migration patterns, we find there is typically no information on people who leave a city or state or job.

2. *Being sporadic.* Data collection may be very expensive. For example, significant demographic changes may occur between the decennial censuses, changes not noted in the special surveys.

3. *Being in the wrong form.* Canned data tend to be collected for bureaucratic rather systems purposes, and to emphasize economic rather than social variables.

4. *Differential reporting or diagnosis.* For example, is emphysema really increasing today because of pollution, stress, tobacco smoking, and the like? Or are more cases which a couple of decades ago would have been "bronchitis" or "respiratory condition" now receiving a more IN and fashionable diagnosis?

5. *Being out of date.* Data may be out of date by years. For example, the latest figures on the incidence of a disease may be several years old.

6. *Collection under incorrect assumptions.* The many biases in opinion polling obtain here, e.g., with respect to people who respond at all and those who do not.

7. *Collection under questionable sampling strategies.* Related to the aforementioned item, this deals with sample size and representativeness.

8. *Coverage of too short a time period.* Differentiating between minor system oscillations and true historic trends may be impossible on the basis of available data.

9. *Inconsistency from category to category.* Data collected by one agency and fitted into one category frequently are not commensurate with another agency's categorized data.

10. *Lack of transferability from laboratory to field.* This is one of the most fundamental—even crisis-generating—problems of modern science; it permeates the pages of the literature today as well as the pages of this book *per se.*

11. *Danger of techniques exceeding meaningfulness of data.* Computers and sensors and other instrumentation seemingly possess an *animus* which requires their use; the data collected may be unrelated either to the advancement of science or to the solution of systems problems.

12. *Crudeness when pooled or aggregated.* Many observations reflect masking or cancellation effects of phenomena which would be evident if data were collected at a more *micro* level. We have already discussed in Chapter 1 the possible cancellation effect of particulate matter on the atmospheric temperature increase theoretically due to CO_2. Similarly, the micro-climate of cities is difficult to determine based on airport readings. And SMSA data may mask behavior evident at the census tract level.

Let's now review a couple of analyses which illustrate some of the problems enumerated above.

Sterne (1967) has looked at deficiencies of ecological analyses of social disorganization. Because detailed itemization of a social system would be unmanageable, it is necessary to deal with simplified models which may be misleading. Six misleading "stereotypes" are examined, based on the author's research in the city of Miami, Florida. The city was divided into 295 analysis districts composed of one or more U.S. census bureau enumeration districts. The rate of occurrence per thousand estimated population of each problem, e.g., juvenile and adult arrests, illegitimate births, and cases of syphilis and tuberculosis, for each district was computed. Principal components analysis (a form of factor analysis) was performed giving a Pearsonian correlation output. Also, weighted social problem scores for individual districts, derived from the above rates, were correlated with various physical attributes using multiple regression.

Sterne's stereotypes and refutations include:

1. Social disorganization operates apart from the general social structure. Refutation: each city constitutes a social system of its own and it is misleading to generalize as to ecological patterns, e.g., the concentric ring formation. (However, compare the alternative ideas of Forrester [Chapter 8].)

2. Certain "components" or factors are always present under conditions of disorganization. Refutation: high mobility, usually associated with disorganization, was absent in the Miami "central Negro district," the area of worst housing.

3. Interrelationships of the "components" or factors within the system are uniform. Refutation: correlations between factors differ as functions of different areas, socioeconomic level, etc.; even when there are apparent uniformities, these may reflect not stable social processes but rather policies like police enforcement and housing code enforcement.

4. Important "components" or factors have been included. Refutation: unknown problems may have been omitted from the model.

5. Observations are complete. Refutation: the apparently simple absence or under-enumeration of adult males in black areas may really represent a complex interaction between the disorganized group and the main society.

6. "Subsystems" in the "system" of social disorganization have been recognized. Refutation: there is danger in simplifying the social system, in producing fictitiously homogeneous areas, and in swallowing up whole areas in statistical generalities.

The social researcher must, therefore, beware of sterotyped models based on previous fashionable, but perhaps limited, research. We must have models that aid our understanding of the interrelationships of people in communities, not just their distributions.

With reference to studies relating environmental variables to health, Lave and Seskin (1970) comment:

1. *Epidemiological studies.* Such data are well adapted to evaluating the effects of air pollution on health. They are in the form of mortality or morbidity rates for a particular group defined geographically, e.g., the census tract of a city. Such vital statistics are tabulated by the government and hence are readily available. However, they may not be valid because of disparities in performing autopsies and in ascertaining the cause of death. Sample surveys, using questionnaires and interviews, can in addition be used to determine smoking habits and residence patterns of the deceased.

2. *Episodic relationships.* This involves attempts to relate daily or weekly mortality or morbidity rates to indices of air pollution. However, there are many complicating factors here. For example, absences from work tend to be high on Mondays and Fridays, and this has nothing to do with air pollution or illness.

Representative Sources of Compiled Data

Data are collected and compiled on a massive scale by government agencies from the international to the local level, and by many private and semiprivate organizations. These agencies differ as to type(s) of data provided, form of data, detail or aggregation of data, frequency of updating of data, cost of collecting and processing of data, and types of statistical procedures applicable. It should be pointed out that published data may be secondary, for example, based on data obtained by local sources using questionnaires.

Following is a summary of representative commonly used and valuable sources of data:

1. International
   a. United Nations (Statistical Office). *Demographic Yearbook. World Health Statistics, World Energy Supplies,* and *Statistical Yearbook.*
   b. World Health Organization (U.N.). *Manual of the International Statistical Classification of Diseases, Injuries, and the Causes of Death.*

2. Federal Government (U.S.A.)
   a. Bureau of the Census. Decennial census, backed up by special surveys, e.g., of scientists and engineers. Also *Monthly National Household Survey and Statistical Abstract of the United States.*
   b. Department of Labor (Bureau of Labor Statistics). *Handbook of Labor Statistics.*
   c. Department of Health, Education, and Welfare. *Vital Statistics of the United States.*
   d. Federal Bureau of Investigation. *Uniform Crime Reports.*
   e. U.S. Air Force (Directorate of Aerospace Safety). Accident depository.
   f. Federal Aviation Agency. *Statistical Handbook of Aviation.*
   g. Department of the Interior. *Minerals Yearbook.*
3. State
   a. Department of Finance. Population projections.
4. Local
   a. From Bureau of the Census. *County and City Data Book.*
   b. *Handbook of Standard Metropolitan Statistical Areas* (from *Statistical Abstract of the United States).*
5. Other
   a. National Safety Council. *Accident Facts.*
   b. Automobile Manufacturing Association. *Automobile Facts and Figures.*
   c. Association of American Railroads, *The Yearbook of Railroad Facts.*

A number of data archives have been formed by governmental and private agencies. Schoenfeldt (1970) describes several of these of special importance to the behavioral and social sciences and to education. We discuss the use and misuse of data banks further in Chapter 9.

The urgent need for more meaningful data is paralleled by the attempts of many agencies to provide these data. For example, the 1970 United States Census has included a number of new features which promise to be of added value to planning. Among other things, counting the population by mail has required much more thorough development and testing. Many of the new features are reviewed by McGimsey (1970) and are summarized from that source as follows.

In the Standard Metropolitan Statistical Areas (SMSAs), a new series of block maps has been produced. Complementing these maps are geographic base files which are computer retrievable. These files can be created in two different ways; the form called Dual Independent Map Encoding (DIME) is of the greater interest to planners.

There is now the capability to aggregate detailed data according to newly conceived and irregular areas, for example, those along alternative routes for proposed highways. Previously, such tasks might have taken months or years by manual methods. Some of the things that can be accomplished are street network analysis, computer mapping, area and distance calculations (and, therefore, density ratios), and analysis of continuity of blocks.

The geographic base files and metropolitan maps should be regularly updated so the whole process need not be repeated for the next census. The Southern California Association of Governments, as part of the Southern California Regional Information Study (SCRIS), is investigating how this can be done.

The 1970 data for small geographic areas are more readily available. Population and housing data for blocks are tabulated for cities of 50,000 or more inhabitants, for the urbanized fringe of such cities, and for some smaller cities. Data are tabulated for block groups and enumeration districts (these are smaller than census tracts but larger than blocks). All SMSAs have been completely subdivided into tracts. Areas with an incidence of poverty 1.25 times or more than national average are so identified. Population and housing data are tabulated for ZIP codes.

The first available census outputs were summary computer tapes. Published data are only a small fraction of that available on magnetic tapes. Census data for individuals, in contrast to that for geographic aggregates, are available as samples (one-in-a-thousand, perhaps eventually one-in-a-hundred) of individual records from which all geographic identifiers smaller than SMSAs have been removed.

The direct observation of housing condition by enumerators has been eliminated. Hindsight had revealed that any two census enumerators could agree as to whether a housing unit was dilapidated or not in less than 50% of the cases. However, the Bureau of the Census has demonstrated that the number of dilapidated units with complete plumbing can be estimated from such "objective predictors" as central heating, overcrowding, years of schooling completed by head of household, and rent or value of the unit.

A second major change in the 1970 census is that detailed information on place of work for very small areas is now available. Detailed socioeconomic statistics in each tract with 1000 or more workers have been published (SMSAs of 250,000 or more). Plans for preparing a traffic zone-of-residence by traffic zone-of-work matrix have been developed.

Need for Current Realtime Data

Data are obviously needed for the advancement of science and for model building and validation. An equally important need is for current realtime or near-realtime data on which to make major decisions relative to the management of society. A suggested design for a near-realtime sociotechnical-environmental management information system is given in the last chapter of this book. In this chapter we shall summarize some of the general features necessary for such a system as follows:

1. The basic variables to be measured must first be recognized. Work on social indicators is a beginning, but still has a long way to go. Among other

things these presently deal with surficial phenomena rather than deep-lying forces. Work on means of determining environmental, ecological, and social impacts of technology and so forth similarly has a long way to go. Understanding and quantification of many physical and economic variables is much further advanced.

2. The people-sensing, -measuring, and -monitoring devices must be within the state-of-the-art and practicable. This is not now the case even insofar as meteorological, air pollution, and other physical variables are concerned.

3. The sampling strategies and placement of sensing and monitoring stations must be well-thought-out and realistic, in order to obtain representative and unbiased data. The national political and consumer opinion polls are only limited attempts in this direction; in addition they have undesirable side effects of influencing opinion and exerting subtle pressures toward opinion change.

4. The system must be capable of responding rapidly to needs for recalibration, for example, in relation to new evidence on subtle attitude changes.

5. Measurements and data reduction and analysis methods must be standardized, in order to preclude the introduction of bias and error.

6. Data must be collected in, or reducible to, a form permitting transmission, integration, automatic and manual storage and retrieval, and display for managerial planning and decision-making.

7. The system must possess a rapid and flexible response to requests for additions, deletions, combinations, patterns, and projections of data.

8. Data banks must be designed absolutely to prevent misuse such as tampering, invasion of privacy, or personal gain such as power and control over others.

ANALYTIC MODELS AND
MORE ON QUANTIFICATION METHODS

Quantification methods play an important role in the study of sociotechnical systems, but mainly at the subsystem level, or at a system level of great aggregation, reduction of number of variables, and associated oversimplification. At the present time, our development of mathematics and of algorithms does not permit quantitative or analytic solutions to the most complex problems. Nevertheless, quantitative techniques, used in conjunction with other methods, will continue to provide a valuable part of our repertoire of expertise.

Among the methods most commonly used are data plotting, curve-fitting and projection; econometrics; matrix analysis; multiple regression analysis (itself a form of curve-fitting); and numerous operations research methods. These categories, of course, are not mutually exclusive. We shall consider curve-fitting and projection more fully in the next chapter, dealing with forecasting and the other areas briefly below.

Econometric Methods

Econometrics attempts to find numbers that correspond to the parameters of economic models. This might involve applying mathematical and statistical methods to already collected data in order to specify equation(s) for demand and supply functions. There has been a tendency to misuse econometric methods, in terms of placing too great stress on attempts to manipulate data collected by other agencies for other purposes. Often there has been too little emphasis on the collection of original data. Too little econometric work has been of use in testing and resolving conflicts among alternative theories. As Boulding (1970) points out, there may have been too great an emphasis on smooth, well-behaved, nicely abstracted, continuous functions, when the "system breaks" are really more important and the mathematics of discontinuity more applicable.

The Bay Area Simulation Study (BASS) (Center for Real Estate and Urban Economics, 1968) is an example of a complex econometric model relating population, land, and jobs. It is one of the methods for forecasting the future, a topic to which we shall return in the next chapter, and which has been used in conjunction with other techniques in urban policy-making and planning.

BASS was developed out of recognition of the need to integrate a wide variety of interdisciplinary material necessary for forecasting regional population, employment, income, industrial infrastructure, transportation, investments, consumer travel and purchasing behavior, building location decisions, government and other land use policies, and so forth. BASS development reflected the *lack of an integrated metropolitan growth theory*, and the need to integrate previous economic base, input-output, location, urban land market, and journey-to-work and other transportation studies.

The model builders attempted to strike a balance between a highly complex theory of regional land use and growth and a feasible empirical operating model. BASS is thus a sophisticated analytic device which permits alternative economic projections to be input in order to produce as outputs various incremental effects on land absorption. In addition to being classifiable as an *econometric* model and an *input-output* model, it can be considered to be an *impact* model in that it measures the impact of changing assumptions of the abovementioned variables affecting future land absorption and utilization and urban and regional growth.

BASS is a series of integrated submodels linked by a master computer program. For example, demographic data provide the basic inputs to the *Population Submodel,* and state and federal economic and financial data to the *Employment Submodel.* The latter consists of two sub-submodels, a *Structural* (regression) *Submodel* and a *Shift Submodel* which, also using regression equations, calculates the difference between national and regional growth rates); the two are then reconciled giving a forecast for the demand for labor. Supply of labor can be obtained from the *Population Submodel* by using an appropriate multiplier. The results of such *throughput* or *process calculations* are the outputs, population forecasts to the year 2020 for thirteen San Francisco Bay Area and San Joaquin-Sacramento River Delta, California counties and employment forecasts for twenty-one industries for the same time span and for the same counties. It should be noted that the final output of these three submodels is a *judgmental* reconciliation of the separate forecasts. These outputs in turn provide the basic inputs to two other submodels, the *Employment Location* and *Residential Location Submodels*. The final output of the model consists of population, employment, housing unit, and land use forecasts for 777 census tracts of the thirteen counties.

The authors state that there are no *explicit* policy variables in the structure of the BASS model, but that these can be introduced implicitly through changes in the input assumptions about zoning, pollution, transportation, land use by industry, business, and private persons, etc. They recognize further that the final outputs must be regarded as probabilities rather than as exact predictions. Thus the BASS model should be used as a supplement rather than as a substitute for alternative forecasting methods.

The authors are also frank in recognizing the deficiencies of the model, which also apply—we add—to other complex models. These deficiencies pertain especially to the faultiness of the basic data for reasons we have already discussed, poor knowledge of industrial and consumer practices, the tendency of one submodel to pass on errors to subsequent submodels, and difficulties in validating models whose "proof" lies in the future world. Validations have been attempted largely in terms of what appears "reasonable" to urban planners, especially as reflected in published master plans. The influence of "party line" on what is "reasonable" is, of course, recognized by the authors. Finally, from the viewpoint stressed in this book, we should mention again the high degree of aggregation common to this and other econometric models of complex systems, and the underlying deficiency accruing from poor understanding of human behavior in the day-to-day activities of working, traveling, and consuming. Also, in the total systems sense, there was little if any consideration in the BASS model of developments of new products and technology; of the influences of national defense and foreign trade; of possible future social, political, and economic changes; of the structure and function of individual industries; and of changes in migration patterns. There was too little appreciation of dynamic systems and too much extrapolation of past trends and relationships into the future.

Matrix Analysis

Matrix algebra has been useful in the study of many social problems. A matrix can be thought of as a set of numbers or symbols arranged as a rectangular set of boxes. A matrix can be transformed into another matrix by means of algebraic manipulations. Matrices can be used as elements of difference systems and to describe successive states of a system An input output matrix of the community represents a familiar example. As a more detailed example, let's consider the following.

Rogers (1966) has developed an integrated interregional population projection model which can be programmed for a computer. He shows that the effects of mortality and fertility can be expressed by matrix multiplication. Migration can be described in terms of transition matrices. Then an integrated matrix model of population growth is discussed, in which effects of fertility, mortality, and migration are applied to an age-disaggregated population and this population is adjusted forward through successive time periods.

Many methods of population estimation and forecasting are too simplistic to be of much value. The *cohort-survival method* is especially attractive because of its feature of disaggregation. Using the conceptually elegant and computationally simple techniques based on matrix algebra, one can move from a single best estimate for a single region to multiple estimates under varying birth, death, and migration rates, allowing for their interaction across regions.

The cohort-survival projection method summarizes the pattern of fertility and mortality characteristic of a population and explicitly introduces the effects of net migration. For example, an initial age distribution can be carried forward through a time period, say five or ten or fifteen years, by the application of age-specific birth and death rates and consideration of changes due to net migration. Further, the researcher can disaggregate the population into sex-and race-differentiated cohorts separately survived through time. Expressing cohort-survival population projections in matrix terms permits treating the projection process independently of the population to which it is applied. To some extent, also, the effects of policy intervention can be investigated.

Rogers traces through the applications of matrix techniques, giving examples. In order, he considers mortality and fertility. He then combines them as a survivorship matrix to find their joint contribution to the total projection process. Next he considers migration and the interregional system. After developing matrix methods for handling each of the major elements of population change, he combines these into a population growth model:

$$W_{t+1} = SW_t + N_t$$

where W_t = a population matrix the rows of which denote age groups and the columns of which denote regions, S = a survivorship matrix constant over time and over the regions of the system, and N_t = a net migration matrix the rows of which denote age groups and the columns of which denote regions.

Rogers' model has been used to project California's interregional population, by five-year cohorts, to 1980. It utilized the 19 state economic areas as fundamental areal units and was calibrated on 1955-1960 data. See Chapter 3 for another example of the use of matrix methods.

Multiple Regression Analysis

Multiple regression analysis, a form of least-squares curve fitting, that is, determining a best-fit function made up of multiple linear terms, enables us to determine the combination of factors ("independent" or "predictor" variables) which will best predict another factor ("dependent," "predicted," or "criterion" variables). It is based on correlation coefficients among all the variables involved.

Solution to a multiple regression equation (see below) involves solving for the b or partial regression coefficients which indicate the slope of the regression line. This is accomplished by solving first for the β or standard partial regression coefficients, in turn obtainable from partial correlation coefficients.

In practice, multiple regression analysis is usually undertaken in the context of matrix algebra which eliminates the algebraic detail. A computer is utilized, and solving the regression equations is the same as finding the inverses of matrices. There are several methods for finding such inverses:

1. *Straightforward multiple-regression analysis* involves solving for all the b coefficients, assuming these are of equal importance as contributors to the variance of the dependent variable.

2. *Stepwise multiple regression analysis* involves adding variables to the multiple regression equation only if it can be shown they are making a significant contribution to the dependent variable. The computer calculates iteratively, reducing the rows and columns of the matrix one by one. Statistical significance is tested by the analysis of variance; that is, the F-test is used to evaluate the contribution made to the variance of the dependent variable by each independent variable in turn.

3. *Mixed-mode multiple regression analysis* is a combination of the first two methods. The computer is programmed to remove first the variables that are experimentally or intuitively believed to be most important.

Many researchers consider multiple regression analysis to be only an interim step, pending construction of more dynamic analytic or simulation systems models which yield greater insight into cause-effect relationships. Restrictions on overuse of multiple regression analysis accrue from the fact that many, sometimes most, independent variables are cross-correlated, yielding misleading results. Further, a statistically significant regression coefficient may not mean that the factor is important; rather, the factor may be correlated with some other factor not included. And, in addition, multiple-regression analysis does not deal with nonlinear, dynamic situations, which are, indeed, representative of most realworld systems.

Now let's look at an example from transportation. Cirillo, Dietz, and Beatty (1969) have looked at the relationship between geometric factors in interstate freeway design, such as interchange and ramp design on the one hand, and traffic accidents on the other.

The model, according to this approach, was a mathematical formulation of the relationship between response (dependent) variables, such as traffic accidents, and other variables of interest, such as traffic volume and design geometrics. There were four types of response variables in this study: number of accidents, number of injuries, number of fatalities, and dollar amount of property damage.

The data for this study were collected by 24 state highway departments as part of the Interstate System Accident Research Study II. All data were submitted on punch cards classified as highway data (e.g., design features), traffic data (e.g., volumes and speeds), and accident data (e.g., number of persons killed in a vehicle). An effort was made to include as many geometric and traffic parameters as possible which were thought to contribute to accidents. However, the objective of this study was to investigate the effects of geometrics, and other road (e.g., roughness), driver (e.g., age), and weather (e.g., rain or snow) variables were not studied. Likewise, time, space, and money constraints were not factors in the models.

The approach was that of multiple regression analysis, that is:

$$Y = a + b_1 X_1 + b_2 X_2 + \cdots + b_n X_n$$

where Y indicates the dependent or predicted variable, the Xs indicate independent or predictor variables assumed to have known values, and the a and the bs indicate unknown parameters or constants. Multiple regression analysis requires that the b parameters be linear; however, it is possible to make such statements as, for example, setting $X_1 = X_2^2$.

The multiple regression models could be used, first, to predict or estimate the average number of accidents, fatalities, and injuries, or the property damage per year on a given type of highway interchange or element thereof; and, second, to compare design alternatives in terms, for example, of average estimates of accidents.

In the final multiple regression equation many variables originally considered did not appear. Which, and how many, of the candidate independent variables remained was based upon a mathematical decision based on step-up and step-down regression procedures. In the step-up case, variables were brought into the regression equation until R^2 (the multiple correlation coefficient) exceeded 90% of the maximum possible value. If now each of the independent variables had a regression coefficient greater than twice its standard error, then the regression equation became the final model. If, however, some of the ratios of regression coefficients to their standard errors (t-ratios) were less than 2, a step-down procedure was used to eliminate independent variables until all the t-ratios exceeded 2. Thus, statistical measures of significance and predictive ability determine which and how many independent variables to retain in the final model. This approach can be considered related to the sensitivity analysis discussed in the chapter on systems analysis.

The square of the multiple correlation coefficient (R^2) can be interpreted as the fraction of the variance of the response or dependent variables which is accounted for by the regression model. R^2 estimates the proportion of variance in Y explained by the regression on all the Xs.

The actual finding of the study was that geometric factors exerted very little effect upon the number of traffic accidents. Although the models were intended to help the highway designer design a safer highway system, weather, driver, nongeometric road, and economic factors were defined as outside the system and beyond control of the designer. There was thus great danger of suboptimization. In addition, the emphasis on representative over high-accident stretches of freeway may have biased the regression results. For future study, the authors recommend a larger scale cost/effectiveness model incorporating safety, economic, right-of-way constraint, and other factors.

Other examples of multiple regression analysis are discussed in Chapters 3 and 8.

Summary of Operations Research Techniques

Operations research attempts to emphasize the objectives of the entire organization and to tradeoff advantages and disadvantages in coping with management problems and helping make optimum administrative decisions. Dealing with problems of system operation, it involves use of mathematical models and arriving at solutions in situations involving conflicting goals.

Operations research looks at the system, abstracts the essentials, and tests alternative ways of manipulating these essentials.

It stresses system performance, clear definition of goals, and quantitative solutions. Solutions are sought which are optimum for the system as defined by the study. With some justification, operations research (but not systems analysis!) can be considered the scientific approach to decision-making.

Often an approach may *suboptimize* the system, that is, one or more elements will be brought to an optimum, but not the entire system. Contrariwise, optimizing the entire system may result in having some less-than-optimum elements.

To define an organization's problems, we must first know what that organization is supposed to do, that is, what its goals are. We should avoid general terms, like the provision of health services. With such general statements, quantification is impossible and actions may conflict. We must define quantitative criteria that measure the extent to which goals are achieved, in ways that preserve the qualitative integrity of the goals. Thus, an early step of operations research should be the development of measurable criteria for the organization. This requires an interdisciplinary team of specialists and administrators.

System constraints must be stated explicity and must not be loosely confused with goals. Some typical constraints are budget, shortages of professional personnel, lack of physical facilities, legal requirements, and transportation problems. Confusing goals with constraints limits the freedom to optimize.

A mathematical model is a representation of the system which can be manipulated on paper or by computer to yield desired results. The model shows how managerial decisions affect the attainment of system goals, and also how constraints limit the range of management decisions. There may be two or hundreds of equations. One type of equation is the *criterion function* or *objective function* which relates the criterion measure both to factors subject to management control and those not so. Another type of equation expresses constraints on the range of management decisions. See below for examples of these equations. See Halpert, Horvath, and Young (1970) for further detail on these and related matters.

An important step in model building is specifying all the fundamental variables that appear to affect the criterion measure; these are those controllable within the system and those representing constraints on the system. Model building can start with collecting data through discussion or observation. As factors are listed and measured, the analyst begins to see how they are related and how to express this verbally and then mathematically. This alone may furnish sizable insights about the system, because the model highlights the important, rather than trivial, factors about the system. Further, as we have seen, it is much easier to manipulate a model than a real system, and a model allows comparison with other systems. Development of such analytic models is a prerequisite to use of operations research.

There are a number of operations research models which are of at least potential interest to the study of sociotechnical and social systems. For example, in the health field some applications could be determining location of satellite facilities, allocating resources between prevention and treatment when resources are limited, organizing appointment schedules and patient flow through a facility, and developing staffing patterns. Some criteria for measuring the effectiveness of a mental health program could be: (1) number of patients treated per time period; (2) number of clinic visits per time period; (3) percentage of discharged patients who do not reenter treatment; (4) cumulative fraction of an admissions cohort discharged after 30, 60, or 90 days; (5) reduction in rates of arrest, narcotics addiction, divorce, or suicide within a catchment area (Halpert, Horvath, and Young, 1970). We must emphasize here, however, that reducing people to numbers may seriously distort the real nature of the problem. The results of the operations research study must be judiciously mixed with other insights.

For futher reading, see Hillier and Lieberman (1967) and Hughes and Mann (1969). An excellent, easy-to-read summary of operations research (OR) concepts and techniques, with particular emphasis on application to the mental health field, is given by Halpert, Horvath, and Young (1970). The following summary of models is based on this source.

Allocation models apply to situations of limited resources, for example, when there are a number of jobs to be done but not enough resources available to achieve results at a desired level. The operations researcher must estimate the amount of resources to be allocated to each of the different competing activities so as to optimize the criterion of system performance.

Mathematical programming is typically used. An objective is specified, alternative ways of achieving this objective are examined, and the optimum alternative selected, while recognizing the numerous constraints. An *assignment model* or a *transportation model* may apply. A representative problem could relate different kinds of patients, different clinics with different available physicians' hours, and some aspect of "return" or quality of care. The over-all objective would be to determine the number of patients of each type to send through the clinics so as to maximize the total value return to the clinic, operating under constraints of time required by each patient and total hours available in each clinic. A simple problem could be solved by analytic geometry; a complicated one involving many equations with many variables would require a computer and an algorithm for solving simultaneous equations (*simplex method*).

The basic linear programming model which, with variations, typifies the models used in operations research follows (Hillier and Lieberman, 1967):

Find $x_1, x_2, \ldots x_n$ which maximizes the linear function

$$Z = c_1 x_1 + c_2 x_2 + \cdots + c_n x_n$$

subject to the constraints or restraints

$$a_{11} x_1 + a_{12} x_2 + \cdots\cdots\cdots + a_{1n} x_n \leqq b_1$$
$$a_{21} x_1 + a_{22} x_2 + \cdots\cdots\cdots + a_{2n} x_n \leqq b_2$$
$$\cdot \qquad\qquad\qquad\qquad\qquad \cdot$$
$$\cdot \qquad\qquad\qquad\qquad\qquad \cdot$$
$$\cdot \qquad\qquad\qquad\qquad\qquad \cdot$$
$$\cdot \qquad\qquad\qquad\qquad\qquad \cdot$$
$$a_{m1} x_1 + a_{m2} x_2 + \cdots\cdots\cdots + a_{mn} x_n \leqq b_m$$

and the $xs \gtreqless 0$ or $\lesseqgtr 0$.

The xs are called *decision variables*, the as, bs, and cs represent given constants, n indicates the number of competing activities, and Z is called the *objective function* or *criterion function*. Z can also be thought of as a measure of total value or effectiveness. The criterion function, or objective function, can be thought of as relating the criterion measure both to factors subject to managerial decision or control and those not so; it offers insight as to how a system objective can be achieved. The xs could indicate units of a given product, ingredients in a diet, grades of gasoline, types of tomatoes, number of acres devoted to given crops, etc.

Game theory deals with any human situation in which there is conflict of interest in economics, sociology, management, the military, and so on. It can apply to competitive corporations, states, or the physician versus nature. Decisions must be made or a course of action selected among many alternatives. The distinctive feature is that the outcome or payoff of a decision may be uncertain and influenced by the strategy of the real or hypothetical opponent. A payoff matrix and selection of strategies typify the game-theoretic approach. A *zero-sum* game is one in which what one decision-maker loses the other must gain. A typical approach is the *minmax* approach in which *maxmin* payoff deals with a situation in which the first decision-maker or player attempts rationally to maximize his minimum gain, and in which minmax deals with a situation in which the second decision-maker tries to minimize his maximum loss. Sometimes maxmin equals minmax and a "saddle" is said to exist. When such fixed strategies do not exist, the players must make their selections on the basis of probabilities. Percentage of time each alternative must be chosen can involve random number selection. Other refinements involve *decision-making under certainty, decision-making under uncertainty,* and *decision-making under risk.* An example from the health field could involve the determination of whether a disease does or does not exist and whether to treat it or not (physician versus nature).

Inventory theory involves costs resulting from different stocking policies. Thus, stocking drugs (or beds) involves costs associated with inventory investment, storage, handling, and obsolescence. Surplus must be balanced against shortages. A problem could involve determining the amount of inventory to be carried and frequency of replenishment so as to minimize the over-all average cost of the supply operation. The effects of shortages, variable demand, lead times, multiple-ordering, etc. must often also be considered. Mathematic input-output models are typically used. In many realworld situations, however, mathematical modeling is impossible and one must resort to computer simulations.

Queuing theory deals with scheduling problems, i.e., the effects of random arrivals of individuals at some service facility where they may have to wait for service because the instantaneous arrival rate may exceed the facility processing time. Arrival and service times are probabilistic, resulting in periods of congestion or idleness. A typical problem could involve patients arriving without appointments at an emergency clinic. Probabilistically, arrivals might average at one every 15 minutes. There could be one physician on duty who spends an average of 12 minutes with each patient. Amount of time to care for any one patient is unrelated to the amount for another. Arrival rate is constant throughout the day and patients are served first-come-first-served.

Replacement deals with the deterioration of physical articles at different rates, and the determination of the optimum point at which to replace the articles. The problem is to balance the cost of preventive maintenance against time lost because of inoperative equipment. "Preventive maintenance" could also apply to determining a replacement pool for workers absent because of illness.

Search problems arise when there is limited time, money, or skills to use in detection. The goal is to maximize probability of detection for a given amount of resources. The technique has been applied to the detection of submarines, minerals, and diseases.

Sequencing or routing problems deal with a number of customers, e.g., patients, who are waiting to be processed at a series of facilities; one must decide the order in which they are to be handled. The objective could be to sequence events so as to minimize the amount of time the facilities are idle or minimize the number of jobs or patients completed behind schedule.

Dynamic programming is a mathematical technique for making a number of interacting decisions so that a criterion function is optimized. It provides an approach rather than a standard set of equations.

Halpert, Horvath, and Young (1970) summarize a number of health problems that should be amenable to operations research study; we add that many of these problems transcend the health field:

1. *Satelite locations.* Study would entail determining the reason for establishing such locations, e.g., to reduce transportation problems and as a result increase demand for services. The number of cases per 1000 population and the desirable size of facilities would have to be determined. Search theory to determine need as opposed to demand and market survey techniques to ascertain clients' feelings could be applicable.

2. *Prevention versus treatment.* This could be viewed as an allocation problem—limited money and skills are to be allocated among several alternatives. However, health disorders come in many forms; thus, it may be necessary to reduce them all to cost estimates, or subdivide the problem into categories with more homogeneous goals. There are many assumptions in such studies, and it will be necessary to perform *sensitivity analysis,* i.e., to see how sensitive the criterion is to each assumption.

3. *Patient flow.* Simulation might be extremely valuable in terms of trying out proposed changes in a computer before trying to change the actual system. The computer model would have to simulate the patients as individuals in terms of where they live, and their preferences for treatment, diagnoses, and progress under treatment. The simulation would have to follow the probabilistic pattern of the real world. There would be no equations that could be solved easily. Rather, individual patients would be simulated one by one to build up data. A year's clinical activity could be simulated in an hour. Then this could be repeated with a different configuration of activities, and so on. Analysis of data should give great insight into the value of various configurations.

4. *Appointment scheduling.* Queuing models could be used. Managerially the problem is affected by whether those who wait in the queue and those who wait to serve are both in the same organization (and, hence, management must pay under any circumstances) or are in different organizations.

5. *Electronic data processing.* The value of the computer derives from:
   a. Its use as a giant calculator to solve complex scientific problems.
   b. Its use as a data processor when calculations are not complex but there are many data, e.g., in payroll applications.
   c. Its use to store and retrieve large amounts of alphabetic and numeric data making possible much more thorough data analysis.

   A computer-based clinical information system, the "automated nursing system" has been developed at the Institute of Living, Hartford, Connecticut. This has two elements: a "nursing behavior report" which contains both check-list and narrative information; and a computer analysis of the nursing behavior report which gives quantitative graphical indices of depression, anxiety, social nonconformity, and exhibitionism.

6. *Pharmacy.* The problem is to minimize the cost of service at a given level of quality. Some factors are staffing, space for storage, emergency deliveries, a given inventory level, and time wasted while waiting for materials. Allocation, inventory, and queuing models are applicable.

7. *Central warehousing.* Should each operating unit have its own warehouse, or should all units share one or more, and if more than one, how many? Inventory levels, warehouse rates, shipping distances, shipping rates, and inventory levels are involved. If inventory calculations are made for one configuration and must be repeated for all configurations, calculations may become immense in numbers. Therefore, a *heuristic* or trial-error approach may be necessary.

8. *Staffing pattern.* How does one determine the proper balance of professional and other specialists given certain necessary levels? A probabilistic model is necessary because of the variability in different patient's needs; each patient will need a specific type of therapy for only a given

time period. System criteria must also be probabilistic. Linear programming could be used.

9. *Nurse staffing.* A great deal of research has gone into creating statistical models describing a medical-surgical patient's need for nursing attention. We need more data for relating patient characteristics to nursing care over a long period of time. Work-sampling and multiple regression techniques have been used. Work-sampling could involve: (a) preparing a list describing the job activities of the nurse, e.g., bathing, feeding, medication, dressing, and supervision; and (b) estimating how much time is spent daily on each. A representative and adequate sample of observations is necessary. Analysis would seek a regression relationship between the variables and the nursing time required. From this a patient checkoff list could be derived.

10. *The impact of a mental health center on the community and how to measure the impact quantitatively, the facility design, and the criteria for evaluating the effectiveness of mental health programs.* These are more complicated problems which will require an assortment of systems techniques.

Bruno (1970) has found that operations research work in a school district requires much more than the expected mathematical skills. In such politically acute environments, communications and human relations skills are particularly important. Otherwise, distrust, alienation, and ineffectiveness will result.

Specifically, Bruno has attempted to develop a salary schedule as an alternative to the fixed-step salary schedule which represents the increment in salary associated with years of experience in the school system. The fixed-step schedule has long been criticized for a number of reasons, for example, equal pay in the slums and in the suburbs and necessity of moving into administration in order to receive additional salary.

Multiple regression analysis, used in many salary evaluation schemes, was found to be inappropriate, because all the factors considered in a salary evaluation cannot be correlated to salary, and multiple regression analysis cannot handle constraint conditions. Hence, a linear programming model was used.

Bruno concludes a mere transference of operations research procedures from the military and industrial fields to school management has not proved practicable. This is true especially because, first, models are a long way from reliably relating the independent variables such as students, subject matter, teachers, and teaching methods to outputs such as learning, skills, and attitudes. The mechanisms of learning are just not well understood. Second, political forces greatly determine and influence planning decisions.

Finally, the operations research activity should be placed close to the highest executive's office. It must have easy access to all parts of the program if the total system is to be approached.

MEANS OF DEALING
WITH QUALITATIVE FACTORS

Complex sociotechnical systems do now, and always will, deal with judgmental, subjective, mentalistic, and intuitive variables and data. This is so not only because of the myriad interactions of variables, but also because we must concern outselves with things like individual needs and values. This does not mean these things are beyond access. Indeed, a number of methods have been developed for achieving order and even quantification in dealing with subjective and other qualitative material. A discussion of methods follows, but it is well to caution the reader against oversimplification and too nice preciseness in using these methods:

Aggregation permits the reduction or elimination of individual differences and the utilization of a collective statistic(s). For example, economics can speak of a collective demand, and is not concerned with individual variations in the appeal of a commodity. However, let us point out here an important distinction, namely, that collective behavior such as that represented by a group of workmen building a house and average behavior such as that represented by the typical consumer are *not* the same as other collective human processes such as those represented by group problem solving, a "collective unconscious," or a collective intelligence (Wechsler, 1971). In the last there is an integration, an interaction resulting in the emergence of something new. There is most likely a hierarchical jump such as those we discussed in Chapter 1. Crude aggregation may produce the most erroneous models of man and of society.

Psychological scaling methods permit the dealing with stimulus variables on linear scales. Although often considered part of the general repertory of psychophysical methods, scaling methods are sometimes differentiated from the latter on the basis that response values are usually unknown. There is no way to relate stimulus to response variables as in the case of pure psychophysical methods. Typical scaling techniques are the method of rank order, and rating scale methods. They are useful where there are no objective measures as in dealing with values, attitudes, preferences, affective tones, desires, esthetics, etc. Scaling methods are often used in the development of criteria of performance or capability in realworld systems and thus in validating tests and other predictors. The Cooper-Harper Rating Scale is an example of a device enabling incorporation of pilot opinion as to aerospace vehicle stability and control into design.

Behavioral decision theory, typically through the applications of *Bayes' Theorem,* permits dealing with subjective probabilities. Historical data, if available, can be employed to estimate probabilities from relative frequencies. Bayes' Theorem can be used to revise prior opinion or prior probability in the light of new evidence to obtain a posterior probability. Probabilities can be thought of as quantifications of uncertainty. Subjective probability is a number between 0 and

1 representing the extent to which a rather idealized person believes a statement to be true. Gustafson, *et al.* (1969) propose utilization of these concepts in a computerized system for medical diagnosis, although problems of conditional independence of symptoms, mutual exclusivity of diseases, and availability of basic data for determining frequencies must first be solved.

The *Delphi technique,* which we discussed briefly in Chapter 4, typically involves the judgments of experts within the same specialty. Sometimes it is referred to as *cybernetic arbitration,* because the experts' deliberation is steered through feedback of a control group. Delphi provides a forecast or estimate by subjecting the views of individual experts to group criticsm without face-to-face confrontation. Anonymity of opinions and arguments is stressed, and the "band wagon" effect supposedly minimized. Delphi typically employs a sequence of questionnaires: the expert is asked to give opinions and reasons for his opinions. At each successive interrogation, the subject is given new and refined information in the form of opinion feedback derived from the computer consensus from an earlier stage. At each stage the median and interquartile values may be calculated. The process is continued until there is little further progress toward consensus. Conflicting views are documented in the results.

The Delphi process can obviously be time-consuming and expensive, even though Delphi has been computerized. It has been widely used in future forecasting studies and to some extent in determining and ranking alternative goals and policies. Some workers question that it gives results any better than those of less formal methods. Among other things, the experts tend to perceive problems within the context of the popular issues, pressures, and fads of the times. For example, in the classical study by Gordon and Helmer (1964), the "experts," physical scientists and engineers with few biologists—and before the popularity of "ecology"—tended to overestimate the promise of "ocean farming." These persons appreciated neither the ecological complexity of the sea nor political and legal restrictions to exploitation of the sea.

The use of *overlays* and *transparencies* to map judgmental and scaling data has been of particular value in studies of land use (see, for example, McHarg, 1969). This permits the combination of estimates and judgments of esthetic and conservation value, as well as housing and industrial value, with measurements of slope, physiographic form, stability, drainage, vegetation cover, etc. to come up with a composite pattern, in color if desired, for decision-making.

In many sociotechnical situations it will be desirable to use combinations of the above methods. For example, O'Connor (1972) has developed two indices of water quality based on an extension of behavioral decision theory known as *multi-dimensional utility analysis,* and utilizing the Delphi technique and multi-attribute scaling procedures. The experts, water quality engineers, were asked to establish a set of parameters to be used in each index, to rate the relative importance of each parameter to water quality, and to rescale the physical value of each parameter. O'Connor found the two indices were associated with the assignment of very different quality values to water samples. Hence, the specific use of the water had to be considered. Further, any index must be periodically revised in keeping with new monitoring techniques, new findings, and new priorities. This approach promises to be of value as one step toward the further refinement of social indicators discussed in Chapter 9.

SUMMARY AND CONCLUSIONS

Complex systems possess a great variety of data requirements. Meeting these requirements is limited by the nonapplicability of many available or "canned" data and by our imperfect understanding of the system when understanding is necessary to acquire new and original data. Nonetheless, available sources should be utilized whenever possible to supplement the well-thought-out acquisition of new data.

A number of analytic models and related means of data quantification are available. These should be viewed as being just one part of the over-all systems decisional structure. Often they are necessary, but never sufficient.

There are a number of methods of dealing with qualitative and subjective data. It is emphasized that future progress in dealing with complex socio-technical and social systems will be dependent on advances in the means of dealing with such data.

REFERENCES

Boulding, Kenneth E., 1970, *Economics as a Science.* New York: McGraw-Hill.

Bruno, James E., 1970, The Function of Operations Research Specialists in Large Urban School Districts, *IEEE Transactions on Systems Science and Cybernetics,* SSC-6(4), 293-302.

Center for Real Estate and Urban Economics, 1968, *Jobs, People, and Land: Bay Area Simulation Study (BASS),* Special Report No. 6, Berkeley, Calif.: University of California, Institute of Urban and Regional Development.

Cirillo, Julie Anna, Stephan K. Dietz, and Richard L. Beatty, 1969, *Analysis and Modeling of Relationships Between Accidents and the Geometric and Traffic Characteristics of the Interstate System.* Bureau of Public Roads Research and Development Report. Washington, D.C.: U. S. Department of Transportation, Federal Highway Administration, August.

Gordon, T. J., and Olaf Helmer, 1964, *Report on a Long-Range Forecasting Study.* Santa Monica, Calif.: The Rand Corporation, September. (Defense Documentation Center AD 607777).

Gustafson, David H., Ward Edwards, Lawrence D. Phillips, and Warner V. Slack, 1969, Subjective Probabilities in Medical Diagnosis, *IEEE Transactions in Man-Machine Systems,* MMS-10(3), 61-5, September.

Halpert, Harold P., William J. Horvath, and John P. Young, 1970, *An Administrator's Handbook on the Application of Operations Research to the Management of Mental Health Systems,* National Clearinghouse for Mental Health Information, Publication No. 1003. Washington, D.C.: U. S. Government Printing Office.

Hillier, F. S., and G. J. Lieberman, 1967, *Introduction to Operations Research.* San Francisco: Holden-Day.

Hughes, James, and Lawrence Mann, 1969, Systems and Planning Theory, *Journal of the American Institute of Planners,* 35(5), 330-3, September.

Lave, Lester B., and Eugene P. Seskin, 1970, Air Pollution and Human Health, *Science,* 169(3947), 723-33, 21 August.

McGimsey, George B., 1970, The 1970 Census: Changes and Innovations, *Journal of the American Institute of Planners,* 36(3), 198-203, May.

McHarg, Ian, 1969, *Design with Nature.* New York: Natural History Press.

O'Connor, Michael F., 1972, *The Application of Multi-Attribute Scaling Procedures to the Development of Indices of Value,* Report No. 037230-I-T. Ann Arbor, Mich.: Univ. of Mich., Engineering Psychology Laboratory.

Rogers, Andrei, 1966, Matrix Methods of Population Analysis, *Journal of the American Institute of Planners,* 32(1), 40-4, January.

Schoenfeldt, Lyle F., 1970, Data Archives as Resources for Research, Instruction, and Policy Planning, *American Psychologist,* 25(7), 609-16.

Sterne, Richard S., 1967, Components and Stereotypes in Ecological Analyses of Social Problems, *Urban Affairs Quarterly,* 3(1), 3-21, September.

Wechsler, David, 1971, Concept of Collective Intelligence, *American Psychologist,* 26(10), 904-907.

7

Projecting and Forecasting

In this chapter we first look at some of the reasons for, and limitations of, forecasting the future. Then we examine some of the techniques of technological forecasting, the area of greatest emphasis and development so far. We conclude the chapter with a discussion of the social and environmental factors that are of paramount importance in all but the tritest forecasts; these are *sine qua non* to sociotechnical forecasting.

There is a growing literature in the field. In addition to a number of books, you should consult the journals *Futures* and *Technological Forecasting.*

IMPORTANCE AND PITFALLS

Projecting and forecasting are important intrinsic features of government and industry. The term, *technological forecasting,* is particularly prominent today, and also somewhat misleading, inasmuch as many people use it synonomously with forecasting in general, thus implying there is no other type. There is, of course. For example, economic forecasts involving growth of the Gross National Product and changes in employment patterns have long been made. Expertise in social forecasting is the least developed, and has been largely the output of individual soothsayers from the fields of history and literature.

Other than, say, the joy of creative expression in literature, the reasons for forecasting are several: (1) the stimulation of a technological development once a "need" has been forecast; (2) the determination of business and market policies, once future markets, competitions, and so on have been ascertained; (3)

the determination of a government policy for intervention, once, say, a pattern of political, economic, or social instability has been forecast; (4) the scientific study of the future *per se.*

A glance at past attempts at projecting and forecasting reveals a path strewn with failures. For example, economists and demographers in the 1930s and 1940s, using data on Depression consumption habits and birth rates, forecast another major depression following World War II, and expressed serious concern about the future low American population. Other examples will follow.

Many people remain skeptical about the value of forecasting, regarding it as imprecise and subjective. However, forecasting need not be perfect—merely better than the situation without it. In spite of difficulties and failures associated with gross oversimplification, failure to understand the changing environment, misinterpretation of contemporaneity or correlation for cause and effect, minimization of side effects and impacts, misinterpretation of up- and down-trends of oscillating patterns, and so on, projecting and forecasting have a definite place in the study of sociotechnical systems.

Ayres (1969) makes the distinction between the "ontological" and "teleological" ("normative") views of technological change. The former stresses technological change as self-generating, the latter as responses to external needs, demands, purposes, and objectives. Undoubtedly, both views are partially correct, and are collectively representative of the sociotechnical approach.

Thus, technological, economic, and social variables interact so that success, say, of a device in the marketplace, in turn stimulates further invention and innovation. This is another example of the familiar positive feedback loop. The military, religious, and cultural context which stimulates or inhibits given developments is also of great importance. Advertising is an especially significant variable. For example, companies in the consumer products industry—makers of cosmetics, detergents, etc.—typically spend 25% or more of their total revenue on advertising and product development. Most of their "research" is devoted to testing customer reactions to packaging, brand names, slogans, etc., resulting in new images for old products.

Forecasting is subject to four main shortcomings (Quinn, 1967). The first is *unpredictable interactions.* For example, post-World War II emphasis on manned bombers over missiles did not account for the interactions among compact higher powered nuclear weapons, increased reliability and decreased size of solid-state devices, computers used in guidance and control, and heat-resistant materials.

Unprecedented demands are another shortcoming. Unforeseeable future conditions may create new areas of demand, e.g., the demand for high-speed computers growing out of nuclear and missile technology. Further, computer and xerographic technologies stimulated their own use in needs not previously anticipated.

Major discoveries constitute another limitation of forecasting. In the past, major breakthroughs such as transistors, superconductivity, and lasers have opened unexpected opportunities. The importance of such discoveries is so great they are often cited as bases for the futility of all technological forecasting. However, these developments are seldom unprecedented, but rather result from long efforts, the pieces of which suddenly fit together in a new insight. (See our discussion of hierarchical jumps in Chapter 1.)

The single most limiting factor may be the *inadequacy of source data.* *Aggregate* figures available through the Census Bureau and Bureau of Labor Statistics rarely have been organized in ways permitting either the diffusion or the impact of technological change. Further, industrial and secondary-source data are spotty or have proprietary limitations, and economists have ignored technology in the past. Thus, forecasters must often develop their own primary data before proceeding to analyses, and cost limitations reduce the population the analyst can sample, further reducing his accuracy. However, the situation has recently improved and the government foundations and corporations have presented trends in technological progress.

Some workers argue that forecasts, even the most accurate, are useless unless they influence action. In a corollary sense, an action might not take place if a forecast were not made. Forecasts may, accordingly, be self-fulfilling. A *contingency forecast* is one in which the strategy adopted affects the future, perhaps in an undesirable way. This suggests that in some cases forecasting may be contraindicated; here is another instance of our ongoing need to monitor and control our technology.

In developing a forecasting capability in business, Quinn (1967) recommends staffing with high-quality personnel, and integrating forecasts into executive decision processes. Outside scientific advisors, in-company staff, and/or "wild men" may be variously appropriate. To sell top management on the importance of forecasting, Quinn urges, first, concentrate on near decisions, not on problems of the year 2000 (societal forecasts must, of course, include long-range efforts); second, establish opportunities and threats in priorities; third, fit the forecast into the organization's regular cycle of executive decisions, especially with regard to committing expenditures; and, fourth, include, as part of executive training, participation in forecasting.

METHODS OF TECHNOLOGICAL FORECASTING

In general, science seems to exceed predictions, and the technological application of scientific discoveries to lag behind predictions. The nature, accuracy, and veracity of a technological forecast, of course, is a function of basic assumptions, scales used, adequacy of data, the means of plotting, and so forth. Likewise, the personality factors of the forecasters, for example, extreme conservatism, must be considered. And a forecast using simple trend or "envelope curve" extrapolation of weights, powers, distances, energies, etc., however accurate otherwise, may be misleading if made outside a systems framework.

Technological forecasts do not have to predict the exact form technology will take, but only the probability and significance of future developments. Technology is not simply a single specific piece of hardware, but knowledge of physical and other relationships applied to some purpose. The typical technology possesses a wide and continuous range of attributes in different applications over time. True step functions are rare. It is such relative continuity that makes technological forecasting possible, technically and economically, within a range of performance characteristics.

Often simple extrapolations can be made, as long as we know a situation exists without knowing why it exists, that is, without our knowing the underlying mechanisms. In most cases, however, there are numerous intercorrelated variables, and higher levels of understanding are necessary.

Ayres (1969) differentiates among the following elements of technology:

1. *Invention,* e.g., of the first germanium transistor.
2. *Innovation,* e.g., the first use of transistors in place of vacuum tube diodes in electronic computers.
3. *Diffusion,* e.g., the rapid displacement of vacuum tubes by transistors in computers, radio, television, etc.
4. *Transfer,* e.g., the use of transistors in areas where vacuum tubes had never been utilized, such as to replace relays or commutators in alternators.

Technological change in fast-growing fields may be graphically represented by a series of escalating S-curves, the envelope of which may itself be an S-curve.

There are a number of techniques for technological forecasting based on analyses of past events combined with the insights of "experts." Measurements of data, trends, and interactions are required. Different kinds of products and different stages in the life history of the same product may require different kinds of forecasting. The appropriate technique should be chosen through a balance of purpose (say, R & D or sales), cost, accuracy, time, and data availability.

There are a number of ways of classifying the methods of technological forecasting, and we shall summarize three approaches below. All authors agree that a combination of methods is necessary for complex problems dealing with the future of whole technologies or broad changes in the economy. Quinn (1967) provides a particularly fine and comprehensive classification as discussed below.

Assessment of perceived demand, not technological capacity, tends to be the primary force stimulating technological change. Technology is utilized only when it responds to a need. Thus, if one can identify future needs, one is in a good position for analyzing technological advances. Quinn doesn't consider, however, how needs may arise, e.g., through the media of advertising and propaganda. Further, he seems overly sanguine as to human motivation and problem-solving once the "need" has been identified. His approach here is basically open-loop or simple cause-effect.

Demographic and sociological analyses such as those related to transportation, pollution, and food are important in the identification of needs. The *rate* must be determined at which the underlying demand factors will become strong enough to overcome political, behavioral, and social patterns counter to it.

Conditional demand analysis attempts to predict conditions under which new technology will be needed; and the probability, timing, and impact of each event can be predicted using Bayesian and/or trend analysis techniques. A final forecast would predict: (1) strength of need relative to seeking a technical solution; (2) performance requirements; (3) present technical advances; (4) probabilities of occurrence of each circumstance at future dates; and (5) the payoff if the event occurs.

Opportunity identification techniques enable management to identify latent demands and to enter unique, nonsaturated areas.

The above techniques for identifying opportunities are essentially extensions of market research techniques and offer no real conceptual problems.

Theoretical limits tests involve pushing a known item or phenomenon to its theoretical limits and then attempting to visualize its potential applications. The logic of such forecasts can be made by a group of experts refining their estimates through successive approximations, i.e., by a Delphi technique.

Parameter analysis is the heart of the forecasting process. It involves selection of key performance parameters which can be quantified. Ranges, as well as most likely values, are identified. Best estimates of the probability of meeting the projection, exceeding it, or falling short are given. There are several specific techniques available, the first of which is predicting technological changeover points. Critical performance characteristics, expressed quantitatively, are defined which will enable the technology to substitute for another, e.g., turbojet aircraft engines for piston engines; and solid-state devices for vacuum-tube devices Changeover points in the future, rather than now, are the important ones. The second technique is analyzing unique properties of a product. Situations are identified in which a product can most readily be substituted for other products.

Trends in plotting technical-economic performance provide the third technique. The method enables one to indicate when a new technology will cross critical thresholds, e.g., when the costs of tunnelling for urban superhighways will be feasible economically as compared to the costs of surface construction. However, data may be spotty and appear as scattered points on a "parameter versus time" chart rather than as a straight line. Technological advance is rarely a linear process, and it is dangerous to extend even the most rigorously analyzed trends very far into the future. Basic science, new approaches, or unforeseen factors may mitigate against an expected process.

Analyzing substitution growth curves, the fourth technique, shows how rapidly one technology will take over from another. Substitution of one technology for another tends to follow the "S" shaped curve; i.e., substitution increases slowly at first, faster as acceptance grows, and more slowly as saturation is reached. The analyst, therefore, attempts to determine where on a growth curve a technology is. Major substitutions of one technology for another may take decades. A number of historic examples show a great similarity in technological substitutions.

Finally, diffusion studies relate to the fact that technological potentials exceed the applications of these potentials. This is associated with conservative user behavior, process debugging, development of new skills, labor relations, etc. Just because a technological potential exists is no guarantee that the technology will receive widespread acceptance. Accordingly, we must forecast both the technological potential and the actual diffusion of that technology.

Systems analyses can identify weaknesses in present systems which are amenable to technological improvements. Another approach poses hypothetical or probable future problems and the technologies required for solution; this technique is commonly applied to military and space problems. *Impact studies* help determine what effects possible new technological solutions would have on existing or anticipated systems; technical, economic, and social effects of the new development are determined. Probability and cost of each performance level can be compared with potential economic and social benefits, and the net incentive to reach each level can be calculated. Results can then be combined with parameter analyses.

Scientific surveys enable us to deal not with technologies but with new basic knowledge, the precise form of which may be impossible to predict. However, we can say relative to basic research: (1) what fields are most likely to be receiving attention in the near future; (2) which fields will possess relevant knowledge; and (3) what problems research is or is not likely to solve in the near future. Surveys help determine what is unknown, rate of accumulation of new knowledge, available personnel, company and government support, etc. Such forecasts are based on previous experience and depend on past patterns continuing into the future. No attempt is made to predict serendipitous discoveries.

Finally, Quinn notes in his classification that some forecasts relate to how a *competitor's actions* will affect the organization.

Ayres (1969) uses a somewhat different classification. *Morphological analysis,* his first category, involves stating a problem to be solved or functional capability in great precision. Then characteristic parameters are identified and subdivided into distinguishable states. The myriad combinations among parametric states are determined by multiplication and analysis made, perhaps by eliminating certain "impossible" combinations. For example, 36,864 distinguishable combinations of jet engines can be made based on such parametric states as medium (vacuum, air, water, earth), state of propellant (gas, liquid, solid), internal or external thrust augmentation, self-igniting or non self-igniting propellant, and so on. Disregarding meaningless combinations still leaves 25,344 possible jet engines. The approach can be embellished using network methods and can be extended to, say, political problems by using conflict scenarios involving various states of such parameters as geographic region, level of conflict, tactics, mission, and so on.

Extrapolation of trends, in the simplest sense, involves determining the general form of a curve such as exponential, logistic, linear, power, etc., and then using perhaps the "least-squares" method to minimize the variance or sum of squares of the errors. Further, a distinction should be made between *component-oriented* extrapolations which tend to be conservative and *envelope-curve* extrapolations which embody all the techniques, say, in aircraft power (reciprocating engine, subsonic turbojet, supersonic turbojet, nuclear powered, etc.) or computer speeds (mercury acoustic delay lines, cathode ray tubes, ferrite magnetic cores, etc.).

Heuristic forecast is based on a model of the future which requires greater understanding than a simple extrapolation. Many of these models are based on, or related to, S-shaped or logistic growth curves. Many incorporate variables (or constants depending on the assumptions), such as number of scientists, amount of information, probability of exposure to information, amount of researcher productivity, and so forth. Large-scale uses of operations research in multivariate models and computer models and simulations are also included here. Most of these are input-output models of the Leontief (1965) type; the Forrester systems dynamics approach discussed earlier is also representative.

Intuitive methods of forecasting involve various combinations of experts, with or without direct confrontation, perhaps utilizing role playing and scenarios, and perhaps aided by computers or other equipment. The Delphi technique is a well-known example.

Chambers, *et al.* (1971) have evaluated a number of forecasting techniques, rather simply classified, as follows:

1. *Qualitative techniques,* such as the Delphi method and market research, that emphasize the opinions of experts, consumers, or others.

2. *Time-series analyses,* such as trend projections and the Census Bureau's X-11, which rely entirely upon historical data and emphasize patterns and pattern change. Rates (say of sales) and changes in rate can also be determined. The assumption is that existing patterns will continue into the future.

3. *Causal models,* such as regression methods, econometric models, and input-output models, which use refined and specific information about relationships between system elements. Historical data are important here. These are viewed as the most sophisticated kinds of forecasting tools, especially for predicting turning points in growth and in preparing long-range forecasts.

Specific techniques within each of the three categories were evaluated in terms of costs, manpower, time, in-house capability, preciseness, and so on. Applications were made to component product (a glass bulb for color television tubes) development and sales. Within the context of their work, Chambers, *et al.*, report success in forecasts for color-television penetration on a national basis utilizing historical information on price, consumer disposable income, and sales of black-and-white TV. They suggest, however, that for undefined markets, such as time-shared computer terminals, modular housing, and electric automobiles, history may be irrelevant.

The techniques to be used over the next several years will be those indicated above, but costs will decrease because of advances in input-output data banks, computer software packages, computer time-sharing, and man-computer interactive systems. Also, computer simulation with probabilistic models will become commoner. However, accuracy problems may remain for one or more decades.

Finally, we must exercise a word of caution. Forecasting is still an art and the judgmental element is always high. The number of historical examples of misinterpreting correlation or contemporaneity for cause and effect, of mistaking oscillations for real trends, of extrapolating past trends too far, and of not recognizing the importance of time lags is legion.

SOCIOTECHNICAL FORECASTING

Sociotechnical forecasting, by definition of a sociotechnical system, must involve an understanding of the dynamics and interactions among a social subsystem, a technological subsystem, and an environment. The difficulty of the forecasting will be a function of system hierarchical level and complexity and of the distance of the future. For example, forecasting the impact of computers on top management within a given industry in 1980 will be easier than forecasting the effects of automation on society as a whole in the year 2000.

An example of a study of the interactions between technological and social changes in a very limited sense is provided by Sulc (1969). Sulc sought to understand changes in social values by using the Delphi technique to compare forecasts of computer technology with those of organizational control of computers.

The experts in Sulc's study included first, eight computer scientists who were asked (1) their opinions as to the probability of given computer developments, e.g., aural-reading computer-input devices, during indicated periods; and (2) how each computer development contributes to particular social impacts (specified on a scale of 0, 1, 2, 3 from low to high). After three rounds of questioning, the median date of all time forecasts was utilized as the most likely time of implementation. Next, a second panel of experts, 45 members of senior courses in industrial management, was asked to express opinions on organizational measures for helping management adapt to computerization. Help might involve various ways of influencing the behavior of employees affected by computerization.

Results were expressed as a three-dimensional model interrelating technological changes, organizational changes, and social impacts. The results were held to help the corporate planner develop appropriate countermeasures, for example, training in computer application, to the respective deleterious social impacts of technological change, for example, redundant middle managers.

Table 7-1 depicts the interrelationship between computer development and social impact. The greater the total relevance number of the computer development, the greater the expected resistance to technological change. Table 7-2 similarly shows interrelationships between computer developments and adaptability of management.

Some of the difficulties in trying to make estimates of even the near-term social future are evident in an article by Bennis (1970). Not only did the future (say, the next 25-50 years) look vastly different in 1970 compared to 1964, but certainty as to that future had decreased. Bennis's original soothsaying was made within the liberal-democratic context of the early 1960s, and involved the evolution of organizations, particularly away from bureaucracy. His arguments were based on things like the continued beneficent growth of science, education, and reason, including more humanistic and democratic management. In particular, Bennis saw a gradual replacement of bureaucracy by adaptive, temporary systems organized around problems to be solved.

Bennis's 1964 prediction of the emergence of a "postbureaucratic" world could have been expressed using Trist's later (1968) framework. This framework is indicated in Table 7-3.

A number of new organizational dilemmas made Bennis's earlier future problematical. These included a crisis in legitimacy associated with the failure of the establishment to live up to its basic values and to maintain a proper relationship between means and ends, and the changing attitudes of people, particularly youth, toward leadership. Further, American institutions may be incompatible with regard to fulfilling both elitist and populist functions. In addition, the old concerns of power, prestige, money, and profit remain the main determinants of decision-making in large bureaucracies. Finally, consensus falters in the face of vested interest and organizational variety and complexity. The future of democracy itself in America is unclear, particularly with regard to impatience with delays of the democratic process. Thus, the inability to tolerate ambiguity and hence frustration leads to the myriad "mini-societies" in America today.

Bennis believes any forecast of institutional trends must account for:

1. The need for fundamental reform to enable adaptive response to exponentially changing environments.
2. The need to develop organization on a human scale.

TABLE 7-1

Interrelationships between computer development and social impacts.*

Developments in computer control / Social impacts of computer control developments	Relevance in process technologies					
	1. Demands for qualification and personal dispositions	2. Redundancy of middle managers	3. Loss of responsibility and decision autonomy	4. Impersonality of procedures and communication	Total relevance	Probable date of implementation
1. Optical character recognition of uniformly styled types, leading to a reduction of 25% of current punch card personnel	2	2	0	3	7	1972 −73
2. Optical character recognition of handwriting and differently styled types	0	0	0	2	2	1977 −78
3. Aural reading computer input devices	1	0	0	2	3	never
4. High speed stores of vast capacity enabling non-stop operating systems	0	3	3	2	8	1974 −75
5. Real time data systems becoming universally feasible in management (production scheduling, inventory control)	1	1	1	1	4	1973
6. Simplification of semantic and syntactic tendencies in the collection and dissemination of technical and managerial information	0	0	0	2	2	1973
7. Programming of all routine operational control decision-making	0	2	1	2	5	1971
8. Programming of advanced operation control decision-making (optimalization)	1	3	3	2	9	1973 −74
9. Simulation of long-range planning decisions	2	0	2	2	6	1979
10. Simulation of human thinking in symbolic logic (computer as a general problem solver, self-teaching computers)	3	0	0	3	6	1985
Total relevance	10	11	10	21	52	

*From O. Sulc, "Interactions between Technological and Social Changes," in *Futures,* September 1969.

TABLE 7-2

Interrelationships between computer developments and
adaptability of management.*

Effects of future trends in computer control engendering the resistance of management / Measures improving the management adaptability to future trends in computer control.	Relevance in process technologies					
	1. Demands for qualification and personal dispositions	2. Redundancy of middle managers	3. Loss of responsibility and decision autonomy	4. Impersonality of procedures and communication	Total relevance	Probable date of implementation
1. Training of operational management staff in computer application, throughout all aspects of the firm's business likely to be affected by computer technology starting from junior graduate posts	2	3	1	1	7	1970
2. Acquiring operational management staff so trained in computer application from outside the company, particularly from research institutes	2	0	0	1	3	1973 −74
3. Development and application of methods for selecting computer system managers and scientists with appropriate intelligence and personal characteristics	3	0	1	0	4	1971 −72
4. Inter-company agreements on the transfer of displaced middle managers	0	3	0	0	3	never
5. Inter-departmental transfer of displaced middle manangers to newly created jobs within a company	1	3	0	0	4	1976 −77
6. Inter-departmental training and experience for middle managers before introduction of computer	3	0	2	2	7	1970
7. Changing the social prestige image from membership in the decision heirarchy to that in a technically expert elite	2	0	1	0	3	1976 −77
8. Greater adaptability of computer programs to conform to the varying qualifications of operators and program users (for example, by more flexible subprograms, and more natural computer language)	3	0	2	1	6	1971 −72

TABLE 7-2

9. Designing the technology of computer maintenance and service with the aim of employing a greater number of semi-skilled operaors rather than a few highly skilled ones	3	1	0	3	7	1972 –73
10. Changing the social prestige image of managers in the environment as a whole, from decision and control functions to coordinating functions	0	0	2	1	3	1974
11. Facilitating and simplifying flow of information between: (a) highly specialised groups or departments (horizontal flow of information)	1	0	0	3	4	1973
(b) staff and line functions such as systems design, computer personnel and operational management (for example, by the introduction of suitably qualified liaison officers)	2	0	0	3	5	1970
Total relevance	22	10	9	15	56	

*From O. Sulc, "Interactions between Technological and Social Changes," in *Futures,* September 1969.

3. The youth movement.
4. The demand placed on organizations to participate in improving the quality of life.
5. The accelerating technical changes requiring development of a scientific humanism.
6. The necessity of bringing man into better harmony with his physical environment.
7. The need for a more sensitive and flexible planning capability by management.
8. The rising demand for social and political justice on the part of the deprived sectors of society.
9. The need for order and peace at all levels of societies.

Here Bennis is guilty of the same *faux-pas* as in the case of his original prognosis: forecasting from the context of the present, rather than from understanding basic societal forces. Yet Bennis's conclusions are general and

TABLE 7-3
Changes toward a post bureaucratic world.*

From	Toward
Cultural Values	

From	Toward
Achievement	Self-actualization
Self-control	Self-expression
Independence	Interdependence
Endurance of stress	Capacity for joy
Full employment	Full lives

Organizational Values

From	Toward
Mechanistic forms	Organic forms
Competitive relations	Collaborative relations
Separate objectives	Linked objectives
Own resources regarded as owned absolutely	Own resources regarded also as Society's resources

*From W. G. Bennis, ' A Funny Thing Happened on the Way to the Future," *American Psychologist,* Vol. 25, No. 7 (July 1970), 595-608. Copyright 1970 by the American Psychological Association, and reproduced by permission.

mild enough and include, first, the organization's response to the environment will continue to be crucial for its effectiveness. Second, large-scale bureaucracies will become more vulnerable to legislative and judicial review. Third, there will be numerous contradictory tendencies, such as more participation in governance of bureaucracies, including lower levels of hierarchy; more formal, quasi-legal processes of conflict resolution; more rapid turnover and varying relationships within organizations; and more direct confrontations when negotiation and bargaining fail.

The difficulties in forecasting the sociotechnical and social future relate especially to our limited understanding of the basic ("genotypic") factors and forces of human society and of the existence, nature, and magnitude of inter-actions. Sociotechnical theory is in an incipient stage; hence, forecasting is still heavily dependent upon intuition and judgment and indirectly upon individual experience and perceptual bias.

A number of additional factors help explain the difficulty of sociotechnical forecasting. For one thing the changes in society are occurring at differential rates. It is often stated, for example, that the rate of person-to-person information flow is increasing much faster than such parameters as population, Gross National Product, and energy consumption.

Further, forecasting must consider how trends come together, e.g., as represented today by the youth movement. Detecting latencies is of critical importance, especially in the context of the hierarchical jumps discussed in Chapter 1. Consider, for instance, that we have been educating for and urging democracy for generations—but only now is it really beginning to sink in, perhaps to the dismay of many. Similarly, society is characterized by shifting coalitions and polarizations, themselves frequently adaptive manifestations to frustration and conflict. Recent beginnings of liaison between universities and labor unions and between conservationists and labor unions provide illustrations.

Behavioral and social changes tend to be at once less concrete and more pervasive than purely technological changes. Forecasters prefer to deal with the concrete, if not with gadgetry at least with dollars, jobs, or numbers of people. The familiar Delphi forecasts, using polygons to summarize estimates made by half the group of panelists, represent forecasted developments in physical and biological science. Even articles dealing, say, with psychology in the 21st century tend to stress things like electronic or pharmacological control of behavior.

Emery (1967) has attempted to identify the needs the social sciences should be prepared to meet in the next 30 years. Man's need for understanding and controlling himself and his societies may be, indeed, different then from now. This is viewed as a challenge to the social sciences.

Emery believes we cannot expect an important new concept seriously to affect the growth and direction of social science in less than five years. (However, see the article by Deutsch, *et al.* [1971] reviewed in Chapter 1.) Further, each wave of planning must create the conditions necessary for planning the next wave. In the social sciences, this would seem to involve a foresight (but not a detailed forecast) of 20 to 30 years.

With planning, the social sciences can play an active role in the oncoming decades, not simply a passive one. Obviously the job of predicting would be easier in the simple passive role. The social sciences must actively seek ways of enabling man better to control himself and his institutions; their role is not reducible to oversimplified predictions or forecasting. The planning in which social sciences engage should seek to extend the choices men can make relative to conditions, responses, and goals, not to dictate these choices.

Emery next looks at concepts and methods that may help the social scientist determine the shape of the future. There are theoretical questions involved in predicting the future as distinct from methodological ones. Also, prediction of repeated processes or processes showing only quantitative change is outside the scope of consideration. Capability for future prediction is a function of how much of a system's life extends up to the present, part-whole relationships, and interactions among systems.

Emery examines methodologies, given the conceptual model of overlapping systems. Two main aspects of the methodological problem are (1) to identify the system in terms of its elements and the dimensions in which they are arranged, and (2) to identify the characteristic generating functions of the system. Insofar as a system generates its successive stages, it will display a temporal series of behavior which might be represented as a mathematical series.

Large social systems are, however, much more complex than are the systems studied by the constituent social sciences. This has been considered by Ashby in *Design for a Brain* (1960). He mentions the insuperable difficulties if we attempt to build a picture of such systems from a representation of all the elements and their interactions.

What system tendencies generate conditions that make adaptive survival behavior possible? Changes in survival conditions should induce changes in values or goals. Direct study of what is valued should enhance the predictions made from study of survival conditions alone. Churchman and Ackoff (1949) believe that when something is valued by a social system we can test the tendencies to pursue this something more efficiently and to use this more efficient means as well as the tendency toward increased conscious desire to achieve the something. This model may be useful, Emery stresses, in resolving relationships between values and long-term shifts in values.

The sharing of elements between subsystems may be so great that their subordination to newly emerging processes can be difficult to detect. The elements appear still to function in the already established systems, although perhaps more erratically. This presents great methodological difficulty. Yet if social life can be characterized in terms of overlapping systems or Gestalten, then many processes critical to the future are already extant in the present.

Why are there significant processes acting in the present which, nevertheless, remain undetected? Emery believes that the sharing of elements by complex social systems enables social processes to continue growth without detection. These elements continue to play traditional roles in existing familiar systems. The analogies to cancer and incipient psychosis are examples here. Once there is a new fully fledged system, we can usually trace the roots of its origin. What sort of methodology do these ideas suggest? Following Angyal (1958), Emery suggests three ways of analyzing social systems. First, when the emerging system is weak, it will tend to manifest itself in parasitic or debilitating effects upon a host system. The latter will find it increasingly hard to mobilize energy or people and to respond to new demands. Eventually, oscillations may occur making the functioning of the system less predictable and encouraging experimentation with new forms of system functioning. The reasons for the increase in uncontrolled variance (error) in system operation will be sought inside the system itself leading to measures to tighten up its integration. Operational analysis of system variance would seem appropriate here.

Second, when the emerging system is stronger than in the above but still cannot displace the existing system, we may see occasional intrusions which still do not reveal the shape of the emerging system. We should be able to develop proper methodological techniques appropriate here.

Third, when the emerging system has grown to be about as strong as the existing system, we may see mutual invasion. The existence of a new system should be evident, but many people will regard it merely as a reaction against the old. Methodology must identify aspects of the new system that are not simply oppositions to the old. Some of the problems of early detection are summarized in Figure 7-1

Most growth processes in social systems appear to assume the sigmoid form. This is mostly because social systems possess the property of highly developed symbological communication. What is absent (because it is past, distant, or as yet only poorly anticipated) can be represented by relating one element to another. Hence, mutual coordination is vastly extended and so is the contagion of change.

Emery points out that much of individual human change or adaptation (e.g., learning) may not be conscious. In addition, social symbols, beliefs, fads, myths, values, language, and fashions change without any necessary awareness of what the change means. Several methodologies may be of value here: (1) symbol analysis, (2) value analysis, and (3) analysis of linguistic usage. Emery feels that these methods will offer a reduction in the complexity with which we must deal, because "men will, if acting unwittingly, tend to symbolize the relevant changes and filter the relevant changes out for themselves (page 215)." In acting

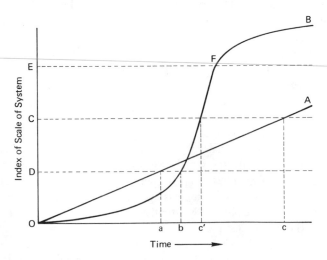

FIGURE 7-1

Growth process in social systems.[1]

[1] From F. E. Emery, "The Next Thirty Years: Concepts, Methods, and Anticipations," *Human Relations,* August 1967.©1967 Plenum Publishing Corporation. Curve A represents a steady rate of growth; Curve B is more typical of social system growth; C is point of critical size; D is point of detection of growth; OF is exponential curve of sigmoid curve B.

consciously, on the other hand, they tend to see things through the ideologies of the times.

Emery thus emphasizes that, first, the future will be largely shaped by human choices and will not be molded by technological forces alone. Second, present processes can reveal some of the choices people must make in the next 30 years. Third, social scientists can provide not only theories, methods, and personnel, but also should play a more active role.

Emery maintains that the *leading part* of the systems under concern is the technological system, i.e., the complex of interrelated sociotechnical organizations concerned with the production of goods and services. What we know of the growth processes of Western-type societies, while not easily amenable to mathematical or graphical extrapolation, seems to permit the Ashby-type analysis. This approach has some precedent in Lewinian psychology, and in the study of economic and military organization. It is interesting to note that Lewinian psychology has also influenced the thinking of Jay W. Forrester and others and can be considered an important general sociotechnical systems link.

One dimension of the environment, viz., *causal texture,* receives special emphasis. This refers to the extent and manner in which variables relevant to the constituent organizations or organisms are, independently of any particular element, causally interrelated. The relevant variables may be considered to be goal objects and noxiants ("goods" and "bads").

Emery goes on to specify four ideal types of organizational environments (causal texturing) from simplest to most complex texture. First, goals and noxiants are relatively unchanging in themselves and are randomly distributed within the environment giving a placid, randomized environment. Second, goals and noxiants are not randomly distributed but are clustered; however, the environment is still placid and static. Third, the environment is characterized as disturbed and reactive. Fourth, the environment is characterized as a turbulent field. See again Chapter 1.

Emery believes the next 30 years will evolve around men's attempts to create social forms that are adaptive to turbulent environments or which downgrade them to less complex types of environments. Complexity can be downgraded through segmentation, fractionation (superficiality), or dissociation. However, these are passive adaptations and the question arises as to what active steps man could take by changing the conditions leading to complexity. He may restrict the range of conditions to which he must respond. There often is fragmentation, however; as a social system differentiates to cope with complexity, there is an increased probability of the elements pursuing their own ends without regard to the total system. In dissociation there is a downgrading of the properties of coordination and regulation. Dissociation (cf. loss of the absolutes and the rising criminal statistics) seems to be a particularly important feature of modern societies. Further, Emery sees these three passive defense mechanisms as being: (1) mutually facilitating and not mutually exclusive; (2) tending to fragment the larger social system, necessitating further adaptations at the local level; and (3) tending to sap the energies and reduce the adaptiveness of the larger systems. However, none of the modern industrial nations seems so handicapped by these features as to lack the power to adapt in other ways.

Men are not limited just to adapting to the environment. The emergence of *values* as a human response to the uncertainty of our emerging turbulent environment is also important. But what values, and how do these values shape the lives of men and the organizations they create? Why do values take such a long time to emerge?

Emery believes that, in the design of their social organizations, men can make the biggest impact upon those environmental forces that mold their values. If these changes are made in the leading part, i.e., the sociotechnical organizations, the effects are more likely to spread than if made elsewhere. See also the suggestions of Skinner discussed in the last chapter of this book.

The first decisions about values for the future control of our turbulent environments are the decisions relative to choosing our basic organizational designs. An unavoidable choice must be made between a population seeking to enhance its chances for survival through strengthening social mechanisms for control or by increasing the adaptiveness of its individual members (apparently the bias of Western societies).

In the design of an adaptive, self-regulating system we must build-in redundancy or else be satisfied with a fixed repertoire of responses adaptive only to a finite set of environmental conditions. An arithmetical increase in redundancy leads to a logarithmic increase in reliability. Redundancy may arise from having either redundant elements or redundant functions for each (or some) element. The last seems more consistent with Western thought and practice.

Emery concludes that developments in systems management and in involving individuals in the control of their working organizations may help lead to effective "democratic" solutions before the passive adaptive modes force us to "totalitarian" solutions. However, these techniques may be misused, given the wrong assumptions. The characteristics of the turbulent field require a different form of organization from the familiar hierarchically structured form.

Mesthene (1968) has looked at ways in which "technology will shape the future." He stresses particularly the effects of technology on values and value change. Technology is seen to add to the available options, that is, to increase and diversify material possibilities. This in turn requires new activities and organizations taking the form of social change.

Because new technology alters the conditions of choice, it tends to be followed indirectly by changes in the hierarchy of individual and social values. Of course values and technological change reinforce one another. In many ways, technology can flourish only in the presence of the proper value predispositions. Accordingly, Mesthene writes of a social drive to develop ever more new technology; this drive is associated with the high probability that new technology will result in physical, social, and value changes. Collectively, this ensemble characterizes a world whose major attribute is change. In turn, pervasive change colors the way in which people understand, organize, and evaluate the world. Thus, ongoing change is more characteristic of the world than is steady state or transition from one steady state to another.

There is a direction or pattern to societal change—it is not aimless, but is directed toward the enhancement of the use of knowledge.

Qualitative and permanent alterations in the nature of human society are seen to occur as a consequence of the perception of ubiquitous change. These alterations affect the person, the family, education, trades and professions, organizations, and governments. But technological change need not result in the destruction of all values. For although particular values may change, the social function of values and the process of creating new values do not change. In this sense Mesthene writes of *valuing,* the human ability to extract values from experience and to use and cherish them. Yet the total pattern of values, attitudes, and activities required by a social posture of expectation of, and readiness for, change will be different from that of a society which perceives itself as mature or in stable equilibrium, a society characterized by an allegiance to the known, stable, familiar, and formulated. The most fundamental political job in a technological world then emerges as the systematization and institutionalization of the social expectation of change that technology will continue to produce. Many of these themes have since been popularized and widely disseminated by Toffler (1970). We shall return to the all-important topic of values and value change in Chapter 9.

For further discussions of projecting and forecasting, see Chapters 2, 8, and 9.

SUMMARY AND CONCLUSIONS

Projecting and forecasting have become integral parts of the operations of business, industry, and government. Economic and demographic forecasts have long been made relative to Gross National Product, population, and employment, and have been used for planning, for example, of schools and highways. Technological forecasting involves a more recently developed body of techniques; it has been used mainly in the development of products, including military systems. The record of all these forms of forecasting is mixed. Sociotechnical forecasting is, by definition of a sociotechnical system, much more complicated. Development of a workable sociotechnical forecasting capability would be among the most valuable contributions of science to society. Such a capability would be dependent upon our ability to describe the subsystems and environment and their interactions in the present. Especially important to forecasting, it would appear, are latencies and time lags, reactions to stress, coalitions and reconfigurations, hierarchical jumps, shifts in motivational level, exposure to information, differential rates of change of subsystems and environment, ability to maneuver, and the specific nature of operating forces within society.

REFERENCES

Churchman, C. West, and Russell L. Ackoff, 1949, The Democratization of Philosophy, *Science and Society,* 13(4), 327-39, Fall.

Angyal, A., 1958, *Foundations for a Science of Personality.* Cambridge, Mass.: Harvard University Press.

Ashby, W. Ross, 1960, *Design for a Brain.* New York: Wiley.

Ayres, Robert U., 1969, *Technological Forecasting and Long-Range Planning.* New York: McGraw-Hill.

Bennis, Warren G., 1970, A Funny Thing Happened on the Way to the Future, *American Psychologist,* 25(7), 595-608.

Chambers, John C., Satinder K. Mullick, and Donald D. Smith, 1971, How to Choose the Right Forecasting Technique, *Harvard Business Review,* 45-74, July-August.

Deutsch, Karl W., John Platt, and Dieter Senghass, 1971, Conditions Favoring Major Advances in Social Science, *Science,* 171(3970), 450-9, 5 February.

Emery, Fred E., 1967, The Next Thirty Years: Concepts, Methods, and Anticipations, *Human Relations,* 20(3), 199-237, August.

Leontief, Wassily, 1965, Input-Output Models, *Scientific American,* 212(4); 25-35.

Mesthene, Emmanuel G., 1968, How Technology Will Shape the Future, *Science,* 161(3837), 135-43, 12 July.

Quinn, James Brian, 1967, Technological Forecasting, *Harvard Business Review,* 89-106, March-April.

Sulc, Oto, 1969, Interactions Between Technological and Social Changes, *Futures,* 1(5), 402-7, September.

Toffler, Alvin, 1970, *Future Shock.* New York: Random House.

Trist, Eric L., 1968, *The Relation of Welfare and Development in the Transition to Post-Industrialism.* Los Angeles: University of California, Western Management Science Institute.

III

TYPES OF SOCIOTECHNICAL SYSTEMS WITH EXAMINATION OF REPRESENTATIVE CASES

In Part III we examine some types of sociotechnical systems backed up by representative cases. The types of sociotechnical systems chosen for discussion are those defined by common parlance and study, for example, transportation, electrical power, urban, and public health. However, it should be borne in mind that, depending on the definition of the social subsystem(s) and technological subsystem(s) and the hierarchical level chosen, the number of sociotechnical systems is theoretically very large. Further, one system chosen for convenience of study may typically be part of another. Also at the macrosystem level all these systems are interlocked.

Common properties for describing these systems, discussed throughout this book, are summarized. Then we look at the most typical problems associated with each system and provide a case(s) showing how a problem has been attacked. Thus, not only general issues and principles but also specific details are offered, as warranted. To avoid needless repetition, all conceivable methods of studying a given system are not offered. However, collectively this part includes essentially all the important systems, problems, and methods of attack. A general hierarchy of approaches is reflected in the chapter as a whole. This represents simulation, mathematical modeling, operations research techniques, multiple-regression analysis, and use of computers in methods not implied in the foregoing.

8

Classification
and Detailed Cases

This chapter, after an introduction, is divided in terms of the major subsystems of the sociotechnical macrosystem. Each subsystem is illustrated by one or more cases, which represent problems and selected methods of solution. Although the chapter as a whole is comprehensive, no one section (i.e., subsystem) contains all methods that have been, or could be, applied to the solution of the recognized problems. The chapter concludes with an integration of subsystems into "Models of Society" and consideration of problems emergent at the higher hierarchical level of society as a whole.

FACTORS IN LOOKING
AT SOCIOTECHNICAL SYSTEMS

A means of classifying complex systems is highly desirable. The following, not necessarily mutually exclusive, factors and questions present a framework for such a classification and a checklist useful in systems analysis:

1. *Age.* In what stage of systems development is the system, or alternately expressed, in what phase of the life cycle? Is the system in planning, fully operational, obsolescent, or senescent? Is it rapidly growing, mature and stable, stagnant and unchanging, or decaying?
2. *Type and variety of users.* How sophisticated are the users? How varied? In what ways are they related to the developers, the managers, and the financers?

265

3. *Management.* Is there a coordinated management? Is there a parallel between the system and its management? Do the management elements operate at cross-purposes? Is the system under its own or other control?

4. *Internal structure.* What types of constituents or elements comprise the system? How formal are the relationships among the elements? How are the elements organized as subsystems? What types of negative and positive feedback loops are there? What time lags are there? What are the hierarchical levels? How ephemeral or permanent is the structure?

5. *Functions.* How clearly definable are the functions of the system? To what extent are they variously operational, maintenance, production, service, steady-state-ensuring, and so forth? How does function relate to structure?

6. *Purposes, goals, and objectives.* Can a single purpose, goal, or objective be defined? Are plural objectives reconcilable? Are the objectives consistent with the structure and capabilities of the system? Are the constituents arranged in terms of a meaningful purpose?

7. *Dynamic or static nature?* Is the system stable or unstable? Is it changing, and if so, at what rate? Is change among the subsystems consonant? Is the system changing in parallel with changes in the environment?

8. *Performance criteria.* To what extent can performance criteria be defined, especially quantitatively? How can these criteria be classified by category? How many different categories are necessary? What dimensions or scales can be used?

9. *Degree of openness.* How much does the system interact with its environment? How much can it be considered "relatively open" or "relatively closed"? Does the degree of openness change with time? Does the boundary become increasingly permeable, perhaps finally disappearing?

10. *Time-space axes.* Does the system change its configuration or structure with time? What is the form of changes, e.g., periodic, oscillatory, reversible, irreversible, etc.?

11. *Type of technology.* Is the system associated with a stable, stagnant, or explosive technology? Is the state-of-the-art being pushed? Is technological impact parallel with other factors, such as dollars? Is the real impact of technology due more to intervening or side effects than to the technology itself? Is the technology changing so rapidly as to make adjustment nearly impossible? How accessible is the technology to control or even to understanding?

12. *Complexity.* How can the complexity of the system be expressed, e.g., in terms of "orders" of integrations or differentiations, number and superposition of feedback loops, number of subsystems, number and variety of basic constituents, number and variety of interactions, rapid change, rapid response, and so forth?

13. *Hierarchy.* What is the hierarchical level of the system? How do structure

and complexity vary with hierarchy? What new properties emerge with change in hierarchy?

14. *Nature of processing.* How can the system be characterized in terms of the processing of information, energy, materials, or people (e.g., education and training)? Are these compatible?

15. *Data availability and characteristics.* Particularly with regard to modeling and simulation, how available are data and in what forms are the data?

16. *Relationship to the environment.* To what extent can the system meaningfully be abstracted, isolated, or delineated from the environment?

One of the salient features of our world today is the degree of interlocking among subsystems, among organizations—indeed, among nations and societies. Consider, for example, the interrelationships among automobile, highway, petroleum, and construction interests. New highways stimulate growth in the number of automobiles using those highways, which both stimulate the growth of more highways and utilize more gasoline, the taxes from which (in California, at least) are used to finance more highways.

In this chapter we have taken what we consider the most meaningful approach to the study of complex sociotechnical systems, namely, the recognition of the interrelationships among cities, transportation, health, education, power generation, etc., in the context of the ecological, social, and political (power) environments.

On Theory and Practice

Our approach to sociotechnical systems has two origins: (1) in *theory* as discussed in Chapter 1; and (2) in practice, particularly, in the application of systems analysis, engineering, and management *techniques,* originally developed in the aerospace and weapons systems fields, to civil systems; many of these techniques have been discussed in Part II. Unfortunately, there is at this time no necessary relationship between theory and technique. There are hopeful beginnings in bridging the gap between theory and practice, however. For example, Baker (1969) has used open-systems theory in the study of community mental health centers, and the Forrester systems dynamics and other cybernetic concepts have been rather widely applied.

Theory, so far, has been based mainly upon observations of lower hierarchical levels of systems. This is true of the classical studies of Tavistock Institute scientists and the related studies of man-machine systems. Even the systems dynamics approach is grounded in techniques based originally on studies within single organizations. As far as we know, the present book represents the first attempt to extend the sociotechnical idea to systems of great complexity. In doing so, theory will most likely have to be modified greatly. For one thing, the earlier theories were based on rather constrained conditions; it was possible to control alternate configurations of men, or men and machines. This is not usually true with the societal systems receiving our major emphasis. Further, earlier studies typically dealt with systems in which the men and machines possessed an apparent balance in relationship to one another, even though technology invariably represented the leading edge. In our systems, either the social or technological subsystem may dominate, and technology includes systems analysis, computer programming, and so forth, as well as hardware. Finally, in our systems, measures of "performance" transcend production data and personnel data (absences, tardiness, etc.); they include basic human values.

The aerospace industry entered the "civil" field much more in search of products and profits than in a spirit of problem solution. The results have been disappointing. For a critique of the four classical "California Studies" and related early efforts, see De Greene (1970). Concepts of systems, systems analysis, operations research, etc., have pervaded the field widely, but the civil area still offers slim pickings for those in search of a quick profit. For example, at the 1971 meeting of the American Institute of Aeronautics and Astronautics (Strickland, 1971), it was concluded that institutions created for aerospace will not penetrate local government; rather, industry must establish entirely new institutions. Among the specific problems facing aerospace are:

1. The fragmented market.
2. The lack of transferability of systems engineering techniques to social and political variables.
3. Lack of R & D funds by most cities.
4. Lack of a stable pattern of local government.
5. The complex web of local sociopolitical structure. This involves many subtle, formal or informal, almost symbiotic relationships between business and politicians, problem sources and problem solvers, criminals and police, etc.
6. Failure of social change to keep up with technological capability.

Systems concepts have, however, diffused widely throughout government, where search for efficiency rather than profit has been the driving force. Also, universities have developed numerous special programs variously called "social systems," "technology and society," "urban studies," etc. Among the university special programs and institutes, the following are noteworthy: (1) the (recently defunct) Harvard University Program on Technology and Society;[1] (2) the

---

[1] See the final review, *Harvard University Program on Technology and Society: 1964-1972* (obtainable from the Harvard Information Office) for a summary of methods and findings. For a look at possible reasons why the program became defunct, see Anonymous (1971).

University of Georgia Center for the Study of Automation and Society; (3) the University of California at Davis Institute of Ecology; and (4) The Massachusetts Institute of Technology program in systems dynamics.

THE CITY AND THE REGION

Outside problems which threaten an entire society, and problems of international scope, urban and regional problems are today's most critical. There is a wide range of theories as to urban decline and decay, how to "save" the cities, why the cities should be abandoned and new towns started, and so forth. For example, for one look at planning problems, factional struggles, and the evolving role of the urban planner in the early stages of the trouble-ridden Model Cities Program, see Warren (1969). For two contrasting views as to how cities of the future might develop, see Downs (1970) and the entire Volume 14, Number 6, July-August 1971 issue of *American Behavioral Scientist.* Downs perceives alternate forms of urban growth primarily in the conservative terms of extrapolation of presently important factors, namely, location of new growth in relation to existing metropolitan areas, contiguity of new growth to smaller existing communities, and types of planning control (centralized, local, fragmented, or unplanned).

The authors of the *American Behavioral Scientist* issue emphasize "conceptual dynamics of change," many of which stem from general systems and open systems theory. As the editors of the issue state, most of the ideas expressed by the authors are unlikely even to be accepted by the establishment, let alone implemented in the near future.

For a look at one effort to mobilize scientific and analytic knowhow to help solve the problems of life and government of one city (New York), see the New York City-Rand Institute (1972). The article summarizes the political, financial, and operational difficulties ensuing from the attempt to set up a nonprofit research organization within the chaotic, cynical, and venal milieu of a huge city. The report also summarizes urban research in such areas as housing, health, migration, "criminal justice," and fire protection.

For a perceptive and much needed analysis of behavioral, as opposed to sociological and demographic, variables characteristic of living in cities, see Milgram (1970). Large numbers of people, high population density and heterogeneity of the populace are demographic factors, but the psychological *experience* of living in cities can better be characterized by sensory and cognitive overload. Much urban behavior then reflects adaptations to ever-present, pervasive overload. The quality of experience is also a function of the differing "atmospheres" of great cities. Much more attention should be paid to these psychological variables.

The need fully to characterize the city or the region as a sociotechnical system comprised of the behavioral-social subsystem, and the technological-physical subsystem in a dynamic environment has not yet been met. However, in this section we shall try to bring together some of the most important ideas and methods.

First, let's look at the pessimistic side. Most solutions to urban problems would seem doomed to failure. This is partly because the lessons of systems engineering have not been learned. A total systems approach, especially in terms of analysis, has not been practiced. Rather, reliance has been placed upon costly and inappropriate retrofits. Requirements, functions, and task analyses have seldom been performed. Tradeoff studies have usually been superficial, for example, simple comparisons of the private automobile versus some form of mass transit. A more meaningful approach would begin with the question: Is travel really necessary, and if so, why? What alternate means of subsuming the needs satisfied by travel can be considered? One might be improved computer-communications media involving more effective use of television and computer terminals in homes and other peripheral locations. Much work could probably be performed other than at formal central-city locations.

In dealing with the city as a system it is necessary to consider factors like zoning, taxation, ownership versus rental, the echelons of government, labor, labor unions, etc. It is much more than buildings and freeways!

Let's explore this line of thinking further. Much planning appears to be done by hunch, government fiat, or superficial comparison to other towns. Planning is usually thought of only in terms of physical design and land use. Theoretical bases related to many factors in housing demand associated with socioeconomic level are usually ignored. And only recently have planners recognized the necessity of an integrated approach to land use, and social and economic planning. These factors are examined further by Broady (1969).

Social factors that could be better applied in planning include ownership versus rental of homes, owner participation in design, presence of an active middle class and of activists (like teachers), and so forth. Sociological research could product quantitative estimates of demand. Application of a kind of organizational theory could help determine social conditions conducive to desirable social results.

Social change, however, takes place very quickly and its directions are not easy to predict. Planning must thus be more realistic and less utopian, more dynamic and less static.

Many desirable contributions to a town stem from civic initiative, which is very difficult to predict in advance. The planning profession, perhaps suffering from a cultural legacy of the 19th century, has not always adapted to such civic groups. Further, tensions are often engendered between planners and an increasingly better educated and active public.

Broady, pursuing these ideas, recommends planning in which the planner interacts directly and actively with the developing social structure. The planner is not concerned with physical structures and layouts as such, but rather seeks to encourage social initiatives within the community so that community members may contribute more fully to its development. Planning is much more than land use and economics—it must be thought of as a process of encouraging the human resources to contribute more fully to community social development.

Broady uses the term "architectural determinism" to describe the situation in which physical structures determine social behavior (hopefully beneficially) in a one-way relationship in which social behavior is the dependent variable. Planners adopt this very form of social theory. However, like all forms of popular determinism, it is not a very good theory. Thus, except in the limiting sense, design cannot *determine* social activity.

Using public health data, demographic data derived from the census, etc., it is convenient to construct urban maps. Using data at the census-tract level, for example, a city can be represented by numerous tiny rectangles of different brightnesses and saturations. Color can often be used. Today, computers aid greatly in the preliminaries of map preparation. Urban and regional maps provide invaluable means of visually correlating concentrations and patterns related to race, income, education, disease, air pollution, and so on.

A number of systems-like approaches are being made to urban problems (but few to regional problems!). They involve various models and simulations of the city, evaluations of housing projects or new management schemes, new urban designs, theoretic conceptualizations of cities of today and of the future, and city-environment interactions. We shall consider examples in four main areas: city size, cybernetic modeling, urban dynamics, and the urban heat island.

Determinants of and Limits to Urban Size

Many factors theoretically help determine the optimum size of cities, that is, help answer the question: For a given purpose within a given region, within the context of possible future change or growth, how big should a city be? Certainly there is justified widespread criticism of "urban sprawl" and of all-encroaching megalopolis, yet a city (or integrated set of cities) should be large enough to provide goods and services for its citizenry while avoiding needless replication. Some of the factors important to answering the above question are optimum benefit/cost for such services as health and fire and police protection, access and congestion, disease and possible epidemics and other sequelae of crowding, recreation, and energy use. Means of dealing with these factors range from speculative to pragmatic. We offer the following example of a rather intriguing suggested relationship between human behavior and urban design and growth.

Access. Doxiadis (1968) has looked at the relationship between man's movement and his city.

Some people oversimplify the relationship of transportation to cities and assume that if we can solve the problems of transportation, e.g., by building new highways, we will be able to solve the critical problems of the cities. Doxiadis views this as an oversimplification because transportation is only one urban factor, and solution requires consideration of all the factors. Thus, the city may be viewed as a molecule, or complex system, with five constituent atoms or elements. If we break this molecule, we no longer have a city. The elements are: (1) nature, or the original environment; (2) man; (3) society or the relationships among men, which may work for or against the interests and values of man; (4) shells or structures and buildings; and (5) networks or systems of transportation, power, water, supply, sewerage, telecommunications, etc. Note that transportation is only one of the networks.

Doxiadis uses Edward Hall's (1968) concept of man as a *system of concentric spheres,* starting with a sphere representing what man sees, and expanding to include what he smells or hears, and then the space his mind encompasses. This concept has been extended by the present writer to include a sphere of resource utilization (see also Chapter 2).

The city must be viewed as a very dynamically expanding system, the real body of which transcends physical limits to encompass various material, economic, and esthetic forces. In order to understand man's movement in his city, the two concepts must be blended so that man's system of spheres is in motion with the dynamic system of the city. These interactions result in many combinations, but the essence is how far man can move physically, by walking, by animal transport, and by using vehicles (kinetic fields).

Doxiadis introduces the term *ekistics* (from Greek words for "home" and "to settle down"), the science of human settlements. See also Doxiadis (1970) in which the author infers that the shaping of human settlements has always followed four principles of human maximization or optimization behavior involving: man's potential contact with nature, other people, and the works of man; man's effort required for achieving these contacts, man's protective space; and the quality of man's contact with the environment. A fifth principle involves the optimum synthesis of the other four principles. Tracing the evolution of human settlements, Doxiadis observes, perhaps occasionally tongue-in-cheek, that people do not want to have to walk for more than 10 minutes in order to reach the center from the periphery. This set the upper limits of city states. Capital cities were exceptions, because of the large numbers of people required to run the empire. Kinetic field circles expanded to 3 kilometers, or more than 30 minutes of walking time. This was too much and hence people used horse-drawn carts, paved the roads, and made them straight. Here Doxiadis's cause-effect assumptions appear to be on shaky grounds; he says nothing about pre-Columbian American cities, e.g., Teotihuacán, Tenochtitlán, and Tikal, where neither horse nor cart was available.

Doxiadis believes the more complex level of organization represented by the capital cities was emphermal until the middle of the 17th century because of inadequate technology to maintain this level. At the beginning of the scientific and technological revolution, the static cities of the past changed into dynamically growing cities. The first cities to grow were the capitals, followed by industrial cities. Characteristics were (1) continuous growth with no sign of change; (2) an apparently unlimited need to grow; (3) irregular shape; and (4) a size which could not be served by the walking pattern of the kinetic field. Subsequently, city evolution involved superimposing diagonal avenues upon the gridiron system of roads, the construction of subways, and the advent of the automobile and the widespread building of freeways. None of these attempts was permanently satisfactory, and today cities are in a difficult situation. Although the four earlier levels of organization (exemplified by very ancient cities; ancient Rome, Constantinople, Peking, and 19th century Paris; late 19th and early 20th century Paris and London; and present day Detroit) have not been permanently realized, a fifth level (that of the megalopolis) is now emerging.

Because of highway growth especially, the average densities in several major cities of the world have dropped by two-thirds in the last 40 years; this means every person uses three times the space used previously.

Man has failed miserably to recognize that there is a small-scale region in the city which must correspond to the human scale. Man has been too impressed with the machine, with communications, and so on. There is a need for the simpler organizations and for designs in which man and the automobile can coexist without conflict.

At present, we are far behind the times with meaningful designs, especially for the fourth and fifth levels of organization. However, we must face a future in which we must organize our communities, which operate imperfectly at the above-mentioned three or four levels of complexity, to operate with five to eight levels. A start can be made by defining the city in terms of its kinetic fields and its transportation needs. Doxiadis's suggestions as to implementation hark back to the magical and mystical distance man can travel, by whatever means, in 10 minutes. He then goes on to draw an analogy from the capillary: aorta blood flow-speed ratio, perhaps an overgeneralization. This leads to urban areas with radii of 150 kilometers, about what many large centers today actually have. Beyond these, Doxiadis sees a universal world city or "ecumenopolis" in which any two points may be covered within the magical 10 minutes by various modes of transportation of equal comfort and safety but of different costs. He believes that increasing the opportunities for person-to-person contact will increase the chances for man's fullest development.

As practical steps, Doxiadis suggests we can begin to transfer the movement of goods (gases, liquids, and solids) underground. Therein we can learn much about the technology of high-speed transportation through tubes. A second stage would then involve the transfer of transportation underground, thus freeing even more of the surface for man's use and enjoyment.

Cybernetic Modeling

Savas (1970) has looked at the over-all dynamics of an urban process, including the information system, administration, goal setting, and disturbances.

The natural time constants of urban systems are unrelated to the term of elected office. Hence, it is impossible for an official to show visible accomplishment in four years relative to problems that may take 25 years to solve. Awareness of such dynamics tends to cause a politician to settle for lesser goals and to emphasize programs only of symbolic value. Emphasis, then, naturally tends to be on programs leading to reelection. Much evidence from industry and elsewhere indicates that differing time constants for related processes can generate instabilities and feast-or-famine conditions. These factors collectively suggest principles of design for societal management systems: design in terms of role rather than of allowing idiosyncratic action by the occupant of the role; that is, design so as to force on the incumbent behavior that is consonant with the long-term needs of society, not with his needs for reelection.

The large time constants and multivariate nature of the city as a system require a very large, complicated control device. However, in complex systems with many problems of coordination, communications, bureaucratic inertia, sterotyped responses, etc., it is usually necessary to provide minor-loop control. Decentralization is an example of such minor-loop control, which may result in some sacrifices.

A mayor has many sources of information, such as personal vision, subordinates, the public media, other levels of government, and the public. The last is expressed in terms of vociferous persons, special-interest groups, civil disorders, and elections. However, these may be biased, possessed of a low signal/noise ratio, may saturate the system, etc. Thus, the cyberneticist can identify ways to improve the quality, quantity, and flow of information: increase the sampling rate, open more feedback channels, increase the bandwidth, enhance weak signals, match impedance, suppress noise, and correct biased signals. Such New York City activities as the neighborhood city halls, mayor's urban action task force, and night mayor program are representative attempts.

Savas maintains administration is the weak link in the urban cybernetic loop. Personnel, structure, and theory are all problem areas. Salaries represent the largest part of local government expenses, yet personnel are mediocre, and mindless bureaucracies appear to function solely for the convenience of their staffs. Also, lawyers represent a disproportionate number in the higher echelons of government, yet the best experience for running large, complex government departments comes from large complex corporations, unions, and universities.

There has been a big effort to develop Planning-Programming-Budgeting Systems for city government. This has entailed specification of departmental objectives, relation of alternative programs to these objectives, evaluation of the alternatives relative to cost and effectiveness, and budgeting the programs selected. Goal-setting has been made more participatory and involves more of the local community.

With respect to many features of urban life, disturbances are more important than actions of the local government. Disturbances may be social, political, economic, or natural. An especially important social disturbance all over the world, as we have seen in Chapter 2, is the revolution of *rising expectations*. Disturbances can be dealt with cybernetically in two ways, through feedback control and through feedforward, or anticipatory, control. In the former, a disturbance acts on the system, performance deteriorates, and information feedback causes control action to be taken to counteract the disturbance and restore the system to the desired performance level. The latter anticipates the effect of the disturbance on the system so steps can be taken to counter it before performance decrement occurs. It thus involves planning and is preferable to feedback control. However, as Savas sees it, there are two limitations to its application, namely, first, problems not perceived as problems by the masses are problems not acted on. (The early concern of the scientific and intellectual elite with the population explosion represents a prime example.) And the second is that predictive models for social phenomena are poor.

Krendel (1970) has applied systems engineering to the study of the quality of urban life. Social indicators measure the extent to which citizens' goals have been achieved. These indicators must respond rapidly and sensitively to the citizens' changing perceptions of the gap between goals and actual achievements. Indicators aggregated over large periods of time, large areas, or large population groups tend to be of historical rather than realtime value and to be sluggish in response. Krendel uses citizens' unsolicited complaints as social indicators.

The interacting parallel or hierarchical physical, economic, administrative, and societal subsystems of a city generate the characteristics sensed by the inhabitants as the quality of life. This concept is difficult to quantify and is usually inferred from indices, selected in terms of the values of the given investigator and usually smoothed over time, numbers, and space. Such indices could be health, social mobility, income, drug addiction, infant mortality, unemployment, air pollution, physical structure, etc. For planned rapid responses or modifications, more dynamic indicators are needed to serve as inputs to the control system. A negative feedback structure in which the citizens themselves generate the objectives and also serve as a comparator to evaluate the extent of realization of these objectives has been suggested by Krendel. Systems that can be structured in terms of negative feedback loops tend to have outputs that are desensitized both to external disturbances and to variations within the system's own elements. However, they may be limited in their ability to respond to *major* changes.

Theories of revolution based on the disparity between expected and actual need satisfaction have been reviewed in Chapter 2. In order to plan for possible civil disturbances, measurements are needed which provide predictive information about the social system's outputs. Otherwise, irreversible processes may arise and result in chaos.

The functional characteristics of such closed-loop, negative-feedback social subsystems are:

1. A definition of the desired set of changing goals as a function of time and so expressed that achievement can be measured. Dimensions of the quality of life might be safety, health, or personal worth.

2. A sensor or comparator to sense discrepancies between goals and actual system output along the above dimensions. In cities, the citizens are the comparator.

3. A controlling decision-making capability to determine the timing and amount of corrective response necessary to maintain the stability of the urban system. This may be the police, fire department, health and welfare agency, etc.

4. An implementation capability. This could be police action, a telephone call, etc.

5. A means of integrating the system elements into a network that transmits information or energy. Such communications might be by letter, by rumor, by violence, etc.

The above are indicative of the kinds of measurements and data required to characterize social subsystems. However, these are difficult to obtain. A start can be made by calibrating the human comparator to serve as a measurement device for system element dynamics and for total system performance.

Krendel goes on to present a case study in which these methods were attempted. This involved an analysis of the time of official response and of the substantive content of letters received by the Philadelphia Mayor's Office of Information and Complaints. These freely emitted comments were analyzed to obviate the effects of the analyst's values on the citizens' responses, and to preclude the familiar limitations of questionnaires and interviews, particularly as applied to the poor. The linking of letters from citizens to municipal responses permitted closed-loop analysis.

Two samples, involving 300 files, were examined. Both time and content data were coded. Composite distributions of various response times were made. These suggested queuing or servicing models, and a gamma distribution was utilized. Adequate fits of the distributions were made.

Krendel, in his article, discusses ways of describing organizations in control engineering terms and thereby improving management practices. Emphasis is more on improving performance than on insuring the organization's stability. This can be done by introducing the equivalent of lead equalization, feed-forward, and feedback elements, e.g., improved routines, better communications, and bypassing certain operations. In the above case study, there was the beginning of a specification of administrative process dynamics and of the urban subsystem which senses and responds to citizen-generated complaints about the quality of life.

Krendel came up with a table classifying nine problem areas (movement, resource needs, health, physical safety, esthetics, information, shelter, self-image, and culture and recreation) by percentage of complaints. The imposition of his own values by such categorization was recognized. For example, should a complaint about an abandoned car be placed in the "esthetic" or "physical safety" category? Much more needs to be done in this area.

With more data sources, it should be possible to correlate predictions made from these and other social indicators with social accounting generated by the usual life-quality statistics. If the citizenry can reliably generate lead times for urban system performance and if more effective citizen involvement in the setting of goals (feedforward) can be implemented, a more orderly evolution into a rich-quality-of-life urban environment can result. Alternative decisions and actions can be made evident both to society's managers and to its citizenry.

This paper is valuable conceptually and in terms of model building. It is stronger in the straightforward analysis of response times (amenable to operations research) than in the analysis of content, which is quite subjective and qualitative.

Dynamic Modeling and Computer Simulation

An excellent attempt at modeling social and sociotechnical systems is provided by Forrester (1969). A systems model of a city is constructed, and development and policy interventions simulated over a 250-year period.

The model is composed of three major sectors, each of which in turn contains three elements or level (or state) variables (see Chapter 1 and the discussion of systems dynamics): (1) a *business sector* containing new enterprises, mature businesses, and declining industries; (2) a *housing sector* containing premium housing, worker housing, and under-employed housing; and (3) a *population sector* containing managerial-professionals, laborers, and underemployed.

These nine elements, or level variables, are combined with 22 modes of interaction, or rate variables, such as new enterprise construction, manager departures, and declining industry demolition, and then linked with the outside world through complex multiplier functions. The City is a *closed dynamic system* as Forrester sees it. It involves the four hierarchies of structure discussed in Chapter 1.

The complete model is detailed as flow charts, equations, graphs, and about 400 statements of the computer program. Model equations are written in an algebraic language for the DYNAMO Compiler. DYNAMO emphasizes *circular* rather than simple linear causality (i.e., a driving force exerts effects which in turn modify that driving force). The mathematical format of this simulation language consists of a system of simultaneous, nonlinear finite difference equations with variable coefficients.[2] The equations are integrated to simulate the behavior of the system over time. Algebraic relations are easily handled, but stochastic relations and matrices are not.

Results are in the form of time series plots and tables. DYNAMO inputs consist of a mixture of parameter estimates obtained from routine statistical work, structural relations and decision rules based on logical considerations, and general knowledge of the system. The model contains no random influences, and thus is a deterministic model.

Forrester regards the urban area as a system of industries, housing, and people which interact to produce growth processes. The growth and goal-seeking processes of the system are organized into the computer model. Three concepts are emphasized; namely, specific land area, relative attractiveness, and a limitless environment.

Forrester's model shows how an urban area evolves; it deals with a fixed land area which might be a section of an older city, but not an entire area within a political boundary. Indeed, the "environment" may include other parts of a large city. The model begins with empty land and ends up with decaying housing.

Urban growth and stagnation do not appear to be dependent on changes in the world environment, Forrester believes, but are dependent on internal economics and on the changing mix of population, industry, and housing (the three subsystems). The urban area is thus "a living system that communicates with an environment it does not substantially influence (p. 15)." Changes in the subsystems are the central processes involved in growth and stagnation; indeed, Forrester believes these are more important than social culture, city government, or fiscal policy. Important changes involve shifting populations as housing structures age and industry falls behind the outside economy. This last point may contradict his closed-system concept. Also, he recognizes that changes from outside may hasten or retard the aging process. And, if conditions in the urban area are more favorable than outside, people and industry will move in, and vice versa. Yet he seems to believe in quite an oversimplified robot model of man, in that urban structure would appear to blindly drive human behavior, in this case migration.

Elements outside the boundary are considered to be related to those inside differently from how those inside are related to each other; the cause-effect relationship between the system and environment is unidirectional, whereas the internal elements are structured into interacting feedback loops. Thus, we learn the "environment can affect the system but the system does not significantly

---

[2]If the coefficients are constants, the equations can be thought of as being formally equivalent to those of multiple regression analysis; if the equations are not interrelated, to simple multiplier methods (Hester, 1969).

affect the environment (p. 17)." There are no loops running from the system to the environment and back again. The fact that cause-effect loops do not reach outside the boundary and return is referred to by Forrester as the "open-loop test of independence between system and environment." For example, the mechanization of agriculture and rural famine may drive people to the city, but these are not the major causes of urban aging and stagnation; contrariwise, urban slums do not affect either mechanization of agriculture nor rural weather.[3] Forrester's urban area is a living, self-controlling system, regulating its own flows of people to and from the outside environment.

The concept of "relative attractiveness" states that if an urban area is more attractive to a given class of people, inward migration will take place, and vice versa. This is perhaps too great an aggregation, and one might wonder if social science data really support such an idea.

Forrester's model is in two parts. The first part shows the urban life cycle within a period of 250 years, starting with empty land, growing to full land occupancy, maturing through a rapid realignment of internal balance, and emerging as an equilibrium characterized by stagnation, with unemployment, faltering industry, and increased taxes. One might ask here to what extent does this concept violate principles of equilibrium of natural systems—is equilibrum in nature characterized by stagnation? (See our discussions of steady state and open and closed systems in Chapter 1.) Also, to what extent is his modeling couched in terms of what he *expects* to find, based on his observations of today's cities? In addition, to what extent is his concept universal, and to what extent strictly time limited?

A composite of computer time-series plots, showing growth, maturity and aging, and equilibrium and stagnation is given in Figure 8-1. See also Figures 8-9, 8-10, and 8-11 which are modified actual computer plots, but of a global rather than an urban system.

The second part of Forrester's model starts with the stagnant condition and explores the effects of urban management policies. Many of these policies were failures. By computer runs, Forrester examined policies providing jobs, training programs, low-cost housing programs for the underemployed, and external tax subsidies. Over a 50-year period, such programs tended to make some things better and others worse. However, in the long range, the results were neutral to detrimental, largely because of the *counterintuitive* nature of complex systems. For example, an innocuous sounding 2.5% housing construction rate for the underemployed led to results unfavorable for all three categories of the population. It actually increased unemployment and reduced the "normal" upward economic mobility of the underemployed.

---

[3]Technically this assumption may be untrue. Compare the discussion of the urban heat island later in this chapter.

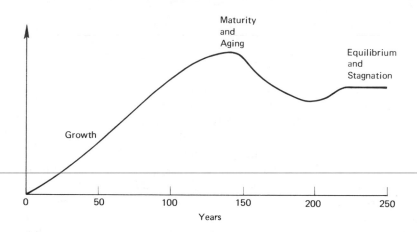

FIGURE 8-1
Representative urban dynamics computer time-series plot.[4]

Forrester believes his model implies much with regard to urban transportation systems—however, he says nothing of the "cause-effect" role of the automobile in urban change and decay. Indeed, transportation is not really considered at all. Forrester concludes:

1. Cities do not need massive financial aid from the Federal Government; problems tend to grow to match the available money.
2. Any outside pressure should be directed toward forcing the city to develop laws and administrative practices conducive to long-term revival.
3. Increase in immigration rate can be delayed best by influencing the type and availability of housing, not jobs. There is typically too much, rather than too little low-cost housing, particularly in relationship to employment opportunities.
4. Aging housing should be removed continually rather than in massive waves.
5. Regulations and taxes should be changed to attract the types of industry that hire many people and offer high wages.

Hester (1969) has provided a particularly good critique of Forrester's urban dynamics approach. In addition, he has extended the model on a small scale to include factors, such as transportation, industrial production technology, and communications, not included by Forrester. A number of other urban models were also reviewed. Hester stresses that in effect no comprehensive model of urban development exists today, although a start has been made toward theory,

[4]Based on data from Jay W. Forrester, *Urban Dynamics,* Cambridge, Mass.: The M.I.T. Press, 1969

and there are models of individual aspects of urban development, such as internal shifts within housing supply.

Because Forrester has not included in his model all qualitatively different areas of the city, the driving force of technology on urban development, and the dynamic effects of the regional environment, his policy recommendations for remedying the stagnation of the central city probably represent suboptimizations and must remain highly suspect.

Urban development is characterized by non-equilibrium, because the city responds to external driving forces as well as to dynamic internal processes. Different parts of a metropolitan area are closely interconnected through accessibility and communication. Accordingly, a city cannot be modeled as the development of independent elements each interacting with its environment.

Factors underlying migration are greatly oversimplified. Migration occurs other than in response to the attractiveness of the specific area being migrated to; rather, it is determined by the activities of the city as a whole. For example, skilled labor can decide where to live and where to work, independently of a given area. Likewise, the location of industry may be mostly a function of cheap, low-tax, available land outside the city. Also population and industry can be stimulated to move out of the city by changes in technology. In summary, both growth and redistribution depend on conditions in all parts of the metropolitan area; the attractiveness of a part of the city need not be based on features physically located in that area.

Urban problems tend to be associated because most activities are differentially concentrated and distributed throughout the city. Theories and models must thus separate the growth and changes in different areas of the city and also describe the interactions among these areas.

Parameters in Forrester's models are estimated in an approximate and nonreproducible manner. However, changes in value by a factor of two or even five of a constant may have negligible results on model behavior. Yet a few constants do make a big difference and their selection remains a problem. Conducting a sensitivity analysis on the parameters in a model with some 200 equations and constants can be a large effort. Interactions require the testing of simultaneous changes in two or more parameters Hester has found.

Misjudging the form of the curve introduced by the table functions might distort the meaning of the model. No formal theory, or even data, exist to explain behavioral phenomena such as attractiveness of an area. Unfortunately, an intuitive feel, based on talking to urban experts, is the method used to estimate attractiveness for migration as a function of housing supply, land supply, or labor supply, and so forth.

Further, Forrester ignores the role of the region in providing the driving force for industrial and economic growth. Once again, let us emphasize, he violates the tenets of open-systems theory. The dynamic city really responds to the external driving forces. Forrester's model presents growth stimulated entirely by internal mechanisms drawing upon a passive environment.

The main effects of technology are on the interactions occurring within the urban area, rather than on its attractiveness. Thus, transportation increases the amount of land effectively available to the city, reducing the need for high densities within the old city. Also distances between home and job or different industries are increased. And third, transportation is discriminatory, in that the old and poor remain trapped within the central city. Improvements in production technology have a similar effect; for example, large one-story assembly-line factories often must be moved to the suburbs where more space is available.

Changes in communications permit greater separation of industries and homes from jobs. But the greatest effect is upon the delays, such as perception of changes in the city.

The equilibrium—growth to stagnation to decay to final equilibrium—is misleading because the model does not consider the driving forces which make an urban area inherently a non-equilibrium system. Instead of reaching a steady state, the city is continuously evolving, and cities differ radically in the way they have developed. Also, the model does not provide for expansion of land supply and use, either horizontally or vertically Hester emphasizes.

Migration is based on a composite attractiveness, in turn based on housing, jobs, etc. These variables are multiplied to yield a composite; in actuality, addition may be better in some cases. Too much intuition and too little use of established theories and data on migration obtain here.

Thus, there are great limitations to Forrester's oversimplified model as a theory of urban development and as a means of either evaluating or recommending alternative policies, such as continual slum demolition and changes in tax policies. Forrester's greatest contribution is in the conceptual approach and the advancement of modeling and simulation techniques.

Finally, validation in large social systems is extremely difficult in the absence of laboratories for carrying out controlled experimentation; in the absence of data relative to dynamically meaningful time series and with data inadequate in terms of disaggregation; and in time scales in years rather than in seconds or days. Yet few constructive solutions have been offered. Hence, new analytic methods for verification and validation and/or success in policy-making are urgently needed; both may take a long time. Until better data and methods are available, evaluation will remain subjective. See also our discussion of model validation in Chapter 5.

Hester concludes that there are these serious limitations to attempts to devise mathematical or quantitative simulation models of large social systems:

1. Results can be valid only in terms of basic premises about individual and group behavior, which are usually overgeneralized and without basis in theory or fact.

2. There are large uncertainties or variations in the key relationships.

3. There is great difficulty in validation with empirical data; among other things, one change in relationships could take months or years to re-validate.

4. Forrester's particular model converges too quickly to a unique equilibrium regardless of variations in initial conditions, ignores the total system context, does not provide for the effects of a number of potential responses to urban problems, and fails to separate government processes from the cultural and social processes of the urban environment. Thus, it is difficult or impossible to study alternate government structures, and to resolve the relationship between government system and urban processes.

For another evaluation of urban dynamics, see Kadanoff (1972).

The "Urban Heat Island"

The phenomenon of the "urban heat island" is of special relevance to the systems study of the city and of urban-regional interactions, because:

1. It is part of a physical system which can be rather easily modeled both *per se* and as part of a larger environmental model involving air pollution and the like.

2. It provides a means of quantifying decisions relative to esthetics that previously had to be accepted only on the grounds of the preference group with the loudest voice and strongest economic and political muscle.

3. It provides a firmer basis for the design of cities and of cities within regions.

Peterson (1969) has reviewed ways in which the climate of cities differs from that of the surrounding rural areas. Areas discussed included temperature, humidity, visibility, radiation, wind, and precipitation. Many of Peterson's points are summarized below.

As metropolitan areas expand, they exert an increasing effect on their own climate; this is potentially of great interest to planners and designers, to health specialists, and to those concerned with the possible global effects of human activities, particularly pollution.

Important source references in this field are Landsberg (1956, 1960, 1962), Tebbens (1968), and Chandler (1968).

Air temperature has probably been the most studied of all the above areas. Indeed, the "urban heat island" has been recognized for over one hundred years. Comparison of minimum daily temperatures of city and land may show differences of 10°F and occasionally even 20°F. The highest temperatures are associated with densely built-up areas near the city center (areas of three- to five-story buildings and parking lots are hotter than areas of high-rise buildings); the degree of warming decreases slowly out through the suburbs, and then greatly at the periphery. The mean annual minimum temperature of a large city may be 4°F higher than that of the surrounding countryside. The greatest differences occur in summer and early fall. A heat-island effect can be observed during the day, but much less easily than at night. In making measurements of the "surrounding area," one must make sure one is measuring the grass- or forest-covered countryside and not the airport Peterson advises.

There seems to be a relationship, not linear, between the heat island on the one hand and city area, population, building density, and morphology on the other. However, other factors such as proximity to bodies of water, topography, wind speed, and cloud cover play a complicating role. Further, small cities and even building complexes may exert a heat-island effect.

There are two primary, seasonally dependent processes associated with the formation of the urban heat island. First, in summer, the pavement and concrete of buildings absorb and store larger amounts of solar radiation than do soil and vegetation. Also, much less energy is used for evaporation, because of the large amount of surface run-off. At night man-made constructions gradually give off the absorbed heat, keeping the city air warmer. Second, in winter, the sun angle is lower and man-made energy from combustion, industry, transportation, and metabolism becomes a significant addition. The annual heat produced artificially may be more than one-third of that received from solar radiation Peterson states.

Year round, pollutants may exacerbate the heat-island situation. Particulates, water vapor, and carbon dioxide absorb part of the thermal radiation directed upward from the surface. A portion of this radiation is re-emitted downward and retained by the surface. However, another part warms the ambient air. In a positive feedback loop, this increases the low-level stability over the city, increasing the probability of even higher concentrations of pollutants. Thus, pollution both contributes to a more intense heat island and alters the vertical temperature structure so as to hinder the dispersion of pollutants.

Reduced wind speed associated with urban roughness also reduces movement of cool air from outside and reduces evaporation.

Other climatic factors also apply to cities. The average relative humidity of the city appears to be several percent lower than that of the surrounding countryside. As a result of air pollution and the associated high aerosol concentrations, urban visibilities are lower and the incidence of all but the densest fog higher than in the countryside. This is because many particulates in pollutants are hygroscopic. Metropolitan areas may have up to 100% more fog in winter and 30% more in summer. Fortunately, though, visibility in many cities (e.g., London) has increased recently, probably associated with the substitution of oil and gas for soft coal and with local efforts at abatement of air pollution.

Particulates over most large cities reduce the amount of solar radiation reaching the surface, particularly in winter at high latitudes and particularly in the ultraviolet range. Solar radiation received in cities in winter may be up to 55% less than that of nearby rural areas. Ultraviolet radiation received at the ground may be reduced by 90% on extremely smoggy days in Los Angeles (Nader, 1967). It is not known whether reduced values of solar radiation at the city surface are compensated for by an increase in infrared energy.

Unfortunately, there have been measurement difficulties associated with these meteorological studies. Most observations have been made at the roofs of downtown buildings, or from parks and open spaces, rather than at street level where most human activity takes place. There is evidence, however, that wind speeds over the city are 20 to 30% lower, and calms 5 to 20% more frequent.

Cities also show strong effects upon the amount of precipitation over them, or, more importantly, immediately downwind. The most dramatic example is that of La Porte, Indiana, about 30 miles downwind from the large industrial complex between Chicago and Gary, Indiana, (Changnon, 1968). Here, the amount of precipitation (31% more annually than in the rural area), and number of days with thunderstorms (38% more days annually than in rural areas) and hailstorms has increased greatly since 1925. Also, there is a correlation between precipitation at La Porte and production of steel and number of smokey days at the industrial complex. Because of the proximity of Lake Michigan, the situation at La Porte may be anomalous; more research is needed on other cities Dettwiller (1968) showed that from 1953 to 1967 the average rainfall in Paris was 31% greater on weekdays than on Saturdays and Sundays. Increases in precipitation in such cities are probably associated with added heat and condensation and ice nuclei.

Policy-making and decision-making, as we have seen, must deal with qualitative and intuitive variables. Some variables, by their nature, will probably always remain qualitative. Others will become increasingly amenable to quantification, as our expertise improves. This is of immense importance to design. For example, in urban design, until recently it was impossible to treat objectively the relative merits of a park, a parking lot, or a freeway. In regional design, a sizable part of "demand" for electrical power comes from home, business, and industrial air conditioning. In both these contexts, studies of the urban heat island are promising.

Myrup (1969), as a beginning toward better quantification, has designed and applied a general purpose, numerical energy-budget model, which predicts the correct order of magnitude of the urban temperature excess. The heat island is the net result of several competing physical processes, especially reduced evaporation in the city center and the termal properties of city building and paving materials. The magnitude of the heat island tends to be positively correlated with city size.

Myrup's model, which concentrates on boundary layer processes, was based on the following simple structure. (It did not, for example, include the effects of pollution or of overcast skies.):

$$RN = LE + H + S$$

where RN is the net radiation flux, E is the evaporation rate, L the latent heat of water (thus LE is the latent heat flux), H the sensible heat flux into the air, and S the flux of heat into the soil.

It is interesting to note that the largest heat island effect reported in the literature (Duckworth and Sandberg, 1954) involved a temperature difference between a large city *park* area in San Francisco and the city center; it was 10°C on one occasion. When this problem was analyzed using his model, Myrup calculated park air temperature to be 11.5°C cooler than city temperatures at midday and 8.1°C at dawn. These striking differences are shown in Figure 8-2.

The relative warmth of the city over the countryside is greatest at the summer solstice and fall equinox and smallest at the winter solstice. Also, temperature decreases with distance from the city center, as can be seen in Figure 8-3.

Sensitivity analyses involved study of the effects of wind speed, albedo, roughness, and evaporation on the city temperature. Results indicate urban temperature excess is the net effect of several competing physical processes, each of which by itself could produce relatively large temperature contrasts. However, generally there is a cancellation effect, reducing the contrast between city and country. Moreover, the most important parameters determining the size of the urban heat island are (1) reduction of evaporation in the city; (2) increased roughness of the city; (3) thermal properties of building and paving materials; and (4) wind speed. In general, reduced evaporation is the most significant parameter during the day, the thermal properties of the substrate by night.

Further work in this area is hampered by lack of data, say on the thermal

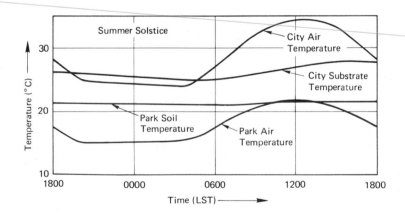

FIGURE 8-2
Temperature differences between city park area and city center.[5]

[5]From L.O. Myrup, "A Numerical Model of the Urban Heat Island," *Journal of Applied Meterology,* December 1969.

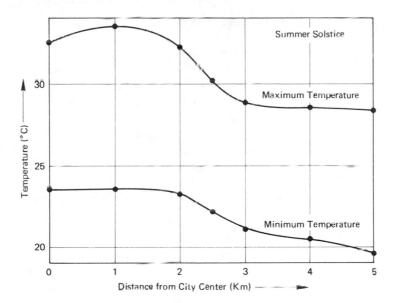

FIGURE 8-3
Temperature decreases with distance from the city center.[6]

properties of the green area and roughness of different parts of the city. Remote sensors can be of value here.

Using these ideas in design could reduce the heat of the sweltering summer nights of U.S. eastern cities. This would include planting at least 20% of the area with vegetation. Rooftop parks would provide one design possibility.

The combined effects of the urban heat island and waste heat from modern technology have been considered by Starr (1969). In a modern industrial society the total per capita energy use is about 10 kilowatts thermal.[7] Assuming release into the city, a population density of 30,000 persons per square mile[8] would make the heat load as large as the solar radiation load into the urban atmosphere. Hence, under extreme meteorological conditions, a city could be 20°F hotter than the surrounding countryside. These ideas should also be reflected in urban design.

[6]From L.O. Myrup, "A Numerical Model of the Urban Heat Island," *Journal of Applied Meteorology,* December 1969.

[7]The annual consumption of all forms of energy in the world has increased about tenfold in the last 100 years (equivalent to an annual growth rate of 2.3%), due both to the increased energy use per person, and population increase. In the U.S., energy usage per capita has grown 1% per annum; economic productivity per capita has grown 2% per annum.

[8]The 1960 densities in persons per square mile, for the following cities, were Manhattan, 77,000; San Francisco and Chicago, 16,000; Los Angeles, 6000.

ENERGY AND POWER

The problems associated with assessing need for, creating and producing, transmitting, and utilizing energy and power are sociotechnical problems par excellence. As is customary in dealing with sociotechnical systems, the tendency is to work within tightly constrained, limited models. Until recently, the environmental impacts beyond both ends of the simplistic input-output system, namely, those concerned with extraction of raw materials and those concerned with the polluting degradation products, have been ignored. Just as serious, nebulous estimates of actual need, or even worse, economic demand, have, without question, been rigorously quantified and incorporated into the system input.

In the analysis and evaluation of power systems, there are several major concerns:

1. The assessment of *real* need and demand.
2. The deleterious impacts on the environment of raw-material extraction or resource utilization.
3. The deleterious effects on the environment, and, of course, on health and the quality of life, of air, water, and land pollution.
4. The danger of accidents and mammoth systems failures.

At a more specific level, most energy and power problems stem from:

1. The production of electrical energy from the combustion of fossil fuels, from nuclear processes, and from hydroelectric dams, and, to a much lesser extent, from solar, eolian, or geothermal processes.
2. The direct burning of fossil fuel to power the internal combustion engines of automobiles and aircraft, and to a lesser extend fuel combustion for industrial and home use.

For an excellent summary of the environmental costs incurred by all present methods of generating electric power, see Abrahamson (1970). For a fine review of the relationship between the generation of electric power and the many forms of pollution see Friedlander (1970a and 1970b). For an excellent and concise treatment of the problems of demand and supply of one state, California, see Lees (1971). These articles examine such important topics as the difficulty of realistic projection of demand, tradeoffs between fossil-fuel-burning and nuclear power plants, differential rates of growth of population and electric power generation, differential use of electricity by residential and industrial and other sectors, possible power failures or "brown-outs," the need to change rate structures, the long lead times in developing new power sources or even in implementing new power plants using present methods of generation, proliferating use of power-consuming gadgetry, and widespread inefficiencies associated with use of electricity.

From these references and from this section and chapter, it should be clear that there is no simple solution to the "energy crisis." Certainly such propaganda of the electric utility companies as the substitution of "clean electricity" for the polluting automobile or coal-powered industry simply "muddies the puddle." Problems of electric power generation must be viewed as just one very important element of systems studies and designs involving transportation, industrial production (especially of metals), waste disposal, pollution, land use, and so forth. Even so, much could be accomplished almost overnight through a joint program of the populace, government, and industry directed toward the elimination or reduction of wasteful practices and cost accounting. Examples of such waste include burning lights all night in many large buildings and poor design of buildings and poor use of insulation materials. However, considering all the above factors, the inescapable major conclusion is that a much reduced growth rate is mandatory over both short and long ranges.

In this section we shall cover the above areas in the context of presenting a long-range forecasting model of the energy balance of the United States, and an attempt to justify the development of controlled fusion power.

An Energy Model of the United States

Morrison and Readling (1968) have written a very worthwhile paper dealing with modeling and technological forecasting (see also Chapter 7). The effort demonstrates the complex systems interrelationships among technology, the environment, resource utilization, the economy, and behavior (by implication); it also exemplifies the difficulties, such as we discussed in Part II, associated with assumptions, future uncertainty, and use of judgments and qualitative data.

Specific forecasts of energy sources and uses are made. The simplified model is quantified for a recent historical period and the results used for 22 analytic case studies that estimate midterm (year 1980) and long-range (year 2000) shifts in energy resource demand and supply. Historical data for the years 1947 to 1965 are presented in terms of energy source, form, and consuming sector. The first 12 case studies involve *conditional projections* of historical trends of demand and supply from 1966 to 1980. Projection is accomplished by correlation of major energy "components" with such independent variables as economic indicators. Simulations of these midterm projections involve varying the assumptions for the determining variables to give high- and low-range projections. The last 10 case studies are *contingency* or *technological forecasts*. These assume technological changes yielding shifts in the pattern of energy consumption and mix of required resources. The forecasting does not include selection of options, specific courses of action, or establishment of programs, "since they are part of the decision-making process." However, the recent introduction of PPBS into the Department of the Interior has provided additional impetus for energy modeling and forecasting, involving planning and programming.

The main emphasis of the report is on the estimation of future energy *demand* rather than *supply*. In the projections and forecasts it was generally assumed that supply, at reasonable cost, would be able to keep up with demand. However, potential shortages of certain resources were recognized.

Historical trends of the major elements of energy demand, by source, form, and sector, can be projected with improved accuracy by single or multiple correlation with such independent variables as economic indicators. Resultant trends can then be fitted to complex growth curves on a conditional or probability basis.

For long-range forecasts, uncertainty naturally increases greatly with respect to the character of the energy market and the nature of the resource mix. Projection of past trends by conditional extrapolation becomes less realistic. The problem is complicated by the inability to predict the precise nature, timing, and impact of technological developments. Also, increasingly, energy resources can substitute for one another. Thus, for long-term forecasts, the new method of quantitative forecasting, viz., technological or contingency forecasting, was used. For example, in a number of the cases, three possible contingency energy situations were variously considered for the year 2000. These were: (1) a continuation of the present conventional energy system; (2) a hydrocarbon-air fuel cell energy system to be used on-site and without the purchase of utility electricity; and (3) an all-electric economy. Projected demands to 1980 assume a 4% average rate of growth of Gross National Product and a 1.6% population growth.

The basic energy model is represented by a series of equations that describe relationships between various determining variables that influence energy on the one hand, and the dependent variable of total energy demand and its major elements on the other. There are two types of variables: independent (exogenous) and dependent (endogenous). The basic model is considered to be either logarithmic linear or exponential and is expressed as:

$$E \text{ or } Y1 = f(X1^b, X2^c, \cdots, X13^n)$$

where (1) E or $Y1$ is the dependent variable representing total energy demand; (2) the superscripts represent the parameters or coefficients of the independent variables; and (3) $X1$ through $X13$ represent quantifiable or nonquantifiable determining or independent variables, such as economic activity, population, industrial production, domestic supply, foreign trade, environmental restrictions, revolutionary technology, and political considerations and tradeoffs.

The major elements (and subelements) of the dependent variable are: (1) major demand sources of energy ($Y2$ through $Y9$) such as demand for bituminous coal and lignite, demand for petroleum and natural gas liquids, demand for hydropower, and demand for nuclear power; (2) major energy markets or consuming sectors ($Z1$ through $Z5$) such as household and commercial sector demand, industrial sector demand; and (3) major forms of energy consumption ($N1$ through $N3$) such as direct fuel uses and utility electricity uses.

Hence, the basic energy model may be expressed as:

$$E \quad \text{or} \quad Y1 = f(X1^b, X2^c, \cdots, X13^n)$$
$$E \quad \text{or} \quad Y1 = Y2 + Y3 + \cdots + Y9$$
$$= Z1 + Z2 + \cdots + Z5$$
$$= N1 + N2 + N3$$

In order to quantify the basic energy model for the recent historical period, before utilizing the model for forecasting the future energy economy under various assumed conditions and contingencies, energy balances for 1947 to 1965 are given in tabular form and trends of supply and demand for energy and its elements are given in graphical form. The historical series are adaptable to computer use. Various yearbooks, e.g., the U.S. Department of the Interior *Minerals Yearbook*, served as main sources of data.

Conditional forecasts and model simulations made use of a number of mathematical-statistical techniques, including econometrics. More specifically:

1. The first step in forecasting was the projection of least squares historical trends for 1947 to 1965 of total energy (E or $Y1$) and its elements of form, sector, and source. The extrapolated trends, representing only a function of time, were subsequently altered as necessary.

2. Projections for total energy (E or $Y1$) and energy demand within three major sectors ($Z1$, $Z2$, and $Z3$) were made by relating these to projections of trends of several economic indicators for which a high degree of historical correlation was determined. Gross National Product or $X1$ was used for projecting total energy demand (E or $Y1$); population or $X2$ was used to project the household and commercial sector ($Z1$); a composite variable for industrial production or $X3$ was used to project the industrial sector ($Z2$); and transportation ($Z3$) was correlated with Gross National Product or $X1$. The projection of the electric utility sector ($Z4$) was taken as given.

3. No relevant economic indicators or other independent variables were available for the projection of the mix of energy resources within the four sectors. Trends were altered on the basis of judgments involving specific markets and speculation as to the impact of economic, technological, social, psychological, political, and ecological factors.

4. Model simulations were done by assigning different values to one or more of the independent variables and their structural parameters while holding the remaining variables and their parameters constant.

The objective of technological or contingency forecasting here is to speculate on possible impacts of alternative technological developments on, for example, future patterns of energy supply and demand. Implied are the actual feasibility of a technological development and the necessary planning and direction to bring an innovation into existence.

Analysis of past trends of supply and demand for energy resources indicates these cannot be entirely explained by plotting classical supply and demand curves in terms of shifts of prices and costs, market patterns, or efficiency. This is because of the strong role played by technological innovations. Examples of such changes are the national network of natural gas pipelines, the dieselization of the railroads, and the utility electric grid. The pace of nuclear development associated with the phasing out of fossil-fuel burning steam electric plants appears to be an evolutionary technological change ($X8$); however, a successful breeder reactor could cause a revolutionary shift toward an all-electric economy.

Examples of projections and model simulations are: (1) Case XI which assumes a low range of natural gas supply and production ($X5$) and a high range of nuclear development ($X8$); (2) Case XII which assumes a high range of natural gas supply and production and a low range of coal and petroleum supply and production ($X5$), caused by environmental restrictions of the use of oil and coal; and (3) Case XVIII which assumes an all-electric economy where total energy requirements are met from utility electricity generated at conventional steam-plants with natural gas the single fuel.

For a typical forecast, a number of conditional assumptions, either quantitative or qualitative, are made for each of the independent or exogenous variables ($X1$ through $X13$). These assumptions affect the dependent variable total energy (E or $Y1$) and its elements, energy sources ($Y2$ through $Y9$), energy markets ($Z1$ through $Z5$), and energy forms ($N1$ through $N3$).

Some of the limitations and problems associated with energy forecasting follow. First, the forecasts are related to the extent the determining variables were correctly identified, quantified, and projected. Only three of the major determining variables were quantified and projected to 1980 and 2000. These were Gross National Product ($X1$), Population ($X2$), and a composite variable for Industrial Production ($X3$). For the other independent variables, assumptions were mainly qualitative. Where quantified they were either simple extrapolations of past trends or contingency estimates for the future made by judgment and intuition. The unknown impact of qualitative factors imposes restrictions on the reliability of such conditional forecasts. Because of the inability to quantify most of the independent variables, the econometric projections were made only in terms of single equations which used two-variable regressions with other variables held constant. However, such shortcomings were partially overcome using model simulation techniques where energy supply and demand were examined under alternative assumptions. This offers advantages over single-point forecasting in that a range of possible choices is provided through establishing the outer limits of the parameters of demand.

Second, historical relationship between energy elements and determining variables may be changed by unforeseen shifts in the character of either. For example, it used to be thought that demand for energy in mature industrialized economies was always a decreasing function of economic output because of more efficient levels of utilization of resources through technology. The shift to an increasing function of Gross National Product seems to be associated with the more rapid growth rate of the electrical utility sector—and utility generation is considerably less efficient in terms of resource inputs. After 1980 there may be a reversal back to energy coefficients as a decreasing function of Gross National Product because of increasing efficiency of electricity generation.

The determining variables themselves are changing. Thus, Gross National Product as an indicator of economic growth appears to be changing as a result of the large contribution services now make. Services do not represent tangible products and are unclearly related to resource expenditures and so distort the picture.

Third, it is difficult to use conditional forecasting for lower echelon energy elements. In descending from total energy to demand by sectors, it becomes more and more difficult to find relevant determining variables. Total energy represents a major segment of economic activity and, hence, can be expected to move in relationship to Gross National Product, Population, and Industrial Production. However, mix of energy resources locally is a function of market or industrial technology which may bear little relationship to the major economic indicators. Thus, the least squares extrapolated trends for given resources were bent by judgments and consultations with experts.

Fourth, projections were limited to the national level. No regional or state analyses of trends were attempted.

In technological forecasting the precise form of the assumed contingency or technological innovation does not have to predicted. However, in addition to establishing the need for an innovation, it is necessary to quantify things like performance and efficiency the innovation will bring. Thus, one must assume different levels of performance efficiency for various technologies. No attempt was made to predict, say through the use of S-shaped curves, the point in time when new technology would begin to displace existing technology. Technological shifts that have occurred in the past have not been linear, but have occurred on a random basis with impacts felt over different intervals. Exact predictions would seem to be impossible in the face of such unknowns.

Morrison and Readling conclude with a look at some problem areas associated with the adequacy of the resource base, expecially petroleum and natural gas but also uranium and low-sulfur-content coal. Only proved reserves of bituminous coal have been quantified and can be said to be adequate. However, if only low-sulfur coals are considered, the reserves may not be sufficient under possible pollution controls or other environmental restrictions. In the case of petroleum, a significant portion of requirements is already being met from abroad, although this, of course, has recognized political and military implications. The adequacy of the future uranium supply will be related to the rate of growth of nuclear power generation plus the evolution of new plants such as those utilizing breeder reactors.

Utility electricity consumption increased from 13% of total in 1947 to 20% of total in 1965. Utility generation is considerably less efficient in terms of resource inputs than is consumption of energy from direct use of fuels. Thus, greater inputs of resources to meet total energy demand will be required if this trend continues as assumed. The estimated resource requirements for an all-electric economy in 2000 are about double that of an all-fuel system based on fuel-cell technology. This is because, regardless of fuel source, the economics of utility power require large plants capable of providing for peak load requirements. However, efficiency declines with part load, and the longer the distance power is transported, the greater the line-loss! Fuel-cell technology is characterized by high efficiency even at part load and by the recovery of heat along with power. Thus, small on-site plants would be efficient.

There seems little doubt that the bituminous coal industry can meet projected demands in both the short and long range. However, the competitiveness of the industry will be dependent upon increasing the efficiency of conventional steam plant generation to compete with an emerging nuclear energy capability and also upon reducing the sulfur content of coal. In addition, synthetic gases and liquids made from bituminous coal could potentially serve fuel-cell, transportation, and other needs.

Natural gas is expected to be limited in commercially competitive amounts, and could not serve as a major supply for fuel cells.

Petroleum also is expected to decline in relative importance because of economic and environmental quality factors. Petroleum is already a declining function of total energy and about one-fifth of total requirements are now met by imports. Improvements would, therefore, have to be made in exploration drilling, and secondary recovery. Alternatives to the use of petroleum and natural gas come from the development of synthetics from oil shales, tar sands, or coal.

Demand for uranium is expected to continue at an accelerating rate. Resources will be limited. If an economic and efficient breeder reactor is not developed in the next decade, it is possible this could adversely affect the growth of nuclear plant capacity (projected as high as 150,000 megawatts for 1980). This could improve the prospects of the coal industry.

On the Development of Controlled Fusion Power

Gough (1970) has attempted to look at the future role of controlled fusion power. He also considers the systems relationships among population expansion, raw materials, living standards, pollution, and raw resources. The following figures summarize some very important relationships. Figure 8-4 shows a plot of energy consumption versus Gross National Product (used as a measure of living standards) for a number of nations. There is a very close relationship

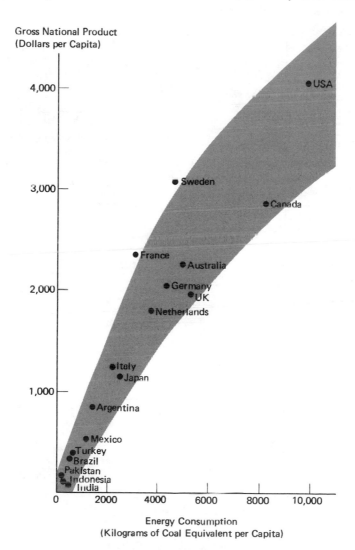

FIGURE 8-4

Energy consumption versus gross national product.[9]

[9]From William C. Gough, *Why Fusion? Controlled Thermonuclear Research Program,* WASH 1165, UC-20. Washington, D.C.: U.S. Government Printing Office, June 1970.

between energy use and Gross National Product. The relationship between energy consumption and solid waste collection and implied pollution is shown in Figure 8-5.

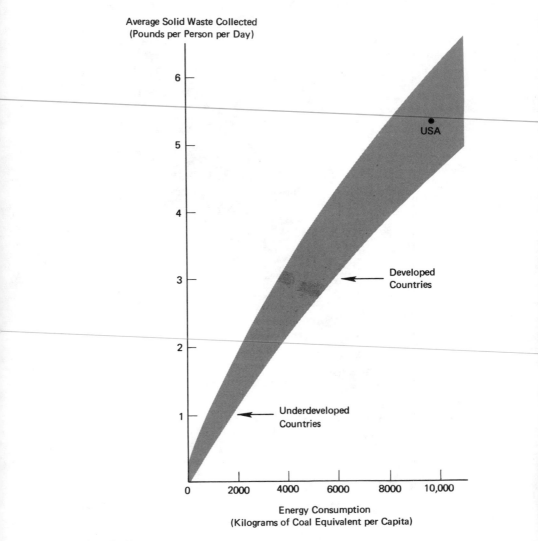

FIGURE 8-5
Energy consumption and solid waste collection and implied pollution.[10]

[10]From William C. Gough, *Why Fusion? Controlled Thermonuclear Research Program,* as based on data from R.J. Black, A.J. Muhich, A.J. Klee, H.L. Hickman, Jr., and R.D. Vaughn, *The National Solid Waste Survey—An Interim Report,* 1968.

As time goes on, known supplies of high quality resources, for example, ore become exhausted, the quality mined decreases, and the cost of extraction increases. Unfortunately, the "demand" is then usually reflected in attempts to exploit previously inaccessible or protected areas, often set aside for purposes of conservation and recreation. These features are shown in Figures 8-6 and 8-7.

Gough examined various kinds of nuclear power sources. Conventional nuclear fission reactors have a very inefficient conversion in recovering the fuel heat from uranium (U^{235}), an exhaustible fuel source. Breeder reactors are more efficient fission reactors and their development is more advanced than that of other "infinite energy sources." However, every ton of uranium produces a ton

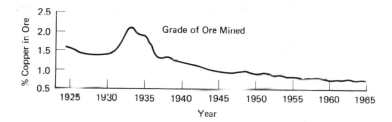

FIGURE 8-6
Grade of copper ore mined in U.S.[11]

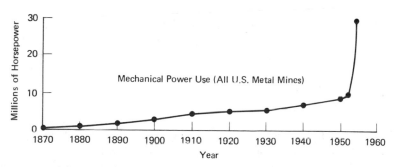

FIGURE 8-7
Increasing energy use for metal production.[12]

[11]From *Resources and Man: A Study and Recommendations* by the Committee on Resources and Man of the Division of Earth Sciences, National Academy of Sciences— National Research Council with the cooperation of the Division of Biology and Agriculture. W.H. Freeman and Company. Copyright 1969.

[12]From *Resources and Man: A Study and Recommendations* by the Committee on Resources and Man of the Division of Earth Sciences, National Academy of Sciences— National Research Council with the cooperation of the Division of Biology and Agriculture. W.H. Freeman and Company. Copyright 1969.

of fission products with unknown or unsolved safety problems and the serious problem of the proliferation of nuclear material. Table 8-1 summarizes some of the pros and cons of various limited and unlimited energy sources.

Without an inexpensive, essentially unlimited, energy source, it will be impossible to support the large world population at a standard of living anywhere near what now exists in the U.S. or even that to which other nations may now aspire. The implications for satisfaction and dissatisfaction, frustration, demogoguery, and aggression, discussed elsewhere in this book, should be strikingly evident. Thus, the main technological emphases must be on developing fission breeder reactors, fusion reactors, or harnessing solar energy. And almost no effort is now being devoted to the last. Fusion, which requires the ability to put three properties, confinement, temperature, and density, into one device, is at an early stage, with serious fusion reactor technology studies underway only since about 1967. Other energy sources are strictly limited. For example, all the water power in the world that could be developed by the year 2000 would produce only about one-tenth of the world's energy requirements. Those individuals who would dam the last of the world's wild rivers should bear this fact in mind.

Fission reactors at present run at about 30% efficiency, as compared to about 40% for first-generation breeder reactors (predicted) and conventional fossil fuel plants. Advanced breeder reactors are estimated by Gough at 50-60% of efficiency, and fusion reactors, depending on the type, at 50-60% to 80-90%. With such a great reduction in waste heat, large plants could be located in the centers of cities. Of course waste heat (thermal pollution) might conceivably have a use in the near future, such as in distilling sewage or heating buildings if the technological expertise were available. Otherwise, this waste heat would be added to other sources of the urban heat island already discussed. Conceivably, a total closed-cycle ecological system could be constructed using fusion also to convert wastes into raw materials and to reduce pollution.

The major problems in obtaining useful fusion energy on earth revolve around generating the hot plasmas and confining them long enough using electromagnetic fields. Controlling the fusion process involves solving a set of equations, intractable even with computer help (see earlier comments relative to analytic and simulation models). The controlling superconducting magnet also requires much more development. Development of a widely useful fusion reactor thus involves a system of elements which must be brought together and integrated at one time. A technological base is thus necessary Gough stresses.

The time necessary to develop a controlled fusion power plant ranges from about 50 years at the present rate of funding, through about 25 years with funding at a planned accelerated rate, to 7 to 12 years with funding as a "national objective." Indeed, this is part of the inter-(national) objective proposed in the next chapter. However, for other looks at the status of the development of fusion reactors, see Mills (1971) and Rose (1971). For reviews of the alternative fast breeder reactors, one program of which has been "blessed"

TABLE 8-1
Some major problems associated with various limited and
"infinite" energy sources.*

(a)   Limited energy sources

Fossil Fuels:

     Concern: A limited and irreplacable natural resource. Widespread pollution and environmental impact from mining and transportation.

     Question: Atmosphere CO_2 and particulate buildup—effect on weather, pH of ocean, photosynthesis.

Fission Water Reactors:

     Concern: Use of irreplacable U^{235} "Seed-Corn"—only 1-2% efficiency for recovering fuel's heat content.

     Question: Fuel availability at low cost; limited uranium and thorium reserves. Fission productions and safety.

(b)   "Infinite" energy sources

Major:

Fission Breeder Reactors:

     Question: Fission products, safety, radioecological concentration processes, and proliferation of nuclear material.

Solar Energy:

     Question: Technological ability to concentrate the low radiation energy density economically and efficiently.

Fusion Reactor:

     Question: Adequate scientific understanding of plasma physics (confinement and scaling laws) safety.

Minor:

Other Energy Sources:

            Insufficient to meet future demands.

World Power Capacity
(Thousands of MW)

Water	2,900
Tidal	1,100
Geothermal	10
Wind	Negligible

BUT: World energy requirements = 30,000 by year 2,000

*Adapted from William C. Gough, *Why Fusion?* Controlled Thermonuclear Research Program, Wash 1165, UC-20. Washington, D.C.: U.S. Government Printing Office, June 1970.

by President Nixon and is being pursued somewhat as a "national objective," see Weinberg and R. Philip Hammond (1970) and Allen L. Hammond (1971). We view the Weinberg and R. Philip Hammond article as conducive both to a very dangerous suboptimization and to the development of very dangerous policies by virtue of such statements as (page 412): "We . . . see in unlimited energy a means for supporting many more poeple than now live on earth." And (page 418): "Thus the limit to population set solely by limits to our energy production is very large indeed—considerably larger than 20 billion." And (page 418): "The assumption underlying these views is that we shall master the technology of catalytic nuclear burning." (That is, the technology of breeder reactors). For problems of nuclear reactor safety, an area which deserves much more scrutiny than it has received, see Gillette, 1971a and 1971b.

Now is a time of crisis. Both human values and other aspects of individual and group behavior and government goals and policies *must* change. Among other things we must learn to adjust to a nongrowth economy with limited resources. At present, only about one-tenth of the U.S. Federal budget is being spent on the really important problems of "infinite energy sources" (solar, breeder, and fusion), materials' recycling, disarmament, and population control.

HEALTH

The health field, particularly public health, is another area receiving large applications of systems-type expertise. Unfortunately, most of it is at a micro-level.

The major problems in health derive from the adequacy of prevention and care, the accessibility to the public, and the uncontrolled, erupting costs. There are profound theoretical and practical problems associated with the very nature of health, well-being, and disease. Part of this difficulty stems from over-reliance on the static, either-or "disease model" of the organism.

Yet we should consider the following. In looking at the health field, we can equivocate forever as to the meaning of health, the meaning of disease, and so forth. More precise definitions here are, of course, important. Nevertheless, we must also determine what can be done now in using the systems approach in a modular sense without compromising the future when understanding will presumably be better. For instance, we could structure a model in which severity of illness or lack or difficulty of treatment are indicated hierarchically, and education in prophylaxis (a lifetime project both in the formal and informal senses) and various counselling, examination, and treatment centers are indicated on the two polyarchic axes. Much can be done simply by dealing with known conditions of large magnitude, for example, pregnancy and abortion, dental problems, accidents, and psychological and psychiatric counselling. The last alone, if effectively accomplished, would take a large burden off the hospitals.

As is the case with all complex systems, numerous intangibles must be dealt with. These include the effect of the observer on the system itself, the need for intuition and judgment in the interpretation of results, and the extreme difficulty in defining and measuring "effectiveness," "benefits," and "costs." Much more research needs to be done relative to research methodology in observing and studying these systems, and to the understanding of intuitive problem-solving and the nature of judgment, motivation, conflict, perception, and so on.

Objectives are typically muddled or confused and even contradictory. This may make comparison of alternative programs, investments, or designs quite difficult. There is usually a "feast" of useless data and a "famine" of relevant data.

Demands for service in the health field are predominantly stochastic and variable. Yet organizations tend to be rigid in the face of such demands. Both need for service, the system input, and duration of stay in the hospital are more or less probabilistic.

The elements of a health system are synergistic, that is, the joint effects of changing the individual elements will not usually equal the sum of the individual effects of the changes of each element. Thus, combinations of programs have to be evaluated against alternative combinations of programs.

Health services require the optimum (if possible), and at least good, utilization of scarce manpower, facilities, and equipment resources. However, there are problems to employing systems techniques in this field. As is the case of all complex systems, the application of traditional mathematical models, e.g., queuing, allocation, and game theoretic models, may be inappropriate.

The simplest models applied are of the input/output variety, similar to those used in econometrics. Even this type of model deals with a vastly complex situation, and ignores many (potentially) key variables. Key variables are those which, if changed, result in the largest effect on the system as a whole. Manipulation of the input/output model consists of varying inputs and calculating outputs.

For complex health systems, heuristic or simulation models may be more appropriate than analytic models utilizing algrorithms as in linear programming. As we have seen, there is no firm distinction between analytic and simulation models, and analytic models may be of value at the subsystem level even when dealing with complex systems. Often the analytic submodels can be incorporated into larger-scope computer simulation models.

Typical applications have involved operations research studies of patient scheduling and staffing of nurses; computer aids to diagnosis; the design of management information systems for patient admissions, records, insurance, pharmacy, and out-patient treatment; and the design of computerized information and display systems for patient monitoring and treatment.

A review of these and other points with examples now follows.

Baker (1969), using open-systems theory, has studied the transition of a state mental hospital to a community mental health center.

General concepts and problems underlying the test and evaluation of health systems have been reviewed elsewhere by De Greene (1971).

Salmon and Altman (1970) looked at some of the elements affecting the formulation, implementation, and evaluation of health programs for the urban poor. Medicaid, a federal effort initiated in the late 1960s, has shown unexpectedly high costs. Variations in state Medicaid plans, problems of coordination and administration, and inadequacy of available data contributed to the lack of an effective program evaluation capability. As a result, requirements for a management information system were indicated.

Unfortunately, in planning, action is deferred until critical symptoms appear and then people jump in with poorly thought out "solutions" directed to evident symptoms rather than to causes. For example, we still know little about health as a system, although Model Cities legislation, for example, has recognized the interrelationships among physical, social, economic, and health factors in blighted neighborhoods. A model neighborhood is expected to develop plans and programs to meet urgent needs of housing, education, crime and delinquency, training and education, transportation, and improvement of physical facilities.

Effective health programming requires a much better understanding of system elements and constraints and the relating of these to objectives and implementation of these objectives. There is a limited ability to estimate health needs. Thus, the plausible premise that increased health services themselves will result in better individual adjustment to the total environment and in improved health status does not hold true. PPBS is of value in identifying points of overlap and gaps between programs.

The interrelationship among system elements may be more significant in planning than the presence or absence of a single element. The salient necessary ability is learning to discriminate between sensitive points in the health system which are strikingly visible and particularly vulnerable to stress on the one hand, and truly critical, perhaps submerged points on the other.

Finally, we must view the individual and his *real* environment as an ongoing, self-perpetuating system structured early in life. Perhaps the Lewinian term "life space" is desirable here. This implies the individual, to some extent takes his environment with him always and to some extent modifies his new, physico-social environment as an extension of his small surrounding capsule. If this be generally so, then all present efforts at social system design, highlighting elimination of urban blight or building community health centers for example, would seem to be gross oversimplifications.

Models and Simulations

Horvath (1966), reflecting an influence by Jay W. Forrester, believes that the medical profession will have to utilize systems analysis in order to understand the interrelationships of different parts of the system. The feedback loops of large social systems such as the medical system are not well understood; hence, he recommends use of gaming and simulation procedures. Like most social systems, the medical system has evolved through trial-and-error modifications rather than by deliberate design. Thus, these systems are developed and modified purely on the basis of experience and intuition.

In Horvath's approach, the players of the game would be professional health experts. The games are quantitative procedures and involve definition of objectives, measures of effectiveness, etc.

Felter and Thompson (1965) provided one of the first relatively comprehensive simulations in the health field. They attempted to provide hospital administrators with the capability to predict operational consequences of alternative designs and policies. They devised the following subsystem simulation models, written and executed in SIMSCRIPT, which are descriptive of a hospital: (1) maternity suite; (2) outpatient clinic; (3) surgical pavilion; (4) clinical chemistry laboratory; (5) a general model to predict the effects of different room arrangements on the economy of operations; and (6) a general model to predict economic and technical consequences of patient organizational schemes based on case requirements.

As we have seen, there is yet no comprehensive body of knowledge, as opposed to the specifics of model construction and validation, relative to the application of general purpose simulation models to the analysis of organizational and management problems. Felter and Thompson's long-range goal was to provide a comprehensive laboratory for testing a large variety of hypotheses regarding hospital design, organization, and operation. They recognized the great difficulty in predicting via a simulation model the technical and economic consequences of changing operating policies in the hospital.

Models were validated with data accumulated at a local hospital. These data were used as input; output statistics were compared to actual system outputs.

As has been pointed out elsewhere by De Greene (1971), the tendency to deal with the most obvious and easily measured health system variables, namely, waiting times, bed and room occupancy, etc., and the need to aggregate patients, may result in findings that are quite incidental to the basic processes of health and health care.

Reid (1969) looked at several problems associated with the development of a cybernetic model of a hospital patient-care system. (See also the section in Chapter 1 on Feedback and Cybernetics.) The health-care system was conceptualized at three hierarchical levels: strategic, operational, and tactical. The object was to build models descriptive of health systems and subsystems so as to allow decision-makers at all levels to allocate resources for the care of patients. Initial work focused on the individual patient at the tactical level. An attempt was made to relate the activities of health personnel to the individual patient's state. The descriptive model was based on feedback and information flow. Eight functional elements, e.g., comparator, regulator, state processor (the patient), and monitor were described.

To test the model, it was necessary to obtain time-series data. All the interactions involving 10 female patients undergoing hysterectomies, from time of hospital admission until discharge, were recorded in narrative form and in a nonparticipating manner, by a team of specially trained registered nurses. All the narrative data were then divided into either hospital activities or behavioral and physiological indices of patient state. The major groupings were further subdivided and each specific activity was given a numeric code. Data were then keypunched onto IBM cards (each card represented the state of the patient-care system at one moment in time) and stored on tape. Computer programs were then developed for data analysis.

The computer programs relate and display as histograms or graphs the hospital actions (resources) and patient states. The relationships between the resources allocated and initial and resultant patient states comprise the main aspects of this model of the individual patient.

Levin, Hirsch, Kligler, and Roberts (1969) have employed the systems dynamics approach of Forrester (1961) to understand the psychiatric patient drop-out phenomenon and to suggest methods of reducing such drop-outs from therapy. They did not attempt to study the causes of health and illness nor the relationship between treatment and health.

Levin, Hirsch, and Roberts (1971) have applied the systems dynamics approach to the problem of narcotics addiction and its control. They deal with an area in New York City with a heterogeneous population of 180,000 persons. The computer model describes the flow of numbers of people in this community through several states of drug use; for example, potential users, heroin users, and addicts in custody, each of which states is regulated by one or more associated rates of change. The model treats migration into and out of the community, attractiveness of the area to pushers, and so forth. Computer experiments assess the probable short- and long-term consequences of various proposed or attempted policies and programs. Information used to construct the model came from reviewing the literature, an area study of an urban community, and interviews with "experts," such as scientists, law enforcement officers, and addicts. As soon as a rudimentary understanding of the system of forces that led to the problem was developed, the formal model was constructed.

The model consisted of about 350 statements about the causal structure of the narcotics problem written in the DYNAMO compiler language.

Addict population growth, community change, and community response were central to model behavior. A number of positive and negative feedback loops were demonstrated.

Preliminary results suggest, first, that there is a need for a balanced set of rehabilitation, education, and law-enforcement programs, as opposed to intensive application of just one type of program; and, second, that the community must perceive the problem, at least in part, as a medical and social problem, as opposed to strictly a law-enforcement problem.

The first simulation was the base run against which behavior produced by various remedial policies and programs could be compared. The base run represented the growth of a serious narcotics problem over a 25-year period. During the first 100 months, positive feedback loops created a growth of addict and user populations because of the growth of the drug culture, exposure to addicts, and increasing availability of hard drugs. This was followed by another positive feedback loop. Crime had become high enough to cause out-migration and the lowering of the socioeconomic level. This resulted in an increase in futility and despair and a heightened use of drugs, causing more crime, more out-migration, and a further lowering of the socioeconomic level. Later a negative feedback loop was associated with police action. However, police action failed because of the counterintuitive effects of pushing up prices of hard and soft drugs, etc. Positive feedback loops then regained dominance and overpowered even a very strong police effort. The narcotics problem had grown out of control and the community had become a slum

Based on the above symptomatic behavior, it is possible to determine the effects of various programs started at different times. The above-mentioned balanced programs are much preferable to simplistic single policies.

Milly and Pocinki (1970) have applied systems analysis to the development and testing of alternative health care delivery systems. Part of the effort to be applied to the evaluation of alternative systems was the development of a simulation model. This included defining the system boundaries, the community, and external constraints. Four submodels were developed for population, the delivery system itself, costs, and finance, and each of these was described in terms of input requirements and resulting outputs. Outputs were related to measures of effectiveness and used to estimate impacts of change to the system.

The simulation emphasized two major constructs, that of "case-type" and that of "service-treatment station." The case-type is the basic element of the population served; the service-treatment station is the fundamental physical element of the system. Statistical, mathematical, and logical relationships depict the interactions of these basic elements. Case-type refers to a class of similar cases, for example, white males, age 35-44, with a diagnosis of coronary heart disease, and who reside in the same census tract. A number of parameters could be utilized to specify the case-types. Parameters were emphasized which accounted for the greatest variance in the need for health services and also could be adequately estimated in most communities. These parameters included demographic and socioeconomic (individual and also family, e.g., age group and family size, respectively), environmental (e.g., residence location), and health (e.g., diagnosis) parameters.

The long-range goals of this effort were to develop a ranked set of alternative medical care delivery systems and plans to implement these systems in communities. To simulate and evaluate the alternative approaches, the complete system model required the four above-mentioned submodels. Attempts were made to determine general methods of estimating the effectiveness of new organizational structures by using a general systems analysis approach.

The community health care delivery system was viewed in supply and demand terms. Demand is provided by community population and supply by community resources in terms of personnel, equipment, and facilities. Such resources can be expressed in terms of costs and financing methods.

Emphasis in this study was on models that simulate the interactions of system variables in probabilistic terms and retain the random nature of the real world. The delivery system model, for example, is basically a queuing model. The health care delivery system may be composed of a number of facilities, each of which may consist of a number of service-treatment stations. Hence, at this rather low hierarchical level the queuing approach may be realistic.

As we have seen, there is no single measure of performance for such complex systems. Measures of effectiveness or criteria against which system performance can be evaluated include measures of health care availability and accessibility, patient satisfaction, provider satisfaction, system capacity, morbidity, and quality of care. Costs must also be measured. Table 8-2 gives these criteria and related measures of performance. Table 8-3 illustrates how such a model can be used to ask "what if"-type questions, that is, to test the impact of various alternative system configurations.

Benefit-Cost and Cost-Effectiveness Studies

Several attempts have been made at measuring the costs of illness, including that of mental illness, and at measuring benefits from various types of programs. For example, Conley, Conwell, and Arrill (1967) estimated that, for the year 1966, the cost of mental illness was almost $20 billion. No precise measure would ever be possible, among other things because of the impossibility of defining mental illness. Thus, reductions in productivity among the employed mentally ill and the costs of treatment can be determined more accurately than the loss of homemaking services and the loss of self-esteem.

Conley, et al. defined the cost of mental illness as "the loss of well-being suffered by society as a result of this disease (p. 755)." Total cost was divided into: (1) cost resulting in a reduction of productive activity; (2) cost of treatment; (3) cost of illegal and other undesirable behavior; and (4) intangible costs due to loss of self-worth, frustration, fear, etc.

Almost half the costs were borne by persons other than the mentally ill. This could be interpreted in terms both of loss of productivity of the mentally ill worker and his treatment on the one hand, and the additional tax burden of the nonmentally ill on the other hand.

TABLE 8-2

Examples of health system evaluation criteria and measures of performance.*

Major Evaluation Criteria	*Related Output Results (Measures of Performance)*
Cost	Total system costs (capital, operating) Total system costs (direct and indirect) Cost by cost center Cost by service (fixed, variable) Cost by case-type (by episode and annual basis) Cost by service unit

Capacity	Number of patients served by type of service—
	   by condition
	   by demographic category
	   by socio-economic category
	 Unused capacity
	 Misused capacity (innappropriate task and personnel assignments)
	 Utilization (personnel and equipment)
	 Residence time in system

Morbidity and Mortality	Derived from services-rendered outputs, and available clinical data
Productivity	Tabulation of services rendered vs. resources consumed
Quality of Care	Spectrum of services—procedures available Services provided by condition Timeliness of service by condition Referral patterns by condition
Investment Potential	Rate of return Time to recover initial investment

Patient Satisfaction	Waiting times
	 Availability of emergency and out-of-hours service
	 Out-of-pocket payments—
	   by episode per person
	   by time period per family unit
	 Predictability of costs (covered vs. uncovered)
	 Quality indicators, e.g., consultants, specialists, equipment

Provider Satisfaction	Income — comparative standing
	              variability
	              method of payment
	 Control over conditions of work—availability of desired services
	 Hours of scheduled duty (by week)
	 Unscheduled duty hours
	 Utilization during duty hours— by scheduled duty
	                                 by unscheduled duty
	 Utilization—by activity
	            by personnel type

Accessibility	Waiting times—to enter system Community-system and intra-system travel times

*From George H. Milly and Leon S. Pocinki, *A Computer Simulation Model for Evaluation of the Health Care Delivery System*, Report HRSD-70, Rockville, Md.: U.S. Department of Health, Education, and Welfare, June 1970.

TABLE 8-3

Examples of health system model applications.*

To Test Impact Of:	Change These Inputs:	Look for Changes in These Outputs:
New physical arrangement of facilities	Service-treatment station descriptions as required	Waiting times, costs, personnel and equipment utilization
	Patient-system and/or intrasystem transit times	
	Possibly: need-demand conversion	
New class of personnel	Entries in specifications-of-care matrix, staffing	Utilization of other classes of personnel
	Possibly: need-demand conversion	
	Enter appropriate pay, etc., in cost model	Costs and capacity
Technological development and new equipment	Specifications-of-care matrix to incorporate postulated new equipment	Personnel and equipment utilization costs, capacity, etc.
Change in standards	Specifications-of-care matrix	Morbidity (requires results of clinical research)
		Capacity, personnel utilization, costs
Change in spectrum of services	Delete columns from specifications-of-care matrix; substitute as appropriate	Record of services rendered; desired services unavailable
	Change service-treatment stations	
Payment of staff (methods and/or amount)	Change cost model rules	Total costs, changes in costs
	Staffing (to reflect change in participation by providers)	All other outputs

*From George H. Milly and Leon S. Pocinki, *A Computer Simulation Model for Evaluation of the Health Care Delivery System,* Report HRSD-70, Rockville, Md.: U.S. Department of Health, Education, and Welfare, June 1970.

TABLE 8-3 (cont.)

To Test Impact Of:	Change These Inputs:	Look for Changes in These Outputs:
Mode-of-payment by clientele	Change rules for charges Possibly: need-demand conversion	Out-of-pocket costs Services used
Needs and demands (e.g., different community)	Change incidence data Add rows, if needed, to specifications of-care matrix	Personnel utilization, costs, capacity

Hallan, Harris, and Alhadeff (1968) have examined in detail the total economic cost of kidney and related diseases of the urinary system. Costs were expressed in terms of direct expenditures for personal and nonpersonal services. The former included the costs of hospital care, nursing home care, professional services, and drugs The latter included expenditures for research, training, construction, and the net cost of health insurance. Total economic costs were estimated at $3.6 billion of which $1.2 billion were direct and $2.4 billion indirect costs.

Le Sourd, Fogel, and Johnston (1968), have produced a very thorough application of benefit-cost analysis concepts to kidney disease programs. Major problems in applying this approach derive from the fact that maximum reduction of morbidity may not coincide with the maximum reduction in mortality, and short-range and long-range optima may not coincide.

Benefit-cost analysis requires that both benefits and costs be expressed in the same units. Somehow the valuation of lives saved and illness avoided must be expressed in monetary units if we are to use this approach. The economic benefits of a certain disease program are the total disease costs reduced by virtue of that program.

Following Weisbrod (1961), the authors give the monetary losses accruing as a result of morbidity and mortality as: (1) loss of economic production associated with the worker's premature death; (2) temporary or intermittent losses in economic production associated with the worker's illness; (3) decreased production efficiency associated with illness; (The above are considered to be *indirect* costs, the below are *direct* costs.) and (4) economic costs of detection, treatment, and rehabilitation and the capital investment in medical facilities.

The usual problems in quantifying worker productivity obtained here, and wages were considered the only objective method currently available. Constant (e.g., 1968) dollars are usually used in such cost estimates. These, of course, do not reflect wage trends.

Both future costs and future benefits were discounted to present values. However, economists differ as to what rate of interest should be used in discounting. Also measures of benefits in terms of salvaged earnings really underestimate true benefits by ignoring the personal and social satisfactions of good health.

Costs may also be considered in terms of who pays them, the individual, the government, other agencies, or society in general. Because total costs are very hard to estimate, the present study dealt only with government costs.

The above-mentioned present-value criterion, of course, implies that the value given to lowered mortality and morbidity is worth less in the future than today. It also distorts values as applied, say, to children, or to programs accomplishing most in the later years of their existence.

In this study, benefits were measured as the discounted value of income losses which were avoided as a result of prevention and treatment activities of the kidney disease program and its elements. Cohort calculations were used computing income on the basis of average earnings by age and sex over the expected lifetimes of persons who otherwise would have contracted kidney disease. A cohort is a group of persons with one or more characteristics in common.

Costs were measured as Federal expenditures per person screened in preventive programs and as annual Federal cost of treatment for dialysis and transplant patients.

The purpose of benefit-cost analysis was to express the measurable quantities of both benefits and costs in monetary terms yielding a direct comparison which could serve as one criterion in policy planning. A benefit/cost ratio greater than unity, by itself, may or may not indicate a given program is desirable.

The report provides in great detail calculations of benefits, costs, and benefit/cost ratios for alternative programs for children, adults, and mixtures of children and adults for two types of prevention or screening programs, namely, *Streptococcus* sort-throat screening and bacteriuria screening; and also for dialysis and transplant treatment programs.

The Program Planning and Budgeting System (PPBS) has been implemented in the U.S. Public Health Service. Le Sourd, Fogel, and Johnston, as a continuation of this effort, recommend a computerized PPBS with extensive data storage and analysis, program structure in terms of objectives, analytic comparison of objectives, continued updating of objectives, continual decision-making, and continual testing of the validity and administration of plans.

Often one uses cost-effectiveness analysis instead of cost-benefit analysis. These differ in that the latter deals only with factors that can ultimately be expressed in economic terms.

Packer (1968) has looked at the application of cost-effectiveness concepts to health services at the level of the individual community. This is a particularly thoughtful study which considers many of the difficulties in applying systems techniques to the health field.

In dealing with complex health systems, a single measure of effectiveness may be hard to come by; even if one is selected, it is almost impossible to relate it to the many correlative factors. A multidimensional scale is thus necessary, and the use of optimizing algorithms ruled out.

Both the effectiveness of alternatives and the costs of alternatives must be estimated in order to allocate scarce resources in complex systems. Effectiveness is quite difficult to measure, but even cost estimating may be a formidable job. There may be difficulty in determining and differentiating among fixed and variable, sunk (historic) and future, and actual (direct) and implied (indirect) costs. For example, estimating potential earnings lost because of illness is more difficult than estimating actual expenditures due to prevention and treatment of illness, itself a difficult job.

DISAFFECTION, ALIENATION, CRIME, AND VIOLENCE

Disaffection, alienation, crime, and violence may represent successive stages of activity along a continuum of rejection of the established majority modes of society. This does not mean of course that all violence is the result of conscious rejection of established values. Rather, many crimes of violence are spontaneous, spur-of-the-moment events.

From a systems point of view, this area is particularly hard to deal with because of:

1. The difficulty in measuring things like disaffection and alienation which, nevertheless, provide the seedbed for the more dramatic crimes and organized violence.
2. The inability to predict individual acts of violence.
3. Outmoded thinking by law-enforcement agencies and the courts as to simplistic relationships between "crime and punishment."
4. The murkiness of the boundaries of the system. For example, at certain operational levels those "inside" the law gradually phase into those "outside" the law. The Knapp Commission, in examining police corruption in New York City, revealed widespread graft in terms of the public offering—and the police accepting or, in some cases, even soliciting—free hotel rooms, free meals, bribes in exchange for looking the other way, and goods in exchange for narcotics. Part of the problem derives from the recruitment of the police mainly from the working class, and their perception of themselves as a marginal, low-status group who at once are deferential to conservative modes and suspect, even brutal, toward

less-favored groups with "radical" ideas. Thus, the police do not spend most of their time enforcing the law, but rather dealing with problems of traffic, alcohol, drugs, psychotics, and family quarrels. Law-enforcement then becomes a public-relations game to sanction these other activities and to justify demands for respect (see, for example, Westley, 1970).

5. The common tendency to think of the "criminal justice system" apart from other subsystems involving overpopulation, education, technological change, job structure, etc. Thus, the offender is viewed as a simple input to the system to be processed and output.

As a result of these deficient concepts, the tendency is to attack one element of the subsystem. This typically takes one of two forms, namely either providing the police with more gadgetry such as new surveillance devices, weapons, and command-control, or hiring more policemen. These steps by themselves are likely to be counterproductive. For example, adding more policemen can contribute to swamping the courts, the prosecutor, the public defender, and the penal institutions.

Let's now examine some instructive models and studies.

A Factor-Multiple Regression
Analysis of Riot Processes

Maloney, a psychologist (1967), reports results of studies relating demographic data to the occurrence or nonoccurrence of riots in metropolitan areas. His study is imaginative and useful, particularly with regard to his interpretations of social dynamics.

Most of the research effort dealt with data from Standard Metropolitan Statistical Areas. SMSAs tend to "average out" some important city-to-city differences, however; hence, use of cities instead of SMSAs would have been preferable. Results still were held to be valid. Disturbances for the year 1967 were the basis for analyses of riot proneness. Factor analyses of data were performed, and the factors obtained from factor analysis used as independent variables for developing multiple regression formulae to predict riot experience. The following seven factors were obtained (including item descriptions and factor loading for the items loaded highest on each factor and also lists of SMSAs most and least characterized by each factor): metropolitan area density, nonindustrial growth areas, southern syndrome areas, blue collar areas, nonmetropolitan versus metropolitan areas, decentralized versus centralized population and employment centers, and low income versus high income areas.

Tables were also given listing 96 metropolitan areas ranked by statistical likelihood of racial disturbances based on the formulas below.

The value of the seven factors as predictors of old riot data for the years 1964-1967, as reported in news magazines, was checked using a multiple regression analysis. The multiple correlation between old riot data and three factors selected and weighed was .51 or "pretty good." Maloney then went on to use 1967 disturbance data as independent variables for regression analysis.

The seven-factor scores were used as independent variables, and number of disturbances or distrubances of different types or rated severities, as in each SMSA, were used as dependent variables. Multiple correlations were then calculated. When relationships were plotted, however, the results did not appear so good and marked skewnesses were noted. This was because almost half the areas had no disturbances at all, and also because severity ratings lacked a property called unidimensionality.

Because of these difficulties in dealing with riot severity, Maloney went back to his earlier approach using simply occurrence or nonoccurrence of *any* disturbance in each SMSA in 1967 as the dependent variable.

A couple of formulas resulted, e.g., the "factors formula":

Riot-proneness = 2.82 − .33 (factor III scores) − .37 (factor V scores) − .42 (factor VII scores).

Multiple correlation was .48. Relationships were also plotted graphically. The 96 areas were divided into four groups of 24 areas each. Each group represented a riot-prone score range and percentage of SMSAs in the score range having racial disturbances in 1967. Statistically, the F value was 9.43 with 3 and 92 degrees of freedom, i.e., it could have occurred by chance less than 1 time in 1000.

In another multiple regression analysis, the dependent variable was as above, but all the individual urban characteristics were used as independent variables. The resulting "items formula" was:

Riot-proneness = − 2.43 + .049 (percentage of families with 1966 income of \$15,000 or higher) + .005 (percentage of blacks in SMSA who reside in central city) − .253 (number of persons per automobile in SMSA) + .056 (percentage of retail sales through food store outlets) + .002 (children per woman of childbearing age) + .011 (percentage of adults voting in 1964 election in SMSA) + .002 (number of special governmental districts in SMSA).

Multiple correlation was .62 and the results calculated from the formula were plotted. The F score also indicated high statistical significance. Further, all the 12 highest scoring areas had racial disturbances and none of the lowest 16 had any.

Both these sets of riot-proneness scores point toward politically active, prosperous, densely populated, northern metropolitan areas as those most likely to have racial distrubances. The rank order correlation between these two approaches for the 96 SMSAs was .79 or "pretty good."

What are possible causes of racial disturbances? The limitations of multiple regression analysis, in answering this question, must be recognized. Regression analysis selects and weights independent variables on a complex, twofold basis. The first independent variable the computer selects for the formula is usually the variable correlating most highly with the dependent variable. However, successive variables are added to the formula on the basis of complex statistical interactions which have as much to do with low correlation with already selected variables as with high correlation with the dependent variable. Hence, many variables can be left out of such formulas, even though they are most directly related to the phenomenon of interest. Alternatively, in attempting to determine causation, one can directly examine zero-order correlations between items. The computer can provide a matrix of thousands of such correlations. Some examples of such correlations follow. The single item correlating most highly (+.42) with the occurrence or nonoccurrence of riots in a SMSA in 1967 was voting activity as reflected by the percentage of adults voting in the 1964 elections. The percentage of sound homes and of persons with high incomes correlated next most highly. There were also positive correlations for number of children in private schools, populous suburban developments, complex or diffused government structures, and central city density of population. Low education and low income correlated negatively. Also total black population in a SMSA correlated less highly than total area population.

Maloney next points out needs for additional information as to what actually causes riots and how to prevent them. He recommends someone repeat his study using the 312 largest *cities* (all cities with populations over 50,000 in 1960) rather than the 96 largest SMSAs. This would provide a more detailed data base. The total group of cities should be divided into random halves (or odd-even halves after being ranked for population). One half should be used for predictive factor and multiple regression analyses, the other half for validation of the formulas developed with primary group data.

Next, there is a need for obtaining unpublished information, particularly with regard to local police operations. For example, police spending per capita correlates +.29 with occurrence of racial disturbances. (With his sample of 96 SMSAs any correlation over .27 is enough larger than .00 [zero] that it could not have occurred by chance as often as one time in a hundred.) Things such as human relations training, mechanization of police operations, personal familiarity, and integration of police forces should be considered. Maloney notes that "police brutality," an attitude or perception more than a tangible picture of beatings, ranks higher than poor housing, poor jobs, or poverty as the perceived cause of riots. An approach, if all cities could not be studied, could involve sample surveys of police operations in both predicted high-riot cities and predicted low-riot cities to see if there are any differences.

Maloney feels greater preparation for riots (riot guns, tear gas, mace) may result in a self-fulfilling prophecy of the form "those who go looking for trouble are almost sure to find it." Accordingly, he has developed a tentative "Model of Riot Proneness." There must be some way of relating, through intervening variables, the demographic variables indicated above and actual rioting in specific cities. He illustrates his model with a simple block diagram (Figure 8-8).

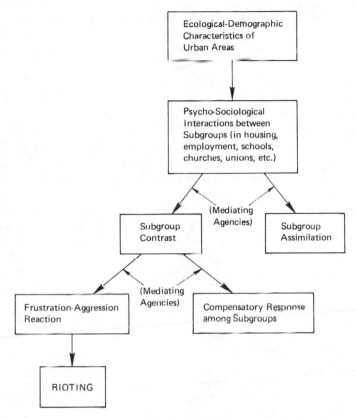

FIGURE 8-8
A tentative model of "riot-proneness" in cities.[13]

Maloney believes that actual rioting is not caused by such "triggering events" as police arrests. These are mere sparks which inflame an already tense and resentful community. There are almost classic examples of frustration-aggression phenomena in these cases.

Minor alleviations of housing, job, and school segregation problems may *intensify* alienation or "subgroup contrast." Other terms which could be employed here are intensification in "relative deprivation," "status incongruity," and "subgroup marginality." All these refer to tensions arising from the "revolution of rising expectations." See also Chapter 2; it is well to repeat here what Alexis de Tocqueville (1856) said about the French revolution: "The evils which are endured with patience as long as they are inevitable seem intolerable as soon as hope can be entertained of escaping them."

[13]From Maloney, 1967.

Similarly, Krech, Crutchfield, and Bellachey (1962) state that upward mobility is not an unmixed blessing, and discrepancies between the ranks of an individual relative to the power, occupational, economic, and social status systems may result in severe frustration. For example, the more active black student protestors come from higher income families and better urban colleges.

There is a contrast or social-psychological alienation or apartness between blacks and whites and between three major black subgroups. This alienation may lead either to an intensified frustration-aggression reaction or to certain compensatory responses among the subgroups (see again Figure 8-8). Maloney believes special attention should be given the mediating roles on riots of social institutions such as schools, employer organizations, financial institutions, and unions.

Although Maloney's interpretations deal with blacks, the basic principles here can be extended to alienated white blue-collar workers and to alienated white upper- and middle-class students and, indeed, to displaced aerospace scientists and engineers.

Maloney urges someone to look into each mediating agency, beyond the cliches and folklore, and determine its relationship to civil rights progress and to the alienations and tensions it causes or cures.

Maloney proposes a number of hypotheses concerning the causes of race riots. Those of general sociotechnical interest are paraphrased below.

Ecological-demographic characteristics of urban areas which attract potentially conflicting subgroups are big-city, industrialized metropolitanism; Northern political liberalism; and economic opportunities for all subgroups including those denied them elsewhere. However, the preoccupation of government planners with the poverty conditions of blacks, especially in Northern city ghettoes, tends to run counter to the economic opportunities available.

The more subgroups are assimilated, the less the tendency to frustration and aggression; and there has been little successful assimilation of blacks. However, we believe this alone is not an all-purpose explanation: what about the white, middle-class hippies?

Subgroup contrast in generally liberal environments gives rise to frustration-aggression versus compensatory (Black Pride, black mayor) reactions. Maloney points out there are at least three types of compensation among blacks. First, there is a submissiveness, perhaps living for the religious afterlife, characterized by southern-born blacks. A second kind of compensation is Black Pride, exemplified by successful black business ownership, and many "Uncle Toms." The third way of compensating is Black Power, represented by a potentially very dangerous "between class" alienated both from white and successful black society. These are northern, lower-class blacks, and many are young or teenagers "to boot."

When subgroup contrast is sustained by the mediating agencies, and these agencies fail to provide channels for constructive compensatory reactions, we can expect the disadvantaged subgroups to become intensely frustrated. Most people today are aroused by the "revolution of rising expectations," but do not personally benefit from civil rights or other reforms.

Between-Group hostility must be channeled into the constructive positive directions of Black Pride if further rioting is to be prevented. If the nation's leaders do not realize this, there will be an increased polarization of blacks and whites and a dangerous "showdown." Urban disturbances will not be prevented by a "war on poverty"—the need is for a "war on frustration."

The greatest racial tension has arisen at the times and places where the greatest civil rights progress for blacks in general has occurred. Purely economic plans and programs are likely to exacerbate the situation, especially massive, cut-and-dried, "made by Whitey" housing, training, educational, and employment programs. (See also Forrester's urban dynamics studies reviewed earlier in this chapter.) These introduce dangerous emotional uncertainties and anxieties. "Guaranteed annual incomes" do not insure self-respect, self-worth, and respect for others. Maloney stresses that too much has been done to, for, and with the black community. It should be allowed to solve its own problems, even though this may at first be inefficient by economic standards. There may be mistakes in housing and business, but the real purpose is enhancing black self-respect. Emphasis would be on enhancing citizen participation and dignity rather than on cost-effectiveness. However, this would be economic in the long run—we cannot afford to spend more and more on the same kinds of programs which have "muddied the puddle" up to now. Maloney predicts a new type of racial disturbance in Western cities within the next five to ten years, unless we learn from the Detroits and Newarks of the past.

You may feel that some of Maloney's interpretations have been invalidated by the reduction in rioting—except in prisons—during the last several years. We suggest otherwise. The forms of violence we have witnessed during the last decade or more—riots by minority groups and students, assassinations, airplane hijackings, dramatic crimes by individuals or small groups—are symptoms which may be individually suppressed or may be abandoned as ineffective. Yet symptoms they are, symptoms the underlying causes of which are poorly conceptualized and hardly amenable to control. We can expect violence to continue, probably expressed in novel and unanticipated forms.

Other Models

Another example of a model of crime and disaffection is provided by Kyllonen (1967), who has related crime rates to urban population density. Kyllonen's model, based on the interaction and energy transport mechanisms of stars, suggests that, in a large population, there will be some social interactions in which the persons have an "energy of collision" high enough to produce a crime. Incidentally, the isomorphism which Kyllonen demonstrates between stellar and urban processes is a good example of the nature of general systems theory.

Concern over the above and other problems of society, technology, and environment is uppermost today, yet there is no simple way to deal with these problems. A straightforward transfer of systems technology from the aerospace field would seem foredoomed to failure. Often the system studied is so abstracted from the real world as to be meaningless. Nevertheless, certain features of complex systems can be realistically abstracted, at least in preliminary analyses. Operations of the police, fire departments, ambulances, etc., which bear a very close resemblance to military and industrial operations (and work methods) are the best example of such cases.

Larson (1970) has modeled urban police patrol operations in terms of answering a call for police service and performing crime preventive patrol. Two models were developed. The first depicted the time required for a patrol unit to travel from its position at dispatch time to the scene of the incident. The second related the frequency of patrols to various physical parameters (for example, street miles in a sector) and could be used to estimate the probability a patrol unit would intercept a crime in progress.

Such applications are, of course, purely technological. In part, they reflect recent federal concern with crime, and legislation aiding the states in planning for improvements in law enforcement. Larson feels such socially important areas call for the analytical skills of engineers.

For example, the President's Commission on Law Enforcement and Administration of Justice (1967) recognized the need for quantitative analysis and recommended that large police departments establish operations research groups.

Larson's models are structured to be relevant to policy; police administrators using them can predict the effects of different operational strategies or allocation levels which reflect not only police efficiency but personnel salaries. Especially important could be the design of controlled experiments to test various methods of deterrence.

However, defining a meaningful set of effectiveness measures is difficult. This is especially true of the effectiveness of patrol activities and other activities in deterring crime. Larson uses the frequency with which a patrol unit passes particular points. Many people believe a large fraction of crimes are not deterrable by police; even if they are, such crude criteria as times and frequencies will afford little insight into basics.

TRANSPORTATION

Transportation, an area of immense importance and far-reaching ramifications, is seemingly among the most straightforward in terms of the applications of systems science. Indeed, there have probably been as many applications to transportation as to any other area. Yet there is surprisingly little to show for it.

Part of the difficulty stems from failure to recognize transportation as a mammoth sociotechnical system, interfacing and interacting with almost every other system in a society. Part of the difficulty is associated with the usual mire of politics and vested interests.

The major problems are summarized as follows:

1. Large elements tend to be pitted against one another, for example, the airlines and the railroads, or the highway users and the railroads, rather than acting in conjunction.

2. Large elements tend to be interlocked with other large elements both within and without the transportation field. Most typically, this involves automobile manufacture, the petroleum industry, highway construction, and special benefits such as Federal support for freeways. This both produces powerful vested interests and makes objective comparison of alternatives difficult or impossible.

3. Federal and other regulative agencies, for example, the Federal Aviation Administration and the Interstate Commerce Commission, may have no common purpose, and, indeed, may operate at cross purposes.

4. The designers, the users, and the maintainers, for example, of automobiles, tend to have a loose connection, if any at all.

5. The producers of automobiles and aircraft tend to be among the biggest elements of the economy. For example, the annual consumption of automobiles is held to contribute 8% of the Gross National Product. Hence, objective evaluation of a means of transportation has far-reaching effects beyond the transportation field.

6. Specific means of transportation, urban structure, and patterns of living, having interacted for many decades, are now almost impossible to unravel, even when the means of transportation and, indeed, the over-all pattern are coming increasingly under scrutiny. And if a means of transportation is allowed to atrophy, there may be unanticipated repercussions throughout society—consider the plight of the postal service following the decline of the U.S. passenger railroads.

7. There is an emphasis on "tangibles" rather than on behavioral and social factors. Thus, there is a proclivity to the solutions to transportation problems in terms of the concrete of freeways, command-control systems, and faster airplanes.

8. There is a tendency to concentrate on existing patterns or projections of existing patterns, even when the underlying structure is deficient. Many studies using cordon counts, the *gravity model* of traffic flow, and so on are in this category.

9. The elements of transportation are viewed as both closed and open-loop systems with no regard for impacts, demands, and so on.

The byproducts and side effects of our poorly designed, mismanaged transportation efforts are, of course, well known. These include:

1 Hastening urban decline; this includes, for instance, the effects of freeways in splitting residential and business areas, or black and white areas.
2. Air pollution and, to a lesser extent, water pollution.
3. Destruction of natural, recreational, and scenic resources.
4. Restricting the opportunity to travel for some groups such as the very young, the old, the infirm, and the poor.
5. Severe acoustic noise pollution.
6. Loss of urban, agricultural, and recreational land to roads and parking lots.
7. Unrestrained "demand" for fuel and other resources that are limited, potentially limited, or can be extracted only at a large economic price or price to the environment.

As an example of the morass of economic and political entanglements which can preclude the objective study and comparison of alternative configurations of transportation systems, consider the defeat of Proposition 18 in the 1970 California elections. Proposition 18 would have allowed tapping the gas tax fund, reserved exclusively for the building of more roads, for purposes of developing mass-transit systems and supporting pollution research. The proposition was defeated, largely the result of a concerted effort by highway lobbies, petroleum interests, and auto clubs, who presented a scare picture that passage of the proposition would result in toll roads and higher taxes. In this election the highway lobby spent hundreds of thousands of dollars, mostly donated secretly by oil companies (Bazell, 1971).

The literature on transportation systems is immense. The Rand Corporation, for example, provides bibliographies of a number of studies. We offer here one example of a large-scale effort.

San Francisco Bay Area Rapid Transit Developments

Developments of rapid transit in and about the city of San Francisco, California, provide a most instructive case history illustrating the effects of vested interests upon transportation system planning, which, in turn, reflects motivations toward real but underlying goals rather than ostensible but superficial goals; the use of systems analysis in integrating proposed and existing transportation networks; and the transfer of systems engineering and aerospace technology to civil systems.

In 1951 a commission appointed by the California legislature to study the transportation needs of the San Francisco Bay Area recommended the development of a high-speed, rapid rail transit system. In 1962 voters in San Francisco, Alameda, and Contra Costa Counties approved the Bay Area Rapid Transit

(BART) system by accepting a $792 million bond obligation, the largest debt ever incurred at a local level. This was to be the first new U.S. urban transportation network since Philadelphia's in 1907 (Bazell, 1971).

The advantages of rapid rail transit are usually considered to include reduction in automobile-induced congestion and air pollution; provision of transportation for the poor, infirm, and very young or very old; and reduction in suburban sprawl. In the case of BART, however, powerful business interests with an eye to profits from land redevelopment in downtown San Francisco provided the initial impetus.[14] Similarly, several large property owners in San Mateo County, fearing that rapid transit would inhibit suburban growth, brought pressure on the county Board of Supervisors, and San Mateo County withdrew from the proposed system prior to the 1962 election (Bazell, 1971).

A great deal of systems expertise has gone into the planning and development of BART; into the integration of BART with existing surface transportation facilities; and into projecting future regional transportation needs on the basis of such factors as population, employment, residence, and present modes of transportation. For example, mathematical models of routings, reasons for travel, operating speeds, fare structures, and so forth have been developed and evaluation of alternatives performed by simulations. Of particular interest behaviorally was the surveying of about 250,000 transit riders for details of their riding habits, especially with regard to origins and destinations. (For further details of a system study of coordinated transit needs projected to 1975, see Simpson and Curtin, 1967.)

Contracting for the BART system and its financing, design, production, and testing also provides a number of instructive lessons. The major contractor was the Rohr Corporation, a medium-sized manufacturer of aircraft engine pods and thrust reversers. The Rohr effort seemingly represents a successful diversification of an aerospace company into the civil system production market. Yet there were difficulties. Costs of course increased as in other huge construction projects. By mid-1967 the BART project had almost foundered; it was rejuvenated in 1969 when the California legislature voted an increase in the sales tax of the three counties, resulting in a needed extra $150 million. The system eventually cost $1.4 billion.

Design, production, testing, and operations reflect a sophisticated aerospace technology, including human factors, such as considerations of noise reduction, safety, esthetics, smooth but rapid acceleration and deceleration, simplicity, and human engineering design of equipment. The complex of aluminum trains, tracks, subways and under-the-bay tubes, elevated rights of way, sensors, telemetry and other communications links, local and centralized control devices, and central computer facility with operator displays and control consoles bears a

---

[14]And because of BART as well as for other reasons common to some other U.S. cities, a building boom has, indeed, followed.

striking resemblance to an aerospace command and control system. Automation applies not only to operation of the trains and overall system control but also to ticketing and passenger ingress and egress. Automation should result in considerable cost savings; over 80% of costs of deficit-ridden East Coast transit systems stem from wages (Bazell, 1971).

The eventual impact of BART upon the environment, upon land use, and upon transportation behavior can only be surmised. Consensus seems to be that BART will not relieve rush hour congestion. Consequently it would appear to be desirable to take further active measures to deemphasize the automobile by restricting further highway growth. Yet, in an egregious example of *not* taking the systems approach to transportation planning, the California legislature approved the construction of a new bridge, the Southern Crossing, just south of the present Bay Bridge!

For further reading, see Bazell (1971), Elson (1972), and O'Lone (1972).

EDUCATION

Education continues to be one of the slipperiest areas with which to deal in systems terms. For one thing education, unlike almost all the other areas, is inextricably always a part of the model of systems science itself. Education is a part of our expertise for systems study and problem solving; it can never be treated as objectively as, say, transportation or electrical energy and power. More than almost anything else, education is associated with the modern model of man, opportunity, and fulfillment. And, as with such other areas as welfare, urban design, and health, there is a particular problem with evaluating the system's *real* performance.

Accordingly, the goals and objectives of education have been questioned only recently. Part of the questioning is associated with recognition that the *real* goals of educational institutions are frequently custodial and indoctrinative rather than the preparation of a person to lead a more productive, successful, or meaningful life through stimulating and developing the learning processes.

Another major difficulty derives from considering education an open-loop system, apart from either the real needs of society, job opportunities, or self-fulfillment, As with transportation, the dominant underlying philosophy is: the more, the faster, and the more powerful, the better. There is need for cybernetic modeling and management of education in relationship to employment and the needs of society; some of this is being done now in the U.S.S.R. In any society, a well-educated person with great expectations but little hope of meaningful employment is likely to make mischief for himself and others.

On a less grand scale, there is much that systems science can do to remove or reduce recognized problems of educational institutions. These include better use and scheduling of facilities and equipment, avoiding replication of resources, and providing more flexible curricula and more meaningful terminal education. There has been a tremendous development of computer-assisted instruction and other use of computers. Much good has been accomplished, at the same time there has been automation of the erroneous and inconsequential and wasted polemics as to the relative worth of teachers and teaching machines.

It should now be evident to the reader from our earlier discussions how systems analysis, modeling and simulation, operations research, benefit-cost analysis, and so on can be applied to problems of education. The limitations of these techniques should also be evident, especially that performance criteria expressed in terms of classroom hours, semester and quarter units credit, and diplomas and degrees granted may be, in the long run, irrelevant. We shall return in the next chapter to problems of superfluous degrees and superfluous education in our changing times. For a readable treatment of systems analysis in the development of elementary teacher education models, see LeBaron (1969).

POLLUTION

Except on a limited scale, application of systems science to problems of air and, to some extent, water pollution, presents formidable challenges in terms of the number of variables and amount of interactions. Nevertheless, some rather comprehensive models are being developed. At the local level, techniques such as cost-effectiveness analysis can be meaningfully utilized to evaluate such things as alternative automobile or industrial emission control devices.

Studies of the effects of pollutants on health and on global climate have been reviewed in Part I of this book. In the last chapter, we consider problems of designing an air pollution surveillance and control system. In this section we shall limit our attention to solid pollutants.

Solid-Waste Management

Of all the areas considered in this chapter, that of solid-waste management probably best fits the straightforward application of systems science techniques. There is little need to advance theory, people can be dealt with essentially as numbers, and quantitative measures are readily available. This does not say that we are dealing with a completely routine, dead-end field. Certainly, new techniques for reusing and recycling, say, junked automobiles or urban sewage sludge, are being developed. Likewise, we are not implying that political problems or neighborhood problems cannot cloud the issue. The automobile industry may not feel it is in its best interest to recycle junked cars. Also not everybody is willing to accept sewage sludge as a fertilizer.

Recognition of the need to take the systems approach to problems of solid-waste management is one consequence of the growth forces and changing attitudes toward the environment discussed in Part I. Recapitulating somewhat,

U.S. population has increased from a little over 130 million in 1940 to over 200 million in 1970. During the same period G.N.P. increased from about $100 billion to approximately $1 trillion. Parallel to these explosive growth changes has been an increase in solid-waste production from about 70 million tons per annum to over 175 million—about 900 million pounds per diem. And not only has the absolute and per capita quantity of solid refuse increased, but the composition has changed to include a much higher proportion of substances which are not easily degradable by either biological or inorganic processes. Plastics, glass, and aluminum are particularly culpable substances in this sense.

These problems are compounded by increasing urbanization; the decrease in the amount of available land adjacent to urban centers; esthetic and health-based objections to older methods of collection, transportation, and disposal; price changes of many products; the rise of the "throwaway" mentality; and decreased demand for junk.

Collectively these interacting factors dramatize the need for an integrated approach to planning. In the geographic sense this must involve regional rather than strictly local design. The Solid Waste Disposal Act of 1965 reflects federal interest in the need to take new and sophisticated approaches and to develop improved technologies.

Several systems analyses of regional solid-waste handling have been performed within the last few years. The analyses have included the development of flow-diagram or mathematical models permitting the evaluation of alternative programs in benefit-cost and other terms. These studies have concentrated on specific areas, but the models and findings are to a considerable extent generalizable to other areas. The Aerojet-General study (1969) dealt with the urban-rural region around Fresno, California, and recommended a system to be attained by the year 2000. The effectiveness of any alternative solid-waste system was based on the rating of 82 different solid wastes according to thirteen environmental bad effects. The proposed system would include at least some recycling or reuse of wastes, namely, the municipal wastes, livestock manure, and agricultural wastes that are compostable. "Solutions" that merely substitute one problem for another, such as simple incineration or transport to remote areas were minimized or avoided.[15]

The systems analysis performed by Morse and Roth (1970) involves the Buffalo, New York SMSA. The analysts explicitly emphasized the need to integrate the often separately handled functions of solid-waste management, that is, collection, transportation, processing, and disposal. The mathematical model involved the selection of facilities and assignment of source areas to facilities such that the total cost of facilities and operations was minimized. Pollutants

[15]Ironically, as late as 1970, in the face of obstinacy on the part of the Peninsula town of Brisbane which had accepted San Francisco's trash, there were serious proposals to haul this waste by railroad to a dump site in remote Lassen County.

and land usage were also considered as measures of effectiveness. Although not reflected in model design, indirect costs received some attention in the discussion,

The specialized but highly significant problem of junked automobiles and their recycling was the basis of the systems analysis performed by Management Technology, Inc. (1970). Although the analysis dealt with problems in the state of Maryland, the conclusions and recommendations can be generalized to other states or regions. Analysis involved consideration of the processes of abandoning, collecting, storing, disposing, salvaging, and processing junked cars as an integrated system. Both the esthetic and neglected resource aspects of junking automobiles received attention. Seven major problems were identified (for example, vehicle abandonment continues at an alarming rate.) For each problem a conclusion was made (for example, actions by the private sector to reduce the number of abandoned cars are, and will continue to be, ineffective), and a recommendation offered (for example, government legislation imposing heavy penalties on those who abandon cars is required). The analysts believe that whereas the esthetic problems require government action, the problems of inadequate demand for processed scrap can be solved by industry.

MODELS OF SOCIETY

The many areas just discussed can be considered submodels of much larger models of regional, national, or even global ecosystems and human societies. In this section, we shall first summarize briefly a social systems model proposed by Gross. Then we shall review in detail two much less theoretical approaches to large-scale modeling, namely, that at the Institute of Ecology of the University of California at Davis and that at the Massachusetts Institute of Technology. Work at both centers, although preliminary, is indicative of the development of powerful new tools for high-level policy-making and decision-making. Theory and concepts and our ability to build models, of course, lag behind events. *We cannot stress too much, though, the urgency of developing better techniques for assessing the state of the world and better managing the world before time runs out.* We shall continue this line of thought in the last chapter of this book.

Gross (1967) proposes a social systems model based on general systems theory applicable to various hierarchical levels from the international to the individual. It is an open systems model which attempts to account for dynamic situations and for the many varieties of social systems. It is held to be applicable to all aspects of organizations and territorial entities.

Gross emphasizes that the source of the system's capacity to perform is found in its structure, i.e., the elements and relations between them. The structure of any social system consists of people and nonhuman resources, grouped into subsystems and lower, that interrelate among themselves and with the external environment, and are subject to norms and central guidance that aid in system performance. Internal relations must be studied in polyarchical (lateral) as well as hierarchical (superior-subordinate) terms. Networks of communications and mobility are of great importance in establishing relations among subsystems.

Gross's model combines the *structural* (interrelated elements) and *performance* (input-output-activity) approaches. It involves seven performance features: (1) acquisition of inputs; (2) transformation of inputs into outputs, especially involving feedback; (3) needs or interests satisfied or not satisfied by the outputs; (4) extent to which certain outputs are invested in the system rather than transferred to the external clientele; (5) the extent outputs are used efficiently; (6) codes of behavior (legal, moral, etc.); and (7) conceptions of technical or administrative rationality.

The model does not establish the value to be placed on elements in the system—this is for the user to do. It does provide a means for describing the changing structure and performance of a social system and for understanding interrelationships among the system elements and between the system and its environment. It is still sketchy and does not provide for prediction or control, or for implementation by computers or other means.

The University of California at Davis Studies

The main effort of the initial two-year study (Watt, *et al.,* 1969) was to determine the feasibility of developing a mathematical model of California so as to perform computer simulation studies of the effects of continuously rising population densities. The multidisciplinary group spent a year searching the literature on theories, models, and data, and in consulting with experts. Four principle techniques were used: (1) reading essays by recognized thinkers in each specialty; (2) constructing tables in which a wide variety of processes were ranked by rate of change so as to reveal especially important processes; (3) using summaries of local government expenditures to make plots of expenses per capita of various categories against urban population density (this helped identify density-related processes); and (4) using mathematical and statistical analyses of other workers which provided ideas as to how to quantify in particularly refractory fields, such as health, and crime and violence.

Essentially the work resulted in a literature survey,[16] some block diagrams, a few regression analyses, and some valuable interpretations. No actual computer simulations were performed.

This study operated at the descriptive-correlative regression analysis level,

---

[16]This is not meant in a pejorative sense. Work in this field is by no means easy and meaningful results cannot be guaranteed beforehand. The results are by no means atypical of large-scale studies of societal problems. The several-year-long Harvard Program on Society and Technology also yielded mostly literature reviews.

rathei than at the dynamic level of differential equations, or at the even more elegant systems dynamics level. The memoiy demand of the model as designed was so great as to preclude its storage in memory at one time; hence, it had to be divided into a series of subroutines and brought into memory as needed. Further, the huge output made time sharing impracticable. Finding a suitable computer presented a problem.

Watt, *et al.*, thus attempted to construct a complex systems model containing numerous submodels interrelated in input-output, and to some extent feedback, terms. All the submodels were in early stages of development based on literature searches, conferences with experts, and preliminary analyses of available data if any. Extant submodels were employed whenever possible. Four general categories of the effects of population densities were sought: (1) competition for resources; (2) biological effects on individual human beings; (3) effects on human society; and (4) environmental degradation.

A summary of the submodels under development in the initial study follows. It should be noted that development of several of these submodels was not pursued in subsequent studies, probably because of model recalcitrance in handling. The submodels were:

Demography. Past population projections have almost all resulted in low estimates even over short time periods. For example, little is known about age specific fertility, and numbers of young, urban, poor are imperfectly known.

Demographic factors often contribute to biases in predictions of technological development. Estimates have been on the low side even over short time periods.

The Bay Area Simulation Study (BASS) (1968) models, discussed in Chapter 6, form the basis of the demographic submodel.

Agriculture. This area was especially pursued in the later study. In this earlier study, the authors noted several examples wherein paucity of hard data precluded establishing functional or causal relationships, in turn preventing detailed modeling.

Public health. Using this submodel, it was attempted to determine the relationships between California population density stratified by race and socioeconomic level, various environmental factors, and the physical and mental health of the citizens. The census tract was selected as the level for data collection and analysis and for the input-output of the model, because statistics on natality, morbidity, and mortality citywide or countywide were found to mask significant differences. This is similar to the conclusion reached by Maloney and cited earlier in this chapter. Inconsistencies in availability of health services and in disease reporting contribute to this picture. It was hoped to build models for such events as emphysema death rate, cancer, pollution and cardiovascular mortality, effects of stress, etc.

Because this area is beset by all the difficulties discussed earlier in this chapter, it was not pursued further in the next study.

Crime and violence. The authors were especially interested in modeling the relationship between population density and socioeconomic variables, and crime and violence. Regression methods were considered especially attractive. Of course, many of the same problems as with public health obtain here, namely differences in diagnosis, classification, and reporting. This area was not pursued in the later study.

Man's effect on climate. This area also has received extensive study in the later report, and illustrates again the falling back on easier-to-quantify physical measures, rather than pursuing the above more nebulous areas. Areas of especial consideration were the urban heat island; rural cooling; and the effects of air pollution upon clouds, fog, and precipitation. Much more detailed knowledge here will provide us with a better rationale for the design of environments.

Transportation. The authors were interested in building a transportation model, but this was not pursued in the later study. Although many simulations have been performed, most have been quite specific and at a subsystem level. The authors feel sufficient data exist to build a model that emphasizes demands and costs, provided nondollar costs, such as those associated with pollution and the availability of new modes of transportation, can be evaluated. Here again, except at the most abstracted levels, there are the tenuous factors of status, advertising, pressure by conservation groups, and other not easily predictable facets of changed social thinking.

Education. This area also, one of the most difficult in all society with which to come to grips, was not seriously attacked and not considered in the later report. Emphasis would have been upon the discrepancy between quality education and high population rates. This would involve considerations of taxation and the ratio:

$$\frac{Taxpayers\ in\ education\ tax\text{-}consuming\ ages}{Taxpayers\ in\ education\ tax\text{-}producing\ ages}$$

City services. This area, not pursued further, would revolve around the questions: How much does the size of a city affect the living costs of its residents? Thus, many essential city services rise in cost per capita per annum with rising city services. For example, the per capita per annum cost of police protection (Cp) and the size of the city expressed as number of inhabitants are related as:

$$Cp = a + b \ln S$$

The same type of curve describes fire protection costs. Such considerations indicate the danger of one-dimensional thinking in design, such as that of Dox-iadis discussed earlier in this chapter.

Taxation and zoning. This was considered central to the whole issue of population expansion Unfortunately, many taxation and zoning policies and much legislation have been conceived in response to pressures by lobbyists to give short-term profits for vested interests. There are innumerable instances; for example, of city planners' wanting to make money for real-estate speculators and zoning farmland so as to bankrupt farmers. Other well-known examples relate to forests and oil.

Watt, *et al.,* provide several interesting and valuable speculations as to the future of society. For example, they hold that the belief that the energy efficiency of society is rising is in error because of the way of defining efficiency. Thus, if efficiency is measured by the number of calories produced by a process as a proportion to calories consumed by it—instead of the productivity of goods, and services per capita—efficiency is dropping. This applies to all human activities because of the increased energy overhead associated with these processes.

Another way of saying this is that, by the second law of thermodynamics, a fixed proportion of the energy going into any activity will be wasted (the same rule applies to matter, space, and information). Thus, the greater the amount used, the greater the amount wasted. We compound these problems by over-designing everything.

In order to deal with the interrelated problems of population growth and extremely inefficient use of resources, and consequent faulty decision-making, Glass and Watt (1971) are attempting to develop a four-level hierarchy of systems models. It is argued that it is often impossible to understand events at one level only in terms of phenomena at that level. Rather, it is necessary to move back and forth through levels of scale and aggregation (see also Mesarović's theories of multilevel hierarchical systems discussed in Chapter 1). The four levels are global, United States, California regional, and subregional. The models will be used to develop alternative scenarios on the computer to aid in the evaluation of alternative strategies.

Four major areas have been studied: (1) energy consumption; (2) the global carbon cycle; (3) land use; and (4) the relationship between biospheric energy transport and agricultural food production.

Energy consumption. Results of the interactive model indicate that countries go through a long, slow stage in which energy consumption per capita increases, but after the rate reaches a maximum value it again drops off sharply. Eventually, the rate of increase in energy consumption per capita drops to zero at approximately 50 barrels of oil-energy[17] per person per year. Thus, advanced

[17]Estimates of fuel use are converted into crude oil equivalents.

societies may reach saturation points with respect to growth in demand; beyond such a point further growth takes place only with growth in population. Especially large rates of increase could be expected in underdeveloped countries if a great influx of foreign capital occurred.

Further results indicate definite, albeit complicated, relationships between energy consumption per capita and birth rates for women in given age groups. Attempts will be made to predict future trends in rates of increase in energy consumption for most of the countries of the world in terms of the use of coal, oil, gas, hydropower, nuclear power, and total energy use.

Glass and Watt speculate on the side effects of large-scale energy consumption. They emphasize that the basic physical principal of conservation of mass dictates that populations cannot continue to grow without limit because space, food, and other resources are limited. Likewise, the first and second laws of thermodynamics indicate continued human energy use will inevitably result in major planetary temperature changes. The belief the earth is an infinite sink into which man can dump all his waste without deleterious effect is now widely held to be wrong. For example, atmospheric pollutants may have a marked effect on the earth's radiation balance, especially on the albedo or percent of total incoming solar radiation reflected back to outer space. For example, a change of about 15% in the albedo might elicit catastrophic changes. See also Chapter 1.

In recent years, the development of somewhat comprehensive numerical models of geophysical processes makes study of these events more possible. For example, at present the total yearly human production of energy is about 1/2500 the solar input at the earth's surface, but Glass and Watt calculate the two values would be equal in 200 years at the present rate of increase in energy usage of 4% per year. Likewise, a fourfold increase in the global equilibrium dust concentration could decrease the mean ground temperature by $3.5°K$. However, such estimates are still based on imperfect models, perhaps associated with the absence of understanding of basic physical processes, which hold many potentially important factors constant and ignore interactions. For example, relatively little is known of the effects of cloud cover on sea ice, which could change the planetary albedo by 100% to 200%. Ironically, science has not always been even so systems oriented as have economics and the military. Perhaps, without realworld pressures, it could continue to afford the luxury of disciplinary and problem fragmentation.

Global carbon cycle. This was studied in the hope of finding a quantifiable prognosis of the effects of man's use of fossil fuels on the environment. As human population grows exponentially, so does fuel use, and there appears to be a corresponding increase in the amount of atmospheric carbon dioxide.[18]

When the dynamics of amounts of carbon stored in various parts of the

[18]Some persons caution this increase may reflect natural system oscillations.

biosphere, hydrosphere, atmosphere, and lithosphere were expressed as equations, and computer simulations performed, some important results were obtained. For example, the biosphere expanded to accumulate all the carbon released into the atmosphere by man. The atmospheric carbon came to equilibrium and the sea lost some carbon. Increasing the time delay in the biosphere may augment or even initiate system oscillations. The effects of selection of time interval, as emphasized by Forrester, have been discussed earlier (see Chapter 1). Significantly, the simulation indicated a "phenomenal growth of the forest biomass required *to extricate man from potential dangers which could result from his industrial activities* (p. 49, emphasis added)." Natural laws themselves might prohibit such growth. But even if not, "it is doubtful that man, in his infinite wisdom, would permit such an intrusion of forests on his land area (p. 49)."

The effects of human exploitation were next entered into the model. Thus, although the biosphere expands phenomenally, exploitation results eventually in ravishing the forests completely. The atmospheric carbon content then triples but again falls to an equilibrium value. Glass and Watt emphasize the importance of a *thorough systems approach* involving human population growth, fossil fuel use and discovery rate, forest growth, and forest practices.

Land Use. Land use was examined at the regional level. As human population growth in California continues, more and more agricultural land is converted to urban, industrial, highway, and other nonagricultural uses. At the same time, demand for agricultural products will increase with population. In the simulation, equations were developed to describe the nature and flow of acreage into and out of the urban-use level and agricultural-use level.

A matrix approach was used. Four submodels were developed, namely, demographic, land inventory, agricultural, and economic; their interrelationships determined; and the submodels synthesized into an over-all regional model. The three other models were driven by the demography model. Validation was extremely difficult because of a paucity of data. The greatest problem dealt with migration information, especially that of inter- and intra-county census tracts.

We see that in rapidly urbanizing areas an immense amount of the world's best crop production land is being lost to agriculture. This is estimated at about 70,000 acres per year, or approximately 0.22 acres per person, as compared to the national average of 0.15 acres per person. And unfortunately the move toward urban sprawl shows little sign of abating. The evils of land speculation coupled with anachronistic tax and zoning laws would appear to guarantee the passing of agricultural land to "higher uses." Concomitantly, the demand for agricultural products has also been increasing steadily. Technological changes and additional irrigation, resulting in higher crop yields per acre, have permitted California to maintain a high level of agricultural productivity. However, nothing comes free, and such gains have placed immense stress both upon other areas, marginal for agriculture and best left as forest and wilderness, and upon wildlife populations (stressed also through use of pesticides, as discussed in Chapter 1).

Various assumptions were made in the simulation modeling as to population growth, rate of urbanization of agricultural lands, crop yields per acre, and water resource development. This provided a range of alternative futures, some with excesses and some with shortages of irrigated acres. Successive runs of the model indicated the great sensitivity of the results to key parameters and the need for much greater understanding of the basic mechanisms of population growth, technological change, etc. The best way to evaluate the output of the simulation would be to compare the results with a field experiment.

The relationship between biospheric energy transport and agricultural food production. In this model, for each crop an attempt was made to determine the quantitative factors governing growth and yield. State variables such as plant growth, temperature of the air and soil, soil moisture and chemical composition, etc.—which define the state of the system at a moment in time—were acted upon by inputs to the system, such as nutrients added, moisture added, etc. The inputs to the system were considered those we desired to control; such control made the system state variables act so a desired output was obtained. A complete mathematical model of the crop production system, which could be used for projecting trends of future yields, involved defining the mathematical relationship between the dependent variable or yield level and various independent variables. The relationship between crop yield and various independent variables was determined from data. Regression analysis was used to determine the equations for the production functions. The next step involved adding constraints to the problem and determining the production yield, given such constraints upon the inputs and state variables. This was done by formulating nonlinear and linear programming problems. The objective function would be a composite of the production functions; the desire was to maximize production. The next stage would be to expand the model to formulate dynamic solutions to the problem.

The Massachusetts Institute of Technology Studies

Jay W. Forrester (1971)[19] has utilized the "systems dynamics" methods previously discussed to model and computer-simulate the global system. Although his attempt is to be applauded, he is strong on assumptions based almost completely upon intuition, personal experience, and the opinions of consultants. He is weak on data. His level of aggregation is impossible. Yet this work is important, for at least two reasons. First, it will focus attention on the

---

[19]It is interesting to note that in this book Forrester uses the terms "socio-technical system," "socio-technical-natural system," and "socio-technical-economic-political system" on and off, but without defining them.

subtle interactions of complex systems and upon counterintuitive behavior following most policy solutions

Second, it places Forrester and his followers, along with Skinner and others discussed in the next chapter, in the arena of the would-be "managers of society." For instance he states (p. 122): "As the next step we can hope that the dynamics of growth and equilibrium will be investigated . . . until a consensus begins to form. After the consensus will still lie the task of implementing the necessary changes in world goals, values, and actions."

Forrester believes his model, rather quickly prepared for a summer 1970 demonstration to the activist Club of Rome,[20] is more complete and explicit than the mental models now being used for national and world planning. Unfortunately, from our image of national and world planning, he is probably right.

Like the present author, Forrester objects to accepting future population growth as preordained and the basis for action. If we make provision for rising population, population responds by rising. Thus, there is a circular process in complex systems in which there is no unidirectional cause and effect. Many programs which "buy time" until "solutions" can be found really reduce pressure to solve the population (or other critical) problem. Behavioral science theory substantiated this conclusion: men are satisficers.

The immediate solutions include the many popular "Green Revolution," water resources, food-from-the-sea, and other programs. Humanitarian efforts tend to make things worse, and (p. 124):

> Rising pressures are necessary to hasten the day when population is stabilized. Pressures can be increased by reducing food production, reducing health services, and reducing industrialization. Such reductions seem to have only slight effect on quality of life in the long run. The principal effect will be in squeezing down and stopping runaway growth.

Forrester recognizes limitations on capital investment may be even harder to achieve than limits on population. People don't yet recognize the threat of industrialization. Yet social values and goals based on growth cannot continue indefinitely. There must be new human goals and values to replace those based on economic advancement and a rising possession of superfluous gadgets.

Forrester stresses that Nature must be helped rather than conquered, civilization must be restrained rather than expanded. I have discussed these ideas

---

[20]The Club of Rome is an informal, international organization with a limited number of members and based on the premise that global problems are so interrelated and multifaceted that traditional institutions and policies are not qualified to deal with them. (See also our discussion in Chapters 3 and 9 as to the limitations of present institutions and policies.) Further, these problems occur to some extent in all societies. The Club's collective activity is called "The Project on the Predicament of Mankind." The results of the first effort sponsored are given in Forrester (1971) and Meadows, et. al. (1972).

elsewhere in this book. Certainly paleontology provides numerous tragic examples of unbridled expansion (cf. the trilobites and ammonites). Forrester goes on to state (p. 125) "Social pressures probably must increase rather than decline, until those pressures can be transformed into a change in social values that take satisfaction from an equilibrium society." Both developed and underdeveloped countries face this choice; indeed, in crisis the latter, being ecologically closer to Nature, may have a greater chance of survival. Perhaps in this context the policies of Brazil to "develop" the Amazon and to "protect" the Indians (Von Puttkamer, 1971) need reevaluation. The Amazon may be among the last refuges humanity has. The long-term future of the earth must soon be faced and goals of nations and societies altered to become compatible with a future in which man is in balance with his environment. The goal of civilization must be that of global equilibrium.

Forrester believes, on the basis of his modeling, that we should be able to plot a course from exponential growth into global equilibrium. Numerous curves are given, reflecting various interactions and policies with regard to population growth, growth of capital investment, pollution, and so on. Yet one serious deficiency of this modeling derives from the long time spans. Many of the predicted results take place toward the middle of the 21st century. It seems likely crisis will occur long before the times approximated in Forrester's model.

Forrester believes we are on the verge of the latest (should we say last?) great era of human pioneering—that of social systems. Certainly, physical science, engineering, and associated technology have long since stabilized. Science is routine; the process of scientific discovery is orderly and organized. Yet Forrester talks of progress over the next 30 years. Will there be time, especially considering his modeling is based on present or past understanding and popular pressures, and we know essentially nothing about the basic levels and rates necessary to model the world of 1980, let alone 2040? A future modeled on the interaction of presently understood forces could be vastly different from that based on realworld forces. Who, in 1960, predicted hippies, drugs, alienation, the success of the conservation-environment movement, internationalism, the rejection of chauvinism and war, etc.? Will 1975 or 1985 show us a simple swing of the pendulum back to 1950 values and behavior, as clutchers for past security would have us believe; or, as is much more likely, will there be behavior manifested which we cannot even anticipate because of lack of understanding of real underlying social dynamics and because we arrogantly shun real behavioral and social science research in the name of expediency?

Forrester apparently assumes unconquerable forces of Nature. This may leave him open to attack by those who maintain we can conquer and control Nature for a long time to come. He urges realistically, though, that we choose a nongrowing and balanced condition. This seems entirely consistent with the organic world.

We know too little of the dormant forces, which exert their effects suddenly once a critical threshold has been exceeded. Fundamental laws of Nature and society will have been waiting until their time has come to suppress the power of growth. Certainly nothing in the natural world—consider cancers, lemmings, mountains, and stars—indicates other than that unlimited growth eventually becomes curtailed, even destructive. Forrester looks at some of the forces that will become barriers when growth goes too far—interactions occuring when exponential growth collides with a fixed environment—and also at some of the changes that can arise to stop exponential growth. Our greatest immediate challenge deals with how we guide the transition from growth to equilibrium. But time is running out.

Forrester constructed his system structure using five levels: population, capital investment, natural resources, fraction of capital devoted to agriculture, and pollution. These were interrelated in the simulation model. They were related also to quality of life used as a measure of performance of the world system. Simulation results indicated population growth, for example, can be limited by depletion of natural resources, rise of pollution, increase in crowding, and decline in food. The results of Forrester's simulations make intuitive sense, but unfortunately are based on such a high level of aggregation and are so unrelated to basic data as to be practically meaningless. For example, there are many kinds of pollutants which, as pointed out elsewhere in this book, may actually have a cancelling effect on each other. The details of relationships between pollution and death, or crowding and death have not yet been firmly established. In level of aggregation and abstraction, Forrester's "top-down" approach differs from the "bottom-up" approach of Watt, et al., and Glass and Watt discussed earlier in this chapter.

Forrester's book deals, as does the present one, with the world system of man, his social systems, his technological systems, and the natural environment. Unfortunately, Forrester pays little more than lip service to our need for better understanding in behavioral science—to understand why people pursue capital investment and industrialization, what procreation means to people, how best to change values, etc. Forrester's modeling is of major value in even attempting to structure complex systems and to show the interaction of basic forces; it is weakest, in common with all other computer modeling, in that it emphasizes overly abstracted, easily quantifiable factors.

Forrester states (p. 112): "The industrial societies have behind them long traditions that have encouraged and rewarded growth. The folklore and the success stories praise growth and expansion. But that is not the path of the future." But he provides no insight as to what to do about it. Certainly behavioral science knowledge, perhaps from psychoanalysis, relative to symbolism (what do growth, bigness, newness, and change really mean in terms of personal needs, and how can we substitute for them? how do we, using what we learn, restructure our entire educational system?) should be brought into action here.

As a final example, quality of life was determined as a function of material standard of living, crowding, food, and pollution. Certainly this neglects any consideration of personal meaning and self-concept, alienation, drug use, and other dramatic manifestations of our modern sociotechnical reality.

The major conclusions of Meadows, *et al.* (1972), conclusions which we heartily endorse, may come as a shock to those who believe growth can go on forever or who simply have never thought of these things before. We shall stress those conclusions here in summary form. The short doubling times of human activities coupled with the immense amounts being doubled lead to limits to growth of these activities in a surprisingly short time. The momentum of present growth may (in less than 100 years) overshoot the carrying capacity of the earth—in arable land, in water, in non-renewable resources, in the capacity of the environment to absorb pollutants, and so on. The closer we come to the material limits of earth, the harder the problems will be to solve (and these problems include

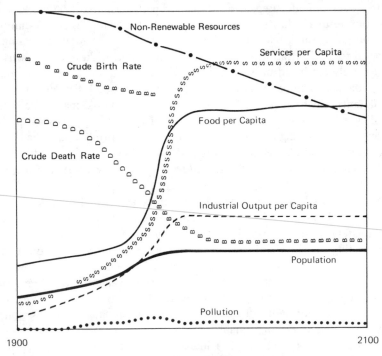

1900   2100

Systems dynamics idealized computer plot showing stabilized growth patterns following "ideal" initiation of technological and growth-regulating policies beginning 1975-90. Technological policies include resource recycling, pollution control devices, increased lifetime of all forms of capital, and methods to restore eroded and infertile soil. Value changes include increased emphasis on food and services rather than on industrial production. Births are set equal to deaths and industrial capital investment equal to capital depreciation.

FIGURE 8-9[21]

[21] Adapted from *The Limits to Growth* by Donella H. Meadows, Dennis L. Meadows, *et al.* A Potomac Associates book published by Universe Books, New York, 1972.

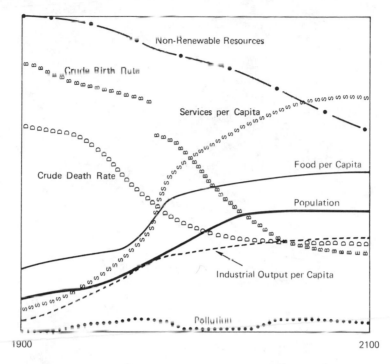

1900

2100

Systems dynamics idealized computer plot showing stabilized growth patterns allowing for some "voluntary" restrictions of population and economic growth beginning in 1975. Population and capital are regulated within the natural delays of the system and the equilibrium level of population is higher and the level of industrial output per capita is lower than in Figure 8-9. The birth rate only approaches slowly the death rate because of delays inherent in the age structure of the population.

FIGURE 8-10[22]

armed conflicts between the Haves within and between societies and the Have-Nots). Technological developments which temporarily remove some limit to growth allow the system to grow to another limit, followed by surpassing that limit and collapse to a much lower level. Figures 8-9, 8-10, and 8-11 illustrate this point. Too much societal "problem-solving" is devoted to attacking and removing naturally curative negative-feedback loops instead of the positive-feedback loops of growth. The transition from a growth ethos to an equilibrium ethos presents problems of unknown difficulty, yet there is clearly no alternative. Finally, although there are profound implications for human behavior, societies, and policy making, the model admittedly doesn't deal with behavioral and social factors. And that's where books like the present one enter the picture.

[22] Adapted from *The Limits to Growth* by Donella H. Meadows, Dennis L. Meadows, *et al.* A Potomac Associates book published by Universe Books, New York, 1972.

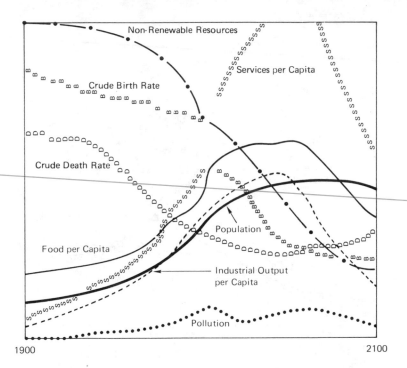

Systems dynamics idealized computer plot showing lack of stability following initiation in the year 2000 of policies allowing for some "voluntary" restrictions of population and economic growth. Population and industrial capital reach levels high enough to create food and resource shortages before the year 2100.

FIGURE 8-11[23]

SUMMARY AND CONCLUSIONS

In this chapter, we have considered a number of examples or cases classified in terms of common parlance, such as urban systems, health systems, transportation systems, etc. These systems differ, of course, in the relative contribution of the social subsystem and the technological subsystem. The greater the social subsystem contribution, the greater the difficulty in applying present systems methodology. For example, crime and violence is much more difficult to handle than is solid waste management. Difficulty in handling tempts many workers to convert social or sociotechnical systems into purely technical systems, or at best, technico-economic or technico-demographic systems.

---

[23]Adapted from *The Limits to Growth* by Donella H. Meadows, Dennis L. Meadows, *et al.* A Potomac Associates book published by Universe Books, New York, 1972.

The examples in this chapter represent the various applications of methodology discussed in Part II, namely, systems analysis, computer modeling and simulation, analytic modeling, benefit-cost analysis, multiple regression analysis, and so on. Problems of defining criteria, benefits, performance effectiveness, and costs have been especially highlighted. Numerous implications for managerial planning and policy-making have been indicated; for example, tradeoffs in urban land use between a park and a parking lot, determining how best to prevent an urban riot, and planning for an energy balance in 1980.

Many of the examples have indicated impacts on and interactions with other subsystems and with the social and natural environments. The first sections of the chapter can be thought of as being prerequisite to building models of society. "Society" of course can be defined at various hierarchical levels, from, say, the study of interactions between the urban subsystem and the transportation subsystem on the one hand to the world society in Forrester's study on the other.

We have defined two different approaches to modeling society; a *bottoms-up* approach, in which a number of extant submodels are synthesized to produce the model of society, and a *top-down* approach in which a large, highly aggregated model is used to predict events at lower levels. The bottoms-up approach can be associated with difficult, even impossible, problems of integrating the submodels; the top-down approach may produce such generalities as to be silly. Nevertheless, experimentation in both approaches is quite necessary—in that we have nothing else that could even remotely promise our control over the macrosystems that now control us.

REFERENCES

Abrahamson, Dean E., 1970, *Environmental Cost of Electric Power.* New York: Scientists' Institute for Public Information.

Aerojet-General Corporation, 1969, *A Systems Study of Solid Waste Management in the Fresno Area.* Report No. SW-5d or Public Health Service Publication No. 1959. Washington, D.C.: U. S. Government Printing Office.

Anonymous, 1971, Program Given Notice, *Science,* 173(3993), 219, 16 July.

Baker, Frank, 1969, Review of General Systems Concepts and Their Relevance for Medical Care, *Systematics,* 7(3), 209-29.

Bazell, Robert J., 1971, Rapid Transit: A Real Alternative to the Auto for the Bay Area? *Science,* 171(3976), 1125-28, 19 March.

Black, Ralph J., Anton J. Muhich, Albert J. Klee, H. Lanier Hickman, Jr., and Richard D. Vaughn, 1968, *The National Solid Wastes Survey—An Interim Report,* presented at the 1968 Annual Meeting of the Institute for Solid Wastes of The American Public Works Association, Miami Beach, Florida, Oct. 24 (HEW, Environmental Control Administration).

Broady, Maurice, 1969, The Social Context of Urban Planning, *Urban Affairs Quarterly,* **4**(3), 355-78, March.

Center for Real Estate and Urban Economics, 1968, *Jobs, People, and Land: Bay Area Simulation Study (BASS).* Special Report No. 6, Berkeley, California: University of California, Institute of Urban and Regional Development.

Chandler, T. J., 1968, *Urban Climates: Inventory and Prospect,* presented at W.M.O. Symposium on Urban Climates and Building Climatology in Brussels, Belgium, October.

Changnon, S. A., 1968, *Recent Studies of Urban Effects on Precipitation in the United States,* presented at W.M.O. Sumposium on Urban Climates and Building Climatology in Brussels, Belgium, October.

Conley, Ronald W., Margaret Conwell, and Mildred B. Arrill, 1967, An Approach to Measuring the Cost of Mental Illness, *American Journal of Psychiatry,* 124(6), 63-70, December.

De Greene, Kenyon B., 1970, New Vistas. In K.B. De Greene (ed.), *Systems Psychology.* New York: McGraw-Hill.

——, 1971, *Concepts and Problems in the Test and Evaluation of Health Systems,* presented at Conference on Health Research and the Systems Approach, Wayne State University, College of Nursing, Detroit, Mich., March 1-4.

Dettwiller, I., 1968, *Incidence Possible de l'Activité Industrielle sur les Précipitations à Paris,* presented at W.M.O. Symposium on Urban Climates and Building Climatology in Brussels, Belgium, October.

Downs, Anthony, 1970, Alternative Forms of Future Urban Growth in the United States, *Journal of the American Institute of Planners,* 36(1), 3-11.

Doxiadis, Constantinos A., 1971, Ekistics, the Science of Human Settlements, *Science,* 170(3956), 393-404, 23 October.

——, 1968, Man's Movement and His City, *Science,* 162(3851), 326-34, 18 October.

Duckworth, F. A., and J. S. Sandberg, 1954, The Effect of Cities upon Horizontal and Vertical Temperature Gradients, *Bulletin of the American Meteorological Society,* 35 (5) 198-207.

Elson, Benjamin M., 1972, Advanced "Avionic" Units Integrate BART, *Aviation Week and Space Technology,* 97(10), 56-61, 4 September.

Felter, R. B., and J. D. Thompson, 1965, The Simulation of Hospital Systems, *Operations Research,* 13, 689-711, September-October.

Forrester, Jay W., 1961, *Industrial Dynamics.* Cambridge, Mass.: The M.I.T. Press.

——, 1968, *Principles of Systems,* Text and Workbook, Chapters 1 through 10, 2nd Preliminary ed. Cambridge, Mass.: Wright-Allen Press.

——, 1969, *Urban Dynamics.* Cambridge, Mass.: The M.I.T. Press.

——, 1971, *World Dynamics.* Cambridge, Mass.: Wright-Allen Press.

Friedlander, Gordon, 1970a, Power, Pollution, and the Imperiled Environment: I. Scope of the General Problem Area, *IEEE Spectrum,* 7(11), 40-50.

——, 1970b, Power, Pollution, and the Imperiled Environment: II. East, Midwest, and West Coast, *IEEE Spectrum* 7(12), 65-75.

Gillette, Robert, 1971a, Nuclear Reactor Safety: A New Dilemma for the AEC, *Science,* 173(3992), 126-30, 9 July.

——, 1971b, Nuclear Reactor Safety: A Skeleton at the Feast, *Science,* 172(3986), 918-19, 28 May.

Glass, N. R., and K. E. F. Watt, 1971, *Land Use, Energy, Agriculture, and Decision-Making,* a report to the National Science Foundation. Davis, Ca.: University of California, Institute of Ecology, 28 March.

Gough, William C., 1970, *Why Fusion? Controlled Thermonuclear Research Program,* WASH 1165, UC-20. Washington, D.C.: U.S. Government Printing Office, June.

Gross, Bertram, M., 1967, The Coming General Systems Models of Social Systems, *Human Relations,* 20(4), 357-74, November.

Hall, Edward T., 1968, Proxemics, *Current Anthropology,* 9(2-3), 83-108, April-June.

Hallan, Jerome B., Benjamin S. H. Harris, III, and Albert V. Alhadeff, 1968, *The Economic Cost of Kidney Disease and Related Diseases of the Urinary System,* Public Health Service Publication No. 1940. Washington, D.C.: U. S. Department of Health, Education, and Welfare.

Hammond, Allen L., 1971, Breeder Reactors: Power for the Future, *Science,* 174(4011), 807-10, 19 November.

Hester, James, Jr., 1969, *Systems Models of Urban Growth and Development.* Cambridge, Mass.: Massachusetts Institute of Technology, Urban Systems Laboratory, 1 November.

Horvath, William J., 1966, The Systems Approach to the National Health Problem, *Management Science,* 12(10), B-391 to B-395, June.

Kadanoff, Leo P., 1972, From Simulation Model to Public Policy, *American Scientist,* 69(1), 74-79, January-February.

Krech, David, Richard S. Crutchfield, and Egerton L. Bellachey, 1962, *The Individual in Society: A Textbook of Social Psychology.* New York: McGraw-Hill.

Krendel, Ezra S., 1970, A Case Study of Citizen Complaints as Social Indicators, *IEEE Transactions on Systems Science and Cybernetics,* SSC-6(4), 265-72, October.

Kyllonen, R. L., 1967, Crime Rate vs. Population Density in United States Cities: A Model, *General Systems* 12, 137-145.

Landsberg, H. E., 1956, The Climate of Towns. In William L. Thomas (ed.), *Man's Role in Changing the Face of the Earth.* Chicago: University of Chicago Press.

——, 1960, *Physical Climatology* (2nd rev. ed.). Dubois, Penn.: Gray Printing Co.

——, 1962, City Air—Better or Worse. In *Symposium: Air Over Cities,* U.S. Public Health Service Technical Report A62-5, pp. 1-22. Cincinnati, Ohio: Taft Sanitary Engineering Center.

Larson, Richard C., 1970, On the Modeling of Police Patrol Operations, *IEEE Transactions on Systems Science and Cybernetics,* SSC-6(4), 276-81.

LeBaron, Walt, 1969, *Systems Analysis and Learning Systems in the Development of Elementary Teacher Education Models.* U.S. Department of Health, Education, and Welfare, National Center for Educational Research and Development, OE-58035. Washington, D.C.: U.S. Government Printing Office, October.

Lees, Lester, 1971, *California's Projected Electrical Energy Demand and Supply.* Pasadena, Ca.: California Institute of Technology, Environmental Quality Laboratory.

Le Sourd, David A., Mark E. Fogel, and Donald R. Johnston, 1968, *Benefit-Cost Analysis of Kidney Disease Programs.* Public Health Service Publication No. 1941. Washington, D.C.: U.S. Department of Health, Education, and Welfare, August.

Levin, Gilbert, Gary Hirsch, Deborah Kligler, and Edward B. Roberts, 1969, *A Model of Interaction Between Patient and Program, and Its Implications for Treatment Drop-Outs Among Severely Disabled Psychiatric Patients,* draft. Bronx, N.Y.: Sound View—Throgs Neck Community Mental Health Center, 7 August.

Levin, Gilbert, Gary Hirsch, and Edward B. Roberts, 1971, *Narcotics and the Community: A System Simulation,* draft. Bronx, N.Y.: Albert Einstein College of Medicine, February.

Maloney, John C., 1967, *Letter to Dr. Anthony Downs, National Advisory Commission on Civil Disorders.* Evanston, Ill.: The Medill School of Journalism, Northwestern University, 14 December.

Management Technology, Inc., 1970, *Automobile Scrapping Processes and Needs for Maryland.* Public Health Service Publication No. 2027. Washington, D.C.: U.S. Government Printing Office.

Meadows, Donella, Dennis L. Meadows, Jørgen Randers, and William W. Behrens, III, 1972, *The Limits to Growth.* New York: Universe Books.

Milgram, Stanley, 1970, The Experience of Living in Cities, *Science,* 167(3924), 1461-68, 13 March.

Mills, Robert G., 1971, The Promise of Controlled Fusion, *IEEE Spectrum,* 8(11), 24-36.

Milly, George H., and Leon S. Pocinki, 1970, *A Computer Simulation Model for Evaluation of the Health Care Delivery System,* Report HRSD-70. Rockville, Md.: U.S. Department of Health, Education, and Welfare, June.

Morrison, Warren E., and Charles L. Readling, 1968, *An Energy Model for the United States, Featuring Energy Balances for the Years 1947 to 1965 and*

Projections and Forecasts to the Years 1980 and 2000, Bureau of Mines, Information Circular 8384. Washington, D.C.: U.S. Department of the Interior, July.

Morse, Norman, and Edwin W. Roth, 1970, *Systems Analysis of Regional Solid Waste Handling.* Public Health Service Publication No. 2065. Washington, D.C.: U. S. Government Printing Office.

Myrup, Leonard O., 1969, A Numerical Model of the Urban Heat Island, *Journal of Applied Meteorology,* 8(6), 908-18, December.

Nader, J.S., 1967, *Pilot Study of Ultraviolet Radiation in Los Angeles, October 1965,* Public Health Service Publication 999-AP-38. Cincinnati, Ohio: U.S. Department of Health, Education, and Welfare, National Center for Air Pollution Control.

National Academy of Sciences—National Research Council, 1962, *Energy Resources.* Report to the Committee on Natural Resources, Publication 1000-D. Washington, D.C.

National Academy of Sciences—National Resource Council, 1969, *Resources and Man, A Study and Recommendation by the Committee on Resources and Man.* San Francisco: W. H. Freeman.

The New York City-Rand Institute, 1972, The NYC-Rand Institute Research in 1970-1971, *Operations Research,* 20(3), 474-515, May-June.

O'Lone, Richard G., 1972, Industry Influences Rail System, *Aviation Week and Space Technology,* 97(9), 36-44, 28 August.

Packer, A. H., 1968, Applying Cost-Effectiveness Concepts to the Community Health System, *Operations Research,* 16(2), 227-53, March-April.

Peterson, James T., 1969, *The Climate of Cities: A Survey of the Recent Literature.* Publication AP-59, Raleigh, N.C.: U.S. Department of Health, Education, and Welfare, National Air Pollution Control Administration, October.

President's Commission on Law Enforcement and Administration of Justice, 1967, *The Challenge of Crime in a Free Society.* Washington, D.C.: U.S. Government Printing Office.

Puttkamer, W. Jesco von, 1971, Brazil Protects Her Cinta Larga Indians, *National Geographic,* 140(3) 420-444, September.

Reid, Richard A., 1969, *Problems in Modeling the Human Component of Man-Machine Systems,* unpublished paper given at the October, 1969, meeting in Boston of the Human Factors Society. Santa Monica, Calif.: Human Factors Society.

Rose, David J., 1971, Controlled Nuclear Fusion: Status and Outlook, *Science,* 172(3985), 797-808, 21 May.

Salmon, Raphael J., and Stanley M. Altman, 1970, Medicaid: From Conceptualization to Action, *IEEE Transactions on Systems Science and Cybernetics,* SSC-6(4), 303-10.

Savas, E. S., 1970, Cybernetics in City Hall, *Science,* 168 (3935), 1066-71, 29 May.

Simpson, and Curtin Transportation Engineers, 1967, *Coordinated Transit for the San Francisco Bay Area—Now to 1975.* Philadelphia, October (Clearinghouse for Federal Scientific and Technical Information [PB 175 733]).

Starr, Chauncey, 1969, *Energy Consumption and Optimum Population Density,* unpublished paper. Los Angeles: University of California, School of Engineering and Applied Science.

Statistical Office of the United Nations, Department of Economic and Social Affairs, 1969, *United Nations 1968 Statistical Yearbook.* New York.

Strickland, Zack, 1971, Urban Areas Called Lean Aerospace Market, *Aviation Week and Space Technology,* 95(19), 56-7, 8 November.

Tebbens, B. D., 1968, Gaseous Pollutants in the Air. In A. C. Stern (ed.), *Air Pollution* (v.1, 2nd ed.). New York: Academic Press.

Tocqueville, Alexis de, 1856, *The Old Regime and the French Revolution,* trans. John Bonner. New York: Harper and Bros.

Warren, Roland L., 1969, Model Cities First Round: Politics, Planning, and Participation, *Journal of the American Institute of Planners,* 35(4), 245-52.

Watt, K. E. F. (principle investigator), *et al.,* 1969, *A Model of Society: Organization of Research and Problems Raised by a New Field.* Report No. 1. Davis, Ca.: University of California, Institute of Ecology, Environmental Systems Group, April.

Weast, Robert C. (ed.), 1969-1970, *Handbook of Chemistry and Physics,* 50th ed. Cleveland, Ohio: The Chemical Rubber Co.

Weinberg, Alvin M., and R. Philip Hammond, 1970, Limits to the Use of Energy, *American Scientist,* 58(4), 412-418, July-August.

Weisbrod, Burton A., 1961, *Economics of Public Health.* Philadelphia: University of Pennsylvania Press.

Westley, William A., 1970 , *Violence and the Police: A Psychological Study of Law, Custom, and Morality.* Cambridge, Mass.: The MIT Press.

IV

IS
ANYBODY LISTENING?
THE
SUPREME CHALLENGE

This part, consisting of a single chapter, presents a synthesis of earlier ideas, together with amplifying information, directed toward today's paramount management problem, the management of society. It should be quite obvious from the preceeding chapters that systems science applied only to industrial and service organizations may be of limited value, if not downright inappropriate. Society—national and world—is both the environment for other sociotechnical systems and itself the ultimate challenge to our expertise and to our very existence.

In this part we first review various approaches to identifying and classifying the underlying problems of the complex macrosystem of our society; in this context we also consider several suggestions toward remedy. Next, we take a further look at societal problem-solving and decision-making. We follow this with an examination of the roles of behavioral science and of education in today's society. We then approach the design of a sociotechnical management information system, using the concept of social indicators to exemplify the social system, and of air-pollution control to exemplify the technological system. This is followed by our look at sociotechnical effects upon political philosophy. We conclude the part and the book with a call to arms to take first steps toward redesign and management of world society. The inescapable fact is, ideas and political muscle must *now be brought together.*

9

On the Management
of Society

In this book we have utilized the term, *sociotechnical systems,* originally coined by personnel at the Tavistock Institute in London and employed in the more limited context of (especially) industrial production and service organizations, to cover a broad assemblage of theory, dynamic forces, practice, applications, and management concepts. We believe the body of theory, concepts, and methodology to be general purpose and applicable to different times, environmental contexts, types of systems, and system hierarchical levels. Numerous illustrations and examples of such applications, to organizations, processes, societal subsystems, and to some extent society itself, have been presented.

The management of society has both similarities and dissimilarities to the management of large organizations. The basic forces of society are much harder to comprehend than are the functions of organizations, and are much harder to reconcile with structure. It is less easy to specify society in terms of simple inputs, throughputs, and outputs. However, starts have been made to develop a theory for the management of society, particularly from the writings on "social indicators," "social accounts," or "social values." Other contributions involve the techniques of social-trend analysis, general and social systems theory, technological forecasting and the examination of alternative social futures, the analysis of national goals, and new developments in political economy.

Some of the concepts for societal management do, indeed, stem from experiences in managing large organizations. Bertram Gross's model of social accounting is an example. Nevertheless, it is probably wise not to extrapolate too far from organizational theory. For one thing, there is the familiar emergence of new properties at each successive hierarchical level. For another thing, we still do not have a complete understanding of sociotechnical interactions, even within single organizations. For recent discussions in this area see Hickson, Pugh, and Pheysey (1969) and Raymond Hunt (1970). Hunt remarks that classical theories of organization are based on industries of narrow technological range. Thus, there is no one best organizational structure or managerial approach, such as participative or bureaucratic. Organizational success is most dependent on meshing design or social technology with the material technology out of which emerge the organization's tasks.

Hunt differentiated between two fundamentally different models for organization, that is, performance and problem-solving. Most management theories pertain to the former and also most organizations evolve toward the former, that is, toward routinization. This is often premature and dysfunctional, with reduction of flexibility, adaptability, and creativity. There thus may be a "natural" force toward bureaucratization, in that technological complexity stimulates concern for coordination leading to further elaboration and formalization of administration.

Collectively, the body of material presented earlier in this book can be thought of as descriptive of dynamic interactions among a social system, a technological system, and an environment. These interactions produce a new whole. In this chapter, we are concerned with the macrosystems of society, and with the identification of problems and design of techniques for the better management of society. What should emerge as a focus in this chapter from what we have presented before is (1) a realization of the capabilities and limitations of systems science for the management of society; (2) a plea for mobilization of behavioral and social science expertise, both the good material that now exists, and the results of vast new studies; (3) the admittedly sketchy preliminaries necessary for furthering sociotechnical theory at the macrosystems level; and (4) the beginnings of plans for implementing designs for the better management of society. The last will conclude this chapter and this book. It's a race against time: development and extension of theory, methodology, and utilization of experience must at least keep pace with the heightened processes of entropy characterizing the world today.

The plan of this chapter follows the general format: identify society's problems, evaluate pertinent non-economic resources and constraints, design systems and formulate concepts toward a better management.

ON THE NATURE AND REMEDY
OF SOCIETAL PROBLEMS

In keeping with themes developed earlier (see especially Chapters 4 and 5), we are stressing problem recognition and formulation above jumping in and applying available techniques. Indeed, we are here at what can be considered a basic fork in the road, which separates our approach from what might be called the "If We Can Send a Man to the Moon, . . ." school of thought.

A large part of the difficulty in identifying and eventually solving societal problems stems from what might be called *frame-of-reference distortions;* particularly in not recognizing oneself (the manager, the governing elite, the systems scientist) as a part, perhaps the major part, of the problem, and consequently projecting the "blame" elsewhere.

We now make a number of assumptions and observations which apply to interpretations made in this chapter:

1. Human behavior is fundamentally nonrational and emotionally determined; this includes scientists and managers, as well as lesser folk. If this assumption be true, explanations of social structure and attempts to influence human behavior based on models of rational man are seriously undermined.   Yet most political, legal, religious, and educational philosophies do assume man is basically rational.

2. Little is known scientifically about the motivations and values of past and present managers of society. Concern still is with lesser people. But today, society's problems are associated as much with the *success* of industrial productivity as with the *failure* of the poor and the criminal. Each of us, as part of the total system, must look into his own motivations and values—to seek enlightenment as it were—and be willing to change as circumstances no doubt will require.

3. The "establishment" itself now becomes an object of critical study and analysis, with the avowed aim toward rapid *evolution.* The alternative most likely will be *revolution.* The consequences of recalcitrance in Nigeria, Bangladesh, and Northern Ireland in the late 1960s and early 1970s should not be forgotten.

4. "Revolts"—youth, left-wing, etc.—today come fast and furious. It can be easy to misinterpret the pulse of the times and react accordingly—and disastrously. Many policies represent quasi-hysterical responses to oscillations rather than to true trends.

5. We can explain the real dynamics of society today less than could our self-satisfied ancestors, less so, because we think we understand or rationally should understand.

6. Society less and less provides a framework by which most people, particularly younger people can support themselves. The familiar forms of tribalism result, but these are only temporarily fulfilling. Sometime in the next decades the separate gropings toward fulfillment of millions of people will be integrated into a mass movement.

7. It is unlikely that democracy, as we know it and want it, can survive the stresses and strains of today's society, and the ensuing attempts at piecemeal control.

8. We do not really understand the degree to which man has drifted from his biological anchor points and at the same time how much he is still rooted in biological reality. For example, what biological factors are

associated with generalized drive, search, exploration, work, excitement, restlessness, and need for meaningful activity? Without inferring the underlying biological mechanisms, we hypothesize that a need for change is built into animals as one feature of the overall process of organic evolution. In turn this provides one component for societal change and evolution and must be accounted for in our designs of society. For no matter how Utopian the objective world we build, there will be those who are dissatisfied with the status quo.

9. We must ask, why should "human nature" continue to become more complex, as many maintain? Why should human motives be unsatiable? How much of this is culture based? To what extent can satiation and restless search be educated for—and directed?

10. We must refuse to accept as "givens" such things as unrestricted population growth; unrestricted economic growth; "demand" for gadgets or for new housing; uncontrolled migration; and so on. Society's problems are insoluble as long as these remain as givens.

11. Many organizations, systems, and policies represent rather straight-forward extensions of the thought processes of the constituents. Bureaucracies may thus reflect functions largely at the level of safety and security needs, with an extreme need for order and preprogramming and no tolerance for ambiguity.

12. Society appears to be evolving toward decreasing distinctions between the sexes. This may be reflected in less overcompensation, less *machismo,* and less need to prove one's manhood in the old competitive, vanquish-the-opposition manner. There may be a widespread change from "*I* own it" to communal values. This could have a profound effect upon corporate and governmental behavior.

13. In politics, in political theory, and in systems management—as in systems technology—we may have exhausted the state-of-the-art. The spectre of diminishing time hovers over us all. Systems science will increasingly catch on in education and in public thinking, but it may already be too late, without a major breakthrough in the further identification of basic societal dynamics and the development of means of acquiring and handling vast amounts of qualitative and quantitative data. Systems psychology, systems sociology, systems ecology, and the science of sociotechnical macrosystems represent fields whose time has come.

14. The crisis of modern times derives in part from the superposition of operations research, management science, systems analysis, and computer science upon a bed of old-fashioned morality and black-white concepts of goodness. Vietnam has been an easily recognized and remembered resulting example.[1]

---

[1] Tragically, the Southeast Asia war may really have been a tremendous success in terms of the (original) values and perceptions of its perpetrators, in that it maintained U.S. combat ability and training under conditions of actual limited warfare—which was all that may have been intended anyway, in spite of such obfuscating superficialities as the "domino theory"

15. The intricate network of subsystems, as emphasized in this book, more than anything else determines the framework of social structure. However, interrelations among subsystems are quite difficult to express both comprehensively and specifically.

16. Society is characterized by emerging coalitions and polarizations. These may involve, e.g., traditional managers and bureaucrats versus academicians, the intellectual elite, conservationists, and some elements from the ranks of labor. Such coalitions can be expected to struggle for the following (and votes) of the undecided "youth," the "poor," and the "middle class." Consider, for example, recent beginnings of liaison between the university and labor unions (Shapely, 1970; Walsh, 1970), the move toward collective bargaining of the traditionally conservative *American Association of University Professors,* and a recent labor-conservationist hint at liaison (Woodcock, 1971).

    Contrariwise, the most stressed elements of society—youth, the poor, minority groups—with more feeling of abandon, display behavior that incipiently represents the later norm for society. In a sense, an insecure, threatened "establishment" is informally led by the resented and despised (youthful and racial) outsiders it secretly envies for their freedom from bureaucratic and organizational sterility and emptiness. The most stressed groups, along with the intellectual elite, represent the best sources of early warning in forecasting social change.

17. It will very soon be necessary to initiate policies that just a few years ago would have been considered heretical by most people. For example, one way of affecting growth, according to Forrester (1971), is to stop planning for growth and allow deterioration of service, congestion, etc. to come into play as limiting factors. For example, halting freeway construction and converting lanes to bus or rapid transit would decrease the use of the automobile. Electrical power "brownouts" would have a similar effect on decreasing use of electrical power. It is interesting to speculate how people might behave, especially the "done to" as opposed to the "doers" under these conditions. But after all we do have a precedent—the U. S. passenger railroads have been practicing these ideas for decades! (As this book goes to press, we observe that the federal government has proposed the rationing of gasoline in the Los Angeles area. This drastic proposal, an attempt to ensure that Los Angeles meets

---

(cont.)

or "the right of a small nation to determine its own destiny." The training value of Vietnam, of course, has the recent historical precedent of the Spanish Civil War of 1936-1939. Certainly the costs of defoliation, craterization, and other bomb damage to the land, bulldozing of forests, and culture shock must be added to the loss of lives in this case. For a presentation of the widespread ecological and psychological effects of waging technological war in Vietnam, see Orians and Pfeiffer (1970) and Boffey (1971). Especially indictable of big, bungling bureaucracy is the following (Orians and Pfeiffer, 1970, p. 553): "The current extent of the defoliation program is not determined by military demand nor by any considerations of saving the ecology and viability of the land and natural resources of Vietnam, but solely by competition for equipment and personnel."

the requirements of the Clean Air Act by 1977, would seem to be one validation of our theory of societal crackdown in the face of insoluble sociotechnical problems.)

Before we can propose a program for the management of society, we should provide a framework(s) for categorizing previously discussed problem areas. Several approaches follow.

Curry (1970) has attempted to identify neglected high-priority societal problems and their causes. Curry's analysis was a good one, because it emphasized problem identification rather than operations research, cost-effectiveness, or similar quick answers. Societal problems were classified as:

1. *Substantive,* such as pollution, poverty, etc.
2. *Process,* associated with knowledge or organizational resources to cope with substantive problems.
3. *Normative,* associated with overemphasis on efficiency criteria, economic goals, etc.
4. *Conceptual,* associated with contradictory premises, etc.

Because of our emphasis on behavior in this book, let's consider further the normative problems, viz., those that involve serious or irresolvable conflicts among values, cultural norms, objectives, or priorities. All these we must change (see below). One example of a normative problem is bureaucratic behavior, the tendency of persons in their institutional roles to treat other persons like objects.

Another problem is the tendency of persons acting as agents for a larger body to seek to maximize the short-term good of their group, that is, doing the job assigned, without conscious sense of wrongdoing, and without accepting the larger role of social responsibility. Michael (1968) calls this behavior "petite Eichmannism."

The My Lai massacre of March 1968 in South Vietnam, the extensive defoliation practices in the 1960s Southeast Asian war, and indeed, the total technological blast of this war may exemplify aspects of both the above. Adulteration of goals and objectives in terms of bombs dropped, "targets" found and destroyed, tons of "cargo" carried, and "body-count," representative of equally serious deficiencies in bureaucratic behavior, also deserves serious mention. The tragic farce that was body-count, with its consequent needless danger to U.S. forces and devaluation of the concept of human life, stands indicted by itself. The other features were more subtle, but are substantiable from numerous servicemen returned from Southeast Asia. For instance, bombs often were dropped on no targets at all or on things like vine-and-plank footbridges which could be simply replaced in minutes. Military cargo often consisted of Boy Scouts, barnyard stock and fowl, or rows of Vietnamese with each row held in place by a single seat belt! The moral here is: *means became an end.* Numbers themselves became the basis of mission completion, with no real relationship to political, military, strategic, or tactical objectives, except in the sense of sustaining and enhancing an organizational structure and its incumbents.

We can also mention similar aspects of inappropriate bureaucratic behavior, such as the various predator-control and pest-control programs of the U.S. Departments of Agriculture and the Interior. The coyote poisoning and fire-ant control programs are notorious.

For example, the Department of Agriculture has unsuccessfully attempted to eradicate or control an imported South American fire ant for fifteen years. This has cost at least tens of millions of dollars, with the expenditure of over $200 million more planned. The latest effort involves a chlorinated hydrocarbon, Mirex, which is held to be carcinogenic, to kill shrimp and other economically beneficial crustaceans, and to have possibly dangerous repercussions throughout the ecological food web like those of DDT which we discussed in Chapter 1. The main motivating force behind fire ant control may be bureaucratic. In Georgia such control reportedly has commanded the largest single amount of money in the state's agricultural budget (Futrell, 1971). In the spring of 1971 the Department of Agriculture was taken to court by the Environmental Defense Fund in an attempt to halt the aerial spraying of Mirex over a 12-year period and an area of 126 million acres (Anonymous, 1971).

Another problem is generated by the "technological imperative," viz., that any breakthrough that *can* be profitably developed *should* be, without concern for market saturation, resource depletion, or unregulated growth.

A final normative problem is legitimacy, or the belief that present institutions are the most appropriate ones for society and that they reflect individually held views.

Curry sees many normative or value problems as having a conceptual element. Examples are (1) the failure to distinguish between the type of property which is the result of personal labor and hence can be "owned" and the types of property (natural resources, for example) that can only be held in trust by responsible persons; (2) the false worship of economic efficiency in terms of short-sighted goals; (3) the emphasis on getting to a certain state rather than doing a job or living or experiencing once one gets there; and (4) the failure to understand the feedback and compensatory reactions of complex social systems when solutions are introduced. Such counterintuitive behavior is widely considered throughout this book.

Problem remedies were identified as *systematic, preventive, ameliorative,* or *compensatory*. Regarding causes and remedies Curry concluded:

1. A shift from the physical to the institutional environment of the human ecosystem as the main locus of man's activity has not been paralleled by a growth in means of coping with institutional threats to individual freedom and well-being.
2. The most serious institutional problems involve the equitable distribution

of goods and services and the regulation of exploitative and manipulative individual and institutional behavior.

3. The march toward degradation of the environment and exhaustion of nonrecoverable resources can probably not be halted within present incentives, constraints, and cultural values.

4. An increasing incapability to comprehend the complexities of today's world exists with associated feelings of inadequacy and anxiety. Frustration, alienation, and myriad coping mechanisms result.

5. Our true national goals, surmised from the study of resource-allocation decisions and indicators of social performance, have essentially no relation to our professed goals or to serious societal problem-solving.

6. Myriad societal problems are the result of past scientific or technological "successes" yielding cries for improved forecasting and management of technology, in themselves only a small part of the total social and economic future.

7. Most policy analysis still is directed at suboptimal ameliorative and compensatory remedies at the substantive and process levels of problems. Essentially no policy analysis deals with the normative and conceptual problem levels, even though recognition and management of differences at such levels itself presents a key problem area. Thus, there may be a serious lag between policies based on anachronistic individualistic-materialistic-competitive values and emerging humane-regulative-cooperative values.

8. The public sector is sorely lacking in determining constituent needs and wants, as compared to the market research activity of large private organizations.

9. There is no cost-effective solution to most societal problems. Similarly, the more efficiently a system fulfills a single purpose, the harder it is to fulfill multiple purposes.

A somewhat different approach to the identification and classification of societal problems is provided by the California Tomorrow Plan Task Force (Heller, 1972). The *California Tomorrow Plan* represents a creditable first attempt at bringing systems thinking—considering totalities, interactions, and alternatives—to bear on the problems and governance of a large state. The Plan and proposed programs entail an evolution from today (California Zero) to a future at about the turn of the century (California Two) which would as a goal make "possible personal fulfillment within an amenable environment (p. 109)." California One, the other alternative year-2000 future, involves a continuation of today's problems and fragmented, contradictory attacks on these problems, with exacerbation of today's chaos and detérioration of society and the physical environment. The choice between the two must be made imminently; soon it will be too late.

The authors characterized the California of today in terms resulting from human or environmental resource misuse. These are illustrated in Figure 9-1.

As stressed throughout this book, policy should be directed toward underlying causes rather than toward symptoms. The disruptions associated with

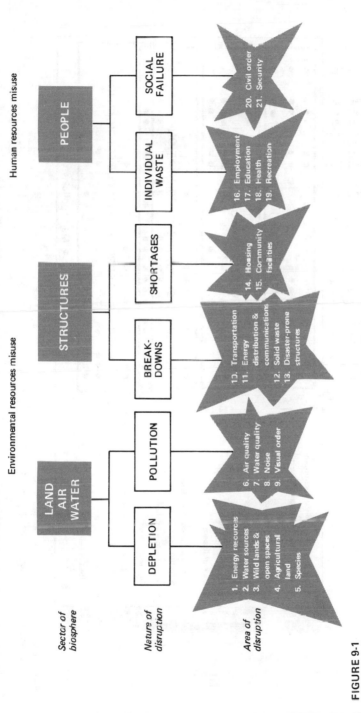

FIGURE 9-1

Contemporary major disruptions in California related to misuse of resources.[2]

[2]From *The California Tomorrow Plan*, edited by Alfred Heller, Published by William Kaufmann, Inc., One First Street, Los Altos, California 94022, Copyright © 1972.

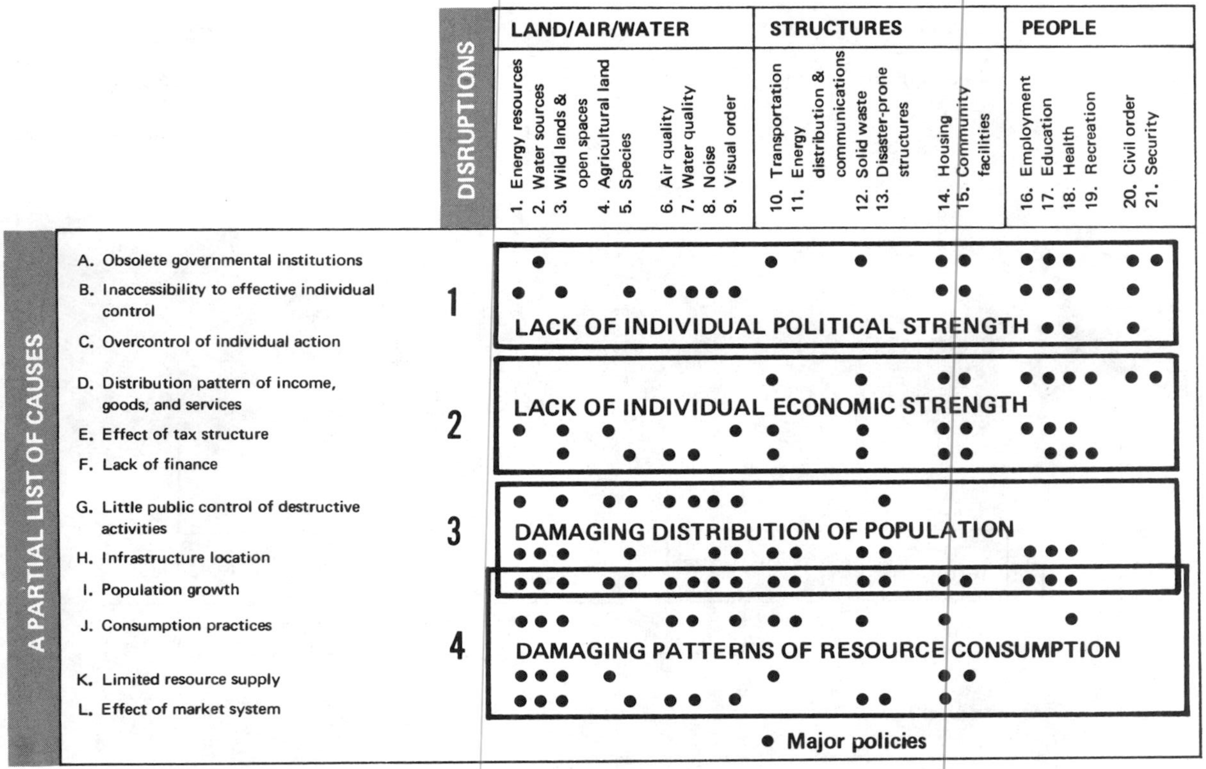

DISRUPTIONS

LAND/AIR/WATER
1. Energy resources
2. Water sources
3. Wild lands & open spaces
4. Agricultural land
5. Species
6. Air quality
7. Water quality
8. Noise
9. Visual order

STRUCTURES
10. Transportation
11. Energy distribution & communications
12. Solid waste
13. Disaster-prone structures
14. Housing
15. Community facilities

PEOPLE
16. Employment
17. Education
18. Health
19. Recreation
20. Civil order
21. Security

A PARTIAL LIST OF CAUSES

A. Obsolete governmental institutions
B. Inaccessibility to effective individual control
C. Overcontrol of individual action

1 — LACK OF INDIVIDUAL POLITICAL STRENGTH

D. Distribution pattern of income, goods, and services
E. Effect of tax structure
F. Lack of finance

2 — LACK OF INDIVIDUAL ECONOMIC STRENGTH

G. Little public control of destructive activities
H. Infrastructure location
I. Population growth

3 — DAMAGING DISTRIBUTION OF POPULATION

J. Consumption practices
K. Limited resource supply
L. Effect of market system

4 — DAMAGING PATTERNS OF RESOURCE CONSUMPTION

● Major policies

FIGURE 9-2
Four underlying causes emerge from cause-effect matrix.[3]

[3]From *The California Tomorrow Plan*, edited by Alfred Heller, Published by William Kaufman, Inc., One First Street, Los Altos, California 94022, Copyright © 1971, 1972.

resource misuse could accordingly be reduced to four basic causes: (1) damaging distribution of population; (2) damaging patterns of consumption; (3) lack of individual economic strength; and (4) lack of individual political strength.

Matrix interrelating of the above disruptions to direct causes with the emergence of the four just mentioned basic causes is shown in Figure 9-2.

A failure to attack underlying causes, with resulting exacerbation of problems, is illustrated by Figure 9-3.

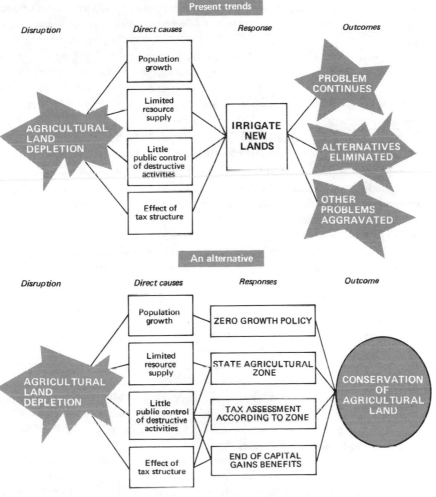

FIGURE 9-3
Comparison of two ways to deal with a fundamental problem.[4]

[4]From *The California Tomorrow Plan,* edited by Alfred Heller. Published by William Kaufmann, Inc., One First Street, Los Altos, California 94022. Copyright © 1971, 1972.

The model consists of political-economic mechanisms and policies for the two alternatives. California One assumes continuation of today's practices, such as fragmented attack on problems with proliferation of bureaucracies, inattention to underlying causes, wasteful patterns of resource consumption, and increased public frustration with decision-making processes. Contrariwise, California Two emphasizes restructuring of state, regional, and local governments; a change in economic growth whereby population levels are stabilized and consumption of space, energy, commodities, and goods is selectively controlled; the pleasantness and attractiveness of the environment become essential to public policy; and individual and groups become effectively involved in policy-making and program implementation.

Some, but by no means all, the deficiencies of the present and of California One are: (1) Single-purpose action agencies and their vested-interest clientele dominate the planning, programming, and budgeting of the state government; for example, the Division of Highways and Department of Water Resources use population growth forecasts of the Department of Finance and their own projections of motor vehicle traffic and water demand to plan highways and aqueducts, quite apart from deleterious side effects and apart from any comprehensive state development policy; (2) state-wide regulatory commissions are captured or dominated by the groups they were created to regulate; (3) elections are dominated by large contributors with overwhelming power for economic vested interest groups; indeed, it is difficult to distinguish between the public and private sector; (4) so-called voluntary associations of government tend to block genuine regional planning; (5) private land-developers circumvent local zoning and tax ordinances in collusion with local officials; and (6) the character of economic growth is determined primarily by private industry.

The California Two Model of the future is based on four *driving policies* which coordinate state policy so that, for example, energy production, employment, and pollution control support one another. The interrelating of policies with causes and disruptions is illustrated in Figure 9-4.

Representative aspects of California Two include: (1) the restructuring of state government, especially with relation to establishing regional government; (2) provision of an "income floor" for support of individuals and families according to specific needs at specific times (hopefully, federal policy applied to all states would greatly reduce immigration); (3) financing of political campaigns with public funds; and (4) integrated financing.

The California Two policies are particularly appealing with regard to land use; achieving a stable population at much below the largest projections of increase; amenities such as transportation and health; changes in the nature of taxes, fees, and fines, so that, for example, excess consumption of electricity, excess automobile horsepower, and use of scarce materials such as redwood would be taxed. To be especially noted is a policy to control immigration. This would

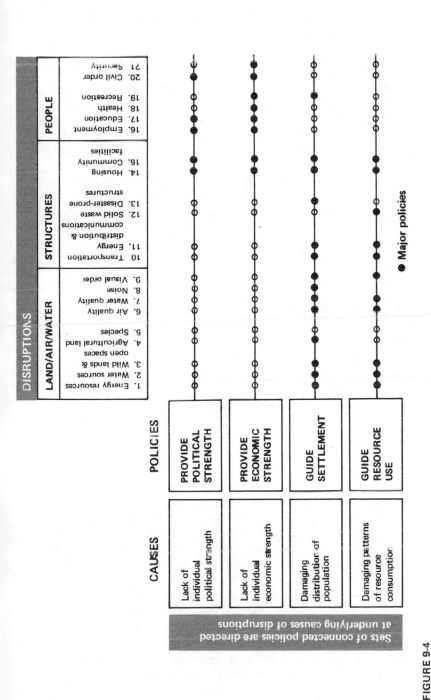

DISRUPTIONS

	LAND/AIR/WATER	STRUCTURES	PEOPLE
	1. Energy resources 2. Water sources 3. Wild lands & open spaces 4. Agricultural land 5. Species 6. Air quality 7. Water quality 8. Noise 9. Visual order	10. Transportation 11. Energy distribution & communications 12. Solid waste 13. Disaster-prone structures	14. Housing 15. Community facilities 16. Employment 17. Education 18. Health 19. Recreation 20. Civil order 21. Security

● Major policies

POLICIES

PROVIDE POLITICAL STRENGTH

PROVIDE ECONOMIC STRENGTH

GUIDE SETTLEMENT

GUIDE RESOURCE USE

CAUSES

Lack of individual political strength

Lack of individual economic strength

Damaging distribution of population

Damaging patterns of resource consumption

Sets of connected policies are directed at underlying causes of disruptions

FIGURE 9-4
Policies designed to deal with basic causes.[5]

[5]From *The California Tomorrow Plan*, edited by Alfred Heller. Published by William Kaufmann, Inc., One First Street, Los Altos, California 94022. Copyright © 1971, 1972.

involve a "capital investment fee" of $1,000.00, to be collected in installments from each new resident of any state.

The document is interesting in terms of the social predictions made, granted that these are made at quite a generalized level and involve mainly extrapolations from today's social structure. Some assumptions are questionable. The population, economic, ecological, and governmental aspects of the California Two model are appealing. Cost comparisons in the areas of open space and transportation seem favorable to California Two as opposed to California One. Although the plan is in quite an initial stage and will improve with time and criticism, it will undoubtedly be viewed as utopian, unrealistic, and impractical, and actively opposed by today's holders of power who have most to gain from perpetuating the status quo. The authors state that phasing in some aspects of California Two could begin within six months. However, this "best-of-all-worlds" idealism ignores the cold realities of economic and political foot-dragging.

Klimberg (1971) has creditably reviewed the area of the mobilization of science for survival, and the over-all morality of scientists. Using a survey, he also examined the attitudes of scientists and engineers. For the most part, they seem content to acquiesce in current, demonstrably harmful relationships with the decision-makers of society; yet many express strong reservations about the wisdom of doing so.

Like others in society, the scientist acts in supreme self-interest; however, he is seen as a hypocrite by righteously insisting on the pure motives of disinterestedness in pursuit of knowledge.

Klimberg believes applications of PPBS and operations research to the Department of Defense, under the most favorable circumstances, resulted in few successes and some monumental failures, for example, those associated with the Vietnam War. Is this a matter or poor application of the techniques and lack of sophistication on the part of the decision-makers? Or, contrariwise, is it a matter of methodology that will never mature because of intuitive underpinnings?

Scientists and engineers are seen to assume value orientations similar to those of the suppliers of funds. They are seen to demand the development of new research areas and to optimize subsystems with no concern for larger system consequences. In field after field, scientists tend to arrive at different conclusions, depending on their employers. See also Chapter 3.

Klimberg believes the original passion for science—the disinterested and objective search for truth—must be fired to win back those who have strayed. Rationalism, as it has existed up to now, has had its day. One cannot expect much of a leadership for a mobilization of science for survival with the above behavioral realities.

The irrationality and shame associated with the linkage between scientists and weapons technology has been noted again and again by writers in *The Bulletin of the Atomic Scientists.* This is to be expected, as this was the first field to experience widespread guilt over the outputs of science.

Scientists thus are often locked in a corrupt symbiotic relationship with society's decision-makers. Many, betraying their own tradition, operate on the basis: maximize public funds for support, minimize public interference.

Technology assessment may be conceptually impossible, because it presupposes agreement on criteria to judge social value. For example, such terms as "maximize the net gain to society" are operationally nearly devoid of meaning.

Klimberg's interpretations tie in well with those of Haberer (1972), who has reviewed three major transformations in science characteristic of the last century, viz., politicalization, professionalization, and a shift from an international to a material orientation. Not only has science become increasingly political, but the major conflicts faced by 20th century scientific communities have become increasingly political rather than scientific. In parallel, scientific leadership has become more and more institutional and less and less *paradigmatic* (that is, based on preeminent achievement). Further, the internationalism of science tends to be shallow. In the wars of this century, scientists have actively supported the political leaderships of their countries. Much of the intellectual effort of U.S. science has become one of analyzing the conditions and institutions that hinder or strengthen the partnership of science and government. Yet the time has come to reexamine the assumptions that guided the study of science and public policy in the 1950s and 1960s, and that have furthered the vested interests of professionalized science.

Hardin (1968), in his much quoted article "The Tragedy of the Commons," has stressed that there are no *technical* solutions to such problems as national security in the nuclear world, population, and pollution. Among other things, as implied in the theory of partial differential equations and stated in the theory of games, it is not mathematically possible to maximize for two or more variables at the same time. For example, maximizing population does not allow maximizing the good things of life.

The concept of the commons, which in English common law antedates the Roman conquest, recognizes there are some environmental objects which never have been, and never should be, exclusively appropriated to the use of any individual or group. The tragedy refers to each user thinking only in terms of his own small impacts or demands without concern for additive properties.

Hardin states it is a mistake to believe we can control the breeding of mankind, in the long run, by an appeal to conscience. He urges a mutually-agreed on coercion (e.g., fines) to prevent tampering with the commons. There may be injustices to some, less endowed genetically, for example, but injustice is better than total ruin.

Thus, the commons as a place for waste disposal must be abandoned; this concept must be extended to eliminating pollution and so on. And every new enclosure of the commons infringes on somebody's personal liberty. Now, *most important of all, we must abandon the commons in breeding, for no technical solution can rescue us from the woes of overpopulation* (emphasis added). Freedom to breed will bring ruin to all. Appealing to individual (family-level) conscience and responsibility abrogates all conscience and responsibility.

Notwithstanding these excellent recommendations, Hardin leaves us with no answer to perhaps the most fundamental question of all. He asks: *Quis custodiet ipsos custodes?*—"Who shall watch the watchers themselves?"

Crowe (1969) sees the situation as even more severe than did Hardin. He stresses the erosion of three social myths: (1) that of a common value system that can be related to national objectives and priorities; (2) that of a monopoly of coercive force the state can employ for effectively suppressing disruptive behavior of dissidents; and (3) that of the basic honesty of the administrators of the commons in protecting the commons against small and organized groups. For example, value positions assumed by groups in society today—students, blacks, hippies, and the middle-class—lead them to make demands, not as bases for bargaining and compromise with the opposition but as points which are *nonnegotiable.* Thus, our philosophies of racial integration, curing the sickness of the cities, etc. may be doomed to failure from the start. Through television, for example, we learn increasingly that others are motivated not by interests, which can be compromised, but by values. Accordingly, our age is more and more not one of accomodation but one of confrontation.

Similarly, the success of numerous guerrilla movements has demonstrated that, although the state can win battles, it cannot win wars of values.

As Hardin remarked (see above), one of our greatest challenges is in developing the corrective feedback needed to keep the custodians honest. This will not be easy. For example, Crowe states that such custodians of the commons as the Federal Communications Commission, Interstate Commerce Commission, and Bureau of Internal Revenue, through hearings and press releases, give the large but unorganized groups in American society *symbolic* satisfactions. Yet the actual day-to-day operations of such administrative agencies aid and legitimize the claims of small, highly organized groups to differential access to resources extracted from the commons. Thus, Adelman (1964) has suggested a common life cycle for all attempts to develop regulatory policies: (1) a widespread public outcry leading to the establishment of a regulatory agency; (2) symbolic reassurance of the offended who hold a generalized but unorganized interest in the commons; (3) conversion of the agency to the protection and furthering of the special interests of highly organized groups; and (4) staffing the regulating agency from the ranks of the regulated.

There may now be structural as well as value problems which make comprehensive solutions impossible. For example, decision-making is in modern institutions sequential and incremental rather than comprehensive. This is exemplified in both budgetary processes and in the conduct of the Southeast

Asian War of the 1960s and early 1970s. Paradoxically, although man's evolutionary success is associated with *generalized adaptability*, modern political and social institutions are dependent on *specialized, sequential, incremental decision* making. This becomes a straightjacket. The many forms of tribal behavior emerging in modern societies may be last hopes of returning to common values and comprehensive attacks on problems.

Crowe concludes: *major problems involving conflicts between individual and social utility have neither technical nor political solutions* (emphasis added).

The above views of the role of technology are not held by all authors, however. For example, Branscomb (1971) believes technology has brought us changes, most of which we should welcome. The impact of technology on social institutions is the most significant thing of recent years, but these problems can be alleviated at least somewhat by technology itself.

To summarize here again, but using Branscomb's points, some of the problems of technology are:

1. It has too much momentum, leaving little opportunity to debate its effect and make tradeoffs.
2. It has failed, in the absence of effective social institutions and clearly defined goals, to solve problems of war, crime, disease, etc.
3. It has undesirable secondary costs and other effects, for example, on the environment.
4. It creates disparities between practices and legal or governmental means of dealing with these practices. This causes tremendous lags in the courts.
5. It creates gadgets of unnecessary complexity and disparities among designer, repairman, and user. There is no "system" and the situation is "open loop."

Associated with the above is the frustration of rising expectations and our inability to deal with them, problems stressed throughout this book. Social institutions have changed with technology in ways not yet well understood. We comment that it is thus sad that schools of management still stress how to adjust to, or even implement, social change, rather than how, on occasion, to prevent social change. There are many unanswered questions associated with rapid change. Are we better able to accept rapid change? Has technology concentrated power in the hands of the few? Is technology helping the unification of Europe? Is individual privacy more or less threatened? Is education able to keep up with technological change? Is there now greater anonymity?

Technology has resulted in a many-body interaction. This means that a large or even a small group of persons can create waves and repercussions which Branscomb in simile likens to the ions and electrons given unstable motions in a plasma. The critical question deals with whether these motions are damped or increased until destruction, "as in present-model controlled fusion machines."

Branscomb believes high productivity is the source of personal leisure and independence. Yet as a society we are very interdependent, and failure modes in any part of the sociotechnical system will soon affect everyone. This is an area of tremendous importance: the failure modes of a complex modern society involving such subsystems as power, communications, transportation, health, large corporations, the military, etc. For a further discussion, see De Greene (1970a). And it is worthwhile to pause here for a moment to ask: What *are* our examples of successes lately?

Branscomb tells us that in order to maintain a high living standard and share it abroad we must continue to increase our productivity, to us a widely felt and dangerous philosophy based on a spurious "model of man in society." The nation wishes to allocate a larger and larger part of its economic effort to service activities, yet these are very resistant to productivity increases and to the effects of technology. Thus, Branscomb stresses, industry must increase its productivity at a doubly increasing rate, based on technology and not on additional exploitation of resources. But coupled with this, world attitudes toward the "rights" to have progeny and use energy without limit must change.

In the 1970s, research previously needed to generate more technology will increasingly be needed to formulate policies for managing technology itself. Up to now policies have been made without adequate information, and more accurate, objective, quantitative measurement is much needed. Otherwise, even if technological fixes are possible, it may be impossible to administer regulations under democratic principles and legal procedures. Yet Branscomb appears to contradict himself, stating (p. 976) that industry "has a very important role and that is to operate within a framework of *demand* (emphasis added) and of social rules, and to meet that demand within those social rules as efficiently as possible." We have pointed out repeatedly the danger in such open-loop thinking. Demand doesn't appear in a vacuum; neither can it be viewed as a static and inviolable "given." And social rules are changing. Branscomb apparently doesn't appreciate the open, closed-loop nature of complex sociotechnical systems (see again Chapter 1). Here the social system and technological system are treated with only a casual relationship to one another.

Finally, Branscomb emphasizes the importance of *managing technology at the source.* The implied alternative, of course, would involve restrictions imposed on technology from without, e.g., by having the government police technology.

One suggested approach for managing technology at the source would try to circumvent today's fragmented "system" of building regulations which stifle technology's opportunity to meet the social need of more and better housing. This would have to be coupled with setting industrial standards *based on performance rather than on design* (emphasis added), admittedly much harder to measure. Branscomb sees this as a solution to taming technology without destroying it, an answer to the antiscientism of many today.

Lindsay (1968) believes a sense of direction and urgency is lacking in the application of American economic, technological, and physical resources. Particularly at fault is society's inability to use the country's knowledge and organizational skills. For example, in 1948 the entire operating budget for New York City was $1 billion in 1968 this amount would just about pay the costs of welfare for 800,000 people, over 10% of the residents.

Cities particularly need innovation, creativity, and new management skills. However, very little is spent on research in urban problems; for example, less than one-tenth of one percent of welfare funds are spent for research in that area, in comparison to five percent of sales spent on relevant research by larger American corporations.

Lindsay cites company disillusionment with civil programs. Most corporations are reluctant to follow through on study recommendations unless there is a possibility for profit. He states (p. 1228), "It is up to business to find ways to serve better the new needs of society, such as the reconstruction of the cities. But it is also up to government to make it possible for business to continue to provide these services." Further (p. 1229), "profit—although by no means an end in itself—is probably the best measure of performance of public services over the long run. . . ." "Moreover, a profit-making corporation stands on its own two feet. If it fails to make profits long enough, it goes out of business, and the government has no continuing responsibility." (This obviously was a pre-Lockheed school of thought![6])

Obstacles to change such as ignorance, apathy, entrenched bureaucracies, and vested-interest groups must be attacked, Lindsay believes, primarily through political processes. Knowledge of the complex interrelationships of the human and physical urban system will give well-motivated political leadership the ammunition it needs to demonstrate the dangers of resisting change. (Yet Mayor Alioto of San Francisco in 1970 may have lost an election issue by urging tapping the California gas tax fund for purposes of mass transit!) And we must ask is there not too much change? And are motivation and education by themselves enough? As we have emphasized repeatedly, the idea that if we only mobilized our great aerospace capabilities, we could clear up society's problems, as we went to the moon, requires careful scrutiny.

Lindsay rightfully feels that greatly needed are increased research, capabilities of systems analysis, massive education and training programs for urban managers, overhauling of existing government organizations, and creation of new forms of government and organization. An apparently important step was the new Urban Institute, patterned after the Rand Corporation, and established to

---

[6]Referring to the 1971 financial difficulties of the Lockheed Aircraft Corporation brought on by alleged mismanagement of the C-5A jumbo jet military transport aircraft, Cheyenne combat helicopter, L-1011 commercial trijet aircraft, and other programs. In late 1971, after considerable controversy, the government advanced Lockheed $250 million, in order to keep the industrial giant afloat.

serve the Federal government on research into urban problems. Yet before generalizing too far, perhaps we should call for a critical evaluation of much of Rand's systems analysis work for the military—with features such as the (ultimate) C-5A aircraft and political-economic-military policy in Southeast Asia as final criteria of effectiveness. Are we in times of big failures in which "systems" methods, as hithertofore applied, may have had little effect, at best "muddied the puddle," or at worst seriously exacerbated conditions by providing an illusory footing in false science?

A FURTHER LOOK AT SOCIETAL
PROBLEM-SOLVING AND DECISION-MAKING

In Chapter 3, we examined a number of facets of the, often faulty, decision process in society. In this section we shall extend the concepts presented there.

As we have seen, almost all planning and analysis of complex problems is defective, with tremendous differences of opinion among experts as to facts. This is associated with how problems are defined, the information available and used, vested interest, bias, disciplinary compartmentalization, and hidden or implicit assumptions. In short, many large organizations have suffered a *breakdown in decision-making capabilities,* partially for the reasons emphasized by Forrester and discussed earlier in this book.

Decision-making is defective, in part, because of long time lags. Thus, it is typical for one party to reap profits now and for somebody else to pay the costs later. Benefit-cost comparisons use the wrong time scales. In addition, data for decision-making are spotty, belated, and out of date.

Causal pathways are long, and there are long-term cumulative effects and long lags; hence, forces are set into operation long before we are aware of them. We are thus in crying need for an *early warning system,* for the alternative might well be disaster.

Complicating the decision-making process is the formidable nature of the system itself, involving as we have seen many-layer interactions among technology, population growth, use and misuse of resources, shifting motivational patterns, economic growth, social stratification, education, and so forth.

Our poor understanding of human decision processes at the behavioral science level presents a further limitation. The literature of many fields illustrates our lack of consensus. For example, there is the rational economic view of man advocated by the game theorists and others; man the "satisficer" (March and Simon, 1958); man who "muddles through," that is, an incrementalist description of political decision-making (Lindblom, 1959, 1965); the economic basis for political behavior (e.g., Downs, 1957; and Olson, 1965); and the behavioral decision theory approach (Schum, 1970).

Schwartz, Sokolow, and Rabin (1971), considering the above, ask relative to modeling of society: What are the decision-making mechanisms of society? How can these mechanisms be described in the model? How can the model be used to influence changes in decision-making?

In answering these questions it is necessary to distinguish between the orientations of different specialists. For example, the orientation of the political-scientist, planner, and public-administrator tends to be much different from that of the systems scientist, management scientist, or engineer. The latter describe the system so that the consequences of different programs or policies can be evaluated, but the information is then presented to a decision-maker for action. This is based on several assumptions; (1) that there actually is an identifiable decision-maker with authority to act; (2) that there actually are organizations to carry out the policy; (3) that there actually are laws, regulations, or economic or other incentives to implement the policy; (4) that there is an agreement as to goals and values; and (5) that the mixture of the above is correct in time, usually a short interval.

Unfortunately, these assumptions apply much more to military and industrial situations than to social or environmental situations, wherein there may be no organizations capable of implementing a policy (see Chapter 3).

In the social area, authority is diffuse, conflicts over goals and values high, institutions often lacking, and the time for decision long (10 years or more, even though usually shortened in terms of electoral cycles). Decision-making is, of course, even more difficult at the global level. Added to this are the great powers of vested interests, for example, of the petroleum, highway, construction, steel, and automobile industries.

Thus, the time required to bring about major changes is long, and the means of effecting such changes indirect. This leaves us with the profound question: Do we have the time? Once again, in this context we must stress the emerging power of *informal organizations,* for example, conservationist organizations, and of informal bodies such as "youth."

Schwartz, Sokolow, and Rabin were concerned with mechanisms for changing decision-making behavior at the individual, corporate, and government levels. One area of great importance involves informing and educating people as to the undesirable effects of the high rate of consumption of materials. People are usually more willing to take action collectively than privately. The psychological, social, and economic disruptions attendant to shortages following exhaustion of resources could be stressed. Governmental action to discourage consumption could involve fees, subsidy, and direct regulation.

Educating people, corporations, and governments could incorporate what Muruyama (1968) refers to as *circular* or *mutual causality*. Industrialization, for example, leads directly to an increase in resource use, to increases in income, and to greater demands for goods and services. Greater demand then requires an increase in production capacity. As a result, growth loops are established and it becomes difficult to introduce negative feedback into the system.

It is important to distinguish between centralized and decentralized decision-making. Schwartz, Sokolow, and Rabin feel it would be extremely desirable to have models of decentralized decision-making, of market behavior, and of supply and demand. However, model building is extremely deficient here because of lack of understanding of underlying mechanisms involving both consumer and industry. It would, of course, be possible to model some decision-making by an input-output ("black box") description of the process. This might involve an aggregate description of decentralized decisions, e.g., of parents to have children.

Another important point involves the strong interaction between the choice of policy and the means of implementation. In this sense, much of the systems dynamics work of Forrester has received criticism, for it offers little provision for considering feedback in the form of government regulation—which is curious considering systems dynamics models are cybernetic models. It can be seen that the recommendations of broad policy objectives (even though correct), such as Forrester's for a large decrease in birth rate, or in the rate of industrialization are deceivingly easy when the responsibilities to achieve them are assigned to someone else. For example, how is it possible to halt further industrialization, without a drastic political and economic restructuring? What incentives can be offered to those who now most benefit from rapid growth to get them to give up these benefits? Why should underdeveloped nations now forego their hopes, through industrialization, for a "better life?" Within this framework, world society today is caught in a situation in which no choice is really possible.

Schwartz, Sokolow, and Rabin distinguish between a *proposal* and a *law*. Both involve many hurdles and a considerable time frame. *Perception* (of a problem) and *time lags* are important in each case. A three-step process of converting problems into formal legislative proposals could be: first, recognition of the existence of a problem defined by objective indicators generated elsewhere in the model; second, perception of the problem among nonlegislative persons, and organization and articulation of concern into political demands for legislation; and third, acceptance of these demands by a legislator who introduces a bill.

Modeling would seek answers to such questions as: What factors can shorten the time lag and heighten legislative perception? How can the effectiveness of the legislation be evaluated?

These authors hope to model the development of policy in the California legislature relative to land use. Initial work involved data coding and preparation of computer programs to analyze 30,000 bills introduced to the California legislature between 1963 and 1970.

Strasser (1971) believes the most critical areas of societal problem-solving involve the formulation of objectives in an implementable form, in the integration or orchestration of problem-solving resources, and in the reform of institutions. Yet there is no clear way to reorder priorities, except in the general sense, away from material values and Gross National Product or a related standard-of-living index based on material goods.

Strasser tells us it is unreasonable to expect DOD and NASA to support science and technology in the manner accustomed to in the 1950s and 1960s. But there is no clear replacement, nor any simple solution to the displaced scientists and engineers. We suggest that perhaps this is another characteristic of large-scale sociotechnical systems: waves of specialists who are used to a certain level of prominence, affluence, and expectation, only to pass on to make way for another wave. History can perhaps be telescoped in microcosm in such waves.

Strasser sees three major problems in applying the systems approach to societal and environmental problems. First there is *the nature of the decision-making process* which may be divided into three stages: (1) an objective stage or deciding what should be done; (2) an approach stage or deciding how to do it; and (3) an implementation stage, or taking the necessary action to get it done. Contemporary systems engineers have obtained most of their experience in the weapons and aerospace fields in the approach stage (doing things cost-effectively). Yet with social and environmental problems most help is needed in developing objectives and implementation measures.

The indicator problem concerns the fact that output measures analogous to the performance specifications of weapons and aerospace systems are difficult to define

Long-range plans are faulty in the social and environmental areas, because of lead times, lag times, vested interests, the nature of the term in office, the behavior of the incumbent relative to reelection, and demands by constituents to solve short-range problems. This third problem is simply part of the much broader and more formidable problem of *institutional obsolescence.*

Sociotechnical systems, as we have seen, are characterized by such features as the following, which further complicate problem-solving and decision-making. First, they make a great impact, both on policy and technology, often cumulatively, with short lead times, and often insidiously. Second, potential mistakes are large and costly. Third, more and more actions become irreversible. Fourth, simple, unified goals are not possible. Fifth, there is less environmental damping. And finally, simple cause-effect relationships do not exist.

Most new organizations are goal-oriented. Yet with the passage of time the means for reaching a goal become entrenched, and the means become an end in themselves. Thus, many of our institutions cater only to past needs.

Strasser sees even further obstacles to societal problem solving as: (1) absence of knowledge as to how to establish parameters to which objectives are sensitive in a manner reflecting economics, behavioral and social science, political science, etc; (2) absense of social, environmental, and other indices for measuring programs, benefits, and impacts; (3) absence of performance rather than design-oriented standards; (4) inability to treat discounted future environmental costs and benefits; (5) inability to popularize for decision-makers such notions as uncertainty, risk, expected value, etc., so as to include potential, and probabilistic impacts and side effects; and (6) inertia of institutions and vested interests, precluding needed reorganization of existing institutions to make them more responsive to national goals.

Strasser urges greater efficiency, increased productivity of goods and services, and better management, without saying how these are to be accomplished or, indeed, why they are desirable goals. And, unfortunately, Strasser's recommendations as to how to overcome the aforementioned deficiencies involve rather humdrum suggestions for universities and government. Thus, "systems thinking," societal problem recognition and definition, and so forth represent the advanced thinking of a group of affluent, self-actualizing elitists.[7] The masses of people, home and abroad, may at first see things in an entirely different light. Obtaining a broad popular base for any meaningful restructuring of goals, policies, and institutions may take much more time than really remains. Popularizing systems science concepts, methods, and findings may be a formidable undertaking. Opposition can be expected from those managers and technologists who have much to lose from changing the status quo. And, as stressed elsewhere in this book, the gaps in our understanding of the behavior of top managers and policy makers are especially critical.

ON BEHAVIORAL SCIENCE
PROMISE AND THREAT

In this book we have frequently made statements such as: everybody must change his values; we don't know enough about the motivations of top management; and behavioral and social science variables are not considered enough in systems studies. In this section we shall summarize some recent work relative to making behavioral science more effective and, at the same time, more dangerous. We shall look at the areas of values and attitudes, motivation and leadership, behavior control, and control of behavioral and social science. For another discussion of the use and misuse of psychotechnology, see G. A. Miller (1969). See also Maslow (1969).

Values and Attitudes and Their Modification

Rokeach (1971) reports that relatively permanent changes in values, attitudes, and behavior can be accomplished using a rather brief experimental treatment. The experimental procedure involved basically the inducement of feelings of self-dissatisfaction as a state of imbalance or inconsistency. While there is considerable social psychological research on attitudes and theories of attitude change, Rokeach emphasizes the less studied concept of value and

---

[7]In many ways probably not different from the Voltaires, Franklins, Jeffersons, and Marxes of the past.

theory of value change. Values are considered to be more fundamental aspects of a person's makeup than are attitudes, and indeed, are determinants of attitudes. An *attitude* is considered to represent an organization of interrelated beliefs focused on a specific object or situation. A *value* is held to be a desirable end-state of existence (that is, a *terminal* value) or a desirable mode of behavior (that is, an *instrumental* value). Accordingly, a person may have thousands of attitudes but only several dozens of values which underlie the attitudes.

Dissonance between attitudes, values, or cognitions or self-dissatisfaction can be measured experimentally by having the subject report how much he is satisfied or dissatisfied with whatever he may have said or done in a given situation. Measures of behavioral effects, as well as of verbally reported value and attitude change, can be made. Differences between experimental and control groups, statistically significant at the .01 level of confidence, remained many months after Rokeach's experimental treatment.

Studies such as this, of course, offer tremendous potential for use and misuse in the area of behavior control. The paramount question remains as to *who* shall decide which values, of whom, shall be changed. Yet I have already stated above we *all* must change our values. In a cybernetic model of society based on the mammalian organism, the controlling "nervous subsystem" and "endocrine subsystem" can be quickly counter-controlled by the "cardiovascular" or "respiratory subsystems." Used judiciously these techniques and others can be effective means of designing a more systematized and saner society.

In passing, it should be noted that 298 university students, when asked to rank 18 terminal values, had earlier ranked them as indicated in Table 9-1. Rokeach's study should be repeated with a greater emphasis on technology and the environment.

Rokeach and Parker (1970) find that rich and poor are distinguished by considerable value differences, but that whites and blacks are not when income and education are controlled. Poor and rich may be regarded as subculturally distinct. Blacks especially emphasize equality more than do whites.

The authors believe people do not differ so much as to the possession of values, but rather in the manner they pattern and rank these values. For example, in earlier studies, different value patterns had been found for such groups as hippies, policemen, college professors, college students, artists, prison inmates, and the religiously devout. In the present study, emphasis centered on the social problems of poverty and race relations, and alternative positions relative to the so-called "culture of poverty."

Many differences were found between poor and rich; especially the values *clean* and *comfortable life* were ranked higher by the poor. This suggests reaction to the unpleasant living conditions associated with poverty. Used judiciously, recognition of this mechanism could be used to reshape values relative to technology, economic growth, "progress," and ecology, factors not considered by Rokeach and Parker. The values *clean* and *comfortable life* in a

TABLE 9-1

University student ranking of terminal values.*

Rank order of importance to 298 Michigan State University
Students

Rank	Value
13	A comfortable life
12	An exciting life
6	A sense of accomplishment
10	A world at peace
17	A world of beauty
11	Equality
9	Family security
1	Freedom
2	Happiness
8	Inner harmony
5	Mature love
16	National security
18	Pleasure
14	Salvation
15	Social recognition
4	Self-respect
7	True friendship
3	Wisdom

*From Milton Rokeach, "Long-Range Experimental Modification of Values, Attitude, and Behavior," *American Psychologist,* Vol. 26, 1971, pp. 453-59. Copyright 1971 by the American Psychological Association, and reproduced by permission.

similar way differentiated between the poorly educated and the well educated. The rich and well educated tended to place more emphasis on competence and self-actualization values, as one might expect.

Motivation and Leadership

In understanding the dynamics of the complex sociotechnical systems of today, it is essential to understand the behavior of each element. One area of especially deficient understanding involves the behavior, especially the motivations and leadership mechanisms, of top managers and executives, whether in private industry, government, or the military. Although myriad studies had been made of the behavior of workers, mostly blue-collar but also including white-collar and professional, little had been done until the 1960s to further our understanding of managerial behavior. The emphasis still continues to be on improving performance and effectiveness more than on an understanding of more basic dynamics. Similarly, treatises on top management may tell us a lot about management policies and practices, but little as to the basic whys of these policies and practices, the behavioral characteristics of the managers concerned, or the dynamics of the organization generalizable beyond the specific cases (see, for example, Holden, Pederson, and Germane, 1968).

Cummings and El Salmi (1968) conclude that a unified theory of managerial motivation does not yet exist. For example, essentially no studies have treated managerial motivation as the independent variable, and measures of performance as the dependent variable. Neither of the two presently most popular theories of motivation, the Herzberg two-factor theory nor the Maslow need-hierarchy theory and its extensions, alone are sufficient.[8] The two-factor theory in its simplest form stresses the motivating and satisfying nature of job *content* (intrinsic factors) and the dissatisfying nature of job *context* ("hygiene" or extrinsic factors). The need-hierarchy theory postulates human needs are organized in the following hierarchy of prepotency: physiological, safety, belongingness and love, esteem, and self-actualization. When needs are met at one level, they cease to be motivating. Actually, the self-actualizing concept is important to both approaches.

Increasingly, individual differences among managers are being recognized. These involve the situational features of specific organization and hierarchical level within organization. For example, job level appears to be a major factor determining managers' perceptions of needs and need satisfaction. Thus, higher-level managers appear to derive more from fulfillment of such higher-level needs as autonomy and self-realization, and lower-level managers from security and social gratifications. The emphasis on self-actualization and autonomy occurs repeatedly in various technological nations studied. However, granted these needs are extremely important, the picture is not complete without an understanding of how and whether the manager's work environment is perceived as gratifying these needs. Perhaps much frustration and untoward social behavior is associated with just such disparities between needs and possibility, in modern organizations, for gratification of these needs.

Much evidence indicates blue-collar workers derive greatest satisfaction from such job-context factors as working conditions, personal life, job security, company policies, and interpersonal relations with others on the job; and white-collar workers, professionals, and managers from such job-content factors as task achievement, recognition, responsibility, advancement, and the intrinsic nature

---

[8]We believe, however, both these theories are of value in understanding sociotechnical systems. Explicitly and implicitly they appear repeatedly throughout this book, as does the important Freudian concept of ego-defense mechanisms. For further discussions of motivation and organizational and societal behavior, see Chapters 1 and 2.

of the job itself. Both intrinsic and extrinsic factors can produce job satisfaction or dissatisfaction, but intrinsic factors appear to be more strongly related to both job satisfaction and dissatisfaction than are extrinsic factors.

Our understanding of leadership is likewise far from adequate, in spite of decades of research. Generally, one of two approaches has been emphasized: (1) that stressing the personal traits of the leader; and (2) that stressing the group task or other features of the situation. Most work has been done at the small-group level. Now the tendency is to examine the broader system, away from the laboratory, because both these approaches are insufficient. Hollander and Julian (1969) have reviewed the literature in an attempt to rectify this polemic approach and have stressed the need for understanding leadership as a social influence process and not as a fixed state of being. This involves recognizing the two-way nature of the influence process and the expectations of the followers. Problems of ongoing or emergent leadership, of give-and-take between leader and followers, and of the legitimacy of leadership require more attention. Evaluating the effectiveness of leadership should and must include the outcomes for the total system, including the fulfillment of followers' expectations. Mutual goals must be defined and respected, perhaps in terms of reciprocal identifications. Further, followers hold expectations as to what the leader should be doing here and now and not absolutely.

Nealey and Fiedler (1968) have examined leadership functions of middle managers. Theory, training practices, and empirical studies are not in agreement as to what are middle managerial functions in large organizations. However, it is evident there are fundamental differences in leadership functions between first-line supervisors, middle managers, and top managers, for example, in the type and amount of interpersonal relations required and knowledge as to the technological details of the job. The first-line supervisor becomes increasingly a terminal position for one who rises through the ranks. Once again we see the importance of hierarchical level. Fiedler's "contingency model" predicts varying degrees of effectiveness for different combinations of leader, followers, and other situational contexts involving degree of task structure, leader-member liking, and position power of the leader.

We believe that among the most important sociotechnical systems research that could be performed would be studies of top management (executive, policy-maker, decision-maker) values, motivations, and leadership attributes in the context of different system configurations; with performance criteria expressed in terms, not only of system success or failure (profits, meeting contract requirements, employee turnover, etc.), but also in terms of inter-relation with other systems and of environmental impacts. Of interest, for example, would be determining the extent to which a manager internalizes the values of the immediate system and the extent he chooses only a system con-sonant with his own long-held values.

Behavior Control

Recently there have been several examples of behavioral science thinking— strangely, representing concepts, theories, and practices that are decades old, and characteristically *American*—which have attracted national attention and which have profound implications for the design and management of society. In addition, such thinking promises to shake our most basic values and beliefs as to science, philosophy, religion, government—and indeed the very nature of man himself—to their very roots. At the same time, there is the danger that, by attacking the specifics, say, of behaviorism or intelligence testing, we may lose sight of the more fundamental issues of societal structure and change.

There are a number of methods by which control over people can be exercised: (1) surgical, including electronic implantation; (2) genetic; (3) pharmacological; (4) motivational; (5) by knowledge of the individual; (6) through various reinforcement procedures associated with learning theory; (7) emotional conditioning; (8) by the use of values and attitudes; (9) through manipulations of the social milieu of the "encounter" and "sensitivity" variety; and (10) manipulation of the actual physical environment. See also W. A. Hunt (1970).

All the above, single or as an integrated system (!) possess the capability for grievous misuse. Most are already receiving formal or informal use to varying extents in varying places throughout the world. Now we shall summarize and discuss one approach that seems particularly relevant to the theme of design and management of society.

B. F. Skinner (1971) proposes the extension of his laboratory-based methods, based on the principles of *operant conditioning,* and variously called *behavior modification, behavioral technology,* and the *scientific analysis of behavior,* to the design of cultures. This emphasizes that we can change behavior by changing the conditions of which it is a function. Skinner believes our problems stem from the hallowed concept of "autonomous man"—that each person is a mentalistic being, such as a soul, a personality, or an ego, that is free rather than having been shaped by and responding to the environment. To change—or *control*—human behavior, one need only change the environment. This thinking, of course, would take some of the strong arguments from the Declaration of Independence. Skinner's book reflects the influence of organic evolution: Man must now design his culture in a scientific manner so as to shape the behavior necessary for survival; to do so means the abandonment of the concept of autonomous man. Thus, Skinner urges the basic reshaping of our image of man.

It should be evident from what we have said already that social and techno-logical change enforce major restrictions on freedom, and that large organiza-tions actively discourage autonomy and individuality. I have pointed out earlier (De Greene, 1970b) that unless we understand the basic forces within society and especially the *interactions* among these forces and control them accordingly, a threatened society will resort to control over individuals. Skinner's proposal must accordingly be viewed as one serious and well-thought-out alternative for the future world we must begin to design now. But is the answer to technological oppression and incipient disintegration more technology?

A strong point in Skinner's arguments is the emphasis on positive reinforcers or rewards, rather than the punishment long aided and abetted by the "literature of freedom and dignity." A weak point is his constant reference to physics and biology, which insofar as the good of society is concerned, certainly have proved to be mixed blessings.

Presumably, the design of a positively reinforcing environment would render those controlled happy and content with the system that controls them.

Skinner stresses there is little evidence that massive technology has advanced the freedom and dignity of man. The basic organization of society revolves around the invention, development, and distribution of tools, gadgets, and materials and the economics associated with these practices. Our gadgets demand our adherence to their logic, our conformity to their strengths and weaknesses; they enslave us far more than they free us. Skinner's world would not be a movement from freedom and dignity to control and anonymity, but rather would be a substitution of a more purposeful "scientific" control for a more haphazard control that promises oblivion.

Skinner must be given credit for being brave and honest enough to present issues and a program many people have found horrifying and revolting. Simplistic his ideas may be, as when he stresses essentially a one-to-one isomorphism between the experimental laboratory and the culture. However, as mentioned above, this is not the point. A more eclectic technocrat might correct theoretical and pragmatic deficiencies by extending the concept of scientific design of and control over society to include phenomenology, group dynamics and humanistic group encounter, and use of drugs, electronic, genetic and surgical methods. Still unanswered, in Skinner's book and elsewhere, are the questions: *Who* makes the decisions? *Who* control *whom*? How are the controllers themselves controlled? How does the system get initiated and how does the interim or transitional period, between now and the optimally designed environment, operate? Would there be a period of ruthless elimination (by death, imprisonment, or exile) of the undesired residual older people, as earlier in Russia, China, and Cuba, while the children were being shaped in the new mold?

Certainly there are notorious examples today of individual freedom and rights threatening the basic structure and future of society. The freedoms to procreate, to pollute, to make large personal economic profits, to squander resources, to despoil Nature, to mislead others through advertising, and to manipulate government as a vested interest block are among the most egregious of abused freedoms.

Skinner's emphasis is upon designing an environment that would modify actions, that is, behavior rather than the inner world of feelings and values (see again the section on values and attitudes). Behavior is thus determined not from within but from without; it is shaped and maintained by its consequences. The problems of society can be traced to defective social environments. Skinner would build a world in which people are "naturally good" by virtue of having been rewarded for wanting what is "good" for their culture.

Skinner emphasizes developing a technology of behavior, much as we now have a technology of physics and biology. He raises the question: Who will use such a technology and to what ends?; but never satisfactorily answers the question.

Skinner stresses that behavior is shaped and maintained by its *consequences,* by what the environment does to an organism not only before but after it responds. Behavior *operates* on the environment to produce consequences ("operant behavior") as a function of environments in which specific consequences are contingent upon behavior. When a certain consequence follows a given behavior, that behavior is more likely to occur again; such a consequence is called a *reinforcer.* However, seldom does the environment elicit behavior in the all-or-nothing manner of a reflex; it simply makes a behavior more likely. The environment itself can, of course, be manipulated. This technology should help to displace two particularly troublesome aspects of autonomous man—his freedom and dignity. Control would shift from autonomous man to that exercised by the environment. Skinner goes on to argue that the social environment should be designed so as to make it as free as possible of negative reinforcers, which are aversive in that organisms turn away from them. We must make life less punishing and replace the time and energy consumed in avoiding punishment by more positively reinforcing activities. The world should be designed so that behavior likely to be punished seldom or never occurs. Behavior would depend upon the environment rather than upon man's purported inner goodness.

Skinner argues that the scientific conception seems demeaning to many because eventually nothing is left for which autonomous man can take credit.

Skinner argues that those who most violently object to the manipulation of behavior try hardest to manipulate minds, and he is probably right here. Also the strongest champions of freedom and dignity are those who most condone punishment.

Design should promote the evolution of a culture in terms of bringing people under the control of the consequences of their behavior. Reinforcers should now include not only those things that aid personal survival or are derived from these personal reinforcers, but also those aiding the culture. Survival is the only value by which a culture is to be judged. The survival of the culture functions as a value. The culture can be thought of as a set of contingencies of reinforcement. Skinner suggests that countercontrol will limit the controllers in terms of the contingencies under which they control, but he isn't very convincing here. The relationship between controller and countercontroller is reciprocal. However, Skinner states the great problem is to design countercontrol and to bring consequences to bear on the behavior of the controller. A world must be designed not to be liked by people as they are now, but to be liked by those who live in it. A world liked by the people of today would merely perpetuate the status quo. The better world will be designed in terms of what is most reinforcing.

Skinner fervently believes that the intentional design of a culture and the implied control of human behavior are essential if the human species is to continue to develop. What is needed is more control, not less, an engineering problem of paramount importance. We have the science, technology, and wealth to act. However, if we continue to value freedom and dignity over cultural survival, possibly some other culture will make a greater contribution to the future. Skinner states: "Those who have been induced by their culture to act to further its survival through intentional design must accept the fact that they are altering the conditions under which men live and hence are engaging in the control of human behavior (p. 172)."

Man must be abolished, not as a species or as an individual achiever, but as an autonomous agent, and this represents a step forward. The functions ascribed to autonomous man must be stripped away one by one and transferred to the controlling environment, for autonomous man has simply been a device used to explain what we could not explain in any other way. Man will not have become dehumanized; he will become freed of the inner demon. Following the strategy of physics and biology, the science of behavior will replace the autonomous agent with the environment in which the species evolved and in which the behavior of the individual is shaped and maintained. I consider this pseudo-Darwinism and as reflecting ignorance of human evolution. Besides, evoking the higher needs of the (reified) state is old stuff in almost all past and present societies.

In a sense, Skinner rightfully is arguing only for the recognition, formalization, and extension of what exists anyhow. Few people are really either free or dignified. The environment or culture which controls man is in turn designed by man and almost always has been. Certainly we must agree with Skinner that there is a connection between the unlimited right of the individual to pursue happiness and the catastrophes promised by unchecked breeding, unchecked exploitive affluence, and imminent nuclear war.

In summary, Skinner, in spite of his several good interpretations, can be attacked on both theoretical and pragmatic grounds. For our purposes here this is immaterial. What *is* of paramount importance is the chaos, contradiction, alienation, anomie, rootlessness—the general purposelessness—of our times. People helpless, hopeless, and adrift will grasp at any security. The many forms of "tribalism" today attest to this. Without well-thought-out and well-presented alternatives, a program based on the scientific analysis of behavior could provide immense appeal to those people disillusioned with present philosophies, practices, and institutions.

Control of Behavioral and Social Science

Once again, taking the total systems approach, there is an intricate, if often informal, web interrelating behavioral and social science[9] thinking and findings on the one hand, and legislation on the other. As far as we know, nobody has ever formally documented this relationship, although we have this project in mind; nevertheless, legislation, particularly in recent years, has undeniably been influenced by thinking and findings in such areas as intelligence, personality, small group dynamics, and the effects of the physical environment. Most people would agree that the new legislation has been on the whole desirable. But wait! Most people—at least until recently—have had deep faith in the new gods, science and technology. Science, nominally at least, has an open charter allowing and encouraging the free, impartial, objective observation, measurement, and interpretation of phenomena of the universe. But science at any one time is incomplete. What if the scientific underpinnings of previous legislation turn out to be *wrong*? Should science now be controlled, at the total societal level as has been the case at the organizational and governmental bureaucratic levels (see Chapter 3 and the first section of this chapter), so that only the *right* findings emerge? Is there *good* science and *bad* science, in the sense that existed in Lysenko's Russia? We shall provide no specific answer here. But, let's now look at this issue further in the context of recent heated debate regarding individual differences in intelligence, particularly as reviewed by Herrnstein (1971).

Renewed interest in intelligence, I.Q., and intelligence testing stems considerably from three landmark social documents which deal particularly with the ancient nature-nurture or heredity-environment controversy and with possible racial differences in intelligence. These are the writings of Moynihan (1965), Coleman (1966), and Jensen (1969). The Moynihan report emphasized blacks had evolved a matriarchal family structure which was inconsistent with the rest of (patriarchal) American society. The Coleman report, representing a very large-scale, two-year long evaluation of American public schools, found blacks lagged behind whites in school achievement in every grade from first to twelfth, with the differences increasing with age. Strangely, a clear effect of school quality on the scholastic achievement of white children could not be found, and Coleman concluded the difference between whites and blacks was probably in the cultural surroundings at home. The Jensen articles suggested the possibility

[9]A similar situation of course obtains for physical and biological science. However, for purposes of simplification, we shall not consider this.

that blacks and whites differ in inherited intelligence. The reaction against all these reports, but especially against Jensen's, was extreme and often violent.

Herrnstein rather dogmatically informs us: "The measurement of intelligence is psychology's most telling accomplishment to date." And "the measurement of intelligence is one of the yardsticks by which we may assess the growing meritocracy, ..." (p. 45, 64)

Herrnstein, quoting Jensen and other sources, states that intelligence is now about 80% determined by heredity and 20% by environment, and our attempts to improve environment are bound to increase the contribution of heredity. This means that a certain portion of the population will be limited essentially genetically to the lower social and economic rungs of the ladder. Automation and technological change, especially by eliminating or changing the nature of jobs, will contribute to unemployment's running "in the genes of a family about as certainly as bad teeth do now (p. 63)." Social stratification will become even more solidly built on inborn differences. As the complexity of human society grows, "there will be precipitated out of the mass of humanity a low-capacity (intellectual and otherwise) residue that may be unable to master the common occupations, cannot compete for success and achievement, and are most likely to be born to parents who have similarly failed." ". . . . a virtually hereditary meritocracy will arise out of the successful realization of contemporary political and social goals (p. 63)." Intelligence will play an increasingly important role, as menial jobs are taken over by machines. Greater wealth, health, freedom, and educational opportunity will not bring about an egalitarian society. Rather they will bring a society with even greater innate separation between the top and the bottom and even less room at the top.

Herrnstein assumes a much greater relationship between inheritance of mental abilities (and our capability to measure these) on the one hand and occupational and societal success on the other than do many workers (cf. Goslin, 1968; Mayeske, et al., 1969; and Mayeske, 1971). For example, Goslin seriously questions the validity and widespread usage of standardized ability tests, and Mayeske and his coworkers have found racial-ethnic differences in academic achievement of students in our public schools—but after a number of social condition variables had been accounted for, these differences almost disappeared. The motivational and attitudinal aspects of family life were found to play a greater independent role in the regression analysis of academic achievement than did racial-ethnic group membership, social class membership, or type of school attended. Herrnstein's writing, like that of Skinner, may be simplistic and perhaps basically incorrect. However, this doesn't deny two factors of paramount importance to the management of society.

First, the capabilities and complexity of modern technological society, above and beyond that created by automation, will increasingly render millions of people, abilitywise, superfluous, regardless of racial background and above and beyond difficulties of adjustment associated with alienation, withdrawal, subgroup fragmentation, etc.

Second, implications that there are heredity differences in intelligence, especially racial differences, that render impotent current social programs are threatening to many. These persons and groups threatened to curtail or squelch the release of such controversial materials. This threatens the very meaning and existence of science as science has been understood up to now. Yet today the use—or misuse—power, inertia, and practice (including gamesmanship) of science are increasingly being brought under scrutiny. This is as it should be, yet, contrariwise, there is a real danger that some persons may attempt to define what is "good science" and "bad science" other than in terms of impartial, unbiased measurement and evaluation.

MORE EDUCATION IS NOT
NECESSARILY GOOD

In Chapter 8, we highlighted some of the major problems associated with viewing education almost as a closed, open-loop system. Especially pertinent are the failure to integrate education with employment and societal needs in general, and a preoccupation with curriculum evaluation in terms of classroom hours and the like. Coupled with these are the simultaneous emergence of new disciplines and rapid obsolescence of knowledge and skills.

Almost all nations today stress the importance of education as a means of advancing their people out of the depths of poverty, misery, and hopelessness. The idea was a good one. But like all variations on the theme "The Bigger, the Newer, the Faster—the Better," its time has come for critical reevaluation.

Much of the problem is associated with the nature of universities. It comes as a surprise to most scholars that the university, dedicated to the pursuit of truth, may be the most conservative, political, fragmented, and bureaucratic of organizations. Universities are characterized by immense time lags in responding to the needs of the society without. Sociotechnical systems analysis (see, e.g., Rice, 1970) applied to the university can be one of the most rewarding uses of our expertise.

Our emphasis here, however, is upon the consequences of the open-loop situation in which supply is poorly related to demand. These consequences are two: (1) educated people will not be available when needed, say, for careers in sociotechnical systems; and (2) superfluous, dissatisfied, hypereducated persons will attack and try to tear down society. The Naxalite terrorism in India provides an excellent example of the latter. This is simply in keeping with the disparity between (rising) expectations and reality as stressed throughout this book.

These problems and the problem of rapid obsolescence of curricula, knowledge, and skills can be further understood from the following reviews.

Cartter (1971) believes there will be an increasing oversupply of Ph.D. scholars and researchers from 1970 to 1985. The problem is not due to a temporary cutback in Federal funds. Decreased contract work in universities and reduced R & D and aerospace expenditures have simply hastened what otherwise might have taken several years to manifest. Cartter thus emphasizes we have created a graduate research and education effort in American universities which is perhaps 30 to 50% larger than can be effectively used in this time period. Readjustment will be painful. The manpower policy of the last decade has been uninformed, and vested interests in universities have continued to push growth and expansion. Physics, chemistry, mathematics, and biology all have surpluses.

Cartter believes total college enrollment will expand at a steadily decreasing rate in the next decade, and in the 1980s there will be an absolute decline in the number of eligible students. In the future there will be many fewer openings for the approximately 50% of new doctorates who take jobs in university teaching; the numbers may soon drop to 25% and then to 10% in the 1980s.

The lead time for developing and funding doctoral programs is five to seven years or more, and cannot readily be reversed.

Cartter estimates there will be over the next 15 years a demand for 210,000 to 255,000 new doctorates (130,000 non-academic and 80,000 to 125,000 academic). Yet we are already 30% beyond that level and will probably produce 325,000 to 375,000 Ph.D.'s in the next 15 years. In the 1980s there may be 50% too many Ph.D's for the types of employment we now know. An increasing number of such persons will not be employed in areas of their specialization. The result will not be so much unemployment as underemployment, and associated erosion of skills and generation of disappointments. There is thus an urgent need to redirect university goals and programs. See also the classical work of Thorstein Veblen (1923) and Firestone (1971).

Shapley (1971) indicates the 1971 oversupply is just the beginning. The situation is particularly bad in physics where an unemployment rate of 6 to 7%, that is, about the national level, is predicted. For example, 1000 new Ph.D.'s will graduate in the next few years in the specialty area of elementary particle physics, although in early 1971 there were only 1500 such specialists in the entire country!

Many industries prefer B.S.'s to Ph.D.'s today, because of increased units now necessary for the B.S., because of unneeded research emphasis for the Ph.D., and because the person holding the B.S. will accept a lower salary.

A SOCIOTECHNICAL NEAR-REALTIME
MANAGEMENT INFORMATION SYSTEM

The managers of society must be provided with the capability of making decisions relative to social, technological, and environmental variables; and interactions, patterns, historical trends, future projections, and policies involving these variables. This is, of course, saying a lot, and the implementation of such an integrated system is at present beyond the state of the art. Also, although we use the term "system" in a general sense here, in actuality there will be many such systems fitting specific needs at local, regional, national, and international levels.

There will be problems of costs, computer capacity, man-computer system design, and so forth. We shall not consider these further. We believe they are relatively straightforward. Much can be gleaned from our experiences with military control and command and control systems, for example. The problems we shall address here deal with deciding what information to acquire and then acquiring it, and protecting the individual from abuse by the new holders of power. We shall present concepts and examples from the areas of social indicators, education, and air-pollution control.

Sociotechnical indicators must reflect new models. The givens of present and past models are now being questioned. For example, the market model, as pointed out earlier, has not considered externalities onto the outer environment leading to pollution, freeway enhancement of incipient urban racial schisms, etc. The indicators must clearly differentiate between production costs, such as pollution, and real social costs. Indicators must reflect both a saturated society and a resource-limited society. This shifts emphasis to priority setting rather than cost-effectiveness. So far, social-systems theories have given us only rough descriptions of societies, seldom specific enough to utilize large arrays of statistics or indicators. However, systems theory can undoubtedly provide a framework for social accounting.

In society, of course, there are no simple, straightforward measures of performance, in contrast to those, say of an aircraft, wherein integration of subsystems and determination of performance criteria present relatively little difficulty. However, we are optimistic and believe we can, in the reasonable future, develop macroscopic assessments of societal structure and function, predict the future, and control social processes. Technology assessment (see Chapter 3) will also be an important management technique to prevent a development going too far.

Springer (1970), envisions the following five interrelated functions as necessary for the rational control of society, the ultimate application of managerial rationality:

1. *Assessing the state of society.* This information should be as quantitative as possible; however, there are no models to determine which parameters are relevant or important. There has been the suggestion that both sociological and economic variables be included, but (we add) little if any thought, until the present book, on the role of ecological, technological, and psychological variables.

2. *Assessing the performance of society.* The development of normative criteria is formidable. There seems little consensus as to what is desirable.

3. *Anticipating the future.* This depends on realistic and accurate assessments of the present, something at present sorely wanting.

4. *Indicating control mechanisms.* This would indicate methods for reaching certain goals, for example, emphasizing family restructure and income instead of increasing police force as a means of reducing crime. Yet, strangely, these things are bound to come.

5. *Guidance of social knowledge.* The present state of social knowledge and analysis severely delimits all the above. Better methods for identifying and solving problems must be developed.

Finally a critical problem remains with regard to the *integration* of inputs from technology, the environment, political science, economics, society, etc., to produce a set of sociotechnical indicators. And such indicators should have at least the properties (Strasser, 1971) of simplicity of understanding to politicians, relevance, and wide acceptance.

Social Indicators

Concepts of the assessment of society and analysis of social trends and change, in terms of data and goals, have been around for several decades. However, the formal idea of a national and local system of social accounts and of an annual social report stems from Gross (1965a, 1965b). Gross intended to extend, and also refute, dependence solely upon economic indicators—I might add political and military intelligence to the things beyond which we critically need indicators.

Gross (1966) has provided a rough social systems framework within which social accounting might take place (see Chapters 1-3 and 8 for more review of his ideas). The general model for an international system of social accounts, originally applied to organizational management, includes but broadens the traditional set of economic indicators. Using the model would permit the past, present, or future state of any nation to be analyzed in terms of two interrelated and multidimensional aspects, *system structure and system performance.* The model supposedly could be applied to any nation regardless of its level of complexity. Gross's model derives from his writings in the first half of the 1960s, and, hence, must be viewed on the conservative side.

Gross states his emphasis is on description preparing the way for explanation, rather than upon prediction and control. Likewise, he does not address the use of electronic computers in implementing his concepts.

Gross hopes to remedy deficiencies related to the existence only of partial systems models, the misapplication of systems engineering and cybernetic concepts, the lack of a conceptual framework into which myriad data already being collected can be fitted, inability to treat comprehensively both qualitative and quantitative information, and the absence of truly comprehensive data. As

Gross sees it, a comprehensive system of national social accounting must provide concepts to structure information on the past and present, formulate goals or objectives or desired future system states, establish criteria for evaluation of present and past situations and trends, and determine side effects of actions.

Further, comprehensive social systems information on structure and performance should provide a conceptual basis for economically scanning over all kinds of relevant data and selecting those most relevant to the given situation.

Gross believes national economic accounting to be one of the modern world's great social inventions. He has been particularly influenced by the concept of *input-output analysis* developed by the economist Wassily Leontief (1965). Nevertheless, he is critical of national income and related economic statistics in that these introduce error from an inadequate data base, fitting of data to concepts, and interpolating to fill gaps. Errors of 10 to 20% may exist.

Unfortunately, highly quantitative economic data detract attention from other deserving areas. This, of course, is highlighted in crude misuse of concepts, such as cost-effectiveness and benefit-cost-analysis. Most economic accounts incorporate manpower and human skills poorly into their reckoning; and omit items such as on-the-job training and special study programs from their accounts of education. By extending the concepts of national economic accounting it should be easier to explain the whys and wherefores of economic performance.

Satisfactions and dissatisfactions are almost impossible to observe directly; hence, a wide variety of "surrogates," usually economic like the purchase of automobiles, is utilized. All too often output is used as a measure of satisfaction; the two should be viewed separately. We shall return below to this implied concept of the *quality of life* and problems of measurement.

Collecting information on social indicators is, of course, one way of assessing system performance. The reasons some people want more data, including social indicator data, are examined by Gross. These may be specialized persons interested in crime, health, or voting behavior data. Only a minority of people are interested in comprehensive data. Inertia, vested interest, and limited resources, of course, will limit any plan for large-scale data collection. There is always the danger of premature acceptance of a plan, however, based on hopes for prediction and control. Gross sees, though, a slow movement toward consideration of how social accounting should be done. One of the major problems will entail just how comprehensive and just how selective the data should be.

Gross concludes that progress in the collection of social indicators will be uneven and may take many decades to mature. However, the world has changed greatly in the five to ten years since Gross's writings and a much more favorable, even urgent, climate now exists. A system such as is tentatively, if implicitly, designed in this chapter is inevitable.

Toward a Social Report (U.S. Department of Health, Education, and Welfare, 1969) provides another very modest beginning for a program of social reporting, indispensable to the establishment of a realistic set of program priorities. The report is based on the idea that the nation has no comprehensive set of statistics reflecting social change, although the set of economic indicators is held to be comprehensive and reliable. For example, it is not easily possible to assess the disparity between rising expectation and actual reality. The fundamental relationship between improvement and disaffection has long been recognized, and in the very significant words of Alexis de Tocqueville, quoted once again for sake of hyperbole (1856, p. 214):

> The evil which was suffered patiently as inevitable, seems unendurable as soon as the idea of escaping from it crosses men's minds. All the abuses then removed call attention to those that remain, and they now appear more galling. The evil, it is true, has become less, but sensibility to it has become more acute.

A realistic program should eliminate overemphasis on the present newsworthiness of problems, which is associated with emotion and drama. Rather, it should attend to basics.

The report asks questions and summarizes the (often meager) state of knowledge with regard to health, social mobility, income and poverty, the condition of the physical environment, public order and safety, and learning, science, and art. Insights into basic cause-effect relationships are slight, and the plea for more information pigeon-holed as "the aged," "youth," and "ethnic minorities" may further discourage the development of insights. In many ways, the report may already be out of date, in both data and interpretation. This may be particularly true with regard to trends such as the retrenchment of aerospace and the plethora of over-educated individuals. In short, the symptoms of a society in decay first affect the poor and weak, then spread to both the stable center and leading edge of that society. This is analogous to the spread of disease in a population.

The report looks at what is needed for better future social reporting. Most deficiencies relate to existing statistics. Typically there is too much of routine, *ad hoc* statistics and too little of comprehensive and coordinated statistics of explanatory value. New ideas are urgently needed. Many present statistics are merely the by-products of the informational requirements of routine management and accounting. Other statistics may be unnecessarily aggregated and not reflect changing technologies and fashions.

The report states an impressive set of social indicators could be developed in the near future at modest cost, but "a complete set of policy accounts is an utopian goal at present (p. 101)."

Springer (1970), after having reviewed various attempts at programs of social indicators, makes these valuable interpretations. He emphasizes that American social science has been developed mainly to aid the rich and powerful governing elites of our political and economic institutions, not to assist the poor, despised, recalcitrant, ruled, disenfranchised, and unorganized. Or even, I might add, to understand the complexities of large bureaucratic industrial, military, and governmental organizations. Yet times are changing and we can expect much more popular involvement, and grass-roots pressures aided and abetted by mass higher education, communications, and movement. Improving managerial rationality has been the driving force of social science, and the conceptual approaches to social accounting stem from these developments. These are extensions of the management of organizations. However, approaches like cost-effectiveness analysis and PPBS are most effective when applied to economic variables and to the goals and activities of one agency. Thus, they are only partly useful. Likewise, simple extrapolations of technological forecasts and decision-making within the firm can be misleading. There are simply too many conflicting values in society, as we have repeatedly stressed.

Programs of social indicators have been at least tacitly encouraged by the last couple of presidential administrations. Yet, Springer notes, these programs are curious in that they have no popular basis for support, but have been spear-headed by a small group of prestigious intellectuals and liberal congressmen. The emphasis of these programs is upon the nature of policy-making rather than upon specific areas. Social indicators represent just one more example of the increasing power and influence of informal groups; the conservationist-environmentalist—ecology versus establishment controversy and rapprochement has already been reviewed (see Chapter 3).

Springer indicates there is concern by many over the danger of encouraging a new breed of technocratic managers, perhaps culled from those who urge the development of systems of social indicators! Thus, the literature on social reporting can be viewed as an ideology justifying the emergence of a new ruling class of "objective," "scientific" individuals. And who are the scientific advisors and who are the rulers themselves? There would be a blending of roles, as has been the case in the weapons systems area. How can these concepts be developed within the framework of a resilient democracy? The development of a system of social accounts could definitely threaten individual freedom (see below). What, though, is the alternative in times of such rampant social and technological change, and the decay of cities, spoliation of the environment, alienation of the population, with no systematic plan for moving into the future? Thus, social indicators represent an idea "whose time has come," but may also represent a reaction against an ecologically normal, however apparently chaotic, evolution of man, the organism, and his society. Also, I should emphasize here that many of the problems of society of concern to government and social scientist alike do indeed spring from the poor, despised, and unorganized. Yet, in many ways these elements represent the real dynamics of society, with panicky government and science dragged along by the leading edge. However, it is not simply a matter of recognizing problems of race, alienation, poverty, pollution, congestion, etc., and the ruling elite's then doing something about these problems. Let me repeat:

Problems permeate all elements and levels of society; those originating with the elite deserve just as much, and no more, social accounting and control as those associated with the ruled.

The distinction between the "advisors" and the "doers" is, of course, of ongoing importance to management theory (see Livingston, 1971). Many shades of relationships from informal to symbiotic among men, machines, and data, in the sociotechnical control systems of tomorrow can accordingly be envisioned.

A Further Look at Quality Versus Quantity in Life

We have commented often that the concept of economic indicators, originally a good idea, has *by itself* outlived its usefulness. Economic indicators provide a summary of the nation's total output of goods and, to some extent, services (Gross National Product or GNP) by types of products and expenditures, and the distribution of national income by type and origin. Yet they undoubtedly mask true social dynamics. And as a society becomes more affluent and more educated, and more people shift upward motivationally, behavior becomes determined by experiences that are difficult to quantify in terms of the purchase of automobiles. The broader emphasis on quality *and* quantity will have widespread repercussions on the structure of society and on its management. For a penetrating look at some of these problems consider the following.

Wagar (1970) provides two useful formulae for the average standard of living (*SL*) and for the quality of living (*QL*):

$$SL = \frac{\Sigma \text{ production} - \Sigma \text{ losses}}{\text{population}}$$

$$QL = \frac{\Sigma \text{ production} - \Sigma \text{ losses}}{\text{population}} + \frac{\text{services/time}}{\text{population}} + \frac{\text{experiences/time}}{\text{population}}$$

As material comforts increase, it is likely that people will want more services, and as services increase the emphasis will shift to experiences. Quantity of experiences may increase, but quality will probably decrease as the environment continues to deteriorate. Wagar suggests values will shift toward what is available (however, cf. Emery in Chapter 7 of this book). Nevertheless, many will remember what used to be, and will be dissatisfied. In emphasizing production and distribution, therefore, most people overlook the environmental base on which our production and enjoyable experiences depend. Thus, we may have to rethink our entire economic strategy.

As Wagar aptly puts it, smog alerts, unemployment, riots, epidemics of hepatitis, and dead birds and fish demonstrate that personal greed does not aggregate to public good in a populous and complexly interrelated society.

The new ideal economy should provide a decent quality of life for every citizen. Individual freedoms should not be overly restricted because of population density and technological complexity. Population growth, the stimulus to all other growths, must be controlled, or representative government will be threatened. Increasing government expenditures would be necessary simply to fight off the external and internal "Have-Nots." Centralized decision-making, required by an increasingly complex society, is likely to decrease individual freedom even more.

Unfortunately, our market system is based only on costs incurred by the individual and the firm. Costs to society are ignored, even though eventually they must be borne by the public. To discourage this, Wagar suggests taxing a person for repairing, replacing, or cleaning up whatever was damaged by his economic activity. For example, there might be pollution charges. Fortunately, legislation in this direction is now being enacted. If environmental protection were considered a legitimate cost of production, many abuses would become too expensive to perpetuate and some presently profitable activities would become unprofitable. Another tax could be a resource-depletion tax to encourage protection of resources for the future. A space-depletion tax would apply to people who replace automobiles and other gadgets frequently. This also could serve as a stimulus to making safer and more reliable products and to discouraging junkyards, mining blight, and industrial smoke. More resources, energy, and leisure would be available for purposes other than building automobiles.

Some Practical Problems of Implementation

A number of additional problems accrue from attempts to implement societal management information systems. Among these are interagency rivalry, increased centralization of decision-making, abuse of individual freedom, and invasion of privacy. Consider the following analyses.

Haak (1967) has examined the technical, political, legal, and data-collection problems associated with the development of a metropolitan data system for San Diego, California.

Government interest in multi-agency data banks is great in the state of California, stimulated particularly by *The California Statewide Information System Study* prepared by Lockheed Missiles and Space Company (1965). This study recommended a system designed primarily for state government, but also serving local levels of government. A computer-based Information Central would not store all data itself; rather it would contain an index to all data and would serve as a communications network among peripheral computer centers and inquiry stations.

Subsequent work by TRW Systems, Inc., in developing a land-use information system, and subsequent attempts at legislation have further stimulated interest in information systems for government. However, there may be problems of compatibility among local systems, and local governments may be suspicious of the state's assuming some of their functions.

Haak states (p. 7), "The intention of a multi-agency, coordinated or federated information system is to promote efficiency and effectiveness in meeting information needs without asking the participating agencies to sacrifice their flexibility or autonomy." However, threats to local autonomy may occur, e.g., emanting from new patterns of intergovernmental relations stemming from computer developments. One result could be state control over local programs.

The San Diego system involves cooperation by the City, County, and Unified School District in establishing a coordinated data exchange without creating initially a data center or joint computer complex. First efforts have been directed toward ensuring compatibility of data. Duplication of effort was minimized. The basis for later development of a joint data center, if desired, was laid.

The following criteria, modified by the present author, may be considered representative. The system should:

1. Be flexible, lending itself to expansion in terms of new requirements.
2. Be related to the regular operating processes of the participants.
3. Be user-oriented.
4. Return benefits to data suppliers.
5. Provide adequate safeguards to maintain confidentiality of data and to determine "need to know" by users.
6. Not exceed the manpower, equipment, or financial resources of the agencies which participate.
7. Enjoy the full support of the heads of the agencies which participate.
8. Reflect the increased need for central coordination and direction as the centralized service and number of participating agencies grow.
9. Interface with other regional information systems.
10. Reflect changes in data-gathering procedures by the Bureau of the Census, etc.

In California, many items of information are legally confidential and may not be released to persons outside the agency, or even outside the department of the given agency, which collected it. This obviously may hinder the development of an effective multi-agency data system. Nevertheless, the present author urges that strong restraints be placed upon the developers, managers, and users of information systems. The horse was a servant to mankind, but the men on horseback came to rule mankind.

Goldberg (1970) looks at the problem of regional, state, and local governments developing large numbers of urban information systems. It is envisioned that hundreds of such systems will be in operation by 1980. Little had been written in the area of invasions of privacy, partly because computer technologists did not consider this a problem, or they considered the technological gains far to outweigh possible compromise of information.

Goldberg considers reasons for developing urban information systems, and insightfully concludes that at least part of the motivation therefor lies in people's preoccupation with gadgetry and with prestige symbols. Regardless of the motivation, there is a great need for *controls,* a need for understanding and resolving the power over the individual a system gives to the holder of the information.

In the past, privacy was protected because locating and integrating widely dispersed information was difficult, time-consuming, and expensive. It is in just these areas of storage, integration, search, and retrieval that computers excel.

Goldberg reviews three existing urban information systems, indicating types of physical and people-related data utilized by each. He further provides literature citations indicating that, once an organization acquires a large computer, this starts a momentum toward the collection of more and more information. The impact of computers on organizational life is to destroy the boundaries of privacy. Needs for information now transcend the needs of policy. Hierarchies of interlocked information systems can provide detailed, comprehensive information from a wide variety of sources to a wide variety of persons. *Intelligence systems* which generate data about individuals, and *statistical systems* which do not *directly* generate data about individuals may both be threats to people's rights.

Some safeguards are possible. These may be both social and technical, and include cryptographic techniques, frequent audits, monitoring requests for information, and so forth. Goldberg urges, however, that legal safeguards be added to these. Legal rights to privacy can be traced back to English law. In the United States such rights were highlighted in 1890 in "The Right to Privacy," by Samuel D. Warren and Louis D. Brandeis. However, the Constitution also reflects concern with privacy. Despite the above, there was no constitutional right to privacy until 1965, as reflected in a Supreme Court decision invalidating a Connecticut law forbidding the dissemination of birth control information. Thus, Goldberg emphasizes that "the implications of the evolving tort law of privacy and the emerging constitutional law of privacy for urban and other information systems are profound (p. 259)." A person has a right *not* to be defamed, either by a man or by a machine.

New laws will be needed to prohibit the eliciting, storing, or retrieving by a government officer or agency of certain types of information for any purpose; to provide each person with the right to inspect information about himself and to correct inaccuracies or omissions; to limit access to stored information to the original recipient thereof; to limit files to a prescribed life span; and to require removal of identification when the files are used for research.

In view of the advantages computers offer in information storage and retrieval and command-control, pressures will be exerted to implement systems without regard to potentially dangerous side effects. Thus, the *totality* of technical, social, legal, and ethical restraints to the invasion of privacy may prove inadequate. Invasions of privacy are bad because they interfere with the individual's control over himself and what (he feels) belongs to him. A civil society cannot exist in the absence of respect for such rights—in respect for privacy as much as in any other respect, a democratic society differs from a totalitarian one.

A Nationwide Air-Pollution Control System

The design of a nationwide air-pollution control system exemplifies features of the interaction between technology and the physical environment. In a systems sense it represents many of the problems associated with a system of social indicators. Many of the concepts of systems analysis, data availability, systems constraints, political environment, and systems design, highlighted in this book, can be summarized in the context of such a system.

The Federal estimate of air-pollution damage in 1968 to health, vegetation, homes, and materials was at least $16.1 billion annually. In addition, many thousands of persons have died in this century during dramatic, if infrequent, episodes such as in Glasgow, Scotland, in 1909; the Meuse Valley in 1936; Donora, Pennsylvania, in 1948; and London in 1952. It should be emphasized that these costs are minimal; little is presently known as to subtle effects on health, agriculture, and the ecosystem (see, however, Chapter 3).

Morgan, Ozolins, and Tabor (1970) summarize types and sources of pollutants, current and anticipated sensors and other instrumentation, and differences between urban and rural air quality. They recognize that management of air resources is increasingly a responsibility of organized society, and that measures must be taken against indifferent, careless, or deliberately negligent persons or institutions.

Air pollutants exist as solids, liquid aerosols, or gases. Of these, gases make up about 90% of the total mass emitted to the atmosphere. Gaseous pollutants are produced primarily from combustion of fuels and refuse. Sulfur oxides are derived primarily from burning high-sulfur fuels by stationary sources. Motor vehicles produce most of the carbon monoxide and hydrocarbon pollutants through incomplete combustion of fuels. The major sources and amounts of pollutants in the United States are summarized in Table 9-2.

Most of the particulates arise from burning of fuels and wastes and from industrial processes. These are a problem because of economic and biological effects; particularly troublesome are those which are respirable. Particulates increase atmospheric turbidity, attenuate both solar and terrestrial infrared radiation, and thereby may have an effect on global climate (see Chapter 1).

TABLE 9-2

Major sources and amounts of pollutants in the United
States. Metric tons per year X 10⁶. Data for 1968.ˣ

Source	Particulates	Sulfur oxides	Nitrogen oxides	Carbon monoxide	Hydro-carbons
Stationary fuel combustion	8.1	22.1	9.1	1.7	0.6
Mobile fuel combustion	1.1	0.7	7.3	57.9	15.1
Combustion of refuse	0.9	0.1	0.5	7.1	1.5
Industrial processes	6.8	6.6	0.2	8.8	4.2
Solvent evaporation					3.9
TOTAL	16.9	29.5	17.1	75.5	25.3

*From G. B. Morgan *et al.,* Air Pollution Surveillance Systems," *Science,* Vol. 170, pp. 289-96 (October 1970). Copyright 1970 by the American Association for the Advancement of Science.

Many gases and particulates react in the atmosphere, yielding secondary pollutants such as those in photochemical smog, for example, peroxyacetyl nitrate (PAN). Solar radiation, particularly ultraviolet, accelerates such reactions.

In cities characterized by good ventilation, pollutants are dispersed more readily than in cities surrounded by hills or where winds are low and temperature inversions common.

There is a need for nationwide forecasting and coordinated control. At present the Environmental Science Services Administration (ESSA), along with the National Air Pollution Control Administration (NAPCA), provide High Air Pollution Potential Advisories indicating stagnant air conditions.

Present-day pollution surveillance involves local, state, and federal air pollution control agencies. There are over 7000 sampling stations, and surveillance is directed toward enforcement activities. Sampling devices range from simple static devices to continuous sampler-analyzers which record the concentrations of numerous gaseous air pollutants. Sampling is mainly for pollutants for which criteria have been established, viz., total suspended particulates, sulfur dioxide, carbon monoxide, total oxidants, and total hydrocarbons. Adequate sensors or analytic techniques are *not yet available* for other pollutants, such as asbestos, pesticides, mercury, selenium, and odors. The Federal monitoring system provides a uniform data base against which other air quality data can be verified.

Present sensors are largely of the wet-chemical variety which are complex, heavy, and unstable. Solid-state devices with high sensitivity, specificity, and reliability, and using physical or physicochemical properties of pollutants are urgently needed. Morgan, Ozolins, and Tabor describe present and future sensors. Some samplers, designed for collection of 24-hour integrated samples, can be modified to collect 1- or 2-hour samples in sequence in order to study diurnal variations. In automatic sensor-analyzers a single device combines the processes of collection and analysis. A continuous analysis output is provided in machine-readable format or in a form which can be telemetered to a central data-acquisition facility. Automatic sensor-analyzers are available for most of the common pollutants, but only a few have been field-tested in terms of calibration, reliability, durability, and capability. Much research is being directed toward developing sensors to be used at ground level, in aircraft, and in earth-orbiting satellites.

A system is being developed for standardizing reporting, storing, and analyzing aerometric data from a number of sources. Associated computer software packages are being developed.

A summary of particulate concentrations at 60 urban stations for 1957 to 1966 showed a slight downward trend at most center-city sites. This derives from urban renewal, substitution of oil and gas for coal for space heating, and more effective pollution control. However, an analysis over 10 years of 20 nonurban stations revealed an upward trend.

Interestingly, tables in this article reveal that the incidence of suspended particles is not directly related to city size. Rather, the highest concentrations are found in medium-sized, heavily industrialized cities where sources are clustered near the urban core. However, sulfur dioxide concentrations are usually higher and more evenly distributed in large cities, because of the combustion of fossil fuel for space heating and power. A linear relationship exists between population and sulfur dioxide concentration. Relative to concentrations of carbon monoxide, nitric oxide, nitrogen dioxide, sulfur dioxide, hydrocarbons, and oxidants, no clear trends have been identified relative to six U.S. center-city sites. Perhaps this is because emissions have reached a plateau because of source saturation of the centers of most cities.

Bibbero (1971a, 1971b, 1971c) urges a compromise or "mixed strategy" between the extremes of complete control and complete "freedom to pollute." He believes economic necessity and fear of power brownouts and automobile curbs will force a benefit-cost-optimization of emission levels somewhere short of absolute safety.

We must be capable of forecasting pollution levels far in advance—but this may far transcend both current practice and theory. The atypical meteorological events underlying the catastrophes mentioned earlier are especially difficult to predict. Also excessive source control alone is no solution.

Forecasting can be thought of as *feedforward control.* Air pollution levels in different parts of a city would be computed several hours, or a day, in advance using source emissions as input; in response there would be an emergency abatement schedule based on priorities of health, production, etc. However, implementation of feedforward control is limited by deficiencies in mathematical modeling, and instrumentation, and by political bias.

Air pollution will continue to grow, because of its association with population growth and increasing per capita energy utilization. There are tradeoffs Bibbero does not really consider. These involve rationing and reduction of energy use and the means of production, and in the use of automobiles. For example, automobile emissions of hydrocarbons can be reduced by enforcement of present Federal regulations; but it is predicted emissions will rise again after 1980 because of growth in the number of automobiles. A similar picture exists for industrial hydrocarbons, automotive oxides of nitrogen, and power and industrial sulfur oxide emissions.

A major problem is that of a *national will* to tackle the air-pollution threat. In addition, there is a deficiency of atmospheric models appropriate to urban and industrial areas. Thus, we need a total system solution, just as did military air defense. We need a realtime capability for surveillance, prediction, decision, and quick control quite beyond the fragmented situation of today, with responsibility divided among local, state, and Federal agencies. Note, once again, the close similarity between the social system and the technological system.

The main functions of the system would be *identification* of air pollutants and their concentration and distribution; the timely *prediction* of the future status of these pollutants; and *control* over pollution sources. For each function, near- and long-term constraints could be identified. As times goes on, the technical constraints may prove to be the most easily removed.

Linear programming might be used to determine, on a cost-effective basis, shutdown of alternative sources of power in abating the threat of severe pollution episodes.

Bibbero sees three long-term constraints. Social motivation, eventually reflected in legislation, and involving population, power, priorities, and allocating costs between public and private sectors may prove to be particularly recalcitrant. Bibbero believes systems analysis has little to offer here, a point with which we would disagree. Assessing the health effects of trace contaminants may also be hard to solve (however, see again Chapter 3). Cost-effectiveness, of all three constraints, appears to be the most amenable to analysis.

Cost-effectiveness can be conceptually summarized as in Figure 9-5. However,

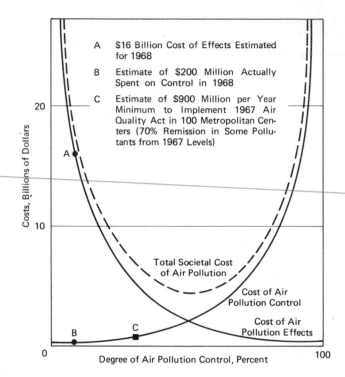

A $16 Billion Cost of Effects Estimated for 1968

B Estimate of $200 Million Actually Spent on Control in 1968

C Estimate of $900 Million per Year Minimum to Implement 1967 Air Quality Act in 100 Metropolitan Centers (70% Remission in Some Pollutants from 1967 Levels)

Total Societal Cost of Air Pollution

Cost of Air Pollution Control

Cost of Air Pollution Effects

Degree of Air Pollution Control, Percent

Costs, Billions of Dollars

FIGURE 9-5

Hypothetical cost effectiveness curves for air pollution control.[10]

it is difficult to quantify such curves because data are unknown and not constant. Much of present prediction deals only with seasonal averages; hence, more refined data are urgently needed.

The most important legislation is the Clean Air Act of 1963 and the Air Quality Act of 1967, amended in 1970 toward more direct Federal control. Through these acts, goals are translated into air quality control regions within which standards are uniform; the states are expected to implement these standards without delay. However, the legal base for regulation and control of pollution sources is still inadequate.

The system should be realtime but should not acquire data beyond those put to use, for example, for early warning. The system should have both national and local features. The latter would reflect pollution sources, topography, and meteorology. The national effort would permit economics of scale, a uniform burden on industry, uniform standards, and interchange of ideas and techniques. Obviously, local exceptions and tax refuges would vitiate the whole idea.

Many present instruments have time lags that make them useless for rapid

[10]Adapted from R. J. Bibbero, "Systems Approach Toward Nationwide Air-Pollution Control. I: The Problem, the System, the Objective," *IEEE Spectrum,* October, 1971.

emergency response. Also the cost of sensors provides a serious limitation Each metropolitan area could require hundreds or thousands of sensors with a consequent heavy telemetry and data processing burden. Digital data communication, the use of digitizers and multiplexers, large-scale integrated circuits, and time-sharing can be used to cut costs and improve efficiency. Bibbero believes display and recording at each station should be minimal. Displays would be conventional printouts, illuminated maps, alarms, etc. Reliable, low-cost computers would permit automatizing even the smaller networks.

There are obviously global implications here, another possibility for international cooperation. This is another example of technology's and technology's byproducts forcing hierarchical changes in social and political thinking. Air pollution is no respecter of political boundaries.

The system would involve both pollution source and meteorological inputs (e.g., wind, stability, and mixing depth). A mathematical model would convert these data into pragmatic realtime decisions.

Yet Bibbero's improved system still represents a suboptimization. For example, viewing the atmosphere as an ultimate sink neglects the problem of water pollution when, say, the acid anhydrides are "washed" from the atmosphere by rainfall.

Mathematical solution of the problem of atmospheric diffusion of pollutants has proved recalcitrant; hence, the statistical properties of turbulence and correlation (regression) features of pollutants have been employed. The properties of pollutants differ, and chemical reactions, important in the generation of photochemical smog, are especially difficult to deal with. Here too, correlation methods have been relied on heavily. These can be applied, for example, to early morning nonmethane hydrocarbon concentrations and maximum hourly average oxidant concentrations occurring later that day.

It can thus be seen that realistic mathematical models present formidable conceptual and solution difficulties. Even if diffusion coefficients (themselves dependent on many factors and interactions), chemical reactions and their rates, and characteristics of wind and turbulence around urban areas and buildings are known, the simultaneous numerical solution of so many partial differential equations is formidable.

These articles recognize the existence of technical controversies, e.g., realtime vs. nonrealtime, digital vs. analog, and automatic vs. manual. The greatest deficiency is that there is constant reference to the cost-effective approach, but few cost-effectiveness results in terms of comparison of alternatives.

SOCIOTECHNICAL EFFECTS
UPON POLITICAL PHILOSOPHY

We have stressed the total systems approach, particularly involving open yet closed-loop dynamic, adaptive systems, throughout this book. Hence, it should not be surprising that the evolution and nature of political philosophies can be interpreted in terms of the social dynamics—really sociotechnical dynamics in even the earliest cultures—at a given time. All political philosophies are a function of man's "real" or biased perceptions and assessments of the world about him. In the past, nomadism, agriculture, pastoralism, deity, anthropocentrism and ethnocentrism played particularly strong roles in the development of political philosophy. More recently, large-scale communinations, mass education, and both the philosophy and findings of science have exerted major effects. The communist writings of Marx and Engels represent the first major efforts to base a political philosophy upon the effects of industrialization, that is, of large-scale technology. And although both Communism and Western-style democracy have evolved greatly since the turn of the century, there is—to this writer at least—considerable doubt either can adapt quickly enough to the stresses, strains, and buffeting of our times. What are the alternatives? One might well be a technocracy very much like that portrayed by Aldous Huxley in *Brave New World* (cf. our discussion of B. F. Skinner's concepts earlier in this chapter). We shall return to our ideas of the interrelationships among sociotechnical systems, political philosophy, and government later. Here we shall summarize two or three other observations or interpretations of the directions our political philosophies and institutions will take.

Bennis and Slater (1968) believe democracy is inevitable, in the family, in the corporation, and in other organizations, by virtue of inevitable rapid change. They emphasize that the democratic family is the most potent and necessary condition for the survival of democracy.

Seeley (1968), in reviewing Bennis and Slater's book, questions whether families which are not authoritarian are indeed democratic. Perhaps the typical family of today (small social distance between parent and child, mild parental authority, and child centeredness) could better be described as anomic. Further, he questions the taking of present mindless, technology-fed, rapid social change as any kind of realistic datum. He doubts any trace of democracy can long survive this and is actually tottering in the face of it. If democracy were really viable, the science of Hiroshima and the technology of pollution would be brought under control.

Gross (1971), looks at societal change and crisis in post-industrial America. Gross sees two alternative futures: First is "Friendly Fascism," an unproclaimed technocratic efficient totalitarianism. This flexible form would need no charismatic leader, no State glorification, no one-party rule, no dissolution of legislatures, and no denial of scientific rationality. In fact, the scientific establishment would be an essential part of this world. To us it appears Gross means *Brave New World* and *1984,* but misuses "Fascism" which has romantic and often racist implications.

Second is a humanist reconstruction of values, rationality, and power systems. This is difficult to present programmatically, but undoubtedly represents significant transformations of social and technological change and political philosophies and institutions and their interrelationships. Major readjustments of technological change would be necessary. This would involve the life style of scientists—and I add managers—and an upgrading of the importance of the arts and humanities. Science-based technology would be shifted from military and economic priorities to areas like health, family well-being, transportation, education, etc. Undoubtedly Gross's concept here is an oversimplification. It probably is the case that the nastiness of our world today is to a large part the irremediable consequence of bigness and complexity. Part of our redesign would thus involve modularization. Also, a lot more thought must be given as to how such changes can be reconciled with human needs.

In spite of inadequate social indicators of fundamental change, Gross sees abundant indications of faster rates of acceleration in three major interrelated areas: technology, institutions, and crisis. In technology, new systems, especially of communication, information processing and storing, producing and transmitting energy, and changing and moving mass, are significant. Acceleration in technology is spearheaded by the needs of military and corporate bureaucracies and technocratic careerism, which in turn shape and change institutional structure. Characteristic of much institutional structures are giant complexes, e.g., military-industrial, automobile-highway-petroleum, communications, and financial which interact as a monstrous web and permeate the entire society including science, research, law, education, and management; a professionalized "salariat" replacing the older industrial proletariat; the polynuclear megalopolis extending across the boundaries of states, provinces, and even nations; and an emerging, highly unstable world society of increasingly interdependent individuals, organizations, and nations.

Technological and institutional change, in turn, is associated with overlapping crises—"revolutions" identified with race, students, youth, women, sex, drugs, hippies, anti-system, alienation, etc. In parallel are crime, urban blight, and environmental abuse and deterioration.

Underlying all the above are a widely felt survival crisis; an aspiration crisis associated with an ever-increasing level of expectancy and aspiration, especially associated with perceptions of relative deprivation, institutionalized injustice, and grossly materialistic values and life styles; a fragmentation in knowledge, family structure, personality, responsibility, and accountability; and an erosion of traditional sources of authority such as parents, schools, government leaders, managers, and scientists.

Gross predicts new crises in the 1970s—but in unpredictable forms. One reason for this uncertainty is that science at least has had much experience in studying transformations within *stable* systems. Instability, however, has usually been studied in terms of restoring equilibrium (the homeostatic model). Similarly, culture analysts have usually focused on degeneration and dissolution. Perhaps our perceptions, distorted by being participants on the scene, can be aided in the general systems sense through studies of cosmological, genetic, ecological, and other natural processes. For example, we should know much more about reactions to sudden crises under conditions of environmental turbulence.

Finally, Gross (1966) views democracy as being expressible as (1) political democracy; (2) organizational democracy; (3) individual democracy; (4) social democracy; and (5) economic democracy. A high degree of political democracy does not necessarily imply the others; organizational democracy, in particular, tends to lag behind the others.

SUMMARY AND CONCLUSIONS: A BEGINNING

United States and world society are characterized by fundamental problems, which many authors feel, given the faulty nature of our present institutions and associated problem-solving and decision-making capabilities and the confrontation of opposing groups, are *insoluble,* at least by technological and political means. No institution—government, private industry, science, the university—is free from taint. Among specific problems of an extremely serious nature are population growth and distribution, economic growth and patterns of consumption, unrestrained technology, misuse of science and technology, and a *growing* disparity between aspiration or expectation and achievement for many segments of the population.

Problem-solving is handicapped by deficiencies in social and sociotechnical systems models and the inability to identify, acquire, and utilize vast amounts of qualitative and quantitative data. At present, the systems dynamics school, which stresses conceptualization based on expert judgment rather than utilization of data in model building, is the most forceful.

The most urgently needed further developments in sociotechnical systems theory should come at the macrosystem level. Likewise, simple extrapolations of organization and management theory to the societal level seem inappropriate.

Societal problem-solving and decision-making could be greatly aided through design of appropriate management information systems and associated command and control systems. We have presented an approach to such a design(s), based on thinking in the areas of social indicators and air pollution control.

A number of serious thinkers and groups of thinkers, greatly concerned not only about the grave problems of our world, but perhaps even more about the superficial, fragmented, after-the-fact attention these problems receive—if any attention—have volunteered their ideas toward the better management of society. They are to be congratulated. Among them are B. F. Skinner, Jay W. Forrester, the *California Tomorrow Task Force,* the Institute of Ecology group at the University of California at Davis, John Gardiner's *Common Cause,* and the Club of Rome. We single out these individuals and groups in particular, because they are *activists*. This does not in any way denigrate the invaluable contributory thoughts of those who prefer to remain on the sidelines. Both types of people are necessary.

In Chapter 1 we noted that most fields today are soul-searching, asking themselves whether they are relevant. We—and you—might also ask: Is systems science relevant? Is sociotechnical systems science relevant? We think so, but go on to add that being timely and being concerned with society's problems alone is not enough. Coupled with these must be *activism*, not merely keeping in step as we prepare to enter the last quarter of the twentieth century—but leading that step.

How do we do this? If our institutions are indeed so faulty, geared to yesterday's world, how do we build new institutions? Space does not permit a lengthy discussion; this is the subject of another treatise (De Greene, in preparation). However, we might recapitulate here the following typical deficiencies of present institutions and practices: very slow change and then only in *response* to a need rather than in *anticipation;* great lag between a stimulus situation and organizational response; an increasing gap between the formally structured goals and the charters and constitutions of a society and its actual dynamics; failure of organizational designs, particularly bureaucratic designs, to meet either the needs of the workers or those of the people to whom the organization presumably offers service; adulteration of organizational function to serve the purposes of a minority; decreasing demonstrations of success by large political, military, and commercial enterprises; frequently blind adherence to dogma and outdated methods; static response to a dynamic environment; definition of the wrong problems; failure to consider repercussions and environmental impacts; lack of coincidence of problem-solving time and time in office; decreasing opportunity for the little man to identify with an impersonal organization; featherbedding, cronyism, and empire building; vacillating resistance to change or too quick response to change; entrenchment of a power elite; organizational momentum apart from the purported goals of the organization; disparities between purported and real goals; profligacy; and management unaware of its own underlying motivations, that is, management unaware it is part of the problem. We offer below a few remarks and questions which we hope will further stimulate your thinking and your action with regard to these many, often contradictory deficiencies.

First, we have asked a number of times; *who* makes the decisions? Suppose I now say, *we* do, we the systems students who are free of governmental, industrial, or other vested-interest bias, who possess the education and knowledge to deal with complexity, who possess as great a capability for impartiality as is humanly possible, and who possess the will and fortitude both to build a better world and to protect our present world from foundering. How do we best pool our collective wisdom so as to shape a forceful policy?

Second, we have discussed the matter of values and the need for everybody to change his values. How do *we,* self-actualizing at the highest rung of the Maslow ladder, ask that the underdeveloped countries, which show little concern for problems of population and the environment and who aspire to rapid industrialization as an only hope for raising their masses from the depths of poverty, now forego the very path we have followed? Yet if you will grant that we are a planet of ever-rising demands and ultimately fixed resources, where nothing (extraction, transportation, and processing, etc.) comes free, then there seems no other choice. Yet perhaps this is a pseudo problem and we're playing the game by the wrong rules. If we were to deal in units of quality of life, rather than of quantity, the problem might appear much easier to handle. What are some alternate paths to a decent quality of life? Certainly the constitution of every country should include a Bill of Rights guaranteeing a quality of life. But the means of implementation need not be the same everywhere. Nevertheless, the elite have an obligation to serve as mentors to the less privileged. In terms of values and motivations, how can this best be done? What must the elite sacrifice in order to insure the less privileged a decent quality of life?[11]

Third, how do we best systematize and institutionalize the concepts stressed in this book—negative population growth, guided automation and technological change, restricted or stabilized economic growth and use of natural resources, guided social changes, and quality of life? Should not a new branch of formalized government emerge? This might, at both federal and state levels, be called the Constituency on Sociotechnical Systems and the Environment, to indicate it is no mere division or department. Such a branch would be designed to overcome the many deficiencies, such as conflict of interest, fragmentation, noncorrespondence of system and management, lack of decision-makers, etc., discussed in Chapter 3 and in this chapter.

Fourth, how should the techniques of value change and behavior modification and new methods of education be employed? Or should they be? What is the alternative?

Considering the extensive environmental and ecological damage from industrial, commercial, and military technological operations, should not the nations of the world now define a new body of crimes, crimes against Nature and the environment, and develop laws to deal with these crimes? Work on environmental impact and technological impact could serve as an initial input to such legislation. Whether the laws would at first "have teeth" in them is a matter of conjecture. Nevertheless, they would undoubtedly have educational value for a new generation and would exert some moral suasion.

And fifth, to become a popular movement, ideas must capture the emotions of people. It is sometimes said that democracy is no longer "sexy." The same

[11]For alternative proposals and views on these issues see Hardin (1971) and the responses in the letters to *Science,* Volume 174, Number 4014, pp. 1077-78, 10 December 1971 to Hardin's editorial.

could be said about communism and socialism. What is necessary to translate scientific studies and analyses into a movement relevant to the people?

These are not the only questions. You no doubt have thought of many more. And here is where you, the readers, come in. If you agree with the basic premises, follow through on the framework presented in this book,[12] filling in details of fact, discovering other convincing examples from your classroom work, daily lives, or jobs, converting new followers, telescoping the processes of sociopolitical change—and most of all harnessing the power and riding the crest of the present revolution of social thinking before others, at once Machiavellian and mischievous, do it for us.

REFERENCES

Adelman, M., 1964, *The Symbolic Uses of Politics.* Urbana, Ill.: University of Illinois Press.

Anonymous, 1971, Fire Ant Control Under Fire, *Science,* 171(3976), 1131, 19 March.

Bennis, Warren G., and Philip E. Slater, 1968, *The Temporary Society.* New York: Harper and Row. (reviewed in Seeley)

Bibbero, Robert J., 1971a, Systems Approach Toward Nationwide Air-Pollution Control: I. The Problem, the System, the Objective, *IEEE Spectrum,* 8(10), 20-31.

———, 1971b, Systems Approach Toward Nationwide Air-Pollution Control: II. The Technical Requirements, *IEEE Spectrum,* 8(11), 73-81.

———, 1971c, Systems Approach Toward Nationwide Air-Pollution Control: III. Mathematical Models, *IEEE Spectrum,* 8(12), 47-58.

Boffey, Philip M., 1971, Herbicides in Vietnam: AAAS Study Finds Widespread Devastation, *Science,* 171(3966), 43-47, 8 January.

Branscomb, Lewis M., 1971, Taming Technology, *Science,* 171(3975), 972-77, 12 March.

Cartter, Allan M., 1971, Scientific Manpower for 1970-1985, *Science,* 172(3979), 132-40, 9 April.

Coleman, J. S., *et al.,* 1966, *Equality of Educational Opportunity.* Washington, D.C.: U.S. Department of Health, Education, and Welfare.

Crowe, Beryl L., 1969, The Tragedy of the Commons Revisited, *Science,* 166(3909), 1103-07, 28 November.

Cummings, L. L., and A. M. El Salmi, 1968, Empirical Research on the Basis and Correlates of Management Motivation: A Review of the Literature, *Psychological Bulletin,* 70(2), 127-44, August.

---

[12] I respectfully solicit comments, criticisms, ideas, and examples and cases from interested readers.

Curry, David A., 1970, *A Systems Approach to Societal Problems*. Menlo Park, Calif.: Stanford Research Institute, October.

DeGreene, Kenyon B., 1970a, Systems and Psychology. In Kenyon B. DeGreene (ed.), *Systems Psychology*, pp. 3-50. New York: McGraw-Hill.

———, 1970b, New Vistas. In Kenyon B. De Greene (ed.), *Systems Psychology*, pp. 534-72. New York: McGraw-Hill.

———, in preparation, *Principles of Percleticism*.

Downs, Anthony, 1957 *An Economic Theory of Democracy*. New York: Harper.

Firestone, Frederic N., 1971, Academic Structure and the Integration of the Social Sciences. In Milton D. Rubin (ed.), *Man in Systems*. New York: Gordon and Breach.

Forrester, Jay W., 1971, Counterintuitive Behavior of Social Systems, *Technology Review,* 73(3), 52-68, January.

Futrell, William, 1971, Action Now, *Sierra Club Bulletin,* 56(1), 12-13.

Goldberg, Edward M., 1970, Urban Information Systems and Invasions of Privacy, *Urban Affairs Quarterly,* 5(3), 249-64, March.

Goslin, D. A., 1968, Standardized Ability Tests and Testing, *Science,* 159(3817), 851-55, 23 February.

Gross, Bertram M., 1965a, Planning: Let's Not Leave It to the Economists, *Challenge,* 14 (1), 30-33, September.

———, 1965b, Social State of the Union, *Trans-Action,* 3(1) 14-17, November-December.

———, 1966, The State of the Nation: Social Systems Accounting. In Raymond A. Bauer (ed.), *Social Indicators,* pp. 154-271. Cambridge, Mass.: The M.I.T. Press.

———, 1971, The Coming Era of Systemic Societal Change, *General Systems Bulletin,* 3(1), 11-4, May.

Haak, Harold H., 1967, The Evolution of a Metropolitan Data System, *Urban Affairs Quarterly,* 3(2), 3-13, December.

Haberer, Joseph, 1972, Politicalization in Science, *Science,* 178 (4062), 713-24, 17 November.

Hardin, Garrett, 1968, The Tragedy of the Commons, *Science,* 162(3859), 1243-48, 13 December.

———, 1971, The Survival of Nations and Civilization, *Science,* 172(3990), 1297, 25 June.

Heller, Alfred (ed.), 1972, The California Tomorrow Plan, Revised Edition, *Cry California,* 7 (3), Summer.

Herrnstein, Richard, 1971, I.Q., *Atlantic Monthly,* 228(3), 43-64, September.

Hickson, D. J., D. S. Pugh, and D. C. Pheysey, 1969, Operations Technology and Organization Structure: An Empirical Reappraisal, *Administrative Science Quarterly,* 14, 378-97.

Holden, Paul F., Carlton A. Pederson, and Gayton E. Germane, 1968, *Top Management.* New York: McGraw-Hill.

Hollander, Edwin P., and James W. Julian, 1969, Contemporary Trends in the Analysis of Leadership Processes, *Psychological Bulletin,* 71(5), 387-97, May.

Hunt, Raymond G., 1970, Technology and Organization, *Academy of Management Journal,* 13(3), 235-52, September.

Hunt, William A., 1970, Human Behavior and Its Control, *Science,* 169 (3948), 901-02, 28 August.

Jensen, Arthur R., 1969, How Much Can We Boost IQ and Scholastic Achievement, *Harvard Educational Review,* 39(1), 1-123, Winter.

Klimberg, Joseph, 1971, *Science and Systems Management,* unpublished paper. Pasadena, Calif.: Jet Propulsion Laboratory.

Leontief, Wassily, 1965, Input-Output Models, *Scientific American,* 212(4), 25-35, April.

Lindblom, Charles, 1959, The Science of Muddling Through, *Public Administration Review,* 19 (2), 78-88, Spring.

———, 1965, *The Intelligence of Democracy.* New York: The Free Press.

Lindsay, Franklin A., 1968, Managerial Innovation and the Cities, *Daedalus,* 97(4), 1218-30, Fall.

Livingston, J. Sterling, 1971, Myth of the Well-Educated Manager, *Harvard Business Review,* 49(1), 79-89, January-February.

Lockheed Missiles and Space Company, 1965, *The California Statewide Information System Study,* Report Y-82-65-5. Sunnyvale, Calif., 30 July.

March, James G., and Herbert A. Simon, 1958, *Organizations.* New York: Wiley.

Maslow, Abraham H., 1969, Toward a Humanistic Biology, *American Psychologist,* 24(8), 724-35.

Mayeske, George W., 1971, *On the Explanation of Racial-Ethnic Group Differences in Achievement Test Scores,* unpublished paper. Washington, D.C.: U.S. Department of Health, Education, and Welfare, Office of Education.

Mayeske, George W., and Carl E. Wisler, Albert E. Beaton, Jr., Frederic D. Weinfeld, Wallace M. Cohen, Tetsuo Okada, John M. Proshek, and Kenneth A. Tabler, 1969, *A Study of Our Nation's Schools (A Working Paper).* Washington, D.C.: U.S. Department of Health, Education, and Welfare, Office of Education.

Michael, Donald, 1968, *The Unprepared Society: Planning for a Precarious Future.* New York: Harper Colophon.

Miller, George A., 1970, Assessment of Psychotechnology, *American Psychologist,* 25(11), 991-1001.

———, 1969, Psychology as a Means of Promoting Human Welfare, *American Psychologist,* 24(12), 1063-75.

Morgan, George G., Guntis Ozolins, and Elbert C. Tabor, 1970, Air Pollution Surveillance Systems, *Science,* 170(3955), 289-96, 16 October.

Moynihan, Daniel P., 1965, *The Negro Family*. Washington, D.C.: U.S. Department of Labor, Office of Policy Planning and Research.

Muruyama, Magoroh, 1968, Cybernetics. In Fremont J. Lyden and Ernest G. Miller (eds.), *Planning Programming Budgeting: A Systems Approach to Management*, pp. 330-34. Chicago: Markham.

Nealey, Stanley, M., and Fred E. Fiedler, 1968, Leadership Functions of Middle Managers, *Psychological Bulletin*, 70(5), 313-29.

Olson, Mancur, 1965, *The Logic of Collective Action*. Cambridge, Mass.: Harvard University Press.

Orians, Gordon H., and E. W. Pfeiffer, Ecological Effects of the War in Vietnam, *Science*, 168(3931), 544-554, 1 May.

Rice, A. K., 1970, *The Modern University: A Model Organization*. London: Tavistock Publications.

Rokeach, Milton, 1971, Long-Range Experimental Modification of Values, Attitudes, and Behavior, *American Psychologist*, 26(5), 453-59.

Rokeach, Milton, and Seymour Parker, 1970, Values as Social Indicators of Poverty and Race Relations in America, *The Annals of the American Academy of Political and Social Science*, 388, 97-111, March.

Schum, David A., 1970, Behavioral Decision Theory and Man-Machine Systems. In Kenyon B. De Greene (ed.), *Systems Psychology*, pp. 217-47. New York: McGraw-Hill.

Schwartz, S., A. Sokolow, and E. Rabin, 1971, Decision-Making. In N. R. Glass and K. E. F. Watt, *Land Use, Energy, Agriculture, and Decision-Making*, a report to the National Science Foundation, pp. 203-28. Davis, Ca.: University of California, Institute of Ecology, 28 March.

Seeley, John R., 1968, Democracy as an Automatic Mechanism, *Science*, 162(3851), 343-44, 18 October.

Shapely, Deborah, 1970, Academic-Labor Alliance Formally Established, *Science*, 170(3958), 614, 6 November.

———, 1971, Job Prospects: Science Graduates Face Worst Year in Two Decades, *Science*, 172(3985), 823-24, 21 May.

Skinner, B. F., 1971, *Beyond Freedom and Dignity*. New York: Knopf.

Springer, Michael, 1970, Social Indicators, Reports, and Accounts: Toward the Management of Society, *The Annals of the American Academy of Political and Social Science*, 388, 1-13, March.

Strasser, Gabor, 1971, Impediments to Societal Problem Solving, *IEEE Spectrum*, 8(7), 43-8.

Tocqueville, Alexis de, 1856, *The Old Regime and the French Revolution*, trans. John Bonner. New York: Harper & Bros.

U.S. Department of Health, Education, and Welfare, 1969, *Toward a Social Report*. Washington, D.C.: U.S. Government Printing Office.

Veblen, Thorstein, 1923, *The Higher Learning in America: A Memorandum on the Conduct of Universities by Business Men*. New York: Viking Press.

Wagar, J. Alan, 1970, Growth versus the Quality of Life, *Science,* 168 (3936), 1179-84, 5 June.

Walsh, John, 1970, Faculty Salaries: 1969-1970 Year May Have Ended an Era for Academe, *Science,* 170(3955), 306-8, 16 October.

Woodcock, Leonard, 1971, Labor and the Politics of Environment, *Sierra Club Bulletin,* 56(10), 11-16, December.

Index*

*References in bold throughout this index refer to figures or tables.